THE MUTUAL CULTIVATION OF SELF AND THINGS

WORLD PHILOSOPHIES

Bret W. Davis, D. A. Masolo, and Alejandro Vallega, *editors*

THE MUTUAL CULTIVATION OF SELF AND THINGS

A Contemporary Chinese Philosophy of the Meaning of Being

Yang Guorong
Foreword by Hans-Georg Moeller
Translated by Chad Austin Meyers

Indiana University Press

Bloomington and Indianapolis

This book is a publication of

Indiana University Press
Office of Scholarly Publishing
Herman B Wells Library 350
1320 East 10th Street
Bloomington, Indiana 47405 USA

iupress.indiana.edu

© Peking University Press 2011
The Chinese edition is originally published by Peking University Press. This translation is published by arrangement with Peking University Press, Beijing, China. All rights reserved. No reproduction and distribution without permission.

中国版本原来由北京大学出版社所出版。此译本由北京大学出版社授权印第安纳大学出版社独家出版发行。未经许可，不得以任何方式复制或抄袭本书之部分或全部内容。版权所有，侵权必究。

© 2016 by Indiana University Press

All rights reserved

No part of this book may be reproduced or utilized in any form or by any means, electronic or mechanical, including photocopying and recording, or by any information storage and retrieval system, without permission in writing from the publisher. The Association of American University Presses' Resolution on Permissions constitutes the only exception to this prohibition.

⊗ The paper used in this publication meets the minimum requirements of the American National Standard for Information Sciences—Permanence of Paper for Printed Library Materials, ANSI Z39.48-1992.

Manufactured in the United States of America

Cataloging information is available from the Library of Congress.

ISBN 978-0-253-02107-6 (cloth)
ISBN 978-0-253-02111-3 (paperback)
ISBN 978-0-253-02119-9 (ebook)

1 2 3 4 5   21 20 19 18 17 16

Contents

Foreword / Hans-Georg Moeller — vii

Introduction — 1

1 Meaning in the Context of Accomplishing Oneself and Accomplishing Things — 28

2 Human Capacities and a World of Meaning — 69

3 Systems of Norms and the Genesis of Meaning — 112

4 Meaning in the World of Spirit — 144

5 Meaning and Reality — 177

6 Meaning and the Individual — 208

7 Accomplishing Oneself and Accomplishing Things: Value in a World of Meaning — 238

Notes — 269
Bibliography — 293
Index — 301

Foreword

Contexts and Concepts: Yang Guorong's Concrete Metaphysics

HANS-GEORG MOELLER

YANG GUORONG IS one of the most creative and prominent Chinese philosophers of our time. He is a truly "Chinese" philosopher not because of his citizenship, ethnicity, or workplace, but because of the nature of his work. Yang makes ample use of the complete range of sources provided by the Chinese philosophical tradition, including all its periods and all its schools (in addition to his reliance on the Western philosophical canon). Thus to call him, for example, a "Confucian" would not do justice to the breadth of his approach. More important, however, Yang is also truly a "philosopher," because he does not only study the history of philosophy or engage in specialized debates within the academic discipline of philosophy but has developed his own comprehensive philosophical system.

The core of his philosophical work is an outline of his "Concrete Metaphysics" (*juti de xingshangxue* 具体的形上学) published in three volumes in 2011: *A Treatise on Dao* (*Dao lun* 道论), *Ethics and Being: Treatise on Moral Philosophy* (*Lunli yu cunzai: daode zhexue yanjiu* 伦理与存在—道德哲学研究), and the present *The Mutual Cultivation of Self and Things* (*Chengji yu chengwu: yiyi shijie de shengcheng* 成己与成物—意义世界的生成). Taken together, these books present an elaborated and encompassing philosophy, addressing perennial ontological, epistemological, and ethical questions. Yang thereby follows the trend of major twentieth-century Chinese thinkers who tried to renew the Chinese philosophical tradition of Neo-Confucianism and its efforts to merge Confucianism, Buddhism, and Taoism into an overarching whole while at the same time incorporating the metaphysical, historical, and existential approaches of modern Western systemic philosophy as represented by authors like Kant, Hegel, and Heidegger. In short, Yang's project establishes a unifying "grand philosophy" by combining traditional Chinese and Western conceptualizations into a systematic synthesis expressed in contemporary language.

Yang's philosophy is called a "metaphysics" for two major reasons. First, he thereby connects with the systematic *methodology* of Western philosophy beginning

vii

(arguably) with Plato and Aristotle. A systematic philosophy integrates all traditional fields of enquiry, that is, ontology, ethics, and epistemology. Thereby, it naturally cannot be confined to one of the contemporary professional "areas of specialization" such as philosophy of science, political philosophy, or philosophy of mind, and much less be concerned with debating (or "solving") specifically isolated or constructed questions as sometimes attempted in contemporary analytic philosophy. A systematic philosophy will, of course, also deal with specific questions, and it will address ontological, ethical, and epistemological issues, but it always does so with an overarching *coherence* in mind. The "truth" that emerges within or from a philosophical system cannot be grasped by summing up the truth values of its propositions, but by developing the capacity to see the connections that bind the various parts of the work together. The reader's task is not to measure up the qualities of each individual component on its own, but rather to appreciate the intricate architecture of the systematic edifice.

A true metaphysics does not "abstract"—in the sense of "de-contextualize"—its objects, but, to the contrary, always looks at them in conjunction with, to speak with Kant, the conditions of their possibility. Any object of cognition, for instance, is to a certain extent constituted by the cognitive subject for which it is an object. In this sense, metaphysics is, methodologically speaking, the art of contextualizing knowledge by not only trying to know something as something, but by also reflecting on the constitutive conditions that make something appear as that which it is. Or, to put it quite simply in Hegel's famous words: "Das Wahre ist das Ganze" (the truth is the whole.)

Second, as to its *contents*, metaphysics, in the sense of the term in the European tradition that Yang relates to, is concerned with reality, or, again, in more succinct Hegelian language, with *Wirklichkeit*. The German word *wirken* shares the same etymological root with the English word *work*. Thus, a true metaphysics is not merely concerned with how the world "is," but more precisely with how it "works." The contents of a metaphysical investigation are thus not just "things," but, in the terminology of Yang Guorong and the Chinese tradition he connects with, "affairs" (*shi* 事). Reality is not an assemblage of "facts" that philosophy can establish or find "out there"; rather, it is a "work in progress," a living body of relations, effects, powers, conflicts, combinations, and so on, within which philosophy itself partakes or "works." Thus, metaphysics does not primarily focus on the simple and narrow "meaning" of whatever it deals with, but on "the world of meaning" (*yiyi shijie* 意义世界) and its genesis, or, in other words, on "significance." A street sign or a word, for instance, may have the specific meaning "stop," and once we become aware that this means that we have to halt whenever we see the sign or hear the word, we may claim to *know* its meaning. This sort of knowledge, however, is "poor" knowledge; it is a form of knowledge a child can acquire, and it may be call it "pre-metaphysical." In order to *understand* the sign or the word, we have to be able to see it as an "affair" that has not only a narrow meaning, but also *significance*. A "metaphysical" understanding that opens up a "world of meaning" will point to the way a word or a sign "works." In fact we can then see that it functions as an expression, for instance, of a context of power relations, of legal institutions, or of moral obligations. In this way, we are no longer limited to a mere perception of a sign—however "true" or "correct" it may be—but by seeing how it "works" we get to comprehend it in a more complex fashion, and rather than being stuck with one and only one particular "meaning" we are *free* to interpret it and not to just do what it seemingly asks us to do. If we only know the meaning of "stop," we will come to a halt. Once we understand its significance, and the genesis of meaning that we, as humans, are engaged in, we can move on. In this way, metaphysical knowledge is intrinsically connected, as Yang Guorong stresses throughout this book, with cognitive and practical freedom.

For both Hegel and Yang, metaphysics is thus first and foremost *wirkliches Wissen* or "working knowledge"—knowledge that works rather than merely informs. For this reason, Yang calls his overall project a "concrete metaphysics," a metaphysics that neither, like the positive sciences, deals with abstracted facts, nor, like a secular theology, with transcendent abstractions. Instead, it gains concrete significance in the sense just described. Yang links himself with Heidegger whom he credits with rightfully criticizing a metaphysics that had deteriorated to a state where it had forgotten about its essential connection with "being." Yang now wants to go a step further than Heidegger and revitalize the concrete dimension of metaphysics and its concern with living, dynamic, and humanist "being." This being "has an essentially historical character" and "as opposed to beings or a being, is rooted in one's own being and unfolds as the humanized world; it differs from any abstract substance hiding behind both individuals and particular beings, and it appears in a concrete form through blending together the universal and the particular as well as the general and the specific."[1] A concrete metaphysics that is thoroughly embedded in the "humanized world" is thus not only reconnected with its Greek ancestors, but also, and even more crucially for Yang, with the Chinese philosophical traditions and their immersion in the living world of human society and nature.

A metaphysics, however concrete it may be, necessarily expresses itself in language. Its core linguistic repertoire consists of concepts. A philosophical system is built from the interrelated concepts representing its constitutive ideas. Concepts are, again, not abstractions, but rather *comprehensive* crystallizations of thought. They are the linguistic manifestation of philosophical *comprehension*. Rather than simply having a meaning, they indicate philosophical significance. Or, in the words of Yang just quoted, they blend together the universal and the particular. The specific meaning of "work," for instance, is to engage in a particular productive activity, and if I say to a child "work," I hope she will understand the meaning and continue her homework rather than watching TV. But one can also have a more encompassing, "narrative" understanding of work, and, for instance, connect the term with images of laborers in a factory or farmers on their land, as in the images of Socialist Realism. A conceptual understanding of "work," however, will "sublate" the understanding of the term to a level where its historical, existential, and cognitive significance is realized. Only on the basis of a conceptual comprehension of work, which is inclusive of and developed on the basis of its particular and narrative understanding, can a metaphysics outline how work is a *universal* aspect of human life that essentially makes us into what we are as human beings. The concept is the integral linguistic form in which an idea can become philosophically relevant.

The conceptual vocabulary of Yang's concrete metaphysics is mainly derived from two sources. First, from the conceptual apparatus of modern Western systematic philosophy, which in turn is to a certain extent derived from ancient Western philosophy, and second, from the ancient Chinese philosophical vocabulary and its modifications and conceptualizations by the Song-Ming philosophers and twentieth-century Chinese systematic philosophy. It is not an easy task to translate this vocabulary into contemporary English. While, on the one hand, English translations of some of the "technical terms" of ancient and modern Western philosophy have been established (e.g., "being," "things-in-themselves," "substance"), this is decisively not so with respect to the Chinese philosophical notions. Moreover, in Yang's new adaptation of the Western philosophical vocabulary and its conjunction with the Chinese terms, an altogether new conceptual network, at least in part, emerges. Given this complex situation, the present translation has to be regarded as an exceptional accomplishment. It succeeds in elucidating the complexities of Yang's system and, at the same time, doing justice to the historical and cultural depth of his work.

In a footnote to the initial publication of Yang's Introduction to the present book,[2] translator Chad Austin Meyers explains in detail the philosophical rationale for his rendering of the book title, and, in particular, of the decisive word *cheng* 成, which he translates varyingly as "maturation" and "refinement" in the title itself, and then in other ways throughout the book. I think that his method is philosophically sound and convincing, and ultimately superior to deciding on one single English term for *cheng*.

Of course, however, a translator of philosophical texts not only has to resolve conceptual complexities, but semantic and syntactical ones as well. As this book progresses, the concept *cheng* evolves as it traverses not only the variety of conceptual components, which compose it from within, but the other concepts and problems that connect to it from without as well. As these conditions amount, conceptual terms must metamorphose if they are to resolve such intensifying perplexities whose dimensions are just as much syntactical as they are conceptual.

As the translator intimated to me, he had only discovered the final stages of development of this term when refining his translation of the book, where he realized that *chengwu*, though encompassing the middle stage of a progressing work, that is, the stage of "refining" or "cultivating" something, stresses more specifically the final stage of "accomplishing" something. His foresight of this was, in fact, the translator's rationale for choosing the term "maturation" for the original publication of the introduction to this book. However, as the translator continued to explain, due to the fact that the present progressive "maturing" doesn't naturally take a direct object, he was left with the following dilemma: either pair "the self" with the semantically fitting, but grammatically forced match "maturing" or with the perfectly grammatical, but more semantically forced match "accomplishing." Since "accomplishing things" is a most natural phrase, and moreover, a most fitting counterpart for the term *chengwu*, and since "having a sense of self-accomplishment" is no less natural in the English-speaking world, the translator has weighed in favor of pushing the reader to work with "accomplishing oneself" as the phrase, which refers to the practice of pursuing and attaining such a sense of self-accomplishment. In translating languages with little in common, there is always a trade-off: a small loss in common familiarity may be a big gain for philosophical consistency. This problem, which the translator has elegantly solved, points to a more general problem regarding translations of a book like Yang's—or that of any other systematic philosopher in both East and West—into current English. Now, the value of a solution must be estimated according to the depth of the problem it grasps. Measured accordingly, *The Mutual Cultivation of Self and Things* is a serious accomplishment in the field of Chinese to English translation.

Contemporary Anglo-American philosophy, for better or worse, has not really embraced the method and "style" of systematic metaphysics. Its conceptual reservoir, therefore, is, comparatively speaking (and again: for better or worse), somewhat limited. Given Yang's extensive reliance on Kant, Hegel, Marx, and Heidegger, it might have been an easier task to translate his book into German. In German for instance, the title of the book could have been translated rather simply as *Selbstbildung und Weltbildung*, making use of Hegel's central concept of *Bildung*, which seems to have strongly informed Yang's innovative usage of the Chinese term *cheng*. In many ways, I think, Yang's whole philosophical project revolves around this very concept. In English, however, there exists no single standard conceptual translation for *Bildung*, not even among the professional translations of Hegel's major works. Translators have therefore chosen to translate it with various different English words in different contexts.

The close ties between Yang Guorong's metaphysics and the Chinese and German philosophical traditions explain its thoroughly historical approach (and thereby distinguish it from current Anglo-American metaphysics). Yang's concrete metaphysics reflects on "being" and on human existence in the world as being in time; only in time there is life, and only in time can life be concrete. Consequently, a concrete metaphysics does not aim at constructing a "museum" of thoughts and refrains from presenting its contents as mummified extractions from passing time. Metaphysics cannot not be abstracted from historical contexts, it finds and locates itself within the history of ideas, the history of culture, and the history of language, and thus contributes to shaping the course of this history. Accordingly, Yang's metaphysics, by incorporating the conceptual heritage of Western and Chinese philosophies, inscribes itself into this history. In order to understand Yang's work, it is therefore necessary to be aware of the past that it makes its own and of the direction it thereby gives to itself.

Yang begins his book by introducing a conceptual distinction derived from the *Yijing* (*Book of Changes*), one of the oldest philosophically relevant texts of China, which served as a source for most philosophical traditions that later emerged. Implicitly, he thereby already claims the deep immersion of his metaphysics into the history of Chinese philosophy. The last two hexagrams of the *Yijing* are named *weiji* (未济) and *jiji* (既济), or in Yang's conceptualized understanding "incomplete being" and "complete being." These two concepts represent the basic dichotomy on which a metaphysical system is built. Humans find themselves in a world of "incomplete being," a world that they have to engage with both cognitively and practically. All human thought and action thus happens as the transformative work between the two poles *weiji* and *jiji*. We are, so to speak, thrown into a world that we yet have to make our own. Our existence consists of manifold efforts to humanize the world. Human consciousness and human practice are the means by which the world is moved from the pole of incompleteness toward the pole of completion.

Human civilization in general is thus described within a framework that Yang relates back to the most ancient philosophical materials of the Chinese tradition. This indicates that for him all philosophy, East and West, and North and South, is seminally contained within these parameters. The unfolding of the history of philosophy is, so to speak, merely the fulfilment of the task of humanizing the world that was already outlined, albeit it in "incomplete" form, in the Book of Changes—and, accordingly, Yang's philosophy, along with all others, is working toward the completion of this task.

Confucianism has conceived of its purpose as "helping transform and nourish the world." The Confucian tradition is accordingly understood as a most fundamental exercise of transforming the world (or "accomplishing things") through self-cultivation (or "accomplishing oneself"). For Yang, the core Confucian value of *ren* (仁) or "being humane" indicates an ethical humanist project of "civilizing" ourselves by forming social relationships, or, in Yang's words, by becoming a "systematic nexus of relationships" (*The Mutual Cultivation of Self and Things,*

p. 112). Ultimately, the transformation of the incomplete singular human being into a more complete cultural and communal being that thinks, acts, and generates meaning within and through social connections also extends to the natural world. Particularly for the Neo-Confucians of the Song and Ming dynasties, the relational form of being humane is extended toward a relational form of being in the world. Meaning cannot only be found in one's social environment, but also in the world as a whole. Thereby, the self-transformative process of "being humane" comes to an even more comprehensive completion. Overall, though, according to Yang, the Confucian tradition, including the Neo-Confucians "limited this process to the ethical domain of cultivating virtue, wherein human capacities are restricted to developing ethical knowledge of what is virtuous, which inhibits the expression of the entirety of human being's essential powers." Yang concludes that, "Orientated in this way, the human state of mind cannot avoid appearing speculative and mystical (ibid., p. 334).

Yang Guorong does not deny differences between the Confucian and the Daoist tradition, but he looks at both as being complementary rather than contradictory. Even Zhuangzi is seen, as is not unusual for contemporary Chinese philosophers, as a "humanist" in a broader sense. Given Yang's systematic premises, all philosophers will by the very act of philosophizing and reflecting on the world necessarily contribute to the humanizing of the world, and the Daoists cannot be an exception to this. They, too, relate to the world as humans, and are, like the Confucians, interested in bringing human nature to completion, even though by different means. While the Confucians seek to embellish humaneness through a kind of social aesthetics, the Daoists tend to be sceptical about the effects of socialization on human nature. They fear that social inclusion may obstruct rather than help human self-maturation.

The Daoist retreat from social and cultural normativity and its pursuit, in Yang's words, of "the authentic person" and "natural human being" is not without problems. For Yang, it "logically leads to the elimination of purposiveness" (ibid., p. 430). Such an elimination of purposiveness can become unproductive and thus cease to further the efforts of self-maturation and world-refinement. On its own, the Daoist way can therefore be accused of a certain one-sidedness.

The history of Chinese Buddhism is highly complex and includes a variety of religious and philosophical branches. Moreover, it first incorporated vital elements of the Daoist tradition and was then in part integrated into Neo-Confucian philosophy. Thus it is difficult to clearly define or isolate Chinese Buddhism "as such." From his metaphysical vantage point, Yang Guorong is specifically interested in the philosophical developments represented by the Chan and the Hua Yan schools. Particularly the latter has considerably contributed to the philosophical understanding of cognitive "world-making," and thus, in Yang's terminology, to the understanding of "the genesis of a world of meaning"—and therefore it deserves attention as an attempt toward the establishment of a systematic metaphysical epistemology.

One important Buddhist conceptual innovation is, for instance, the notion of *jingjie* (境界) or "state (of mind)." This term was taken over by the Neo-Confucians and others, and generally referred to a spiritual dimension that can be reached through, for instance, aesthetic or philosophical activity. It thus represents a specifically Chinese conceptual reflection on the human capacity to construct and to experience the world and one's self within it as significant.

The most immediate historical context within which Yang Guorong's Concrete Metaphysics is located and from which it stems, however, is much more recent than traditional Confucianism, Daoism, or Buddhism. Yang's work continues the efforts of modern Chinese philosophers to establish, on the basis of the Chinese textual and semantic inheritance, larger philosophical systems comparable to those of Western "masters" of metaphysics such as Kant or Hegel. Yang thus connects directly with twentieth-century Chinese thinkers such as Xiong Shili (1885–1968), Feng Youlan (1895–1990), Mou Zongsan (1909–1995), and, perhaps most importantly, his own teacher Feng Qi (1915–1995). All these predecessors were, like Yang, not only highly familiar with the history of Chinese philosophy, but also with both ancient and modern Western thought. They adopted the form, and parts of the contents, of "philosophy" as it was taught at major Western academic institutions of the time and succeeded in filling classical Chinese thought into this (from their perspective) new mold. Thereby, (academic) Chinese philosophy was born.

Although Yang Guorong does not expressively discuss Feng Qi's philosophy in the present book, his way of doing philosophy follows, but also extends, the path of Feng. In an earlier text, Yang wrote that Feng Qi, thanks to the profundity of his thought and his intellectual openness for a wide range of sources, "could make his own imprint on contemporary Chinese philosophy." He adds that Feng "traversed the paths of Western wisdom as much as he delved into the long stream of Chinese wisdom" and that "his intense reflections on the history of human knowledge were accompanied by a Marxist baptism by fire and a continuous interest in contemporary issues."[3] All this can equally be said of Yang Guorong himself.

The influence of Kant on Yang's philosophy is remarkable. Yang not only adopts some of the basic conceptual apparatus of the Kantian Critiques (such as the distinction between things-in-themselves and phenomena), but also Kant's critical intention to transform philosophy into a truly "scientific" (in the sense of *wissenschaftlich*) metaphysics that will not only clarify the cognitive relation of human consciousness to reality, but also the purpose of human life and the foundations of ethical normativity. For Kant, metaphysics opens up the avenue for human freedom. The most foundational goal of human liberation expressed by the philosophy of the Enlightenment is quite emphatically shared by Yang.

Hegel, though, in Yang's assessment "discovered a much broader horizon" (ibid., p. 22) than Kant. It seems obvious that two of the main pillars of Yang's concrete metaphysics are highly indebted to Hegel, namely, as already indicated earlier, the notion of *cheng* ("accomplishment," "maturation," "refinement," or, in Hegelian terms, *Bildung*) as well as the thoroughly historical nature of Yang's thought. The mutuality and reciprocal accomplishment of self-maturation and world-refinement is essential to Hegel's account of the self-establishing and the growth of consciousness from simple forms of cognition to the "absolute knowledge" of the "world spirit." In the constant engagement of (human) consciousness with the world, and, of course, with other human consciousnesses, humanity matures and history evolves. Subjectivity develops in its cognitive and practical engagement with objects. This process is always active and productive, and leads, as with Kant, to increasing "spiritual" awareness and stages of liberation.

Yang is not an outright Hegelian, though, and agrees in principle with one of Marx's most basic criticisms of Hegel as an Idealist who failed to do philosophical and systematic justice to the importance of human practice. When Yang says that with Hegel "'being' itself, as well as the question of how 'what ought to be' transforms into actuality, stops and remains in the spiritual realm (including what he called objective spirit)" and that therefore his philosophical system as a whole was incapable of 'shaking off its speculative character,'" (23) he clearly echoes Marx's judgment. Yang agrees with Marx that the attainment of human freedom cannot mainly be a spiritual endeavor. It cannot be reduced to an effort of "self-cultivation" or it runs the risk to end up in forms of "mysticism" that not only German Idealism, but also the Chinese traditions (Confucianism, Daoism, Buddhism) could not altogether avoid. Marx embraces Hegel's radically historical view of human "maturation" or the "refinement of the world" through human activity, but for him, this activity is a concrete material exercise of human power, constrained only by the material laws humans find themselves subjected to. Yang agrees with this Materialist turn of Hegelian dialectics.

But, for Yang, a Marxist Materialist appropriation of Hegel alone cannot complete a Concrete Metaphysics. He uses Heidegger to add an existential dimension to metaphysics that he misses in Hegelian, and, ultimately, in Marxist philosophy. Yang says that it was Martin Heidegger who "relegated the meaning of the individual's existence to a comparatively more important position" (23) than those before him. Heidegger's concern with (human) *Dasein* adds dimensions of the concrete experience of being in the world into the equation that neither Hegel nor Marx fully recognized. A concrete metaphysics has to properly take this dimension into account, which points to the "genesis of meaning" that occurs on the level of individual existence.

In the end, however, Yang Guorong is no more a Heideggerrian than a Hegelian, Kantian, or Marxist, just as he is no more a Confucian than a Daoist or Buddhist. His philosophy is rooted in the past, but it is supposed to point toward the future. Yang shares the hopes of his systematic predecessors in China and the West that philosophy can newly establish itself as a synthetic world philosophy that proves capable of integrating, or, perhaps better, "sublating," the philosophical, religious, cultural, aesthetic, and, of course, materially productive traditions of all civilizations within a dynamic and growing (concrete) metaphysics.

THE MUTUAL CULTIVATION OF SELF AND THINGS

Introduction

THAT WHICH HUMAN being faces is neither an already-completed world nor primordial beings in-themselves.¹ From human being's perspective, the world is incomplete by nature and in appearance. By "the world" we mean actual beings relative to the being of humans. Beings in-themselves are indeed really there, but they might not be actual for human beings. To be actual, beings must become objects of human being's cognition and practice, and consequently, present actual meaning to human being. In this sense, actuality is characterized by becoming. The transformation of beings in-themselves into actuality is thus a historical interaction. In ancient Chinese, this interaction is characterized by the relationship between complete being (*jiji* 既济) and incomplete being (*weiji* 未济).² Confucianism has stressed this dimension of the actual world in advocating that human being ought to "add nourishment to the cultivation of the Heavens and the Earth" (*zan tiandi zhi huayu* 赞天地之化育), which implies that the world is not yet complete and human being's participation is indispensable to its completion. Corresponding to the incomplete nature of the world is the incomplete nature of human being. Just arriving in the world, human being is to some extent merely biological, similar to a thing in-itself. There is a step by step process whereby human being overcomes this mode of being in-itself, gradually moves toward a state of freedom, eventually attains a free mode of being, and consequently realizes the maturation of her own being along with a sense of self-accomplishment. Thus, on the one hand, things in-themselves are characterized as actual when they merge into human being's process of cognition and practice; on the other hand, human being affirms its own essential powers in the process of cultivating the world, that is, through participating in the formation of the actual world.

We can easily see the two-fold dimension of human being's relation to the world in the historical process of nourishing and cultivating the world: on the one hand, human being is a being immanent to the world; on the other hand, human being is the being who is capable of questioning the world and changing the world, and thus the world is immanent to the very being of humans as the object of human being's cognition and practice. Here, there is a sense of self-accomplishment human being may achieve in the process of self-cultivation while simultaneously accomplishing things, and this genesis of a world of meaning develops being out of the primordial state of being in-itself. Philosophically speaking, the self-accomplishment human being achieves in the process of accomplishing things is the result of human being knowing and transforming the self along with the world.

Accomplishing things brings us first to the question of what things are. "Things" is "the most general term," which refers to all that there is, all beings.[3] In more detail, "things" could be distinguished into two categories: things that have entered the sphere of human being's cognition and practice and things that still lie outside of this sphere. In *What Is a Thing?* Heidegger distinguishes two distinct objects indicated by this word "thing," including whatever is touchable, reachable or visible, that is, what is present-at-hand (*das Vorhandene*); there is a thing in the sense of something that is in this or that condition, the things that happen in the world; then secondly, there is a thing in the sense of what Kant speaks of as the "thing in-itself."[4] The first two "things" involve human being, while the latter remains beyond the sphere of human cognition and practice. We will temporarily lay aside Kant's definition and understanding of the thing in-itself. From the perspective of accomplishing things, we will call those things that exist outside of the sphere of human cognition and practice things that exist in the primordial state of being, each of which encompass two basic determinations, that of being primordial and that of being in-itself; being primordial is said here in opposition to the process of humanization. Things that exist in the primordial mode are those that do not yet concern human being; their being and the vicissitudes of their being have nothing to do with human activity. What is in-itself corresponding to this primordial nature refers to the properties of the thing in-itself, first, the thing's physical properties. Now, even if things overcome the primordial mode of nature, their own physical properties nevertheless still exist in-themselves. This state of being in-itself represents the reality of things; being in-itself in this sense refers to the common attribute shared by beings that have entered the sphere of human practice and cognition and the beings that have not.

These attributes of things mentioned above correspond to the inquiry concerning "What is a thing?" However, this inquiry concerning things is not limited to things themselves. According to Heidegger's understanding, the question "What is a thing?" always leads back to the question "Who is man?"[5] Even though Heidegger never really gave a concrete and clear exposition of the interconnection between these two questions, he undoubtedly engaged the most important aspect of the relation between human being and things. The interrelatedness of the two questions could be stated thus: the thing's meaning is only open to human being. In effect, the quality of primordialness and that of being in-itself, as the two different attributes of things, can only be distinguished in relation to human being: The primordial nature of things may only be understood in opposition to the humanized form of things, while the being in-itself of things reveals the independence of things in relation to human being (even after things undergo humanization, their physical attributes still subsist). Broadly speaking, as this book will show later on, regardless of whether it is at the cognitive level of understanding or at the evaluative level of ends, the meaning of things always emerges solely in the process of human practice and cognition.

As far as the interconnection between things and human being goes, the concept of affairs (*shi* 事) is an aspect that can by no means be overlooked. Here, an affair may be understood in two senses: in the static sense, an affair could be seen as a thing that has entered the sphere of practice and cognition; in the dynamic sense, an affair refers to the activity of practicing and cognizing in the broad sense—just as Han Fei, the great legalist of ancient China, defined affairs: "by affair we mean doing something."[6] The former involves the things human being encounters in the sphere of her activity, while the latter refers to things such as events, matters, business, work, and so on. Chinese philosophy took notice of this connection between things and affairs very early on. When discussing how to accord with *dao,* the *Great Learning* (*Daxue,* 1.1), a Confucian classic that dates back prior to 220 B.C.E., points out: "Things have their roots and branches. Affairs have their beginning and end. To know what is prior and what is posterior will lead one near *dao.*" The statement that things have their roots and branches highlights the form of the thing's being or the ontological structure of things; the statement that affairs have their beginning and end emphasizes the practical order of affairs in the process of human activity. Here, the ontological structure of things and the practical order of affairs are seen as two mutually interconnected aspects, and moreover, grasping this structure and order is understood as a process of coming into accordance with *dao.* This viewpoint reveals the ontological horizon of practical wisdom as it affirms the original unity of things and affairs. The unity of affairs and things gained even clearer affirmations in later Chinese philosophy. When explaining the notion of "things" in *The Great Learning,* Zheng Xuan (127–200) states that "things are like affairs." This understanding again reached further consensus in the philosophy that followed: It was directly adopted in Zhu Xi's well-known Neo-Confucian commentary on *The Great Learning;* Wang Yangming, another great Neo-Confucian, goes even further, arguing that "the thing is an affair";[7] Wang Fuzhi (1619–1692) then follows with an even more profound elucidation of this, stating: "Things are called affairs, because it is said that there is nothing if affairs end up unaccomplished."[8] To say that there will be nothing if affairs remain unaccomplished is to point out that the transformation of "Nature in-itself" (*tian zhi tian* 天之天) into "Nature for human being" (*ren zhi tian* 人之天)[9,10] or the formation of humanized things, can only be realized through human activity; it also implies that the meaning of things may only emerge through human being's cognitive and practical activity. Here, we can see further corroboration of the approach primarily advocated in *The Great Learning*, that is grasping the relation between things and affairs in terms of the ontological structure of things and the practical order of affairs. In fact, we can find the same approach to understanding things in terms of their place in human activity in the following:

> Open things up to accomplish affairs.[11]
> The wise initiate things and the skilled inherit them.[12]

Reforming things (opening things up) unfolds as a process of accomplishing affairs, but the success of affairs is realized through human being's practical activity; to initiate things is to create things that correspond to human needs and human ideals, and to inherit them is to get a hold of those things in the continuity of grasping them. We can easily see what is expressed here: bring things (primordial objects) into affairs (human activity) and open things up or initiate things through affairs. Corresponding to this connection between things and affairs is "things" themselves displaying their ontological, axiological, and epistemological significance.

Bringing things into affairs and initiating things through affairs is the background of the process of accomplishing things. Accomplishing things then unfolds in this context as a process of developing things out of their primordial state. Things in the primordial state belong to Nature in-itself, and accomplishing things demands transforming Nature in-itself into Nature for human being, which implies leading things deeper into the sphere of human being's cognition and practice so as to become forms of being that suit the needs of human beings. Of course, as stated earlier, we shouldn't lose sight of the distinction between primordialness and that of being in-itself: to overcome a thing's primitive state doesn't imply eliminating what it possesses as being in-itself. Things move from Nature in-itself (a primordial state) into Nature for human being (a humanized state), which is essentially a transformation from the form of being that has nothing to do with the being of humans to the formation of being that does; even though the thing's form of being is transformed in this process, its physical and chemical qualities, as well as other such qualities, do not for that matter disappear as a consequence. These qualities of things neither depend upon human practice nor human cognition (consciousness). As independent qualities that exist in-themselves, physical and chemical properties embody the reality of things.

Conjoining things to affairs (human activity) develops things out of a primordial state without destroying the being they have in-themselves, and at the same time, leads things deeper into the humanized world. When they become handled as affairs in human activity, things in a primordial state are made to become humanized real beings, which marks them with human impressions and henceforth makes them belong to the human world. Of course, it is true that a content of meaning takes shape through one's cognizing and practicing, whose historical content is accomplishing oneself and accomplishing things, which constitutes the real source of meaning and also makes the ultimate concern at the level of the way of Nature as a whole concretize within the historical process of one's own being.

As a historical process, accomplishing oneself and accomplishing things primarily involves understanding the world and oneself. Refining oneself (accomplishing oneself) and refining the world (accomplishing things) both presuppose a grasp of authentic being. On the level of knowing what is actual, the meaning of being consists in being understood or being understandable. The content of this level of understanding is knowing or cognizing. From within this understanding-knowing dimension, meaning involves two aspects: form and substantial content. As for form, what is meaningful must first be something that accords with the laws of logic. Jin Yuelin, a modern Chinese philosopher, once stated that the law of identity in formal logic is the basic condition of possibility of meaning. According to the law of identity, a concept must have a definite intension or connotation, which cannot be arbitrarily changed in a determinate discursive context. Besides the law of identity, the law of contradiction and the law of excluded middle also act as the formal conditions of possibility of meaning. As for substantial content, however, meaning is primarily linked to cognition in the factual dimension: with understanding as its aim, meaning always contains some cognized content. Yet, meaning at the cognitive level of understanding is formed in the process of accomplishing oneself and accomplishing things and is also precisely what enters one's horizon and what one henceforth grasps in the process.

Refining oneself (accomplishing oneself) and reforming the world (accomplishing things) is not only a task of grasping actuality, because it also unfolds as a process of cultivating oneself and the world according to one's ends and ideals. With an end as the object of concern, the meaning of being presents values. Or more exactly, at this level, meaning is understood in terms of value: If a relevant person, thing, or idea has a positive function or value in relation to realizing some end, then it presents a positive meaning, or on the contrary, if it has no function or value in relation to realizing the end concerned, then its meaning will be presented as having a negative quality. From the perspective of accomplishing oneself and accomplishing things, meaning in this sense involves ends, functions, and actions, and what has meaning in relation to the latter not only demonstrates the intrinsic values which the process of accomplishing oneself and accomplishing things contains but also concerns the effect and function that various things, affairs, conceptions and actions have in relation to this process.

The concrete content of meaning implicates both an "understanding-knowing" dimension and an "ends-values" dimension, which entails that meaning itself must simultaneously reach clarification in the discursive domains of the meaning of one's own being; one grasps the world and the meaning of the self in a conceptual way and also endows the world with a diversity of meaning through practice. In this sense, we can see human being as the being who aims at meaning. Heidegger once claimed: "The question of the 'meaning of being' is the question of all questions."[14] To say that human being questions after being is also just to say that human being questions after the meaning of being, and this questioning is never just a concern of semantics or the philosophy of language, because it also concretely unfolds in the epistemological, ontological, and axiology domains as well. Historically speaking, several changes of core concern have occurred in the process of philosophy's evolution. These changes have often been marked as philosophical "turns," but behind this variety of so-called turns we can always find an implicit concern for meaning: regardless of whether it's a philosophical system that puts weight on epistemology or a mode of philosophy that focuses mainly on ontology or axiology, it is not hard to see that they all involve a particular intrinsic concern for meaning, and it is precisely in this sense that the question after "the meaning of being" truly has an originative nature.[15]

Connecting the genesis of meaning to the cultivation of self and things will be quite different from a concern with meaning at the transcendent level. Within the transcendent horizon, the ground of meaning is always ascribed to some ultimate being, and pursuing meaning is always understood to be the ultimate concern corresponding to this kind of being. However, in actuality, ultimate being can be nothing but concrete being as a whole or an integrity which takes itself as the cause, and the concern for meaning that corresponds with this being implies facing this authentic world so as to ceaselessly overcome the tension between the finite and the infinite and consequently improve human being's own existential condition. This process can only be realized in the continuation of one's own cognitive and practical activity. In ancient Chinese philosophy, being in the ultimate sense is understood as *dao* (道) or *tiandao* (天道), the Way of Nature as a whole, but *dao* or *tiandao* does not estrange the being of humans. The well-known statement that "*dao* is not distant from human being" (*zhongyong*, paragraph 13) affirms this intrinsic connection between the being of humans and the meaning of *dao*; and moreover, positing human nature (*xing* 性) together with the way of nature as a whole (*tiandao*) (*The Analects,* 5:12) as well as positing *dao* and humans as the two greatest beings in the universe (*Laozi,* chapter 25) are two different ways of making this point clear. Understandings such as these have the following implications: the meaning of ultimate being (the way of Nature as a whole) is actualized in the process of one's being. A concern that suspends one's own being in the reverence of some transcendent being may indeed give one some sort of spiritual rest or speculative satisfaction, but the meaning of being that is revealed through this type of concern will never express the concrete relation between oneself and the world, and thus will never be able to avoid abstraction. The actual

Here, refining the world (participating in the cultivation of Nature) is a process of extending oneself to the other. In effect, accomplishing things doesn't just express the relation of human being to things. Behind the relation between human and things is the implied relation between human and human. In brief, accomplishing oneself and accomplishing things is tied to refining human being in the broad sense and involves inter-subjective interaction.

As the basic precondition of the being of humans, accomplishing oneself and accomplishing things unfolds in different directions. The process of refining things involves one side that moves from human being to object as human being comes to know the world and reform it. As opposed to accomplishing oneself, whose direct object is oneself, accomplishing things is nuanced by the characteristic of externality, which scientism has emphasized time and again. However, on the other hand, since the ideal of accomplishing oneself is self-refinement, the process of accomplishing oneself often falls into an excessive concern for individual existence, inwardly directed spiritual pursuits, and so on. Heidegger posits this as the core of fundamental ontology, while turning the individual's existence and the return to the self's authentic mode of being into the core of concern of Dasein, and the so-called authentic mode of being is tied precisely to the individual overcoming his own fallenness into being-with while comprehending the uniqueness and irreplaceability of her own being. Such an understanding as this reveals the tendency to over-emphasize the dimensions of individuality and internality pertaining to the process of accomplishing oneself. In actuality, however, accomplishing oneself is impossible without accomplishing things, and knowing the world and changing the world is inseparable from raising the state of one's being. In the same way, accomplishing oneself cannot be limited to either the narrow process of survival or the spiritual realm, which is to say that the fruit of self-cultivation only attains richness and concretion in the process of knowing and transforming the world. *The Doctrine of the Mean,* which uses "the Way (*dao* 道) of integrating the outside with the inside" (*zhongyong,* paragraph 26) to elucidate the unity of accomplishing oneself and accomplishing things, seems to have already noticed this. Through this union of refining oneself and refining things, the externality of the process of accomplishing things is overcome, and the process of accomplishing oneself avoids falling into either the one-sided process of survival or introverted self-experiences.

With knowing the self and knowing the world, reforming the self and reforming the world as its concrete historical content, the mutual cultivation of self and things is at the same time a generative process of becoming wherein meaning and a world of meaning is brought about: whether it is opening up the world and knowing oneself or transforming the world and accomplishing oneself, both intrinsically refer to the manifestation of meaning or the genesis of a world of meaning. One questions after the meaning of the world and also questions after

ing oneself and accomplishing things remain open without falling into the transcendent.

As discussed previously, metaphysically speaking, human being is at once a being and also the being who questions being and changes being. At first sight, questioning and changing being is primarily qualified as a process of cognizing and practicing, but in essence this process concretely unfolds as a process of accomplishing oneself and accomplishing things. As human being's way of being-in-the-world with ontological meaning, accomplishing oneself and accomplishing things constitutes the basic condition of the being of humans: once human being acts as the being who faces the world in the mode of questioning being and changing being, accomplishing oneself and accomplishing things becomes the human sphere of being. It is precisely this sphere of being that distinguishes humans from other objects. From participating in the cultivation of Nature to accomplishing oneself, the genesis of the actual world in the process of self-cultivation are the accompaniments of one's questioning and reforming of the world. We could say that were human being to desist from the process of accomplishing itself and accomplishing things, human being would lose actuality and henceforth cease *to be* authentically in the world.

The actual process of accomplishing oneself and accomplishing things does not solely concern the self as an individual and the world as an object. The self is not an isolated individual. Rather, the self is mutually engaged with others in a state of being-with; this state of being-with or mutual affiliation also constitutes the precondition of the being of humans. Thus, accomplishing oneself is inseparable from the accomplishment of others. On the one hand, there is no way for the self to grow without interacting with others; on the other hand, in the process of self-cultivation, the self must acknowledge and respect the other's right and will to cultivate herself and thus contribute to "refining the virtues of others." Confucianism already noticed this when arguing for the unity of *liji* (立己) and *liren* (立人): one must establish oneself and take one's stand in the process of helping the other establish herself and take her stand. In the same way, in the process of accomplishing things, one's effect on the world is not limited to reforming society, since it always exceeds the individual domain as it unfolds as a unified historical process based on the interaction between the self and the other and the unity of the self and the group. *Zhongyong* (中庸) once pointed out:

> Only those who are fully genuine can fully develop their natural tendencies. If they can fully develop their natural tendencies, they then can develop the natural tendencies of others. If they can develop the natural tendencies of others, they can fully develop the natural tendencies of things. If they can fully develop the natural tendencies of things, they can then assist in the cultivation of the world. If they can assist in the cultivation of the world, they can thus fully join the world.[13]

were. Human being, on the other hand, is able to overcome what she was or develop out of the primordial form of being (Nature in-itself) and become what she wasn't (a social being).

In terms of developing being out of the primordial form, we can see that accomplishing oneself is quite similar to accomplishing things. However, corresponding to the distinction between things and the self there is the difference in the content of their value. As the concrete unfolding of knowing and practicing, accomplishing oneself and accomplishing things involves ideals. The object of accomplishing things is to make things suit the historical needs of human beings: in the process of transforming primordial things into humanized reality, making things harmonize with the ideals of human values and making things suit the historical needs of human beings are intrinsically identical processes. Here, the meaning of things is shown through human being, whose ideals possess some degree of externality. By contrast, since the self is in each case one's own being, accomplishing oneself doesn't aim at making things come into accord with needs that are external to oneself, but rather posits one's own accomplishment as an end, which is to say that it has internal meaning for human being. In effect, in the process of accomplishing itself, human being is at once the embodied form of meaning and also the subject who seeks meaning; this is to say that the genesis of meaning is the self-realization of the agent of meaning.

The evaluative dimension of accomplishing oneself and accomplishing things differentiates being from a vague and general interaction between human being and beings or abstract transformations without any real content. In one's cognitive and practical activity, variations that do not carry any values are empty, lacking substantial meaning. However, on the other hand, accomplishing oneself and accomplishing things does not presuppose an ultimate end, which, as the absolutely invariant, would always be of a closed or transcendent nature, and, as the final and ultimate, would be in some sense identical to the thing in-itself existing forever beyond the reach of knowledge and practice. If such an ultimate end were taken to limit and qualify the process of accomplishing oneself and accomplishing things, both self and things would be induced into another state of pure abstraction. In effect, accomplishing oneself and accomplishing things aims at some value and unfolds as a concrete process. Consequently, these ends-values, that is, values as ends, are not transcendent objects: In other words, they are always characterized by concreteness in the process of historical evolution and present themselves as ideals based on reality. Accomplishing oneself and accomplishing things is also the very process through which these ideals of value continuously emerge into being and gradually attain some kind of realization. Thus, the importance of values and ends lies in enabling the process of accomplishing oneself and accomplishing things to overcome an empty and abstract state, and the processuality and historicality of values makes this mutual unfolding of accomplish-

humanized real being still contains objective characteristics in spite of the fact that it is attributable to the being of humans. In contrast, social reality shows a greater degree of intrinsic links to human beings. Both the being and working of social reality—as a world that takes shape through the cognitive and practical activity of human beings—is inseparable from human being. Human beings construct social reality, but the being of humans is also ontologically grounded in social reality; this interaction between human being and social reality exhibits the connection between things in-themselves and things as affairs on the one hand, and yet also makes this link transcend the nature of being merely objective by exhibiting the human mode of being.

From the perspective of the unity of things and affairs, the humanized world is simultaneously the world of "affairs-things" or "things-affairs." So, what the humanized world contains is things as affairs or affairs as things rather than pure things isolated from affairs or pure affairs isolated from things. Pure things isolated from affairs are nothing but primordial beings, while pure affairs isolated from things lack actuality and being in-itself. Corresponding to the mode of being of this "affairs-things" world, refining things concretely expresses itself as the historical unfolding of knowing and practicing, wherein the interaction of things and affairs opens up the world's meaning and leads the world into harmony with the ideals of human values. In this sense, the humanized world is a world of meaning and meanwhile, "things-affairs" or "affairs-things" constitute the ontological ground of the generative becoming of meaning.

Relative to accomplishing things is accomplishing oneself. While the content of accomplishing things is knowing and reforming the objective world, the process of accomplishing oneself posits one's own being as the object of knowledge and cultivation; here, "one" refers to "someone," "human being," or every actual social agent. Just as knowing and reforming the objective world involves developing the world out of its primordial state or mode of being in-itself, human being's own self-cognition and self-cultivation also involves transforming Nature in-itself into Nature for human being. As mentioned, when human being arrives in the world, she is still just an individual with life in the biological sense, and at this level, human being is but a primordial being. Similar to the process of accomplishing things, the process of accomplishing oneself first entails developing oneself out of the primordial form of being by imparting social characteristics to oneself so that one may become a social being. To accomplish oneself is to some extent to become a new self that one has not embraced, or rather, to be what one was not: As a mere biological individual, human being doesn't possess social characteristics from the very beginning but rather acquires and refines these social characteristics continually throughout the process of self-cultivation. Herein lies the difference between humans and animals: animals never develop out of the primordial form of being (Nature in-itself) and thus cannot but be what they

epistemology, axiology, and ontology. However, modern philosophers have often been partial in their treatment of meaning. Theories of meaning in analytic philosophy are often limited to the domains of language and logic. Opposed to this are the phenomenological and existentialist schools which focus on internal consciousness and the relation and communication between the question of meaning, human existence, and values. As for its actuality, meaning can be reduced to neither the semantic content of words nor the existential or axiological dimensions. The multiplicity of relations of human being to the world fundamentally determines that there must be a multiplicity of expressive forms of meaning. In other words, the multiplicity of forms of meaning originates from the multiple dimensions of the process of accomplishing oneself and accomplishing things. As stated earlier, with knowing the self and knowing the world, refining the self and reforming the world as its concrete historical content, accomplishing oneself and accomplishing things involves multiple dimensions—ontological, epistemological, and axiological. Different questions correspond to these different dimensions of meaning implicated in the process of accomplishing oneself and accomplishing things, which could be explicated as "What is it?" "What does it mean?" and "What should it become?" The question "What is it?" engages the level of meaning concerned with knowing and understanding; "What does it mean?" points to the value of beings; and "What should it become?" leads us further into the practical dimension and changes the direction of thought from a concern for the actual form of being of the world and oneself toward a concern for what the world and one ought to be. The multiple intensions of meaning here are intrinsically identical to the multiple dimensions of the process of accomplishing oneself and accomplishing things.

In summary, since the intrinsic origin of meaning is the process of accomplishing oneself and accomplishing things and the historical precondition of meaning is the transformation of primordial objects into humanized actuality, meaning doesn't only appear in conceptual form, because it is manifested in humanized actuality as well. The former (the conceptual form of meaning) is being that is known or understood, but it is also invested with values through the act of evaluating and unfolds as various states of mind as well; the latter (humanized actuality) implies transforming Nature in-itself into Nature for-humans through human practical activity, and by virtue of this process, the mark of human is imprinted upon primordial things, which henceforth come to embody the ideals of human values. These different forms of meaning are interconnected in the interaction of human beings with the world and concretely display the diversity of worlds of meaning. As the historical product of accomplishing oneself and accomplishing things, a world of meaning refers to human being's understanding and prescriptive formulations of being (the being of the world and the being of humans) as well as human being's impact upon the latter. In a wide sense then, a world of meaning could be seen as being that has entered the sphere of human practice and cognition, that is, being that has been imprinted with the mark of human and has come to embody the ideals of human values. Here, we see the unity of the conceptual form of meaning and meaning in actuality. Through the creative activity of reforming the world and refining itself, human being ceaselessly constructs diverse forms of worlds of meaning in the human quest for meaning.

Historically speaking, in the process of understanding the essence of meaning, various partial and one-sided trends have emerged. As regards the formation of meaning, some one-sided trends or biases have taken meaning to refer to the object's properties and attributes that exist in-themselves while others have taken meaning to be built solely upon human being's evaluation, self-understanding, or conscious constructions: the former overlooks the relationship between the genesis of meaning and human being's cognitive and practical activity, while the latter limits the genesis of meaning to the level of subjective consciousness and thus pays inadequate attention to the real ground of meaning, that is, the process of accomplishing the self and accomplishing things, in which meaning is essentially rooted and through which a world of meaning is actually generated.

At the level of values, the two skewed understandings of the question of meaning are expressed in the forms of nihilism and authoritarianism. The characteristic of nihilism is to eliminate meaning, and its fundamental problem consists in denying the intrinsic worth of human creative activity and caring less about the historical connection between the quest for meaning and the movement toward freedom. As a historical phenomenon, the birth and growth of nihilism has an actual social origin. Since the modern age, following the development of the commodity economy, "a general social metabolism" gradually took center stage, the result of which could be seen as the formation of human being's "objective dependency," which has kept human being hooked on things through the alienation of human labor and through the propagation of commodity fetishism. At the same time that this "objective dependency" invests things with purposive qualities, it also makes purposes themselves become extrinsic endowments: being dependent on things not only turns external things into the foundation of value, but also turns external things into the origin of human purposes. Linked to externalizing the ground of values and externalizing internal purposes is a dead loss of meaning, whose result is the widening variety of nihilisms. Nietzsche criticized nihilism for founding values and purposes on "another world." This viewpoint reveals the connection between traditional value systems and metaphysics, but also in some sense engages the historical origins of nihilism. In connection with these premises, there are two aspects that must be considered in overcoming nihilism: one consists in returning values and purposes to their actual foundation, and the other consists in committing oneself to meaning, protecting meaning, and seeking meaning.

Opposite and yet complementary to dispelling meaning is coercively enforcing it. This latter tendency is concretely embodied in authoritarianism. As stated, the generation and presentation of meaning as well as human being's pursuit of meaning all have an essentially open nature. With creating values as its historical content, accomplishing oneself and accomplishing things unfolds in diverse forms, and moreover, there is a multiplicity of meanings generated in this process, which is the precondition of the diversity of values and of one's freedom to choose one's own values. In this way, the generation and presentation of meaning displays one aspect of the freedom of refining oneself and refining things: the open nature of the process of knowing, practicing, and generating meaning reveals the dimension of freedom in the process of human creation. Authoritarianism attempts to employ dictatorial means to enforce some system of meaning upon humans, which obviously doesn't just negate the open nature of meaning's generation, but also terminates the free process of human creation. We can see here that although nihilism and authoritarianism are different in form, the former intending to dispel meaning and the latter tending to coercively enforce it, both are similar in the way they terminate human being's path to freedom.

To borrow Kant's way of posing the question, accomplishing oneself and accomplishing things as well as generating a world of meaning are all intrinsically related to the question "How is it possible?" Now, the question "How is it possible?" primarily involves grounds and conditions. As the grounds and conditions of accomplishing oneself and things and of producing a world of meaning, human capacities can by no means be ignored. Comparatively speaking, Kant was mainly concerned with logic and form when he raised the question "How is a priori knowledge possible?" Although it is true that Kant touched upon the issue of human faculties, he never unfolded an adequate investigation. In addition, even when he discusses human faculties, Kant again starts his critique with the issue of form. This is similar to his exposition of intuition, where he emphasizes the importance of the a priori forms of space and time, positing them as the universal conditions of possibility of intuition. It is true that Kant also emphasized the importance of the synthetic role of the "cogito;" however, the latter is further interconnected with the distinction between the transcendental self and the empirical self, and yet Kant was much more concerned with the former, which is also to a large extent an a priori supposition. We see the same thing in the case of practical reason, where Kant considered questions of morality mainly from the perspective of the formal conditions of moral behavior (universal moral law). In short, we can safely say that the aspects of logic and form are the main objects of Kant's concern.

As the internal conditions of accomplishing oneself and accomplishing things, human capacities obviously need further consideration. As for their mode of being, human capacities have an ontological character, that is, they are inseparable from humans and are equal to the being of humans. In contrast, logical and formal elements may integrate into human being's cognitive systems, but they may also be considered as external to human being. In a broad sense, human capacities are the manifestation of the essential powers of human being in the process of knowing and reforming the self and the world. Concretely speaking, human capacities involve multiple aspects including the "known" and the "knower." The known refers to the knowledge that has matured and piled up in the historical process of humanizing being. In one aspect, human capacities are always founded upon such cognitive achievements in the broad sense, and the maturation of these capacities is always linked to the internalization and consolidation of these cognitive accomplishments. If severed from the latter, human being's cognitive capacities would just degenerate into abstract generalities. In another respect, if the cognitive achievements of knowledge were unable for some reason to gain embodiment and actualize practically in the expression of human capacities, then all we would have is but a possible tendency; as formal conditions that have not yet been actualized, they lack the internal force of vital life. In the process of accomplishing oneself and accomplishing things, formal conditions and internal vitality interact and fuse together. At the same time, it must be granted that human capacities have the logical and formal aspects that Kant emphasized, but they also involve conscious processes and mental activity, and thereby express in a certain sense the unity of logic and psychology.

Starting with an emphasis on a priori knowledge, Kant maintained a detached and distant attitude toward the psychological and conscious aspects of human being. As stated, Kant could not hide his fervor for a priori forms and their purity. However, as soon as we turn from a priori form to actual application, we immediately notice that it is impossible to draw a dichotomy between the logical and the empirical. In this respect, the thought of Karl Marx is a step forward. Marx once compared the realm of necessity and the realm of freedom, pointing out that the development of human power (die menschliche Kraftentwicklung), which is "an end in itself" (sich als Selbstzweck) can only begin beyond the realm of necessity.[16] Worthy of attention here is the claim that the development of human power is "an end in itself," which entails positing human capacity as an end in itself; this has both ontological and axiological meaning. At the ontological level, the fact that human capacities are ends in themselves indicates that human capacities cannot be treated in isolation from the being of humans: as ends, human capacities merge with the whole of one's being and express the existential characteristic of human being in a form that differs from external relations. At the axiological level, the fact that human capacities are ends in themselves indicates that human capacities are different from pure means and cannot be considered simply as tools. As ends in themselves, human capacities have intrinsic value. In brief, human capacities, as the concrete embodiment of the essential powers of human being, are ends in themselves.

Insofar as they unify sensibility and reason as well as the non-rational and rational, human capacities merge with the whole of one's being and reveal the internal attribute of human nature. At the level of rationality, human capacities express themselves in the form of logical thinking and aim at unifying what is and what ought to be, that is, unifying what is true and what is good. Knowing what is (true) and evaluating what ought to be (good) is also related to the validation of ends that accord with reason (validity) and grasping the rational means to reach those ends (effectiveness). This is not only a process of forming knowledge; it is also a process of making wisdom coherent and improving it as well. Regardless of whether it is through opening up this world or producing a world that ought to be, the faculty of reason always expresses the depth or profundity of its powers. Yet, complementary to logical and rational faculties are irrational ones, including imagination, intuition, and the capacity of insight. These irrational faculties are all similar insofar as they demonstrate one's inherent powers to grasp the world and oneself in a way that differs from the way normal reasoning or logical thinking would grasp the world and the self. Imagination is characterized by the power to transcend what is actual and already known upon the basis of what is actual and already known and thereby open up more expansive domains of possibility (including possible connections between things, affairs, and concepts). Imagination points to possible worlds and thus provides free space for grasping the world creatively. In the same way, through surpassing ordinary thinking procedure and transforming ways of thinking, intuition enables one to go beyond the limits of an already bounded domain and reach new understandings and comprehensions of the world and oneself in a non-deductive way. The capacity of insight, which interlinks imagination and intuition, then, with a creative grasp of "degree," as the qualitative quantum of thinking, aims at the essential attributes of things or aspects with decisive meaning, and thus endows understanding with the characteristic of consistency and integral order. Finally, human capacities gain a more synthetic expression in the power of judgment. Judgment's concrete mode of being could be expressed as the reciprocal interaction of reason, perception, imagination, and insight and the combined unity of analytic, comparative, deductive, determining, and decisive faculties. Judgment thus involves a harmonic mixture of different capacities, and aims at connecting conceptual form to the object itself. Within the horizon of accomplishing oneself and accomplishing things, human capacities constitute the precondition of explaining the world and changing the world and express the inner conditions of self-cognition and self-transformation.

Relative to internal human capacities are external systems of norms. Systems of norms prescribe what ought to be. Now, accomplishing oneself and accomplishing things from the level of what ought to be involves the questions "What should one do?" and "How should one do it?" While the former inquires after which goal or direction of action ought to be established, the latter guides one in an inquiry concerning how one ought to behave in a manner that is appropriate for reaching a goal. Opposite and yet complementary to guiding behavior is limiting or restraining behavior, which, by means of negation, prescribes what ought not be done or what ought not be selected as a way to do something. Guiding and restricting express the same normative principle in respectively different ways: one positive and the other negative. As a historical process, accomplishing oneself and accomplishing things embraces the human capacities as its internal conditions and finds itself networked into multiple forms of normative systems: in one respect, cognitive and practical processes are prescriptive in different senses; and in another aspect, by externalizing and becoming universal systems of norms, the knowledge and wisdom formed in cognitive and practical processes further constrains the latter.

Norms play an effective role in accomplishing oneself and accomplishing things. On the one hand, norms are linked to purposive prescriptions and thus encompass the dimension of value; on the other hand, they are also based upon reality and necessity and thus have their ontological ground. Knowledge of what ought to be, what is necessary, and what is actual not only constitutes the concrete content of the various systems of knowledge, for, in the process of practice, rational reflection and the self-verification of virtues transform this knowledge into wisdom. Knowledge and wisdom, embracing what ought to be, what is necessary, and what is actual, then merge with the value orientations and practical needs of human beings so that they transform into or coalesce into different systems of norms, which further guide the process of accomplishing oneself and accomplishing things at different levels. In a broad sense, norms could be understood as the universal standards according to which "doing" or human conduct and human forms of being are evaluated and even prescribed. Forms of being involve what one should be or what one ought to accomplish, and norms in this sense serve as a guide; doing or human conduct thus refers to practicing and in an extended sense also includes conscious activity (i.e., cognizing, thinking, etc.). Systems of norms contain general principles (such as general value principles), special principles that guide behavior in different domains, and even logical and conceptual systems that constrain cognitive processes as well. Prior to or during activity, norms exercise a modulating influence through constraining and guiding activity; after activity has been performed, norms then constitute standards according to which activity could be evaluated. This function of norms is realized through the individual's understanding, accepting, identifying, and choosing. On the other hand, the individual's conscious activity is itself constrained by norms in various ways; such a relation between norms and the inner consciousness of the individual concretely embodies an important aspect of the unity of the affective mind (*xin* 心) and principles (*li* 理), to borrow a pair of Neo-Confucian categories.

As stated, as the internalization of knowledge and wisdom, human capacities are the internal ground of the process of accomplishing oneself and accomplishing things. By contrast, systems of norms, identical to the externalization of knowledge and wisdom, express themselves as the external conditions of accomplishing oneself and accomplishing things. It isn't hard to see that the knowledge and wisdom formed in cognitive and practical processes assure that there is an intrinsic unity between human capacities and systems of norms on an original level. With the genesis of a world of meaning as the objective, the process of accomplishing oneself and accomplishing things originates from internal human capacities but also depends upon external universal norms as well. If treated in isolation from human capacities, systems of norms would hollow out into nothing but formalized abstractions, deprived of the actual vital energy that pump them with life; in the same way, without the guidance of systems of norms, human capacities would unavoidably succumb to arbitrariness and contingency and even lose self-awareness. In the interaction between human capacities and systems of norms, the process of accomplishing oneself and accomplishing things gradually tends to unify creativity, individuality, actuality, procedure, universality and self-awareness, and it is this unity that concretely guarantees the genesis of a world of meaning.

From the perspective of conceptual form, a world of meaning first shows the understandability of being. In the unfolding of the historical context of accomplishing oneself and accomplishing things, the presentation of things and the direction of intentions reciprocally interact; due to this, the world enters the conceptual domain and gains a conceptual form. As the objects of cognition and understanding, things in the conceptual sphere emerge in meaningful world-pictures respectively conjugated to the perspectives of common sense, science, and metaphysics. The content of common sense includes perceiving, understanding, and recognizing the world. To an extent, by arranging things into order, common sense overcomes the alienation of human being in relation to the world, and thereby makes possible the conventional form of life practice. This orderliness that common sense displays enables the world to present itself in an understandable fashion, and also endows the world with its own intrinsic meaning. On the contrary, with experiments and mathematical methods as means, science generates an understanding of the world that differs from pure and simple intuitions of phenomena and presents specific features that are much more positivistic and theoretical. Science shows a world order that is also distinct from the conventionality or irregularity found in everyday experience: in mathematical models and symbolic structures, the world order gains a unique expression distinct from that of common sense. While the scientific picture of the world as a whole refers to objects in the empirical realm, the world-pictures drawn in metaphysical perspective have a different stress. In contrast to science's positivistic and empirical ways of grasping the world, metaphysical perspectives are much more linked to speculative approaches. However, in so far as they both understand the world as an ordered system, the perspectives of science and metaphysics seem to also share quite a bit in common.

The world of meaning in conceptual form is not only being that is understood and cognized but also being that is invested with values through the act of evaluation. In terms of the way the world is grasped, the meaning that a world-picture reveals is primarily linked to the question "What is it?" Although a world-picture itself contains multiple aspects of meaning, in so far as it is being as it is understood by humans, it first expresses what being presents to humans from different perspectives, and thus more directly corresponds to the question "What is it?" In fact, what humans understand the world to be is precisely what the world is from the human perspective. Of course, the ground of this identification is once again actual being. Linked to "What is it?" is "What does it mean?," which leads the world of meaning in its conceptual form further into the domain of values. The world of meaning is invested with values from ethical, political, aesthetic, and religious perspectives. Due to the active functioning of a consciousness of values, the genesis of the world of meaning involves the unity of the subject endowing the object with meaning on the one hand and the object presenting meaning to the subject on the other.

Going out to open the world up and then returning back to one's own being implies a corresponding shift from the inquiry concerning the object's meaning back to a concern for the meaning of one's own being. When one reflects upon why one exists, what one is concerned with is precisely the meaning of one's own being. Linked to the self-investigations of the meaning of being are different states of mind or levels of the world of spirit. The meaning contained in states of mind or levels of the world of spirit not only involves objects as it also engages one's own being in correlation with one's reflections, intuitive comprehensions and sensuous perceptions. In effect, in a state of mind or the world of spirit, thinking and intuitively comprehending the meaning of one's own being has already started to become the leading aspect in contrast to understanding and grasping external objects.[17] As regards thinking and intuitively comprehending the meaning of one's own being, the core of a state of mind or the world of spirit is concentrated and manifested in the pursuit of an ideal and the consciousness of a mission. The pursuit of an ideal refers to "What can one hope for?" or "What should one expect?" Becoming conscious of a mission then unfolds as an investigation of "What should one take responsibility for?" With the consciousness of a mission and the pursuit of an ideal as its core, one's state of mind or world of spirit then expresses the essential attribute of human being qua human at the conceptual level. In this sense, the world of spirit could be understood as the human world, that is, a world in harmony with human nature.

In accomplishing oneself and accomplishing things, the world of spirit is closely related to human capacities. The world of spirit reveals one's internal characteristic as a moral subject primarily at the level of values and ends, while human capacities present the meaning of one's being as a practical subject at the level of value creation. Of course, even though human capacities embody the essential powers of human being, this doesn't mean that their actualization and mode of being will definitely accord with the developmental direction of human nature. Just as the alienation of labor will always lead to the alienation of human being in a definite historical period, human capacities also contain the possibility of becoming alienated as extrinsic means or tools. In another aspect, it is true that the human state of mind contains senses of value, yet if it were closed in a pure conceptual realm in isolation from human capacities and their concrete expressions in cognitive and practical processes, the spiritual realm would easily degenerate into abstract, lofty, vague, and empty spiritual enjoyments or spiritual commitments. From the perspective of the history of philosophy, the Neo-Confucian theory of affective mind and human nature represents this tendency to a large degree; the spiritual realm of the perfectly purified Confucian, which Neo-Confucianism advocated, unavoidably succumbs to silent mysticism and empty vagueness, because in such a spiritual realm there is no room for actual human energy to reform the world, and thus nothing except inner cultivation and speculative experiences of the affective mind and human nature can occur. In the same way, as stated earlier, if human capacities in practice lack the necessary support of virtues, they may lead human being down the wrong path of value. As regards the being of the individual, free personality could be presented as a practicing subject who creates values, as well as a virtuous subject who is a valuable aim. The being of such a practicing subject refuses to be reduced to an abstract blend of cognition, emotion, and will; rather, it unfolds in a concrete way as the unity of human capacities and human spirit. This fact further endows the world of meaning with deeper value through one's own being.

Meaning doesn't only emerge in cognitive and evaluative activity at the conceptual level; grounded in practice, meaning also externalizes into the sphere of actual being or the actual world. As the externalization or actualization of meaning, this domain of being that takes shape in cognition and practice could simultaneously be seen as the actual form or the external form of the world of meaning, which includes "Nature for-humans" or "things for-us" in the world of life or social reality.

The world of meaning in its actual form must be understood mainly in opposition to primordial being. As stated, primordial being still lies outside of the human sphere of practice and cognition and its meaning is still closed off from human being; in contrast, the world of meaning in its actual form has already been marked with human impressions and thus expresses itself on different levels as things for-us. As the kinds of being that are external to the cognitive and practical domain and still without any actual connections to human being, primordial things neither constitute meaningful objects at the conceptual level nor possess actuality at the level of practice. Considered abstractly, however, "being" in a broad sense is attributable to both human being and the primordial world, and thus the latter two cannot be considered to be absolutely isolated from one another. Yet, when the primordial world exists outside of the cognitive and practical domain, the two appear more in a separated rather than combined form.

Under the precondition that one is opening it up out of its primordial form and reforming it, being acquires actuality for the first time. As mentioned, from the viewpoint of one's relation to being, we can make a distinction between "reality" and "actuality": Primordial being is without any doubt real, but it's not actual for human being. If we can say that one affirms one's essential powers in the process of "adding nourishment to the cultivation of Nature" and participating in the formation of the actual world, then we can also say that the primordial world actualizes while fusing into one's cognitive and practical processes, which transforms the form of being of the objective world through the objectification of one's essential powers in the expression of human being's unique way of being. In fact, these two aspects discussed here are intrinsically unified.

Of course, the human world isn't simply a world of beings marked with human impressions. In the social sphere, the human world has the most profound meaning of harmonizing with the natural human tendencies or human nature. In a broad sense, suiting human nature means manifesting the universal essence of human being, which distinguishes humans from other beings, and social reality constitutes the concrete measure and mark of whether or not something accords with human nature or to what degree something suits human nature. As regards the being of humans, the meaning of social reality is inseparable from whether or not something accords with human nature. Whereas the human core of social reality constitutes the specific characteristic that distinguishes the latter from the objective world, suiting human nature gives social reality the meaning of being at the level of essence. As the intrinsic attribute of the world of meaning, suiting human nature is a reality, which warrants different levels of understanding. Since human nature consists of sociality to some extent, according with human nature implies achieving social characteristics or social attributes. A much more substantial and intrinsic expression of human nature, however, involves human freedom and the multi-sided development of human potentials.

While nature expresses nothing but necessity and contingency, only human being demands freedom and is capable of being free. In brief, the question of whether or not and to what extent social reality accords with human nature is identical to the question of whether or not and to what extent social reality manifests the historical tendency of human being's movement toward freedom.

The internal and external dimensions of a world of meaning are not mutually unrelated. The pursuit of conceptual form or the internal world of meaning makes one continuously take up a concern for the meaning of being of the world and the meaning of one's own being and continuously avoid the absolute predomination of things in the forgetting of being itself. If this internal aspect of the world of meaning is overlooked, then one faces nothing but a world characterized by the alienation of human being and the absolute predomination of things. Nevertheless, when one overlooks the external dimension or actual form of the world of meaning, one suspends and forgets to reform the actual world, and consequently one remains trapped within the limits of an abstract, mystical, yet empty world of spirit.

In contemporary philosophy, in one respect it was Heidegger who overcame the transcendent form within Hegel's logic, and at the same time surpassed the "non-human" horizon (prior to the emergence of human being) of Hegel's philosophy of nature. In some sense, he transformed the speculative form of Hegel's philosophy of spirit, and enabled human being in the philosophy of spirit to be understood in a new way as human being in the process of existing. Therefore, he placed the meaning of the individual's existence in a comparatively more important position.[18] However, this led Heidegger into an excessive concern for the internal dimension of the world of meaning, which is entirely relative to the existential meaning of human being. In this sense, Hegel's philosophy of spirit and Heidegger's philosophy of being seem to share some intellectual and historical connections in spite of their differences. In fact, the core of Heidegger's philosophy, Dasein, limits the being of humans to the level of individual existence, and his understanding of the internal lived experience of anxiety and care as the authentic mode of Dasein, although expresses a tendency that differs from Hegel's speculative philosophy, still shows a failure to shake off a tendency that is intrinsically speculative in nature.

Wittgenstein gave a considerable amount of attention to the world of meaning. In his later period, he stressed the role that one's own activity plays in the construction and understanding of meaning. In this way he linked one's practical life to the genesis of meaning. However, he seems to have reduced the world of meaning to the world of semantics. One of the logical consequences of this approach is abstracting the world of meaning from values. Although he did not completely overlook other extra-linguistic questions (including the question of value), Wittgenstein primarily examined these questions from the perspective of the philosophy of language. Within the broader sphere of analytic philosophy, this tendency is quite prevalent.

As a whole, analytic philosophy is concerned with meaning at the cognitive level of understanding. It is true that analytic philosophers also touch upon the issue of value, but do not really discuss actual relationships of value. Take "good," for example. Meta-ethical theories in the analytic tradition of philosophy are principally concerned with the connotations and intensions of this word or concept "good." They have little interest in discussing what good things are in actual life. In the same way, when considering what is "morally good," they also just interest themselves in what the intensions of this concept "morally good" happen to be or what kind of behavior "morally good" refers to when we use this concept. The mainstream of analytic philosophy thus suspends such important questions as "What is the actual form of the morally good?" and "What does morally good behavior mean?" As a matter of fact, as analytic philosophy investigates meaning at the cognitive level of understanding, it fails to account for meaning at the evaluative level of ends. Even though analytic philosophy did eventually begin to discuss topics involving political and ethical issues in actuality, such as justice, it has hitherto taken a formal and procedural approach roughly identical to the way analytic philosophy has asked metaphysical questions from within the limits of semantic analysis. These tendencies all express a linear pursuit of meaning, which reveals the connection of these tendencies to scientism, which primarily concerns itself with questions at the material and technological levels and unfortunately ignores the meaning of being in the dimension of values, the world of spirit, and so on.

In summary, while traditional Chinese philosophy of the affective mind (*xin* 心) and human nature (*xing* 性) and modern existentialism are both principally concerned with the internal (conceptual) dimension of the world of meaning and overlook the actual world of meaning (as humanized being), both scientism and positivism pay more attention to the external material world and neglect the internal dimension of the world of meaning. However, as a concrete being, one transforms primordial objects into humanized beings and thereby creates the actual world of meaning and exists within it, and on the other hand, one continuously investigates the meaning of one's own being in the direction of the internal world of meaning. From the perspective of axiology, a much more viable approach is to sublate the opposition between the internal and external forms of meaning, that is, overcome the opposition between the conceptual world of meaning (the internal form) and the actual world of meaning (the external form) so as to realize their unity in a historical process.

Whether it is presented as an external humanized being or in an internal conceptual form, a world of meaning is never separable from the being of humans. As for the tie between a world of meaning and the being of humans, the individual is an essential element, since meaning first opens up to and presents itself to concrete individuals or individual persons. So, the individual being has some kind of ontological priority, and the process of accomplishing oneself and accomplishing things concerns the concrete individual in various senses. This priority of the individual is expressed in the metaphysical dimension and also unfolds in the social sphere.

At the ontological level, even though the individual belongs to a definite species, it however cannot be taken further as a specimen. This inability to take the individual as a specimen as well as its link to proper nouns reveals the uniqueness of the individual. An individual moves and changes in space-time and hence continuously forms its diverse particularities. However, an individual can belong to a species at the same time, which presupposes that the individual contains the general attributes of the species. Generality internal to the individual could be understood as concrete universality in two senses: in one sense, it enables different individuals within the same species to reciprocally differentiate themselves; in another sense it provides the inner ground for the individual to maintain its enduring self-identity throughout the transformation of its particularities.

In the sphere of the being of humans, the concrete form of the individual is the person. The person is the unity of the corporeal body (*shen* 身) and the affective mind (*xin* 心) and unfolds as an enduring identity, which not only concerns the (physical and physiological) sense of "body" (*xing* 形) and the (psychological and conscious) sense of "spirit or mind" (*shen* 神), but also the enduring continuity of virtues and personality. An individual in the sense of a thing is often understood as a specimen or an example of a species; on the contrary, however, an individual as human being is a singular and unrepeatable being that ontologically exists only for one time and contains irreplaceable value. As far as things go, the transformation, birth, and death of an individual, as a specimen of a species, has no substantial influence on the existence of the species itself; from the human perspective, though no individual (person) will ever disappear in essence and should not be ignored. The intrinsic attribute of the individual person is purposiveness and the individual person possesses a unique personality. In ontology, personality expresses the unique characteristics of a person; in axiology, personality merges with the purposive determination of the individual and manifests the existential orientation of the person. The historical content of the generative and developmental process of personality is the interaction of the individual (person) and society. In sum, the individual person is the unity of individuality and commonality.

The unity of the person not only touches upon the mind-body relation. In a much broader sense, it also concerns personal identity. From the perspective of accomplishing oneself (human being refining itself), the self-identity of a person is obviously unavoidable: The basic precondition of self-accomplishment is the self's enduring identity. Diachronically speaking, if the "I" of yesterday weren't the "I" of today and the "I" of tomorrow will also be different from the "I" of yesterday and today, then self-accomplishment would lose its ground; from the synchronic perspective, if the individual were to differentiate into different social roles and lack intrinsic unity, then self-accomplishment would likewise become practically impossible. In terms of its actuality, even though the individual undergoes transformations in time and undertakes different social roles, the individual is still an identical "I" and maintains an enduring identity in the aspects of body, spirit, social relationships, and practice of life. The identity of the individual thus first provides the precondition of self-accomplishment at the ontological and axiological levels. It is precisely this enduring identity of the individual, which is the foundation of self-cultivation, and which provides the ground for its continuity so it can unfold as one unified subjective process.

From the perspective of accomplishing oneself, the true realization of the intrinsic worth of human being is connected to the development of "free individuality." As far as the derivation of society is concerned, free individuality is first achieved by transcending relationships of dependence. According to Marx, the specific feature of the primordial form of social development was personal dependence. Within these relationships of dependence, individuals belong to other people or an external social system (including hierarchical structures), lacking authentic personality and autonomy. Human being's attainment of independence and autonomy by overcoming relationships of personal dependence is essential for the development of free individuality. Related to personal dependence is objective dependence. The former (personal dependence) entails the dissolution of human individuality and autonomy; the latter (objective dependence) entails that human being as an end in itself and the intrinsic worth of human being are concealed in human being's subjection to things, which engenders human being's estrangement from itself, whereby human being degenerates into a mere means. Aside from transcending relationships of personal dependence, free individuality also calls for overcoming human being's objective dependence, which simultaneously entails the confirmation of human being's intrinsic value and the affirmation that human being is an end in itself.

The process of accomplishing the self, which aims at free individuality, concretely reveals the meaning of the individual's being in terms of her value and historical derivation. While purposiveness and other such attributes make the meaning of the individual's value stand out through human being's difference from things, free individuality along with the whole-sided development of human being endow this meaning with more concrete historical implications. Overcoming personal dependence is the precondition of free individuality; this is the realization of human being's purposiveness with the historical evolution of society as an aim; by virtue of overcoming this two-fold dependency, the meaning of the individual's being gains deeper value and broader historical significance, and the production of meaning through this historical process reveals the dimensions of history and value at the level of the individual being.

Free individuality, human capacities, and the internal world of spirit directly involve the space of the self or the personal domain. The latter in a broader sense involves the relation between the individual domain and the common public sphere. As individual, human being has an internal world of spirit and a domain of individuality; as social, human being is simultaneously situated in such public spheres as the economic, political, legal, and cultural. Historically speaking, some philosophers only accounted for the public sphere, while others the inner personal domain. This is still the case for contemporary philosophy. With human being as the agent of history, the unfolding of the accomplishing the self and accomplishing things in the social realm concerns both the individual domain and the public sphere in many ways. As regards its actual form, the process of accomplishing the self and accomplishing things is inseparable from a diversity of social resources, while the acquisition, occupation, and distribution of resources then breaches the issue of social justice. Just as accomplishing the self is inseparable from the process of accomplishing things, so the public sphere isn't really isolatable from the individual domain. Here, the realization of the self and social justice present their integral inseparability. As far as the derivation of society goes, justice itself has historicity and will be transcended in accompaniment with the evolution of society. With the growth of social resources and material wealth as historical preconditions, the genuine realization of the value of the being of humans is concretely expressed as the development of human freedom, which essentially demands the mutual accomplishment of self and things. Therefore, through the free development of each and the free development of all, accomplishing the self and accomplishing things, as the process of generating a world of meaning, fully demonstrates its historical meaning.

In light of this introduction, the most condensed summary of this book's chapters would unfold as follows: this a concrete investigation into the different forms and deeper connotations of a world of meaning, and a world of meaning first concerns the broad sense of "meaning," so chapter 1 discusses the meaning of meaning.

Now, the genesis of meaning is grounded in accomplishing oneself and accomplishing things, which then begs the question of how this process is possible. From the perspective of how it is possible, human capacities are the internal grounds of possibility of accomplishing oneself and accomplishing things, along with the world of meaning it points to, so chapter 2 focuses on the connection between human capacities and a world of meaning.

However, accomplishing oneself and accomplishing things, along with the world of meaning it points to, isn't only conditioned from the inside by human capacities, for it is also constrained from the outside by systems of norms, which constitute the external conditions of possibility of accomplishing oneself and accomplishing things and the genesis of a world of meaning. So, chapter 3 discusses the relationship between systems of norms and worlds of meaning.

A world of meaning unfolds into two sides, that is, the internal world of spirit and the external humanized world. Because of this, chapter 4 first discusses the internal world of spirit and chapter 5 mainly discusses the humanized world or the actual world of meaning.

The formation and being of a world of meaning is always inseparable from human being. Whether it is the ideal form of the world of spirit or the actual form of the humanized world, neither are separable from human being. As for this relation between a world of meaning and the being of humans, the individual or the person is obviously an essential factor: so-called meaning first opens up to and presents itself to the concrete individual or person. From a broader perspective, the individual being possesses some sort of ontological priority, and the agent of self-cultivation in the social sphere similarly is the particular individual. As a historical process, accomplishing oneself and accomplishing things along with the genesis of meaning all concern the being of the individual at both the metaphysical and social levels. Because of this, chapter 6 discusses the individual dimension of meaning.

The being of the individual is inseparable from the social or public sphere, connected to which is the relation between the individual and public spheres. As interrelated sides of the social sphere, the individual and public spheres co-constitute the concrete background of the historical process of accomplishing oneself and accomplishing things along with the genesis of a world of meaning. The actual process of accomplishing oneself and accomplishing things is inseparable from diverse social resources, and the acquisition, occupation, and distribution of social resources involves the problem of social justice. In correspondence with the unity of "accomplishing oneself" and "accomplishing things," the "individual domain" and the "public domain" are inseparable, and self-realization is inseparably tied to social justice. Because of this, chapter 7 discusses accomplishing oneself and accomplishing things along with the genesis of a world of meaning in terms of the connection between the public and private spheres.

The originative nature of the question of the meaning of being is itself rooted in this basic existential quest of human being—to accomplish itself and accomplish things. Primordial being does not pose questions concerning meaning. The birth of meaning is inseparable from the process of being human: beyond human being's cognitive and practical sphere, objects can only be said to simply be there or "exist," but this kind of "being" or "existing" doesn't yet present any concrete meaning. It is only through the historical unfolding of human being accomplishing itself and accomplishing things that primordial things gradually enter the cognitive and practical sphere of human being, become objects of human being's cognition and reform, and due to this, present meaning at various levels, including the levels of fact and value. Through knowing and practicing in the broad sense, human being ceaselessly transforms primordial things into humanized reality, and as this process changes the objective world, it also pushes the world into a meaningful sphere. Linked to this is the meaning of accomplishing oneself: in the development of one's own potentials and in the process of self-realization, one seeks to comprehend the meaning of being and endow one's being with intrinsic meaning. Although it is a unified process, we can say that refining things accentuates the side concerned with bringing the world into a domain of meaning and refining oneself stresses the side concerned with making oneself become a meaningful being. In brief, accomplishing oneself and accomplishing things opens the world up and imprints the variety of human impressions upon the world, and is thereby the actual source out of which the genesis of meaning arises. As a historical process, accomplishing oneself and accomplishing things cultivates diverse forms of meaning and nourishes a world of meaning.

1 Meaning in the Context of Accomplishing Oneself and Accomplishing Things

Accomplishing oneself and accomplishing things is a concrete historical process of knowing the world and knowing oneself and reforming the world and refining oneself, which simultaneously generates meaning and produces a world of meaning. The world in-itself cannot pose for itself the question of meaning, which is to say that there is no way to dissociate meaning from one's own being. Humans question the meaning of the world and the meaning of their own being; therefore, the genesis of meaning owes its origin to the "being" of humans. As the introduction to this book has already demonstrated, from the perspective of one's own being and its relation to the world, the intension of meaning or "the meaning of meaning" implicates within itself several questions: "What is it?" "What does it mean?" and "What should it become?" The question "What is it?" specifically refers to which things exist and how they exist (in what form do things exist?), which involves the connection between the presentation of things and the human being's intentional activity. The question "What does it mean?" refers to the value or worth that a being may have.[1] With regard to objects, such a question asks whether or not something accords with the needs and ideals of human beings and to what extent; such needs and ideals concern not only life as a process of survival on the material level, but also cognition and practice in spiritual life and the social sphere. With regard to the human being, "What does it mean?" is directed at the very meaning of one's own being: Why, or for what, in the end, does one exist? The meaning of one's own being or the confirmation of the meaning of human life is always grounded in the ends and ideals that human beings value. When the process of one's own being is consistent with the specific ends or ideals one finds worthy, life appears to be richly fulfilled with meaning; and vise versa, when one is either lacking or distantly separated from a valued goal, human life then inevitably strikes one with a sense of meaninglessness.

Referring to properties and attributes at the factual level, "What is it?" primarily concerns cognizing or knowing, whereas "What does it mean?" concerns qualities of relevance and relationships of value, and hence involves evaluating. The meanings, which cognizing and evaluating respectively reveal and confirm, always exist in the mode of ideas. By contrast, the question "What should it become?" has more practical meaning, referring to both how the object should "be" and how oneself should "be." As regards the object, "What should it become?" implies transforming "Nature in-itself" (*tian zhi tian*) into "Nature for human being" (*ren zhi tian*) through the practical activity of human being, by means of which values at the level of ideas are actualized, that is, obtain an actual form. For oneself as human being, "What should it become?" implies moving toward an ideal mode of being through the activity of cognizing and practicing in the continuous realization of the meaning of human life.

From cognizing facts to evaluating values, from knowing the world and changing the world to knowing oneself and changing oneself, from linguistic description to linguistic expression, meaning concerns a variety of domains. Yet, clarifying "the meaning of meaning" is a task that cannot be accomplished if solely confined to logical analyses of the intensions of the word "meaning"; at a much more original level, such a task concerns the genesis of meaning. Here, the historical unfolding of the process of accomplishing oneself and accomplishing things (knowing the world and changing the world, knowing oneself and changing oneself) is the actual source of meaning, insofar as meaning is generated in the processual interaction of human being with the world. Through the creative activity of refining the world and refining oneself, human being continues the quest for meaning and simultaneously fills the world of meaning with concrete historical content.

What Is Meaning?

As the human's own way of being, which differs from that of things, accomplishing oneself and accomplishing things opens the world up and impresses the mark of human upon the world, which consequently generates different domains of meaning.[2] Broadly speaking, meaning is precisely a form of being that has entered human being's horizon of cognition and practice, be it a concrete being or an idea. Opposed to the domain of meaning is the domain of non-meaning. Here, however, a distinction must be made between non-meaning and the meaningless. Meaninglessness is itself a phenomenon belonging to a domain of meaning; something is either meaningless in the sense of being incomprehensible or meaningless in the sense of lacking value. What is meaningless can only be said in a relative sense, relative to the "meaningfulness" of a domain of meaning. In other words, the meaningless pertains to the domain of meaning. By contrast, non-meaning essentially does not belong to the domain of meaning; it could be understood in a broad sense as the beings that have never entered human being's cognitive and practical horizon. As objects that human being has never encountered, such beings still exist outside of the domain of meaning. Neither the issue of meaning nor that of meaninglessness ever occurs with regard to such beings.

In contemporary philosophy, Heidegger gave extensive consideration to the relationship between meaning and Dasein. According to Heidegger, "Meaning is an existential of Da-sein, not a property which is attached to beings, which lies 'behind' them or floats somewhere as a 'realm between.'"[3] Dasein here primarily refers to the being of the individual, and an existential is something related to the activity of individual existence. A property of beings he opposes to this is an attribute that is contained within the object but subsists outside the process of human *existence*. For Heidegger, meaning is by no means a pure and simple objective determination; it essentially comes into life through individual existence, which he understands as a process of projection. This "projecting" refers to the human being's self-determination and self-realization, which entails transforming the being of the possible into the being of the actual through the act of existing. It is precisely from this perspective that Heidegger links meaning to human being's projecting and stresses that projecting consists precisely in the opening up of possibilities.[4]

Heidegger therefore notices that the birth of meaning is inseparable from human being. However, Heidegger understands human being as Dasein, and the being of Dasein is first of all individual existence. In fact, the content of the existential of Dasein is individual existence. As for this link between meaning and individual existence, Heidegger is quite clear, declaring that the phenomenon of meaning "is rooted in the existential constitution of Dasein."[5] From the perspective of accomplishing oneself and accomplishing things, individual existence mainly concerns the dimension of accomplishing oneself. However, the process of accomplishing oneself simultaneously consists of a plurality of aspects pertaining to one knowing oneself and refining oneself, among which individual existence is only one. Placing the focus entirely on individual existence implies restricting meaning to merely the one dimension of accomplishing oneself. What needs to be pointed out here is that in Heidegger, in correlation with his phenomenological background and the importance he finds in the existential of Dasein, meaning is always related to care, anxiety, and other internal experiences of individual existence, and thereby in substance deals much more with the domain of ideas. As the second half of this book will demonstrate, at the level of actuality, human being's existential condition is not only directed at accomplishing oneself, but also unfolds as a process of accomplishing things in the broad sense (knowing the world and changing the world). The latter at once exhibits the practical character of human beings and also constitutes the real source and historical ground of meaning at much deeper and broader levels. In so far as Heidegger came to understand the meaning of meaning from the perspective of Dasein's existence, his insight into the interrelation between Dasein and the genesis of meaning must be acknowledged. However, at the same time, he ignored the process of accomplishing things (knowing the world and changing the world) and placed too much importance on the ideational dimension of internal experiences like anxiety and care, and thereby failed to genuinely grasp the real relation between the genesis of meaning and the being of humans.

What is meaning itself; that is, what is meaning within the domain of meaning? A concrete analysis of the process of accomplishing oneself and accomplishing things could unearth an intrinsic clue to the solution of such a problem. As stated previously, the historical content of accomplishing oneself and accomplishing things is one knowing the world and knowing oneself as well as changing the world and changing oneself. So, this process first concerns one understanding the world and oneself: knowing the world and knowing oneself, in essence, consists in self-understanding and understanding the world, but changing the world and changing oneself is also inseparable from understanding the world and oneself. Whether it is one refining oneself (accomplishing oneself) or refining the world (accomplishing things), both presuppose a grasp of true being. To grasp true being is to concretely know, and hence, understand what is actual. As for knowing what is actual, the meaning of being lies in being understood or being understandable. For those who have no knowledge of paleontology, a fossil of an archaic organism simply does not have meaning associated with an archaic organism: even if a fossil, when human being encounters it, enters human being's horizon of cognition and practice and henceforth acquires a meaning that would distinguish it from being in-itself, for humans who are unable to understand it from the perspective of paleontology, its meaning will simply consist in being some form of rock, which obviously is not the meaning that it, as a fossil, truly possesses. A fossil is a specific kind of being, whose intrinsic meaning is presented through human understanding, and this act of understanding is itself attributable to the process of knowing the world. We can see that at the level of knowing or understanding what is actual, meaning mainly involves the question "What is it?" and in pointing to questions such as "What things exist?" and "How do things exist?" meaning itself acquires cognitive content as well.

Logically or formally speaking, meaning at the level of understanding is also exhibited as comprehensibility, whose basic precondition is following the laws of logic, and first and foremost the law of identity. Jin Yuelin once pointed out that "the law of identity is the most basic condition of the possibility of meaning."[6] The law of identity demands that a concept has a definite intension, that is, a concept in a defined context must express a meaning without arbitrarily shifting. For instance, "father" refers to father and cannot at the same time refer to son, "teacher" expresses teacher and cannot at the same time mean student. Disobeying the law of identity, concepts become confused, which makes it impossible to establish meaning and think about or understand objects and questions. In addition, it is necessary to obey the law of non-contradiction: "The limit of thinking is contradiction. What is contradictory is unthinkable."[7] What the law of identity affirms is that $A=A$;

the law of non-contradiction then emphasizes that A cannot at the same time be non-A. Ideas only have meaning and moreover thinking and understanding only become possible once contradictions are eliminated. So, whereas cognition at the level of fact mainly concerns meaning at the level of content, then according with logic, as the necessary condition of possibility of understanding and thinking, formally determines meaning at the level of ideas. In brief, at the level of form, being meaningful means according with the laws of logic, and hence, being understandable; what is meaningless is thus something that is not understandable, because it disobeys the laws of logic.

In everyday expressions we can see further into the connection just noted between logical form and meaning at the level of understanding and cognition. "Plants need sunlight and water to grow" is a meaningful statement, because it envelops some content that can be cognized, and moreover, the way it is expressed is also permitted by the rules of logic, which makes it understandable. However, the statement "the daytime is heavier than water" is meaningless, not only because it fails to provide substantial content to be cognized, but also because it is not understandable due to the illogical connection it draws between two objects belonging to different categories. Of course within certain contexts, even if an expression were to lack logical connections in the narrow sense, after undergoing certain transformations, it could still be seen as expressing some kind of meaning. As for the statement mentioned previously, if daytime were used as a metaphor for things containing positive value and water for those with negative value (for instance, sinking), then the two would acquire comparability insofar as they would be referring to the same category, that of value, and the statement concerned would thereby also acquire some kind of meaning. The following statement is similar in kind: though death befalls all men, it may be heavier than Mount Tai or lighter than a goose's feather. While Mount Tai and a goose's feather originally belong to types of phenomena differing in kind from life and death, at the metaphorical level of values, they express a communicability in kind. As metaphors, Mount Tai and a goose's feather refer to different values of death and thus also express a certain meaning. It needs to be pointed out that in the earlier case, logical laws in the broad sense still constrain the declarative process and values also pervade cognitive content that is understandable; the metaphor here first expresses an idea of value through a linguistic transformation, and so the meaning associated with it much rather concerns the domain of value, which we will discuss at greater depth later on. Such phenomena of meaning can be seen in artistic works (like poems).

Refining oneself (accomplishing oneself) and refining the world (accomplishing things) is not only a task of grasping actuality, it also unfolds as a process of changing the world and changing oneself in accordance with human ends and ideals. One of the differences between human being and other things lies in the fact that human being is a kind of being, but one who is also not just "there"; human being exists in this world but does not merely exist in the world, because human being is never satisfied with the form of the world as it is already constituted. Human being faces what is, but at the same time also ceaselessly contemplates, what ought to be. What ought to be is precisely an ideal mode of being, whose basis is an understanding of *what is,* and which is also simultaneously infused with human ends, which in turn contain values in the broad sense. With an end as the point of concern, the meaning of being correspondingly presents its intrinsic content as that of value: Considered from the purposive dimension of accomplishing oneself and accomplishing things, having meaning consists precisely in having value. The Chinese proverb "fetching a glass of water to put out a flaming cart of wood" is usually taken as an example of meaninglessness, but the meaninglessness found in this case does not have anything to do with one not being able to understand some phenomenon or action; the meaninglessness here points to the lack of real value or effect a glass of water would have in relation to the end of extinguishing a cart of wood engulfed in flames. Similarly, "the praying mantis raised an arm to block a moving car" is another Chinese proverb taken as an example of meaninglessness. The content of the meaningless found here lies in the lack of any substantial or positive value that a praying mantis's arm would have in relation to a certain aim (like halting the momentum of a moving car). By extension, meaning in this domain simultaneously involves ends, actions, and functions, and being meaningful consists in both the intrinsic value that accomplishing oneself and accomplishing things envelops within itself as well as the effect and function that different things, ideas, and actions may have in relation to this process. So, it is clear that meaning at this level predominantly corresponds to the question "What does it mean?" and ends and values constitute its substantial contents.[8]

Meaning at the level of ends and values could also be understood in much broader terms. With regard to the moral domain, morality is one of human being's ways of being and also makes the being of humans possible to some degree. In the historical evolution of society, it is morals, together with other factors, that serve as the internal forces that bind the members of society together through common ethical ideals, value principles, behavioral norms, evaluation criteria, and so forth. Here, the function of morals not only lies in enabling human beings to attain an ethical determination, aside from a biological one at the natural level, but also to attain economic and political attributes at the social level; more profoundly, the ontological meaning of morals consists in providing a ground and guarantee for the realization of the value of human being by overcoming the tendency of society to dismember into a disordered state. In connection with this, the meaning of what is morally "good" lies in its fundamental affirmation of the value of human beings in so far as it is a subjective confirmation of the value of one's own being as well as an inter-subjective affirmation of and respect for the value of respective human beings;[9] this kind of affirmation and confirmation expresses the being of humans as an end in itself in different ways: only an action that expresses this confirmation of human being as end in itself has moral meaning or positive moral meaning, which demonstrates from another perspective meaning at the level of values.

Meaninglessness at the level of values is usually expressed as absurdity. Camus used the Greek myth of Sisyphus as a figurative explanation of meaninglessness and absurdity. Sisyphus disobeyed and angered the gods. In order to punish Sisyphus, the gods sentenced him to push a gigantic boulder up a mountain; however, due to the weight of the massive rock, it fell down as he reached the peak of the mountain. Sisyphus once again pushed the rock all the way up, and the massive rock came crashing down again. Like this Sisyphus went through the same cycle repeatedly without foreseeable end. As human behavior, Sisyphus's action here could be seen as an example of meaninglessness: ceaselessly repeating the same action without ever being able to reach the established end. An action without any value or effect in relation to realizing a certain end lacks concrete meaning. When Camus labeled Sisyphus "the absurd hero," he in fact took the aforesaid exemplar of meaninglessness as the very mode of being of the absurd.[10] Using the mode of being of absurdity to illustrate meaninglessness certainly brings the relationship between meaning at the level of values and purposive activity into striking relief, if only from a negative angle.

The process of refining oneself (accomplishing oneself) and refining the world (accomplishing things) always involves different objects and the diversity of human activities. External objects and human activity also enter into multiple relationships in the process of accomplishing oneself and accomplishing things, and these relationships are always qualified as either being affirmative or negative. When external objects and human activity constitute positive conditions for accomplishing oneself and accomplishing things, the relation between the two is then qualified as affirmative; if the opposite is the case, then the corresponding relation is qualified as negative. Therefore, meaning possesses different dimensions. What is ordinarily called meaningful and meaningless in everyday speech respectively express the affirmative and negative dimensions of meaning. As for understandability, to say that something is meaningful is to say that something is understandable and to say that it is meaningless is to say that it is not; the former is of an affirmative nature and the latter expresses a negation of meaning. When a proposition in the cognitive domain is falsified, its meaning presents a negative quality.[11] If on the contrary a proposition is proven to be true, it acquires positive meaning.

In the same way, the distinction between affirmation and negation also pertains to meaning at the level of values. Determining the harvest as an end, working the farm, and in the end actually reaping the gains of farm work is a kind of meaningful activity; just passing the days away without tending to affairs and idling one's potentials away is on the contrary a meaningless killing of time. Here, meaning has contents of value and the distinction between what is meaningless and what is meaningful shows us that meaning at the level of values can be either affirmative or negative. Tied to the affirmation and negation of meaning at the level of values is positive meaning and negative meaning. In the practice of reforming the world, external objects may present either positive or negative meaning. The same phenomenon may often present different senses of value relative to the different conditions in which human activity is conducted. For instance, prolonged rains doubtless have a negative meaning in relation to the human endeavor to prevent flooding, but in the struggle to circumvent the harmful effects of draught, the same phenomenon undoubtedly has positive meaning. So, it is evident that the different senses of value that meaning may have is inseparable from human activity in the process of reforming the world (accomplishing things).

The emergence of meaning is by nature relative. This relativity not only lies in the fact that meaning is always relative to the process of one refining oneself (accomplishing oneself) and refining the world (accomplishing things); it also lies in the fact that the genesis of meaning is conditional. At the level of understanding and cognition, the genesis and emergence of meaning itself presupposes a certain background of knowledge. For humans who lack knowledge of mathematics, mathematical signs and formulas have no meaning or are without the meaning that comes with a system of mathematical knowledge. Here, a distinction must be made between understandability and actually understanding: mathematical signs and formulas acquire understandability when a mathematical system of knowledge has taken shape, but actually understanding them demands possessing certain mathematical knowledge as a precondition. These signs and formulas are only presented in the mode of being meaningful when they are actually being understood.

In the same way, meaning at the level of ends and values also has its relativity. Human being's knowing and practicing has unfolded and will unfold in different historical ages and in different social contexts, and hence, different cognitive and practical agents will have different ends and value orientations. For example, consider the peasant movement in China's Hunan Province in the 1920s: for the gentry landowners calling for the preservation of the traditional order, the peasant movement mainly presented negative meaning, "it's terrible!" they cried, which is precisely a judgment regarding the nature of its meaning; as for those aspiring to reform the established order, the same movement presented positive meaning, "it's great!" they cheered, which is precisely an affirmative judgment regarding the nature of its meaning.[12]

The relativity of meaning also manifests itself as the individual differences that meaning presents. As Marx pointed out: "the sense of an object for me goes only so far as *my* senses go (has only sense for a sense corresponding to that object)."[13] A formation of being, like a song or scenery, may have a special nostalgic meaning for some particular subject; the meaning that a person or a thing in life may have for a corresponding subject may supersede that of another person or thing, and so on. Meaning here carries with it a personal significance.[14] Broadly speaking, the use of language also involves this personal "significance," which is always infused with the individual's emotions and intentions, which touches upon what Frege mentioned as the "third component" of an indicative sentence,[15] and which is also linked to the concrete application of language in the process of communicating and practicing. Those so-called implied messages, which a speaker nonetheless expresses but which a listener can only "read between the lines," are all manifestations of a certain significance.

It is clear in the previous cases that the presentation of meaning involves an interaction between the genesis of new meaning and pre-established formations of meaning. On the one hand, every presentation of meaning involves the genesis of new meaning. On the other hand, this genesis can only be initiated on the basis of a pre-established formation of meaning, which is the background or context from which such a genesis emerges. From the processual perspective, the presentation and genesis of meaning cannot occur without a pre-established formation of meaning. Human being always faces external objects in the process of cognizing and practicing in the process of accomplishing oneself and accomplishing things; now, the system of knowledge and values that take shape throughout the unfolding of this cognizing and practicing (accomplishing oneself and accomplishing things) constitute a definite formation of meaning or a world of meaning. When an external object presents itself to human being, one effectively already exists in a pre-established formation of meaning or a world of meaning, which conditions the presentation and genesis of meaning, but which also determines and influences the quality and content of meaning in different ways. At the level of understanding and cognizing, possessing or lacking the system of knowledge of a certain field will always act as a constraint upon what kind of meaning a correlated thing or phenomenon will present or whether it will present any meaning at all; at the level of ends and values, one's ideas and ideals of value will influence one's evaluation of the meaning that an external object presents.

Of course, that there is this relativity between the emergence of meaning and the individual's being, and moreover, that there is this constraint of a pre-established formation of meaning upon human being does not entail that meaning is entirely without universal and determinate content. When Jin Yuelin mentioned his conception of a presentation, he distinguished a "perceiving" pertaining to the individual and a "perceiving" pertaining to the species. When there is a presentation of an object, it is simultaneously perceived by a human being. In this sense, "in any presentation there is always a perceiving." For Jin Yuelin, an individual perception is subjective insofar as it is always tied to a specific perceiver; but a perception pertaining to the species is a perception commonly held by all the individual members of the species, and is thereby objective. Epistemologically, the presentation that corresponds to a species perception is precisely the given.[16] The presentation and the given of which Jin Yuelin speaks predominantly concerns meaning at the level of perception. Speaking in broader terms, the grasp that human being has of the world and the meaning that the world presents to human being is always twofold on a more universal level; human being as the subject of meaning is at once a particular individual and also a member of the human species: the former determines a human being to have what Jin Yuelin called "individual perception," and due to this, the meaning of the presentation of an object is always different for distinct individuals in each and every case; the latter thus determines a human being to have a species perception, and the meaning presented in such a perception thus possesses universal content. In the connection between human being and the world, perception has an immediate and direct character, but the combination of "individual perception" and "species perception" in the process of perceiving establishes a unity of individuality and universality, relativity and determinacy in every presentation of meaning.

Considered from another angle, the relativity of meaning is often tied to the different understandings and experiences of being that individuals from different backgrounds of knowledge and different value orientations may have. Yet, the relationship between being and one's cognizing and practicing cannot be characterized as being merely relative, for such a relationship is also characterized by universal and determinate aspects, which constrain the formation of meaning while making it present different degrees of universality and determinacy, regardless of whether it is at the level of understanding and knowing or ends and values. At the level of understanding, although mathematical formulas and signs appear as meaningless to those individuals who lack mathematical knowledge, these signs and formulas nevertheless present universal meaning to those with mathematical knowledge. Similarly at the level of relationships of value, although it is entirely true that a particular historical phenomenon of a certain historical age will present different senses of value to concrete individuals of different value orientations, we can still evaluate the intrinsic significance of such an event in terms of its relation to the whole historical trend of humankind advancing towards a state of freedom; from this perspective, meaning already transcends the value orientations of concrete individuals and possesses some universality.

As the two basic forms of meaning, the meaning linked to understanding and knowing and the meaning linked to ends and values are by no means unrelated. What is essential for accomplishing oneself and accomplishing things is knowing oneself and knowing the world or the process of knowing, throughout which cognizing and evaluating cannot be dissociated. The interrelatedness of cognizing and evaluating also establishes a link between meaning at the level of understanding-knowing and meaning at the level of ends-values. In the aesthetic appreciation of music, whether or not a rhythm, rhyme, or melody presents aesthetic meaning to an individual depends upon whether or not the individual has the capacity to appreciate music, or as Marx put it, "the most beautiful music has *no* sense for the unmusical ear."[17] Having the capacity to appreciate music or having a musical ear thus involves an understanding of music.[18] However, on the other hand, the aesthetic process of appreciating beauty (including the appreciation of music) is also tied to the aesthetic taste of the human being, which involves having a sense of value. Confucius once heard the music of Shao and for the following three months did not notice the taste of meat.[19] The reason for this is that the music of Shao harmonized with his aesthetic standard of value. At the same time, Confucius repeatedly demanded to "banish the music of Zheng,"[20] due to the discord with which the music of Zheng struck him from the height of his aesthetic standards. Evidently, the two kinds of music here, that of Shao and that of Zheng, presented a difference in aesthetic meaning to Confucius, and this difference not only involved his understanding of both, but also concerned his internal value orientation, which is to say that the understanding of meaning and the evaluating of meaning are here integrally combined.

Mysticism also displays this link in a unique fashion. The principal characteristic of mysticism lies in rejecting discursive analytical knowledge and insisting upon an indivisible unity.[21] That which mysticism seeks after is principally individualistic experiences of rapture and feelings of awareness, which constitute its domain of meaning. Considered from the outside, this group of experiences and feelings seem to lie beyond all understanding, and the meanings they may have also seem to lack cognitive content. How should this horizon of meaning be approached? We could approach this question from two perspectives. First, what mysticism attributes to a field beyond the realm of knowledge (a phenomenon transcending understandability) could itself become an object of explanation: mystical experiences in religion could be examined as religious experiences in the broad sense; the metaphysical whole, the one, and other such ideas could become objects of philosophical analysis. In the process of explaining it, mysticism and the variety of phenomena associated with it could be expressed in a form that accords with logic, and thereby acquire cognitive content as unique objects of explanation. On the other hand, from the mystic's perspective, a unique mystical experience is linked to one's spiritual striving and ultimate concern, and when this experience is able to fulfill such spiritual needs, this experience, which seems to emerge in mystical form, presents a kind of meaning to oneself. Whereas mysticism in the first case (taking mysticism as an object of investigation) implicates within itself some kind of meaning at the level of understanding and knowing, in the latter case (referring to the mystic's own experience) the mystical could be said to present some kind of meaning at the level of ends and values. As two interconnected aspects, both cases always pervade mysticism simultaneously.

Chinese philosophy's understanding of image-signs (*xiang* 象) more concretely displays the interrelatedness of the valuing and understanding dimensions of meaning. *Xiang* thinking first appeared in the *Yijing* (The book of changes): in the hexagrams of the *Yijing,* the idea of *xiang* achieved a rather concentrated expression. Composed of unbroken (*yang* 阳) and/or broken (*yin* 阴) lines, the *xiang* of a hexagram appears as a sign. As a sign, the *xiang* of a hexagram envelops a multitude of connotations and possesses its own distinctive feature. The nature of *xiang* is twofold, and it unfolds respectively on two different levels. On one hand, the *xiang* of a hexagram is a formed image, presenting a particular sensible form; this distinguishes *xiang* from general abstract concepts. Yet, on the other hand, *xiang* also represent different modes of being in a universal way; by synthetically uniting into *The Book of Changes,* they "envelop the principles of the natural way of change of the cosmos (*tiandi zhi dao* 天地之道)."[22] On one level, the *xiang* of a hexagram refers to and represents a concrete thing or affair. As the *Yijing* puts it, "the *xiang* are used to figure things out, to characterize them in a proper way."[23] On the other level, *xiang* signify principles, and were specified as a form of sign expressing universal meaning. As the *Yijing* puts it, "the sage prescribes a *xiang* to fully express meaning."[24] Again, on one level, the *xiang* of a hexagram is composed of broken and/or unbroken lines in a fixed order, which gives the *xiang* a relative fixity, but on another level, by changing any given line (from broken to unbroken and vise versa) or by changing the position of any given line within a hexagram, the hexagram transforms, and thus *xiang* exhibit fluidity and transformability. Furthermore, a *xiang* is a particular kind of sign composed of broken and/or unbroken lines and so differ from ordinary language on the one hand, but they are closely associated with language on the other: Every hexagram has a name that is expressed through language, and the explanation of each line in a hexagram (called the judgment of the line) always unfolds with the aid of language. In summary, as a sign containing meaning, a *xiang* in the form of a hexagram expresses the unity of the particular and the universal, the imagistic and the eidetic, the static and the dynamic, the linguistic and the non-linguistic.

Further consideration of the intrinsic nature of the hexagram system will reveal even more profound implications of meaning underlying such a unity. The *Yijing* is firstly related to divination, which involves the relation between human action and the objective world (including predictions concerning outcomes of actions). The *Yijing* links up with the external world through the hexagram symbols, which represent different things, events, and affairs: "change and transformation, the symbols of advance and retreat; rigidity and flexibility, the symbols of day and night."[25] The change and transformation spoken of here refers to the transformation of the line symbol (from the broken to the unbroken and vice versa) in hexagrams, and advancing and retreating then point to vicissitudes in the natural and social domains; rigidity and flexibility refer to the unbroken *yang* line and the broken *yin* line, and becoming-day and becoming-night are natural phenomena. However, in yet another respect, in connection with human action, hexagram symbols are signs portending "fortune and misfortune:" "the sage prepares the grams, observes the symbol, and makes a judgment, and thus sheds light on what fortune or misfortune awaits."[26] Fortune and misfortune are attributes of phenomena within the realm of value since they express the upside of positive and affirmative values and the downside of negative values respectively; using *xiang* symbols to foretell fortune or misfortune implies that values are attributed to divinatory symbols. If we can say that representations of natural and social phenomena envelop contents pertaining to the level of understanding and cognition, then the telling of a pending fortune or misfortune reveals the level of value implications that such representations have. In this way, as a system of signs, the symbols found in the *Yijing* envelop and are pervaded by both dimensions of meaning, that of understanding and knowing and that of ends and values. The twofold nature of *xiang* here concretely demonstrates that these two dimensions of meaning cannot be strictly dissociated in the process of cognizing and practicing.

Considered from a deeper perspective, as the substantial content of the process of accomplishing oneself and accomplishing things, knowing the world and knowing oneself and changing the world and changing oneself, whose content is understanding the world and the self, also consists in the realization of values and meaning. As noted, meaning at the level of understanding and cognition is linked first of all to the question "What is it?" and the concrete content of "What is it?" lies in the nature and properties of things and events, the relations between things, the meaning of signs, and so on. The concrete content of "What does it mean?" concerns the benign and malign, the advantageous and the disadvantageous, good and evil, the beautiful and the ugly, and so forth. Broadly speaking, the question "What is it?" is based on what actually is, and the question "What does it mean?" refers to what ought to be. However, while one is in the process of refining oneself and refining the world (accomplishing oneself and accomplishing things), what is and what ought to be are inextricably intertwined.

According to its substantial content, the process of accomplishing oneself and accomplishing things is grounded in what is, but is also directed at the genesis of what ought to be (giving shape to ideals by integrating the possibilities that actuality provides with the ends of human values); this also unfolds as a process of transforming ideals (what ought to be) into actuality (what actually is). At the same time, refining oneself and reforming the world, as a process of accomplishment, not only involves "ought" (what ought I do); it is also inextricably tied to the question "how" (how is it to be done?). If "ought" as an end expresses the demands of values, then the "how" connected to the concrete unfolding of any practice is inseparable from understanding and knowing the actual constitution of being. Here, "What is it?" and "What does it mean?" the "ought" and the "how" present their intrinsic relatedness insofar as they point to the refinement of both the human being and the world as an achievement of accomplishing oneself and accomplishing things. "What is it?" presents us with meaning at the level of understanding and knowing; "What does it mean?" presents us with meaning at the level of ends and values; and it is precisely the interrelation of these two aspects in practice that constitutes the real ground of the interconnection between the cognitive dimension and the evaluative dimension of meaning.

Signs, Value, and Meaning

Aside from having two dimensions of concrete content, that of understanding and knowing and that of ends and values, meaning also has different forms of expression. At the level of understanding, meaning is first linked to signs in the broad sense, and the connotations and denotations of signs constitute its modes of being; at the level of values, meaning is intrinsic to the humanization of being, and is expressed in two forms, the conceptual world of meaning and the actual world of meaning.

Signs can be broadly divided into two forms, linguistic and non-linguistic. From the perspective of understanding, the linguistic form is obviously more fundamental. Perhaps it is precisely this which Dewey had in mind when he stated, "language, [being the tool of tools] is the cherishing mother of all significance."[27] Yet, there are different perspectives on the meaning of language, which in a sense reflects the multiple facets of linguistic meaning itself. From the viewpoint of etymology, words associated with the word "speech" in Western languages are tied to the words associated with "illuminating," "shedding light on," "displaying," and so on. John Macquarrie undertook a relevant etymology, showing that the Greek word *phemi* (I speak) shares roots with the word *phaino* (to bring to light), which in turn ties them to the word for light (*phos*). He shows further that the Latin word *dicere* (to speak), the Greek word *deiknumi* (to show), and the German word *zeigen* (to show) could all be traced back to the same source, and these three words could all be traced even further back to the Proto-Indo-European root *di*, which expresses the meanings *to shine, to illuminate*.[28] To show and to illuminate means to bring that which lies out of view into the human horizon. In this sense, using language is identical to the process of knowing the world.

Language cannot be dissociated from human being's knowing and practicing. Historically speaking, it is the evolution and unfolding of human being's knowing and practicing that serves as both the foundation for and driving force behind the formation and development of language. Linguistic meaning should not be considered without this fundamental fact in mind. Grounded in human being's knowing and practicing, the functions of language are concretely manifested in describing, expressing, and prescribing.[29] Describing brings to light the properties and attributes of things themselves; at this level, linguistic meaning is manifested in grasping reality as it is. Even simple descriptions like "this is a tree" already contain this sense of linguistic meaning. The contents pertaining to expressions consist in the ideas, attitudes, desires, and emotions internal to human being; at this level, linguistic meaning is infused with the attitudes and positions humans have in relation to what-already-is (already existing phenomena and actions). Typical expressions like "this tree is really beautiful" are already infused with this kind of linguistic meaning. Finally, prescriptions are at once based on reality and what-already-is but aim further at changing reality and what already is; the meaning of a prescription thus contains the demand of what ought to be. This sense of linguistic meaning is concretely displayed in prescriptions of the type "this tree ought to be protected" (cutting this tree is prohibited). So, if there is a logical connection between descriptions and the inquiry "What is it?," and expressions more directly concern the inquiry "What does it mean?," then prescriptions involve the question "What should it become?" These three senses of linguistic meaning are intrinsically linked to the original form of meaning, which is rooted in both the being of the world and the process of human being.

The meaning of a word first brings us to its referent. For instance, the meaning of the word "Mount Tai" lies precisely in the corresponding object to which it refers, that is, Mount Tai. Even though we can neither say that linguistic meaning is simply reducible to referring nor write off the relationship between words and their referents as a simple relation of correspondence, determining the meaning of words with the act of referring and the referents to which they refer nevertheless reflects one aspect of the relation between language and reality. Here, however, we need to distinguish between words directly and indirectly referring to objects. When we say "book" to refer to some book on the shelf, this book we refer to initially presents itself as a particular form that we can directly perceive through our senses, for instance as a hardback (or paperback), as having a certain thickness, and so on. The word "book" in this context directly refers to those perceivable characteristics of the said book. However, at the same time, the said object (that particular book) contains those other attributes and properties that make a book a book: for instance, it contains a certain amount of words, which discuss some theory or concept. Although these other properties cannot be directly perceived, they still constitute the intrinsic properties of the said book; when we use "book" to refer to the said object, the word "book" simultaneously refers to those other properties in an indirect fashion. The meaning of a word linked to direct reference appears in an immediate form, and the meaning of a word under the power of indirect reference has a mediated quality. Here, directly and indirectly referring as well as the direct and indirect meaning that corresponds reveals different aspects of the link between the meaning of words and objects, and provides words and concepts with the possibility of concretely grasping real objects.[30]

Of course, this explanation of the relation between words and objects by no means implies that every word must necessarily refer to or express a real being. There can be some distance between words and real beings. People often list such examples as the "winged horse Pegasus" and the "golden mountain," which seem to have no directly corresponding referents. However, this does not prove that these words lack a ground in reality. In terms of the construction of such words, "winged horse," and "golden mountain" are combinations of the words "winged" and "horse," "golden" and "mountain." Considered separately, "wings," "horse," "gold," and "mountain" are all names of real beings, and thus although "winged horse" and "golden mountain" are names without actual things to correspond to them, we obviously cannot say that the formation of such words has absolutely nothing to do with real beings. Broadly speaking, "a winged horse" and "a golden mountain" also express possible ways for things to be: they are entirely different from such expressions as "a black whiteness" and "a squared circle"; that is, they do not involve logical contradictions, and logically speaking, anything that does not contain a logical contradiction belongs to possible being. The meaning pertaining to possible worlds is much broader than the real world (logically speaking, the real world is only one of many possible worlds). Thus, corresponding to the mode of being of the possible, "a winged horse," "a golden mountain," and other such names have their ontological ground in the broad sense.

Linguistic meaning is not only manifested through the relationship between a word and its referent, since it also concerns how the referent is reached, which is also just the given way a thing is expressed. As is widely known, Frege made a distinction between sense [Sinn] and referent [Bedeutung]: the referent is the object to which a linguistic sign refers, while sense is manifested in the mode of expression of the sign that refers to the object. The same referent can often be expressed with different linguistic signs to the effect that the referent of distinct signs is the same but the senses that they express differ. For instance, the referent of "morning star" and the referent of "evening star" are identical (they both refer to Venus), but as different signs expressing the same object, their senses differ. Whereas the referent primarily reflects the cognitive relation between linguistic signs (words) and objects, sense primarily concerns the way in which human being grasps or expresses objects. The former rests on the question concerning what it is that human being grasps through the use of linguistic signs, while the latter rests on the question concerning what form of sign or what expressive means human being adopts in order to grasp objects.

Grasping objects by referring to them is the descriptive function of language. Aside from describing, language also plays a role in expressing human being's own self (oneself), which involves emotions, desire, attitude, standpoint, and the like. Ogden and Richards distinguish the symbolic use of words from the emotive use of words: while the former involve statements, the latter is "the use of words to express or excite feelings and attitudes."[31] "Exciting" here could be seen as an effect, which self-expression generates in the listener(s). In this sense, expression constitutes the most basic aspect of the emotive use of words. In the form of expressions, the meaning of language is connected to the external display of internal intentional states. When human emotions, desires, attitudes, and standpoints just exist in the form of internal intentional states, it is hardly possible for the other to understand or come to know of them, but after they are linguistically expressed, they acquire an understandable form, and at the linguistic level, these emotions, desires, attitudes, standpoints, and so on, constitute the meaning implied by the form of language.

Of course, although expressions consist in revealing internal intentional states, this by no means implies that the facts respectively involved in expressing and describing are entirely unrelated. It seems that some philosophers have missed this point. The emotivists in moral philosophy, for example, point out that moral language has meaning at the level of expression while often ignoring the other aspect of meaning that moral language implies. For instance, A. J. Ayer argues that when I say that an action is right or wrong, I am only expressing moral sentiments. For example, when I say to someone "It was wrong of you to steal that money," I do nothing more than express "you stole that money" in a particularly angry tone and with an upset attitude in relation to that action.[32] According to this view, the expressive meaning and descriptive meaning of moral language seem mutually exclusive. But in fact, even though the sentence "It was wrong of you to steal that money" primarily expresses the speaker's attitude and position, there is also some descriptive content contained therein. Initially, as an object of evaluation, the act of "you stole that money" is a fact that has already occurred, which is the factual reference of the aforesaid statement. At the same time, linking "you stole that money" and "wrong" together (using "it was wrong" to modify the action "of you to steal that money") also is not just purely and simply an expression of an emotion or particular mood as Ayer puts it; it is rather a confirmation of an institutional fact of a certain historical age (stealing money is illegal, it is an institutionalized and socialized kind of fact within a certain property relationship or system of property ownership). Ayer considers this statement to be a simple emotional release, which overlooks the concrete socio-historical context of language usage, and consequently, he unduly dissociates the descriptive and expressive meanings of language.

The connection between expressive and descriptive reference just mentioned also shows that an expression cannot be entirely without actual content. In fact, when human beings use expressions as a way to reveal their own emotions, desires, attitudes, and standpoints, these forms of expression are always in some way referring to actuality and are pregnant with opinions regarding the beings concerned, and such opinions first and foremost involve evaluating. Emotions, desires, attitudes, and standpoints concretely consist of love or hate, joy or sadness, acceptance or rejection, yearning for or resisting, agreeing or opposing, and undergirding these intentional states and attitudes is an evaluation of the object concerned: loving, accepting, yearning for, and agreeing with something all presuppose a confirmation of the positive value of the object concerned; hating, rejecting, resisting, and opposing something all presuppose a confirmation of the negative value of the object concerned. From the perspective of the expressive form of language, an evaluation refers to a relation between a human need, a human end, and an object that concerns them, and its meaning will consist in a concrete elucidation of the question "What does it mean?" In correlation with this connection between expressing and describing (or referring), "What does it mean?" in the evaluative sense and "What is it?" in the cognitive sense are inseparable. Chinese philosophy discovered this early on. In *Lüshi chunqiu* we find a summary of the distinctive feature of a speech: "If able to accord with the principle [in things], a speech can determine whether gain or loss, benefit or harm is to come."[33] Here, "according with the principle [in things]" belongs to the cognitive domain, and "gain or loss, benefit or harm" is the content of an evaluation. From the perspective of *Lüshi chunqiu*, a speech "accords with the principle [in things]" in the cognitive sense, and at the same time involves an evaluation of attributes of value such as "gain or loss, benefit or harm."

Evaluations are inseparable from norms. The meaning of an evaluation and the meaning of norms are interrelated in language. When we confirm that a mode of being or action is good or has positive value, such a confirmation also simultaneously entails that we ought to choose the action concerned or attain the mode of being concerned. Austin's notion of speech acts and Hare's affirmation of the meaning of moral language as guidelines for action both show the normative function of language from different angles. In contrast to the descriptive and expressive, the normative nature of language spoken of here embodies the prescriptive function. Corresponding to the inquiry "What should it become?," the prescriptive or normative meaning of language in actual life involves reforming the world at a deeper level. While propounding the theory of rectifying names, Confucius stated: "If names are not rectified, then what is said will not sound reasonable (*bu shun* 不顺); if what is said does not sound reasonable, then affairs will not be accomplished; if affairs are not accomplished, then rituals and music will not flourish."[34] Here, "names" refers to titles and nomenclature associated with an institution or normative system. Rectifying names demands that actions suit the institutional order or normative system expressed by the names. In the same sense, Confucius stated, "the ruler ought to be a ruler, the minister a minister, the father a father, and the son a son."[35] Here, the ruler, minister, father, and son all must follow the norms prescribed by the names concerned. Worthy of interest here is that Confucius ties the accomplishment of affairs and the flourishing of rituals and music to the process of rectifying names. "Affairs" (*shi* 事), broadly referring to human practical activity, reaches the goal of "accomplishment" (*cheng* 成) and "rituals and music" including the political and cultural order reach the goal of "flourishing" by means of rectifying names, which is an affirmation of the role of names in the political-cultural structure of institutions. In a similar sense, *The Book of Changes* (*yijing* 易经) asserts: "That which incites the movement of the world is conserved in language."[36] Asserting that language in the form of speech can "incite the movement of the world" is but another affirmation of the effective role of language. Wang Fuzhi further elaborated upon this passage, stating: "Language incites the movement of the world due to revealing things, which further enables action upon things."[37] To reveal things consists in describing and explaining actuality and the external world, and "acting upon things" implies proceeding from "what ought to be" so as to prescriptively determine and reform the external world. The unity of using language to "reveal things" and "act upon things" involves the relation between language and actuality at different levels. Here, the prescriptive meaning of language further demonstrates the connection between language and human practical activity.

Charles W. Morris once made a distinction between semantics, pragmatics, and syntactics in his research on the meaning of signs. The field of semantics studies the relationship between signs and objects, pragmatics the relationship between signs and the interpreter, and syntactics the relationship between different signs.[38] Among the signs of which Morris speaks are linguistic signs. This distinction undoubtedly holds at the linguistic level and points out different aspects of linguistic meaning. Yet, such a distinction also harbors the tendency to dissociate language and syntactics from human being, leaving the connection between linguistic meaning and human being aside as an issue to be taken up solely at the level of pragmatics. Moreover, although Morris affirms this connection at the pragmatic level, he only does so from the perspective of interpretation. In fact, however, the actual constitution of language is such that linguistic meaning can only be generated in the process of human being cognizing and practicing, and hence, syntactics and semantics are also inseparably bound to human being. So, although from the perspective of semantics it remains true that the meanings of linguistic symbols involves the relations between signs and objects, and moreover, that using different signs to grasp different objects has its ontological ground (using different names to differentiate objects from one another is to cut form out of chaos and thereby overcome a state of chaos, which itself presupposes that there are intrinsic differences between things themselves in the first place, or in other words, the condition of possibility of using names to make distinctions among things lies in things themselves being already distinguishable), however, to designate a sign to refer to an object is a matter of convention, which is determined through the historical process of reforming the world (accomplishing things) and reforming the self (accomplishing oneself), and it is also precisely within the historical unfolding of this process that the relationship between a linguistic sign and a signified object is gradually fixed, stabilized, or as Bartes worded it, "naturalized."[39] Here, the genesis of semantic meaning clearly does not just involve the relations between signs and objects; it concretely unfolds as an interaction between signs, objects, and human being's cognizing and practicing. In other words, the connection between a sign and the object to which it refers is itself established through the process of human being cognizing and practicing. As for the relationship between different linguistic signs (the syntactic dimension), it is true that meaning first involves the function of signifiers to refer, however, the differences between the referents of linguistic signs are essentially inseparable from the being of humans. Taking the different meanings of "morning star" and "evening star" as an example once again, such a distinction only has meaning for human beings as a species: the same object (Venus) acquiring the different meanings of "morning star" and "evening star" is to a great extent still founded upon human life practices, including the conditions of labor and way of life of humankind for a considerably long historical period, wherein working time begins at sunrise (morning) and resting time begins at sunset (evening). Finally, the relation between a linguistic sign and the interpreter (the pragmatic dimension) directly shows the inseparability of human and linguistic meaning. Of course, the relation between the two is not just limited to an act of interpretation. In fact, interpretation itself always happens and unfolds in a much broader process of cognizing and practicing, and always presupposes the different concrete conditions of the reciprocal interaction between human being and world. When Wittgenstein affirmed in his late period that the meaning of words lies in their use, it was undoubtedly this connection between the meaning of linguistic signs and the process of human being living and practicing of which he became aware.

To discuss linguistic signs we must first begin with words. From the epistemological perspective, single words standing alone do not express knowledge, for instance, just saying the word "horse" doesn't demonstrate that the speaker has obtained any concrete knowledge; only forming statements like "This is a horse" or "A horse is an animal" will demonstrate that the speaker has some knowledge of things. Wittgenstein affirmed this point with great clarity: "Only the proposition has sense; only in the context of a proposition has a name meaning."[40] In terms of linguistic form, propositions or judgments are sentences. Whereas the principal characteristic of a word is to be separable and hence differentiable and determinate, it is a sentence that connects together different words. Words refer to different objects, and as the intension of a sentence, a proposition reflects the connections between things and ideas. Just as the meaning of a word is grounded in actuality, so the connections among the words within a sentence only acquire sense under the condition that they are based upon relations in actuality, and these actual relations fundamentally appear, open up, and take shape in the process of reforming the world (accomplishing things) and reforming oneself (accomplishing oneself). At the same time, the meaning of a sentence is presented as a proposition: just as different words are capable of denoting the same referent, so the same proposition could also be expressed by different sentences. As Frege noticed, as opposed to propositions, there is also a variety of other elements attached to a sentence, including emotion, attitude, and the like, each of which makes the meaning of each sentence increasingly complicated. Insofar as this variety of external attachments do not inhere in propositions, propositions could be seen as logical abstractions of sentences; or in other words, sentences are the actual mode of being of propositions: without a sentence, there is no way to express a proposition. As actual modes of being of thought and meaning, such attachments like emotion and attitude demonstrate that in actuality the genesis of linguistic meaning and the understanding of linguistic meaning are inseparable from one's being and doing.

Words and sentences all fall under the broad category of linguistic signs. Opposed to linguistic signs are non-linguistic signs, which could be divided further into two categories: artificial and non-artificial. Artificial signs are those that humans have directly created. At the level of non-linguistic signs, artificial signs constitute a much broader domain consisting of anything from traffic signals to electrical codes and chemical symbols, from postures or behavioral signs (body language like facial expressions, and hand gestures) to artistic symbols (like paintings, statues, music, and dance) and even architectural symbols as well; the category of artificial signs contains all the variety of aspects of the cognitive and practical activity of humankind. As for their origin, all the different forms of artificial signs are generated along with their meaning in the historical process of knowing the world and knowing the self and reforming the world and refining the self. Traffic signals, for example, are one of the means to ensure the fluid circulation of traffic along circuits of roads and to maintain the order of transportation in a city. As such, traffic signals are the product of the development of transportation and city technologies having reached a definite historical stage, and understanding the meaning of them as signs (for instance, a red light is a sign that means driving and walking is prohibited, and a green light is a sign that means driving and walking is permitted) presupposes a background of education and a practice of life.

Aside from artificial signs, there are also non-artificial ones, which could be seen as natural signs. An aura around the moon means that wind is coming; moist stepstones mean that rain is coming. In each case, the prior term constitutes a kind of natural sign. The meaning of one is linked to the coming of wind, and the other to the falling of rain. To take an ordinary Chinese proverb for example, when one says "It takes but one fallen leaf to know autumn has come," what is affirmed in this case is the relationship between one fallen leaf and the autumn season. Here, "one fallen leaf" is a sign of "autumn," a natural sign. Aside from this, there is also smoke as a sign of fire, rising body temperature as the omen of sickness, and the like, which all belong to the category of natural signs. Aside from this rather simple form of signs, there are also more complicated natural signs like fossils. As imprints representing archaic organisms, fossils differ from relics of culture and civilization insofar as the latter are things of human artifice and so could be seen as artificial signs, whereas fossils are natural signs that express archaic biological things. In an extended sense, natural signs also include natural things that may have a representative function like the snow, which is commonly seen as a natural sign representing cleanliness and purity, and the flower, which is a natural sign that is often seen to represent beauty.

At the level of form, natural signs seem only to present relations between natural objects. Whether it is the moon and the wind, stepstones and rain, a fallen leaf and autumn or fossils and archaic organisms, the two related terms in each case are all natural beings. Does this demonstrate that the meaning of a natural sign is entirely "natural" due to not having anything to do with human being at all? The answer is obviously negative. Granted, there is a multitude of real relations between natural objects themselves, and though such relationships must first be understood as being in-themselves, the capacity of natural objects to appear as meaningful signs is inseparable from the capacity of understanding and interpreting, which is relative to the process of human being knowing and practicing. Of course, there can be no doubt that such relationships also involve the natural dimension of cause and effect: an aura around the moon is formed from rays of light refracting against cirrus clouds and ice crystals at high altitudes, and the emergence of an aura around the moon testifies to the presence of cirrus clouds, which are linked, in turn, to the formation of wind currents; moist stepstones are linked to the humidity of the air being rather high, and an increase in air humidity is causally linked to the falling of rain. In the same way, the yellowing or falling of tree leaves is an effect, whose cause is linked to the climatic conditions of autumn. Fossils of ancient organisms are formed out of the reciprocal interaction between archaic organic bodies, the geological environment, climatic conditions and the like. However, when an aura around the moon, moist step stones, yellowing or falling leaves, and fossils appear as natural signs with meaning, there is more than just a relationship of cause and effect working between them and the phenomena they represent, since such causalities have already entered the cognitive and interpretive relationship of human being to such objects. Purely as natural objects, the moon encircled with an aura of light and moist step stones are themselves nothing but natural things and natural phenomena that exist and occur beyond the domain of meaning; it is precisely human being's cognizing and practicing that brings natural objects into a world of meaning and henceforth makes them become meaningful signs. So, clearly some kind of deductive or interpretive relationship has already connected these natural signs and the phenomena or things that they represent: the aura around the moon foreshadowing wind, moist stepstones forecasting rain, fossils representing archaic life forms—the formation of any such relation of meaning always involves deduction, inference, and interpretation at the cognitive level. Disassociated from this capacity of inference and interpretation linked to human being's cognition and practice, there is neither a way to understand the meanings of natural signs nor a way to generate them either.

Showing the connection between natural signs and language can also further our demonstration of the interrelation between the genesis of the meaning of natural signs and the cognizing and practicing of human beings. As already mentioned, the category of signs in the broad sense could be divided into linguistic and non-linguistic ones, but linguistic signs constitute the most fundamental among them. In fact, the meaning of a non-linguistic sign can often only be understood through language. In the words of Roland Barthes, "to perceive what a substance signifies is inevitably to fall back on the individuation of a language," because "every semiological system has its linguistic admixture."[41] Signs of a non-linguistic artificial semiotic system only become meaningful and understandable once they have been translated or transformed into language. In the same way, the presentation and understanding of the meaning of natural signs always involves language in some way or other. Language constitutes the condition under which meaning can be presented and understood not only in the cases of lunar auras, moist stepstones, or fossils appearing as signs of wind, rain, and archaic life or other such cases involving a relationship of inference, but also in those other cases of signifying activity like a flower symbolizing beauty and snow symbolizing cleanliness, since linguistic elements like the words "flower," "snow," "beauty," and "cleanliness" are in each case used. This infusion of language into natural signs thus reveals another aspect of the human activity of grasping the world while generating meaning.

The meanings that are correlated with signs mainly concern understanding. Considered at the level of understanding, the formation and presentation of meaning is logically grounded in the understandability of being. Now, the understandability of being concerns the ground or cause of beings: if the existence of things were to have neither ground nor cause, there would be no way to understand them. This point has both ontological and epistemological meaning: Ontologically speaking, the existence of any given thing has its ground or cause; epistemologically speaking, understanding things presupposes their understandability, which the ground or cause of things provide. Heidegger once asserted that "nothing is without reason" (*nihil est sine ratione*) is the principle of reason. Here, "reason" is at once cause or ground in the ontological sense and also the reasons involved in inferences, deductions, and explanations. According to Heidegger's view, the principle of reason states that "every thing counts as existing when and only when it has been securely established as a calculable object for cognition."[42] The establishment of an object of cognition involves knowing or cognizing in the epistemological sense, and "to count as existing" includes an ontological confirmation; combining the two entails linking the understanding of objects to the process of human being cognizing through the fusion of the epistemological and ontological horizons. In brief, at the ontological level, there is nothing without either cause or reason; at the epistemological level, if a thing is without either cause or reason, it strictly cannot be understood. As regards the dimension of understanding meaning, the principle of reason provides the ontological and epistemological ground for the genesis of meaning. Davidson also deals with this issue when discussing the constitution of action and the understanding of action. According to Davidson, "the reason *rationalizes* the action."[43] This so-called rationalization of an action is a rational justification of an action, which means that the action itself may be understood or explained in a rational way. Even though Davidson did not directly focus on meaning here, his argument still holds as an affirmation of the connection between reason and the understandable dimension of meaning at the level of human practical action.

The previous discussion mainly focused on the meaning that appears in the form of signs. The content of this kind of meaning primarily involves understanding and the process of cognizing. In contrast to the meaning of semiotic systems, which have more to do with the dimension of understanding, the kind of meaning that is linked to human purposes to a greater extent involves the dimension of value. According to the purposive dimension of accomplishing oneself and accomplishing things, to have meaning and to have value are two ways of saying the same thing, and hence at this level, the form of meaning cannot be dissociated from a mode of valuing. Now, signs always represent other things. As Husserl worded it, "Every sign is a sign for something."[44] This characteristic of signs makes their meaning such that they always refer to something other than or beyond themselves. By contrast, meaning at the level of value is first and foremost linked to the being of humans and is intrinsic to this process of being. As the agent who is accomplishing the self and accomplishes things, human being seeks value in a process of self-affirmation.

Broadly speaking, in the domain of value, meaning may present itself in the mode of ideas, but it may also present itself in the mode of humanizing being. At the level of ideas, the intrinsic content of meaning primarily involves the true, the beautiful, and the good. The true is linked to opening up the world as it truly is, but the true may also become embodied in ethical practice. The former shows the meaning of truth-value by providing a true picture of the world, and the latter refers to the formation of truthfulness as a virtue. The good in the broad sense appears as the realization of ideals of value, and the mode of the good as idea is a moral ideal, which unfolds as a normative system that reforms the world in a broader sense. The beautiful, in turn, takes shape through the process of one objectifying one's own essential powers. Through the union of lawfulness and purposiveness, aesthetic ideals overcome the tension between the humanization of nature and the naturalization of humans, provide humans in their creation of values with the guidance of ideas, and also manifest the intrinsic value of the beautiful in the process.

In the process of accomplishing oneself and accomplishing things, one inquiring into the meaning of the world is always interconnected with taking up a concern for the meaning of one's own being. When one thinks about why one exists, that which one is concerned with is the very meaning of one's own being. Linked to the self-investigation of the meaning of one's own being are different forms of spiritual worlds or spiritual states. In the form of internal reflections, realizations, awakenings, felt experiences and the like, the meaning contained in a spiritual state not only involves objects, but also directly concerns one's own being. In fact, as this book will reveal later on, in a spiritual state, one thinking about and grasping the meaning of one's own being starts to become the predominant issue in comparison with grasping the meaning of external objects. In the case of one thinking about and grasping the meaning of one's own being, the core of the world of spirit is concentrated and manifested in the pursuit of an ideal or in the consciousness of a mission. The pursuit of an ideal is guided by the question "What can one hope for?" or "What ought one hope for?" and the consciousness of a mission unfolds as an investigation of the question "What should one take responsibility for?" With the consciousness of a mission or consciousness of responsibility as its core, one's spiritual state is the essential attribute of human being qua human at the level of ideas.

The meaning of value is expressed through the act of evaluating at the level of ideas and is also grounded in practical activity in the broad sense as it externalizes as the actual world of being. As the externalization or actualization of meaning, this realm of being that takes shape through cognizing and practicing could also be seen as the actual or external form of value, which consists of things for-us but also the world of everyday life and social institutions, which are all forms of being that could be seen as humanized actuality in the broad sense.

The meaning that is presented in the form of humanized actuality must be understood in contrast to the beings that have not yet entered the domain of cognition and practice. The objects, which lie beyond or outside the realm of cognition and practice, are things in-themselves, but forms of meaning whose content is humanized actuality have already been impressed with the mark of human being and appear as things for-us on various levels. The traditional Chinese term for "things–in-themselves" is "Nature in-itself" (*tian zhi tian*). As the mode of being of that which has no real cognitive or practical connection to human being and hence exists beyond the realm of cognition and practice, such beings do not yet constitute objects with meaning at the level of ideas nor have they obtained any actual meaning at the level of practice. Abstractly speaking, both human being and things-in-themselves belong to "being," and thereby cannot be absolutely dissociated from one another, but since things in-themselves exist beyond the realm of cognition and practice and hence have not been encountered by human being, the relation between things in-themselves and human being would be qualified more as that of separation than as that of integration. By transforming things in-themselves into things for-us, human being begins to impress the mark of human being upon Nature in-itself, and by virtue of this beings in-themselves acquire senses of value.

So, it is evident that meaning involves linguistic and non-linguistic signs and consists in being understandable, but it is no less evident that it always implies values in connection with human ends and ideals. Whether in the domain of signs or in the domain of values, actual meaning always emerges in a relatively determinate form on the one hand, and develops concrete properties by means of forming associations with the related terms constitutive of a determinate system on the other. In linguistic systems, while each different word has its own relatively determinate sense, a word in actual usage by no means presents its meaning solely by itself in isolation; a word is always in a reciprocally determined relationship with other words and sentences, and it is precisely through such a nexus that it acquires its concrete sense. Furthermore, the concepts and propositions, which words and sentences express, are also connected to other concepts and propositions within a determinate theoretical system, and thus their meaning can only concretely appear and be grasped through these connections, which the theory of holism in epistemology and linguistics clearly demonstrates. In the same way, the meaning of ideas and principles within a domain of values can never appear in isolation from a determinate system of values. Historically speaking, Pre-Qin Confucianism put forward the idea of being-humane (*ren* 仁), and posited it as the core principle of values. Yet, it is impossible to grasp the intrinsic meaning of *ren* solely within the limits of this word itself. In fact, for Confucianism, the idea of *ren* simultaneously involves the relationship between human being and the natural world, between being-humane and observing ritual propriety (*li* 礼), between being-humane and practicing filial piety (*xiao* 孝): as far as the distinction between the human world and the natural world is concerned, *ren* means affirming that human beings have an intrinsic value that is different from the value of natural objects; *ren* is also linked to ritual propriety, since being-humane constitutes the substance and inner core of the observance of ritual propriety, which in turn could be seen as the external form of being-humane; being-humane is no less related to filial piety, which is its ethical source and foundation (filial piety is the root out of which a humane sensibility grows). It is precisely through such a system of values that *ren* presents the many implicated facets of its meaning, and the rich meaning of *ren* can only be grasped as it is rooted within this systematic nexus of relationships. So, meaning can only emerge within a determinate system, because it is inseparably tied to the multi-faceted nature of both the world and human being's doing and cognizing, and the systematic and relational character of meaning is grounded in the systematic nature of being itself and the concrete nature of practice and cognition.

From a much broader perspective, in the process of reforming the world (accomplishing things) and transforming the self (accomplishing oneself) the cognitive level of meaning, which involves understanding, is inseparable from the evaluative level of meaning. So by the same token, meaning in the form of signs is intrinsically related to meaning in the form of values. On the one hand, both linguistic signs and nonlinguistic signs envelop implications of value. In the case of linguistic signs, the significance that words have for human beings as well as the emotions that sentences carry both contain value. At the same time, implications of value are no less involved when considering the case of non-linguistic signs like national flags, cultural relics, and historical architecture. On the other hand, every form of value contains some meaning that can never be entirely isolated from signs: values in the form of ideas are always expressed in linguistic form; moreover, the value of actual beings (humanized actuality) exists in the form of signs, which represent the essential powers of human being. At the same time, meaning in the form of values could never emerge without the involvement of understanding. Dilthey formulates this same point as follows: "something of which understanding is not possible cannot have meaning or value."[45] In this regard, the different forms of meaning are identical with meaning itself insofar as they integrate and fuse together. In effect, different contents of meaning can be presented through the same form of meaning (in the form of signs or in the form of systems of ideas or humanized actuality, etc.): in a cognitive relationship, meaning is predominantly linked to understandability; in an evaluative relationship, however, the content of a meaning will primarily be a value. So, as two interrelated aspects of the process of accomplishing oneself and accomplishing things, both have different dimensions but never cease to interlace and fuse together.

Two Tendencies and Their Limits

Our examination of meaning has so far shown that even though there are different dimensions of meaning, meaning's different forms of being along with the genesis and emergence of meaning cannot be dissociated from the process of accomplishing oneself and accomplishing things. How are we to understand this link between human being and meaning? This question involves the meaning of meaning itself and the meaning of one's own being from a much broader perspective. But, two different one-sided tendencies to understand these two aspects continuously arise. So, to investigate the meaning of meaning requires a close examination of these tendencies.

The being of meaning is inseparable from the way in which meaning emerges. However, some philosophers have failed to notice this characteristic of meaning. For them, it seems that meaning can only be the internal properties of objects. As for this tendency, Michael Polanyi's view is highly representative. In the book *Meaning,* which he co-authored with Harry Prosch, it is stated that aside from human beings, "living things, individually and in general, are also oriented toward meaning."[46] Moreover, meaning here is not only seen as the object pursued by all living things, but also as being internal to everything we have knowledge about: "We might justifiably claim, therefore, that everything we know is full of meaning, is not absurd at all, although we can sometimes fail to grasp these meanings and fall into absurdities."[47] According to this understanding, meaning seemingly constitutes the properties of things in-themselves: regardless of whether or not things have entered human being's domain of cognition and practice, and regardless of whether human being has already grasped these things or not, they still possess their own unalterable meaning. But, this view fails to account for the link between the genesis of meaning and the process of accomplishing oneself and accomplishing things. In fact, although things do have their own properties, which exist in-themselves, such properties acquiring the form of meaning and appearing in a meaningful way is impossible in isolation from the process of knowing and reforming the world (refining things) and knowing and refining oneself: for things to become meaningful beings they must have first entered human being's domain of cognition and practice. Theoretically speaking, Polyani emphasizes the in-itself nature of meaning, because he desires to overcome the merely subjective nature of meaning, which we can see clearly in the following statement: "If we believe in the existence of a general movement toward the attainment of meaning in the universe, then we will not regard any of the kinds of meaning achieved by men to be merely subjective or private."[48] However, even though overcoming the subjective nature of meaning is a rational intention, attempting to achieve this by universalizing meaning and making it a thing in-itself is obviously one-sided. In essence, understanding meaning as objective properties implies abstracting meaning from its authentic existence in cognitive and practical processes and hence entails divorcing meaning from its actual ground and very precondition. It is obviously hard to say that this so-called meaning, which lacks the characteristic of being-actual, has truly overcome the one-sided subjectivity of meaning. Although Polanyi indeed notices the link between meaning and the being of humans in other places,[49] his viewpoint undoubtedly still has its problems.

As opposed to emphasizing the in-itself nature of meaning, other philosophical systems choose to stress the interrelatedness of human being and meaning. Here, pragmatism is of relevance. The distinctive feature of pragmatism is to link the question of meaning to the being of humans and human activity. When discussing the idea of things, Charles Pierce, an early representative of pragmatism, once pointed out: "Our idea of anything *is* our idea of its sensible effects."[50] The "sensible effects" spoken of here involves human activity and the results of this activity. Pierce took "hard," the concept of one of the qualities of things, as an example, stating, "let us ask what we mean by calling a thing *hard?* Evidently that it will not be scratched by many other substances. The whole conception of this quality, as of every other, lies in its conceived effects."[51] Whether or not something can be scratched is something that humans come to know through practical activity. For Pierce, the meaning of the concept "hard" is formed through the results of human activity, that is, the repetition of the result of things being scratched or remaining unscratched. Different representatives of pragmatism of course still have their respective theoretical orientations, but they all affirm that meaning originates from the being and doing of humans. In contrast to Pierce, who concentrated on the sensible nature of the results of activity, James and Dewey placed more emphasis on the connection between meaning and the life practices and living needs of human beings. Taking truth as an example, for James the meaning of a truth lies in providing a leading function that is worthwhile.[52] This function primarily refers to the satisfaction of human being's various needs. Insofar as they affirm the connection between meaning and the practical doing of humans, pragmatists most certainly overcome the idea of meaning as natural properties that exist in-themselves. However, these ways of understanding meaning seem to remain trapped in the dimension of value and fail to account adequately for meaning at the level of knowing facts. Further inspection will reveal that without ever ceasing to view things from the human perspective, pragmatism still often fails to adequately grasp the links between meaning and the actual world.

Adding yet another affirmation of the interrelatedness of human being and meaning, yet from another angle, is hermeneutics. Taking Gadamer as a representative, what is under consideration for hermeneutics is primarily the problem of understanding. From a broad perspective, understanding concerns the being of humans and the interpretation of texts. In the case of interpreting texts, hermeneutics emphasizes that meaning by no means exists in-itself; rather, it is something that is generated through the interaction between text, author, and reader. This interaction concretely unfolds as a dialogue between the reader and writer: it is through the process of questioning and responding that the meaning of a text is continuously generated and understood. This idea shows that the interaction between different subjects is significant for the process of understanding, and simultaneously confirms the leading role of the interpreter and affirms the creativity involved in the process of understanding while avoiding the tendency to reduce meaning to an unchanging object in-itself. Due to revealing the generative nature of meaning, hermeneutics also points out the historical dimension of interpretation, which further enables the actual beings within history and the actual beings within the process of understanding history to communicate, insofar as understanding is seen as the result of an event in history of effect. Gadamer elucidated this point as follows: "The true historical object is not an object at all, but the unity of the one and the other, a relationship that constitutes both the reality of history and the reality of historical understanding. A hermeneutics adequate to the subject matter would have to demonstrate the reality and efficacy of history within understanding itself. I shall refer to this as 'history of effect.' Understanding is, essentially, a historically effected event."[53] Gadamer here touches upon the historical nature of understanding and interpretation, and as he emphasizes the notion of historical understanding, he also gives higher priority to the role of the understanding subject (the interpreter): history of effect also means the product of the understanding subject. So, in the case of interpreting texts, although hermeneutics affirms the dialogical nature of understanding, in the concrete interpretation of a text, dialogue always proceeds in the mode of the interpreter himself questioning both the text and the author, and hence, searching for answers within the text. The author acts as the other half of the dialogue, yet insofar as his participation in the dialogue is exhausted through the act of providing the text, the author himself recedes into a state of being an absent interlocutor. This asymmetry found in the process of dialogue once again points out the leading role of the interpreter. At the same time, Gadamer also likens such a dialogue to playing a game: "Many aspects of the dialogue between men point to the common structure of understanding and playing,"[54] and "first and foremost, play is self-presentation."[55] So, interpreting the text through a dialogue is characterized as self-understanding: "To understand a text is to come to understand oneself in a kind of dialogue."[56] That aside, hermeneutics also raises the notion of "a fusion of horizons" in the understanding of texts, which is certainly a noble attempt to overcome the one-sided nature of understanding as a one-way path leading outwards from the reader's perspective; this is so that the interpreter may be thought of as reaching the author's perspective half-way at a point where their distinct horizons mesh and fuse, but such a fusion itself presupposes the interpreter's prejudices and is initially, in logical terms, based on the interpreter's sympathetic understanding of the author and the text. With this in mind, hermeneutics does indeed reveal to us a serious insight into the interactive, creative, and historical nature of understanding meaning, but it still leans too much to one side in its tendency to excessively emphasize the subject's (read: interpreter's) role.

This tendency to emphasize the subject's role can be seen even more clearly in the phenomenology of Husserl. In terms of derivation of thought, the fountainhead of Gadamer's hermeneutics could be traced back to Husserl's phenomenology. The focal interest of Husserl's theory is, of course, linked to intentional activity. By stressing intentionality from the outset in *Logical Investigations*, Husserl links meaning to what is given by consciousness. In the case of speech, included in every speech is always the intention to share something, but in Husserl's view, "such sharing becomes a possibility if the auditor also understands the speaker's intentions. He does this inasmuch as he takes the speaker to be a person who is not merely uttering sounds but speaking to him, who is accompanying those sounds with certain sense-giving acts."[57] Broadly speaking, according to Husserl's understanding, sense [meaning—Trans.] is given through intention. Here, the formation of meaning is identical to some extent with the act of intending. The turn in Husserl's late period could be explained as a change of focus, which he placed on the structuring activity of consciousness. In phenomenology, meaning involves the object of consciousness, and in Husserl's view, this object is itself constituted: "In the *broader* sense, however, the object is 'constituted'—'whether or not it is actual'—in certain concatenations of consciousness."[58] The logical presupposition of such a constitution is the suspension of being: after the question regarding the existence of the object is suspended, its presence only involves this constituting of consciousness itself. Corresponding to the constituted nature of the object is the determined nature of meaning: "In no noema, however, can it or its necessary center, the point of unity, the pure determinable X, be missing. No 'sense' without the '*something*' and, again, without '*determining content.*'"[59] The X here points to the "bearer of sense" pending determination, which *as carrier* is originally empty of content. The X is then filled with content through the determination of consciousness, which is the very process through which meaning is generated, and this determination of the X has a synthetic character: "the ray of the pure Ego's regard, dividing itself into a plurality of rays, goes to the X which arrives at synthetical unity."[60] The pure Ego, for Husserl here, is but pure consciousness, the synthetic "determination" of which is constitutive. According to this understanding, meaning is mainly something constituted by consciousness or pure consciousness. Even though here in Husserl's investigation we also seem to find the notion of an identity between meaning and object, the object itself is seen as something "constituted" within the noematic complex of consciousness; from this we must deduce that this identity between meaning and object as a whole has no way to overcome one-sidedness—here, staying solely in a domain constituted by consciousness.

Similar to Husserl, Cassier paid a significant amount of attention to the constitutive dimension of meaning formation. The philosophy of Cassier is characterized by its focus on signs, defining human being as the *animal symbolicum* (symbolic animal)."[61] As a neo-Kantian, Cassier was deeply influenced by Kant, but in Kant's philosophy he found the constitutive principle to be more important than the regulative. Proceeding from this bias, Cassier repeatedly emphasized the creative role of spirit, and found the meaning of reality to originate from the autonomous creation of spirit. In *The Philosophy of Symbolic Forms*, Cassier elucidated this as follows:

> True, we still remain in the world of "images"—but these are not images which reproduce a self-subsistent world of 'things'; they are 'image-worlds' whose principle and origin are to be sought in an autonomous creation of spirit. Through them alone we see what we call 'reality,' and in them alone we possess it: for the highest objective truth that is accessible to the spirit is ultimately the form of its own activity.[62]

The creativity of spirit spoken of here means precisely the nature of the mind to constitute. For Cassirer, the meaning of reality or the world is formed in the constitutive acts of spirit itself. A similar relationship, moreover, exists in the domain of value. According to Cassirer, the symbolic form is the condition of possibility of expressing and understanding meaning, but the symbolic form is itself based on humans creating. As one of the domains pertaining to values, the aesthetic domain concretely demonstrates this: "... the conception of an aesthetic form in the sensible world is possible only because we ourselves create the fundamental elements of form."[63] In brief, human being creates meaning in the act of creating symbolic forms.

As opposed to viewing meaning as the property of objects in-themselves, Husserl and Cassirer understood meaning in its connection to human being, and noticed the role played by human consciousness and the activity of spirit in the formation of meaning. As for the process of generating meaning, it is easy to see the importance of sense-giving and meaning-constituting acts: broadly speaking, intentionality is the condition of possibility of things emerging. In the absence of intention one could be looking at something without seeing it, and therefore, although whatever that something is may indeed exist, it would do so without any way to be present for human being. At the symbolic level, that an object has obtained meaning presupposes that it has already entered human being's domain of cognition and practice, and so, the formation, expression, and understanding of meaning all involve human being actively creating. Similarly, the genesis of values linked to aiming at ends is inseparable from the process of accomplishing oneself and refining the world: there is no way to dissociate the genesis and exhibition of values from the act of human being evaluating and consequently engaging the practice of creating values. However, on the other hand, the presentation of things in the process of knowing and practicing endows intentional activity with actual content, and thereby enables intentional activity to be more than just an empty flow of consciousness.[64] Grounded both ontologically and epistemologically in the actual relationship between humans and being itself, things emerge as whatever human being understands them to be, but nothing ever emerges without something actual entering and meshing with human being's intentional activity. Both Husserl's theory of sense-giving and meaning-constituting as well as Cassirer's theory of the mind's creativity seem to overlook the actual ground of meaning while affirming the role of human being in the process of generating meaning. They both restrict the genesis of meaning to acts of consciousness or spirit and thus fail to see the process of practicing in the broader sense: Husserl's suspension of being and Cassirer's abstraction of reality both present meaning as the product of a one-sided effort solely on behalf of human being, who gives meaning and constitutes meaning, which dissociates the genesis of meaning from the actual world and places human being before nothing but constituted or created objects.[65]

Both taking meaning to be the property of objects in-themselves and solely establishing meaning upon either the constitutive acts of consciousness, human being's self-understanding or evaluating happen to be the two one-sided tendencies to understand meaning. Theoretically speaking, while the former overlooks the relationship between the genesis of meaning and the cognitive and practical activity of human beings, the latter restricts the genesis of meaning to the domain of the subject and the limits of consciousness while failing to give an adequate account of the actual conditions of the genesis of meaning. In fact, in the historical unfolding of cognizing and practicing, the emergence of things, the bestowal of meaning, the cognition of facts, the evaluation of values, the being of objects, and the creative activity of human beings are always interrelated. From denotation at the level of understanding signs to evaluation in the domain of values, from knowing the world and knowing the self to reforming the world and reforming the self, the process of generating meaning is always based on the actual connection and historical interaction between human being and object. In determining the nature of meaning along a one-way path, both sides obviously overlook the way to a genuine understanding of meaning.

The Commitment to Meaning and the Openness of Generating Meaning

Logically speaking, despite the fact that the two opposing theories of meaning just mentioned—that of meaning as object in-itself and that of meaning as constituted by consciousness—skew the understanding of meaning in opposite directions, they still have quite a bit in common as regards their confirmation of and commitment to meaning: their explanations of meaning are premised on an affirmation of the existence of meaning, and here, meaning involves both understanding and evaluating. Opposed to these two tendencies to affirm meaning in one way or another is that other position—the tendency to deny meaning and eliminate it. This tendency can be clearly seen in deconstruction, post-modernism, and the variety of nihilisms.

In terms of the evolution of thought in the modern age, whether under the flag of anti-essentialism, deconstructing logo-centrism, or saying farewell to reason,[66] depreciating rationality and casting doubt upon both meaning and the pursuit of meaning seems to have become the very spirit of this age, and what seems to have followed in its shadow is the elimination of and dead loss of meaning. This tendency has become quite typical in post-structuralism in general and deconstruction in particular. The end with which deconstruction is concerned is indeterminacy: disassembling ready-made structures, disposing with the whole integral order of logic, denying all determinate explanations, in brief, ceaselessly transcending pre-established horizons and continuously negating any meaning that has already been reached is its aim, without ever giving any commitment to a new world of meaning. Derrida deployed the concept of différance with this intention. One of the meanings of différance is difference, which means that there is always a space or distance of meaning between the text and the author's intentions. The content, which the author has written, already does not lie securely within the limits of the author's original intentions, and because of this understanding should transcend or break through the original structure in order to reveal the meaning within the text that exceeds the meaning the author endowed the text with through his intentional sense-giving activity. The second meaning of différance is deferral, that is, the presence of meaning is always deferred (the meaning of the text is not limited to the meaning the author endowed the text with at the time of writing; its meaning is continuously expanding after the act of writing), and because of this, the understanding of the text should continuously surpass and negate any presently existing interpretation.[67] In summary, deconstruction emphasizes the indeterminacy immanent to the process of understanding, yet by emphasizing this point, deconstruction seems to simultaneously close down the path that leads to a world of meaning. Such a perspective carries with it a relativistic tendency and embodies the theoretical characteristics of so-called post-modernism.

Nihilism goes even further, embodying the tendency to eliminate meaning altogether. According to Heidegger, the philosophical use of the word "nihilism" might have started near the turn the eighteenth century in the works of Jacob. Later however, the concept of nihilism became popular due to the works of Turgenev.[68] Of course, the philosophical content of nihilism was not concretely elucidated in the works of Turgenev and Jacob. It was Nietzsche who truly took nihilism to the philosophical level of analysis. In *Will to Power* and related works, Nietzsche repeated the theme of nihilism, elucidating it through variations upon that theme. With regard to the intrinsic implications of nihilism, Nietzsche once deployed the method of self-inquiry and response to arrive at a simple definition: "What does nihilism mean? *That the highest values devalue themselves.* The aim is lacking; 'why?' finds no answer."[69] Here, Nietzsche first points out the connection between nihilism and values, and furthermore, the connection between the problem of values and ends. As already discussed, corresponding to ends and purposes is meaning at the level of values. Without a purpose, there is no meaning at the level of values. Lacking a purpose, values are devalued as concrete meaning, and nihilism expresses precisely this dead loss of meaning: "The philosophical nihilist is convinced that all that happens is meaningless and in vain."[70]

Without a doubt, Nietzsche captures the fundamental feature of nihilism in his analysis of its intrinsic implications at the level of values and ends. But Nietzsche does not stop there. Rather, he proceeds, tracing nihilism all the way back to its origin. We have already noticed that according to Nietzsche's understanding, the characteristic of nihilism lies in the highest values devaluing themselves. Yet the question that corresponds to such a characteristic could be formulated as follows: why do the highest values devalue themselves? This question concerns the very ground of values. According to Nietzsche's examination, the highest values are tied to the so-called true world, which is precisely the "metaphysical world." The metaphysical world spoken of here is typified by the transcendent ideas, which Plato set forth as the true world. As "true" or "genuine" being, the metaphysical world is simultaneously seen as the ultimate ground of all values. However, this so-called true and genuine world is essentially a fiction, and taking such a world as the ground of values implies rooting all systems of values in an illusory foundation. The source of nihilism lies here: once the illusory nature of the ground of values has been unmasked, the existing basis of any system of values rooted in such a ground rots away. In the wake of such an event, the idea of nihilism emerges: "As soon as man finds out how the world is fabricated solely from psychological needs, and how he has absolutely no right to it, the last form of nihilism comes into being: it includes disbelief in any metaphysical world and forbids itself any belief in a true world"[71] and "Now that the shabby origin of these values is becoming clear, the universe seems to have lost value, seems 'meaningless.'"[72]

A commitment to meaning at the same time concerns ends: at the level of values, meaning is relative to purposes. However, along with the construction of a metaphysical ground of values is the corresponding tendency to understand purpose as something given from the outside by a transcendent being. In the context of the evolution of Western culture, this kind of external given primarily stems from the Christian religious tradition. In the context and horizon of the Christian religion, God himself not only appears as the ultimate end, He also endows man with a purpose for his existence: the process of man's being always aims at reaching God, and the entire meaning of his being is correspondingly determined by God's will. In the wake of the collapse of the metaphysical world, man began to cast doubt upon ends that are given to him from outside of himself, and nihilism is the logical consequence of this: "The nihilistic question 'for what?' is rooted in the old habit of supposing that the goal must be put up, given, demanded from outside."[73] As nihilism denies the "true world," it simultaneously denies this "divine way of thinking."[74]

Although these two features just mentioned stress different things, they are not for that matter unrelated. Boiled down to their essence, the point they both share in common is their presupposition of two worlds. Taking a metaphysical world to be the ground of values presupposes a distinction between a true world and an untrue world; in the same way, determining an end as something that must be given from the outside presupposes a belief in a transcendent world external to or beyond the being of humans. Here, the important point is that the presupposition of two worlds implies the division of the actual world from *another world*. According to Nietzsche, in philosophy and religion we find different formulations of this other world: for Nietzsche, whereas philosophers contrive a rational world or a place suited for the employment of rationality and logical functions as the true world, religious figures fabricate a divine world—a denaturalized, even anti-natural world.[75] The rational world spoken of here corresponds to a metaphysical world as the ground of values, and the divine world here corresponds to a transcendent world as the source of purpose. Despite the fact they differ in form, insofar as they both fabricate "another world" and separate one from the other, they share something in common. For Nietzsche, as fictions, every other world lacks reality and fails to accord with human will: "The 'other world' ... is a synonym for nonbeing, nonliving, not wanting to live." Holding such fictional "other worlds" as the ground of both values and ends conceals within its depths the very source of nihilism: as soon as the transcendent being comes to its end, the value systems that are established upon that transcendent being follow suit and are overturned. When Nietzsche states that God is dead, he simultaneously exposes the fact that the bedrock of traditional value systems dissolves in the wake of the death of some other world.

Through his investigation of nihilism, Nietzsche discovered that the question of meaning not only concerns the domain of values, but the horizon of ontology as well. As already discussed, the intrinsic feature of nihilism lies in eliminating meaning through a denial of the value of being and the purpose of existence, and this denial of purpose and value is again linked to the fact that such values and purposes are rooted in an illusory world: when the ground of values and purposes is not immanent to the actual world, but found rather in another world, the authenticity of such a ground is put into doubt. Here, the illusoriness of values and the fictitious nature of being are unquestionably correlated: fabricating another world in ontology logically leads to a denial of the meaning of being in axiology.

As for Nietzsche himself, his philosophical position seems twofold. On the one hand, by pointing out that traditional value systems were grounded in an illusory metaphysical world, Nietzsche went further to critique and deny these value systems themselves, and due to this, he called for the revaluation of all values, and thus also expressed a nihilistic tendency. On this point, Nietzsche himself was quite explicit: he repeatedly claimed himself to be a nihilist.[76] On the other hand, he also distinguished between positive nihilism and negative nihilism, considering the distinguishing characteristic of the former to lie in the elevation of spiritual power and that of the latter to consist in its decline. The former kind of nihilism embraces the following intention, that is: to reestablish new value systems through the negation of traditional value systems and to revaluate all values. It is easy to see that the positive kind of nihilism contains within itself the demand to overcome nihilism. However, theoretically speaking, Nietzsche was never able to truly overcome nihilism. One of the sources of nihilism lies in giving meaning to being through something beyond it, and despite the fact that Nietzsche raised much criticism concerning ends given from an outside or beyond, and rejected all such external ends, he simultaneously viewed the "overman" as an aim: "Not 'mankind' but overman is the goal!"[77] So-called overman is precisely the being who, for Nietzsche, transcends mankind, and according to its substance, this kind of being is still transcendent in nature. In this way, hailing overman as the aim implies substituting one kind of transcendent being for another, thereby grounding values, once again, in an illusory foundation. At the same time, Nietzsche also saw the being of life on the ultimate level to be a meaningless eternal recurrence: "existence as it is, without meaning or aim, yet recurring inevitably without any finale of nothingness: 'the eternal recurrence.'"[78] This eternal recurrence is similar to Sisyphus pushing the boulder up the mountain over and over again for eternity to demonstrate that existence is merely a cycle without any meaning. Looking at it in this respect, it seems that, in the end, Nietzsche himself also falls into the trap of nihilism in the effort to trace nihilism back to its source.

As for the theme of eliminating meaning, of course Nietzsche's philosophical standpoint is not the only expression of the nihilistic tendency. The latter appears in diverse forms. Under the flag of a rebellion against rationality, the expression of irrational passions always has the effect of suppressing the rational understanding of meaning; in the denial of determinacy, the pursuit of meaning is once again repelled to the margins—from "anything goes" in scientific research to existence taking precedence over essence in the orientation of human life—in both cases, meaning loses its determinate content; under the slogan of anti-metaphysics, any meaning aside from empirically verified truths and logical form is callously rejected; from the scientistic perspective, human beings are thingified or objectified and simultaneously lose the intrinsic meaning of their own being; the phenomenological approach of suspending being in the movement toward pure consciousness also suspends the actual being of humans and its very meaning; in the experience of angst and the anxiety of being, the process of human life dimly appears in the dimension of hopeless finitude; Foucault's dreary assertion that man has disappeared along with his grave inquiry into the "death of man," pushes human being further into nothingness.[79] That aside, doubt is also cast upon the intrinsic meaning of the evolution of culture, the development of history, the continuation of culture and the value of the very being of community—ethnic, social, and political. At the same time, in accompaniment with the ceaseless reform of social history, the tension between pre-established value systems and the rocky vicissitudes of society also protrudes into the foreground in different ways, which engenders a confusion of values and a loss of meaning. Although these tendencies have different expressive forms, insofar as they all replace the quest of seeking meaning with the skeptical tendency to doubt meaning and the drive to eliminate it, they all seem to reveal different embodiments of the same nihilistic tendency.

This historical phenomenon shows that nihilism in its various guises has gradually penetrated into the very spirit of society and the realm of ideas, and has thereby become a pressing issue that needs to be taken up earnestly in today's age. Historically speaking, the occurrence of nihilism has its actual historical origin. Since the modern age, the market economy has developed to such a degree that it has been accompanied by the predominance of a "general social metabolism" due to which human beings have formed more and more of a dependency on things, or what Marx called an "objective [*sachlicher*] dependence,"[80] to which corresponds quite naturally the increasing alienation of human labor and the intensification of the human fetish for commodities. As this dependency on things bestows upon things the property of being ends, this turns ends themselves into things that are given to human being from outside itself: it not only turns external things into the entire ground of values, it also turns things into the very source of human ends. Linked to the externalization of both the ground of values and internal ends is a direct loss of meaning, which is further accompanied by those forms of nihilism mentioned previously. Nietzsche critiqued the founding of values and ends upon another world, which not only reveals the connection between traditional value systems and metaphysics, but also in some sense reflects the aforesaid historical origin of nihilism.

How is nihilism overcome? Let's first take our previous analysis of the sources of nihilism as our background. We must turn away from transcendent being and this dependency on external things and return to the actual world, and from there, establish the ground of values upon the real relationship between human being and world, so as to avoid determining human ends as external givens. Of course, this will be a long historical process linked to the whole-sided development of human being. Re-engaging the relationship between meaning and rationality first involves the rational location of reason itself: in the context of an opposition to reason, a commitment to meaning will never be truly realized; from Nietzsche to deconstruction, the elimination of meaning is always accompanied by the alienation of reason and a skeptical attitude toward reason. So, overcoming nihilism is the same as values and ends returning to their actual ground, which points to a commitment to meaning, as well as a will to protect meaning and to seek meaning.

Nihilism, with its characteristic destruction of meaning, falls into a negation of meaning, of which the opposite tendency must be seen as the external enforcement of meaning or the coercive imposition of meaning. In traditional societies, the external enforcement or coercive imposition of meaning usually emerges in the form of authoritarianism. While establishing the domination of an orthodox ideology, authoritarianism always declares a set of ideas to be the absolute truth or the highest principle of values, and further, demands people to unconditionally accept this system of ideas, which is a highly coercive way of giving meaning: in essence, it adopts coercive measures to install some system of meaning inside human being from the outside, this imposing of meaning by force and coercion implies restricting or expropriating people's autonomous power to create, choose, and accept different systems of meaning. Since the Han dynasty, traditional Chinese society had demanded "banning the hundred schools of thought, and allowing only the Confucian school to be respected," that is, prescribing the Confucian doctrine of ideas to be the sole legitimate system of meaning, and hence make such a system become the only object that people can legitimately choose. This standpoint in some sense could be seen as an authoritarian enforcement of meaning. Fascism in the twentieth century adopted a variety of coercive means to indoctrinate people with Nazi thought, which is another extreme expression of this same tendency.

This coercive enforcement of meaning also appears in the broad process of knowing the world and reforming the world. This tendency is evident in the epistemological and axiological domains in the form of dogmatism. Dogmatism will view some idea, theory, or principle either in the process of cognizing or in the domain of values to be an absolute truth by denying the positive meaning of opposed ideas, theories, and principles; this is a tendency to dogmatically enforce a system of meaning upon a social community. In the modern age, although authoritarianism seems to be a gradually receding form, the tendency to coercively enforce meaning is still far from disappearing. In the international community, this can be seen in the tendency to enforce one idea of human rights as the only legitimate form and use that idea to oppose every other understanding of human rights while enforcing one model of democracy as the only universal form and sole standard across the globe in a denial of all other possible democratic political institutions; in the same way, praising Western culture and entirely idealizing it is no more or less dogmatic than conservatively protecting Confucian orthodoxy and rejecting every critique of the Chinese tradition. Even though not all of these positions are necessarily authoritarian in form, their intrinsic standpoints all show the authoritarian tendency to enforce meaning coercively to varying degrees. Although this authoritarian tendency and the nihilistic one are to be taken as two extreme poles, they still may be opposed and yet essentially complementary: if nihilism consists in eliminating meaning, then on the deepest level authoritarianism consists in alienating meaning.

Historically speaking, the elimination of meaning and the enforcement of meaning, the withdrawal of meaning and the alienation of meaning mutually coexist just as nihilism and authoritarianism (dogmatism) do; this, moreover, is inseparable from the rise of relativism and the enforcement of universality fusing together in the modern age. On the one hand, the historical tendency of economic globalization is the intrinsic undercurrent of a growing concern for universality—from global justice to universal ethics; from the confluence of aesthetic tastes in mass culture to the rise of common concern for ecosystems and the environment, etc.—in each case the same historical tendency appears in different ways. In correspondence with the daily increase in prominence of the universal dimension of being, seeking universal value ideals has become increasingly pervasive in every field—ethical, social, cultural, and political. On the other hand, a great variety of relativistic tendencies are not inhibited by such strivings for universality: those strivings for certainty that we have seen in the scientific, ethical, religious, and cultural realms are accompanied by an intensifying relativistic undercurrent that seeks to replace all certainties with doubt concerning any possible certainty; as more specific groups (women, minority groups, etc.) move toward gaining self-awareness, self-recognition, and a consciousness of their rights, more differences between the cultural traditions of distinct ethnic groups are coming out of the shadows and into the spotlight as such groups encounter one another in the process of globalization. In the philosophical domain, more and more concepts like language games are fashioned in order to eliminate absolutes, and so on; all such phenomena incite different forms of this relativism into action. The blending and fusing of abstract universalism with the movement of relativism provides authoritarianism and nihilism with the thinking resources and social conditions they need to survive and co-exist. In effect, there is a complex theoretical and historical connection between the one side wrought of abstract universalism and authoritarianism (dogmatism) and the other side forged of relativism and nihilism. So, overcoming nihilism and authoritarianism (dogmatism) logically presupposes overcoming the opposition between abstract universalism and relativism.

Meaning is generated and henceforth emerges through the cognitive thinking and practical doing of human beings. Under the condition that one is engaged in the process of coming to know the world and oneself while reforming the world and refining oneself, the world and the being of humans are presented in the mode of being meaningful. As the precondition of generating meaning, one's cognizing and practicing is essentially a creative process; it is precisely through the creative process of accomplishing oneself and accomplishing things that one continues to open up the true world, make it present its multifaceted meaning and advance toward a state of freedom. The fundamental problem with nihilism eliminating meaning lies in denying the intrinsic value of human creative activity and turning a blind eye to the historical connection between the search for meaning and the ascent to a state of freedom. At the same time, the process of seeking, generating, and presenting meaning is also by nature open. Creating values is the historical content of the process of accomplishing oneself and accomplishing things (one coming to know the world and oneself while reforming the world and refining oneself), which unfolds in a multiplicity of ways. Similarly, the meaning that is generated through this process is itself multiple, which provides the precondition for many kinds of values and consequently the power to autonomously choose. This way in which meaning is generated and presented thus reveals the intrinsic freedom of the process of accomplishing oneself and accomplishing things: the openness of cognizing and practicing and the openness of the process of generating meaning reveals the free dimension of the process of refining the world and refining oneself. In opposition to this, authoritarianism attempts to coercively impose a system of meaning upon human being in a dogmatic fashion, which not only negates the open nature of the genesis of meaning, but also denies the free creativity of human beings. We can see that nihilism, which intends to eliminate meaning, and authoritarianism, which tends to coercively enforce it, are formally distinct, but insofar as they both force human beings to deviate from the path to freedom and subvert their free creativity, they have much in common indeed.

Referring to the manifold process of one coming to know the world while changing the world and coming to know oneself while changing oneself, accomplishing oneself and accomplishing things intrinsically unfolds as a quest for meaning. While a double commitment to meaning, which combines the understanding-knowing dimension and the ends-values dimension, makes accomplishing oneself and accomplishing things the very process, which generates a world of meaning, overcoming the opposition between nihilism and authoritarianism entails at once both confirming the nature of this process as one that is creative of values and also giving the construction of a world of meaning the historical significance of advancing toward a state of freedom.

2 Human Capacities and a World of Meaning

DIRECTED AT THE genesis of a world of meaning, accomplishing oneself and accomplishing things unfolds throughout the whole process of one's being. But as the basic way in which human being exists, how is this process possible? The question "How is it possible?" primarily concerns grounds and conditions. Here, the capacities of human being intrinsically condition the genesis of a world of meaning as the internal conditions of accomplishing oneself and accomplishing things. Similar to "wisdom," the phrase "human capacities" has its everyday connotations, but as a concept, it has philosophical meaning as well. In everyday terms, just as being wise is seen as a synonym for having some perspicacity or intellectual aptitude, a capacity is usually understood to be some ability to solve concrete problems in the process of cognizing or practicing. At the philosophical level, however, wisdom differs from such specialized kinds of knowledge in the empirical realm and consists much more in deeper thoughts concerning human nature and the way of Nature as a whole.[1] In the same way, as the deepest underlying conditions of the process of accomplishing oneself and accomplishing things, capacities are also distinct from a set of particular abilities. As human being's intrinsic properties, capacities encompass multiple facets. Differing from extrinsic means, capacities are the embodiment of human being's essential powers; differing from abstract logical forms, capacities integrate into the process of being and become one with human being. So, capacities not only have epistemological meaning, but ontological and axiological meaning as well, and so we name them human capacities.

Human Capacities in the Process of Accomplishing Oneself and Accomplishing Things

Broadly speaking, capacities first of all refer to the real powers that human being expresses in the process of cognizing and practicing. They emerge in each facet of the process of accomplishing oneself and accomplishing things as the different faculties and powers with which human being grasps and reforms the world and the self. In the case of actually cognizing and practicing, human capacities are immersed in the reciprocal interaction between the knower and the known and in the process of concrete practice as well; the depth and breadth to which knowledge and practice may reach, is always correlated with different human capacities. We can see that in reality, human capacities constitute the intrinsic conditions of possibility of knowing the world and changing the world (accomplishing things) and of knowing oneself and changing oneself (accomplishing oneself).[2] These capacities are by no means external forms of being. From beginning to end, they are one with the being of humans and permeate the whole of human being, and thereby constitute the ontological properties of human being. Constitutive of "human nature," these capacities are the embodiment of human being's essential powers and contain an ontological dimension. In brief, human capacities could be understood as the essential powers intrinsic to human being (being indistinguishable from the being of humans). These essential powers at once both constitute the conditions that make accomplishing oneself and accomplishing things possible and are also that which gains actual confirmation in the process of accomplishing oneself and accomplishing things.[3]

In connection with the processual nature of accomplishing oneself and accomplishing things, human capacities are themselves generative, but this involves the interaction of human capacities with pre-established ways of thinking and backgrounds of knowledge. We can by no means simply consider these capacities as abstract attributes of the mind or consciousness; they are always grounded in the state of knowledge human being has already attained and are constrained by a determinate way of thinking. Regardless of the case at hand, whether in grasping the world or in reforming the world, what we can know is always inseparable from the already known (achieved knowledge in the broad sense).[4] In brief, already having attained some knowledge and already having grasped a way of thinking is a necessary precondition of shaping and refining human capacities, which from a certain perspective reveals their social character. On the other hand, if this already achieved knowledge and this already developed way of thinking were to be divorced from the actual process of applying them, they would only exist in the mode of being merely possible; it is precisely through human capacities in the actual process of cognizing or practicing that methods of thought and achieved knowledge gain actual vitality and real meaning. So, we can see that human capacities still presuppose a pre-existing accumulation of knowledge and a way of thinking without ceasing to be that which endows both the former and the latter with concrete life and actuality.

Aristotle made a distinction between the theoretical, practical, and productive forms of knowing and thinking.[5] Underlying such a distinction between forms of knowing is an essential distinction between capacities: the distinct types of knowing listed earlier correspond to the different capacities human being possesses. In fact, Aristotle already linked human being's knowing and practicing to these capacities in his *Nicomachean Ethics*.[6] At the same time, Aristotle was particularly concerned with virtue (*aréte*), and by virtue he did not only mean it in the narrow sense of moral character; virtue is said here primarily in the ontological sense of the properties of the being of humans. As the intrinsic conditions of knowing and practicing, human capacities have the meaning of being virtues, and are thus ontological.

There are also some modern philosophers who already considered human capacities while investigating the process of knowing. From Leibniz to Locke, and from Spinoza to Hume, human understanding has been one of the core topics of the modern age of philosophy. Here, human understanding is tied to the form of knowledge and involves cognitive capacity achieving a certain form of knowledge. Modern philosophers concretely examined the capacity of human being to know from a number of different perspectives revolving around the topic of human understanding, and demonstrated that the event of knowing is inseparable from certain internal conditions, which are always connected in different senses to the very being of humans. The term "human understanding" itself has highlighted the link between understanding and the being of humans. Of course, modern philosophers also limited the capacity of human understanding to the realm of knowledge,[7] stressing either the role of perception or that of reason, which are just a few particular facets of the human capacity to know, and so they generated rather narrow understandings of human capacities in a twofold sense.

In contrast to Locke, Hume, and the other modern philosophers, Kant considered the conditions of how universal and necessary knowledge is possible from a much broader perspective. However, as opposed to Locke, Hume, and the others, who discussed the occurrence of knowledge in terms of how it is connected to human being's conscious activity, Kant found more importance in logical and a priori conditions such as the forms of intuition, that is, space and time, and the pure categories of the understanding, and so on, but he never focused on the concrete content of human capacities. Kant also discussed intuition, apperception, imagination, and even ethical ideas like autonomy, but his interest in these epistemological and ethical elements remained tied to their formal a priori conditions. Apperception, for instance, is a synthetic activity originally linked to thinking (the cogito), but Kant's distinction between the empirical self and the transcendental self endows the latter, as the apperceiving and thinking "I" or subject, with universal a priori form. Likewise in the case of intuition, Kant was much more concerned with the universal forms of space and time, which make intuition possible. The power of imagination, for Kant, seems to present a much more complicated form. As I will demonstrate, in some ways Kant also understood the imagination to be a faculty of knowledge, affirming it as "one of the basic powers of the mind,"[8] but once again, he emphasized that the synthesis of the imagination is a "pure form"[9] of all possible knowledge. On the same token, Kant further connected the imagination to schemata,[10] which play a double role, one facing the "shapes" corresponding to sensibility, and the other facing the pure forms corresponding to the imagination, which contain a universal structure and hence also logical and a priori meaning. In the domain of moral practice, Kant indeed affirmed that the subject is capable of autonomous self-legislation, but again, legislating for Kant here means overcoming and purifying all empirical passions and inclinations stemming from the sensibility. For Kant, the good will, as the legislating subject, is the rationalizing will, which he invests with formal meaning. We can see that drawing dichotomies—form/content, transcendental/empirical—is the distinctive feature of Kant's philosophy. For Kant, examining human capacities at the level of content implies falling into the empirical realm and failing to reach universal necessity in the transcendental sense.[11]

In order to return to concrete reality and the substantial process of being from abstract logic and formal structure, human capacities become an unavoidable issue. Here, the thought of Marx is worth close consideration. Marx once distinguished between the realm of necessity and the realm of freedom, pointing out that "[t]he true realm of freedom, the development of human powers as an end in itself, begins beyond it [Trans.: the realm of necessity], though it can only flourish with this realm of necessity as its basis."[12] Here, what is of importance is "human powers as an end itself": being an end itself means that human capacities possess purposiveness, which pertains to axiology no less than to ontology. At the ontological level, being an end in itself shows that human capacities are inseparable from the very being of humans; as purposive properties, human capacities pervade the whole of one's being, and embody ontological characteristics of human being that by no means stand in an external or extrinsic relation to human being; at the axiological level, "being an end in-itself" reveals that human being's capacities are different from pure and simple means or instruments; as an end in itself, rather, human being's capacities possess intrinsic value. Therefore, human being's essential powers are concretely embodied in human capacities, which are an end in itself.

Of course, to say that capacities overcome being-instruments is by no means to say that human capacities have no essential connection with instrumental activity. Considered historically, the formative genesis of human being's capacities was and remains inseparably linked to the human production and manipulation of tools and instruments. In effect, it was precisely through manufacturing and manipulating tools that human being gradually acquired capacities differing from those of animals, expressing the essential powers intrinsic to human being. From the perspective of the historical evolution of the species, the development of human capacities has been inseparably linked to the development of this production and manipulation of tools. As a kind of activity with synthetic meaning, the manufacture and manipulation of tools involves many things which accelerate the development of such capacities as logical thought, imagination and intuition, and which has the corresponding effect of heightening human being's capacity to attain the truth of things (the object of knowledge) and to illuminate the goodness of things (assess values), which in turn deeply influences human being's practical activity of reforming the world: as it pushes this practical activity to unfold at greater depth and breadth, it substantially heightens the practical capacity of human being.

We can see that human capacities, as the intrinsic conditions of the process of accomplishing oneself and accomplishing things, are at once distinct from abstract, logical, a priori forms and are also different from pure and simple functions of the mind or consciousness. As ends in themselves, they are the unified manifestation of ontological properties and axiological contents, which shows in a deeper sense that human capacities constitute the precondition of knowing the world and changing the world (accomplishing things) and knowing the self and changing the self (accomplishing oneself) and give this process directionality at the same time: when Marx ties the development of human capacities as an end in itself to "the true realm of freedom," he also sees the development of human capacities as the intrinsic determination of knowing the world and changing the world (accomplishing things) and knowing the self and changing the self (accomplishing oneself).

Multiple Forms

The concrete forms of human capacities could be distinguished in different ways. With reference to the true, the beautiful, and the good, human capacities involve the domains of knowledge, morality, and aesthetics. Linked to the question "What can I know?" is the capacity to know, which is manifested in knowing that and knowing how. Connected to the question "What should I do?" is the capacity of moral practice, which unfolds as the unity of self-awareness, self-willingness, and spontaneity in the moral choices and moral evaluations intrinsic to moral actions. Corresponding to the harmonic unity of purposiveness and lawfulness is aesthetic capacity, which expresses itself in creating and judging the beautiful. From the perspective of accomplishing oneself and accomplishing things, human capacities pertaining to the previous domains are concretely manifested in practice in the broad sense of refining the self and refining the world and are actualized in different ways and in diverse modes. The following section is a concrete analysis of this latter aspect (the different forms of human capacities).

Perception and Reason

As the intrinsic properties of human being, human capacities are inseparable from the being of humans. As a form of being, human being involves both the mind in the broad sense and also a particular body. At the bodily level, the primary issue concerns perception. Perception could be seen as the direct channel that links human being to the world. As a way to grasp the world, perceiving is inseparable from the body's sense organs: perception is "knowing" by virtue of "sensing."[13] Here, the source of "sensation" is the "body" (sense-organs) and unfolds as the reciprocal interaction of human being with the world on the basis of the body. But in a broader sense, a sense organ is not limited to "the body." The sense-organs of human being have acquired various forms of extensions in correspondence with the development of tool production. Optical instruments (like the telescope and microscope) can extend human being's organs of sight; diverse electrical apparatuses for distinguishing tastes and measuring sounds can extend human being's auditory and olfactory organs, and so on. In this way, although human being's visual, auditory, and olfactory capacities are not as strong as those of other animals (like the hawk's or dog's), by means of attaching certain tools, the capacity of human being's sense organs can be amplified to the degree that he can see further than hawks and distinguish sounds and smells that for dogs remain undetectable.

The more intrinsic form of perception involves reason. The body and the mind are the two main inseparable facets of human being, and correspondingly, perception is not a capacity that stands in opposition to reason The most profound difference between human perception and that of animals lies in the fact that human perception does not just depend on sense organs, because it is also constrained by reason in a variety of ways. From everyday perceptions to scientific observations, rationality is always infused into sensibility. In the case of everyday perceptions, when we form judgments like "This is the color red" and "This is a circle," the "red" and "circle" contained in such judgments are no longer limited to particular objects, but represent universal properties, which involve the domain of reason. Phenomenology speaks of such concepts as "eidetic intuition" and "categorical intuition" with just this point in mind. This "intuiting" of universal properties is already far beyond the mere capacity of "seeing" through a sense organ, and demonstrates the persistence of a rational "intuiting" that is already pervading sensibility. This rational intuition fuses together the diversity of reasoning functions such as generalization, deduction, inference, and classification, just to name a few. In actuality, there is no clearly defined boundary between sensible intuition and rational intuition: just as words always encompass both direct and indirect references (at one and the same time referring to the sensible presentation of the object before me and also indirectly to the whole object as a concrete being),[14] so intuition always involves this compound intuiting. Similarly, observation in scientific research can never be entirely divorced from theory, and by correlation, the statements that arise from observations are always infused with some theoretical content.

The characteristic of perception just noted provides a ground for the connection of mind to matter and mind to principle, and enables a true movement toward the world. The world itself is diverse and yet concrete. Truly grasping the world requires affirming and representing this plentiful manifold of properties, and perception takes this richness of the world in by directly encountering it. Within this radiant flux of sensible presentations, diversity and singularity are confirmed as the true attributes of the world as the world itself presents a diversity of concrete forms. At the same time, through the act of perceiving, the mind and body of the human being start to reciprocally interact, fuse together, and overcome the opposition splitting them apart. As a mode expressing human capacities, perception opens up a unified world at the level of sensibility and reveals the wholeness of human being.

As I have shown, as a concrete being, human being has a mode of being which is not only "bodily," for "mind" is attributed to it as well. The capacity of perception does indeed involve the mind, but the way in which perception functions is first based on the body. Yet, relatively speaking, the mind is more closely connected to the power of reason. There are of course different viewpoints regarding reason and the capacity of reason. Broadly speaking in terms of form, the predominant form of reason is logical thought. When Kant took understanding as a conceptual capacity and a power to think, he stressed precisely this dimension.[15] In terms of substance, however, reason is directed toward the true and the good. As the union of both, the capacity of reason is manifested in conscious (mental) activity, but is also employed in the process of practicing.

At the level of logical thought, reason demands thought to maintain self-identity from the beginning to the end of a thinking process. Concretely speaking, the concepts, theme, and context of a thought must all be consistent and identical from beginning to end; whether it is the concepts, the theme, or the context under consideration, if they do not remain consistent or identical throughout the same thinking process, thought will plunder into chaos or confusion without being able to generate a rational conclusion. In connection with the identity of thought, thinking must avoid contradiction in the logical sense. The basic demand of the law of non-contradiction in thought includes: two mutually contradictory propositions can neither be simultaneously affirmed nor simultaneously denied (they both cannot be true and they both cannot be false). Engaging a thought while simultaneously denying this principle would of necessity betray that thought to self-contradiction and profound confusion, out of which no accurate thought could ever take shape. Here, the capacity of reason concretely expresses itself in avoiding logical contradictions and maintaining the identity of thought throughout the process of thinking.

Another one of reason's demands at the formal level is: there must always be a reason or ground to accept or form an idea. Making a judgment without any ground whatsoever amounts to nothing more than the expression of an emotion, which cannot really be seen as a rational act; believing something without any reason is to be a blind follower, which is similarly irrational. Whether it is drawing a conclusion without any grounds to back it up or believing and affirming an idea without any reason to do so, all such cases demonstrate acts that directly conflict with this principle of reason. As for the positive side of reason, to deduce or accept an idea on the basis of certain grounds or reasons is to unfold a justification, and engaging thought on the basis of this principle and procedure demonstrates the very capacity of reason.[16]

At the level of content, a variety of elements express the capacity of reason, from cognizing to evaluating and practicing. In the case of cognizing, grasping actuality constitutes an important dimension of rationality and concretely unfolds as genuinely knowing the true world and the true self. As an intrinsic condition of the process of refining the self and refining the world, the capacity of reason gradually provides a true picture of the world through a harmonious unification of analysis and synthesis, induction and deduction, logical inference and dialectical thinking. Relative to seeking the true world and the true self is striving for the good; this is a process of evaluating. Concerned with the rational needs of human being, to evaluate means to confirm and choose what is good through judgments based on what is beneficial or harmful, good or evil. Even though the distinct meanings of good or beneficial and of bad or harmful as well as that of good and evil are indeed just as relative as they are historical, only choosing good over evil can be seen as rational behavior insofar as a determinate principle of evaluation is affirmed and accepted: on the contrary, knowing that something will bring harm and still intentionally choosing to do it is irrational. Nozick pointed this out when discussing the nature of rationality with his particular emphasis on the utility or benefit expected from holding a particular belief.[17] Here, reaching the truth in the cognitive sense and striving for the good in the evaluative sense could be seen as constituting two sides of the same rational principle. The capacity of reason thus concretely expresses itself as simultaneously seeking the truth (what actually is) while striving for the good (what ought to be).

The union of those two aspects just noted leads us further to the practical level in the relation between means (including procedure) and ends. As the most basic phases of a practice, means and ends both lead to questions concerning rationality. Of course, there is the rationality involved in considering means and that involved in determining ends, so rationality has two different meanings. Ends are formed on the bases of human being's needs and desires and the possibilities that actual situations provide, and whether a determinate end grasps or embodies a human need or desire directly affects the legitimacy of the end considered. In substance, only those needs and desires that accord with the historical tendency of human being moving toward a free mode of being can be considered rational in nature. Such an accord ensures the legitimacy of the end considered. So, it is clearly the rationality of ends that gains legitimacy. Relative to this, the meaning of means consists predominantly in how such ends are to be realized, so the rationality of means lies in how to ensure the effective realization of ends.[18] In brief, the rationality of means consists primarily in their effectiveness. If legitimacy primarily refers to the pursuit of the good, then effectiveness presupposes correctly grasping the background and relationships of an actual situation (reaching the true world). So, in being directed at the legitimacy of ends and the effectiveness of means, reason manifests another aspect of the unity of the true and the good.

As interconnected phases in the process of practicing, the rationality of means (effectiveness) and the rationality of ends (legitimacy) show the two sides of reason. Through this, we can also see that the distinction between instrumental rationality and value rationality only has relative meaning. Rationality may be divided into the instrumental and purposive dimensions and understood accordingly, but viewing these two aspects as merely parallel or separable in actuality logically dismembers the unity of rationality. In practice, this leads to splitting up being, which concretely presents the following disjunction: either hold on to an abstract kingdom of ends or take the process (means) as everything. Since the dawn of the modern age, we have seen both of these one-sided tendencies in humanism and scientism respectively. The integrity of rationality is identical to the unity of cognizing and evaluating (knowing in the broad sense): as stated previously, the legitimacy of ends and the effectiveness of means cannot be divorced from the cognitive process of seeking the truth and the evaluative process of striving for the good. The capacity of reason is thus embodied in the unity of cognizing and evaluating, which ensures rationality in the dual sense (in the legitimacy of ends and the effectiveness of means). In the history of philosophy, different philosophical systems and philosophers of different backgrounds have usually emphasized one of these two sides of rationality. The mainstream of Neo-Confucianism in ancient Chinese philosophy was more concerned with the rationality pertaining to ends. Its arguments were based on a distinction made between moral knowledge (*dexing zhi zhi* 德性之知) and empirical knowledge (*jianwen zhi zhi* 见闻之知): moral knowledge refers to a meaning that is value oriented, and is directed toward the moral end of becoming a sage on the inside and a king on the outside. For Neo-Confucianism, accomplishing oneself and accomplishing things aims at just such a value oriented end. Directly correlated with its neglect of empirical knowledge, Neo-Confucianism always failed to give an adequate account of the concrete way in which such a value-oriented end should be attained through the practical process of administering affairs and ordering the state, in spite of emphasizing the purposive dimensions of rationality and legitimacy. In opposition to this approach is the tendency typified by Hume's philosophy. From the standpoint of empiricism, Hume put weight on the distinction between reason and the passions. For Hume, in relation to the passions, reason always performs an entirely subordinate role: "reason is perfectly inert, and can never either prevent or produce any action or affection."[19] Due to this, Hume saw reason as subordinate to the passions: "Reason is, and ought only to be the slave of the passions."[20] According to its basic definition, a slave has the meaning of being a tool or a mere means, and a slave's role consists in merely being fit for manipulation and use, and taking reason to be the slave of passions implies tying reason mainly to means. According to Neo-Confucianism and Hume's understanding, reason is either limited to the domain of ends or reduced to a mere means. This opposition has appeared in an even more universal form since modern times in the tendency to dissociate instrumental rationality from purposive rationality.

In the form of logical thought, the act of reasoning has as its substantial aim the unity of what actually is and what ought to be, the unity of what is true and what is good, and reason acts effectively throughout the whole process of accomplishing oneself and accomplishing things. To cognize what actually is (true) and to evaluate what ought to be (good) is simultaneously to confirm purposive rationality (legitimate ends) and to grasp instrumental rationality (effectiveness). This very process consists precisely in the formation of knowledge and the consolidation and improvement of wisdom. Thus, whether in opening up the true world or in generating a world that ought to be, the capacity of reason in both cases displays its most profound powers.

Imagination, Intuition, and Insight

From the perspective of the relationship human capacities have to the being of humans, the interrelated human capacities of perception and reason are ontologically grounded in the link between the mind and the body. The issue concerning the mind furthermore involves the relationship between the rational and the irrational. The interaction between reason and perception confirms both the connection between sensibility and rationality and that between the body and the mind in different ways, and so constitutes one of the most important aspects of knowing the world and knowing the self. In the process of accomplishing oneself and accomplishing things, how can we open up the world more profoundly and understand being more trenchantly by means of an affirmation of this relation between the mind and the body? This question leads us to other dimensions of human capacity—imagination, intuition, and insight. From the perspective of "the mind," imagination, intuition, and insight—in contrast to the logical form of thinking that arises from the power of reason—present the tendency to transcend logical procedures to a considerable extent; they are characterized by exhibiting human being's capacity in irrational ways, or rather, in modes quite distinct from rational ones.

Let us first look at the imagination. Kant himself dedicates a considerable amount of attention to the imagination while examining the conditions of possibility of universal and necessary knowledge at the formal level, stating "without imagination there would never be any knowledge."[21] Although Kant tends to account for imagination in terms of its a priori form and structure, imagination originally presents itself as an intrinsic capacity of human being. As a capacity of human being, imagination is inseparable from the possible: ontologically speaking, imagination is grounded in and presupposes the realm of possibility; imagination has space to actively function solely within the realm of possibility. All that is needed for pure actuality is to perceive and observe, but imagination is not required. Wittgenstein already noticed this when he stated: "When I am looking at some object, I have no way to imagine it."[22] Correlatively, perception and observation depend on the presence of an object: perceptions and observations regarding an object can only occur under the condition that this object is present. The condition under which an object can be imagined, on the other hand, is the non-presence of the said object: if an object is present, that which is presented is an actual form of being, and the only thing human being can do is actually perceive or observe this actual form of being itself without anyway to imagine it. Logically speaking, possibility is the adequate and necessary condition of imagination, or in other words, whatever is possible can be imagined; and vise versa, only that which is possible is imaginable (whatever contains a logical contradiction belongs to the impossible, and is therefore unimaginable).

Corresponding to the logical and ontological conditions discussed here, imagination, epistemologically speaking, manifests itself in searching, discovering, and displaying diverse possibilities and establishing possible connections between different objects and ideas. In a perception or observation, a horse only has four legs and appears without wings, but through the imagination, a horse can be connected to a pair of wings to form the image of Pegasus. Having four legs and no wings presents the actual form of a horse's being, but having a pair of wings expresses a possible form of a horse's being, which although different from its actual being still does not contain a logical contradiction, and so displays a possible connection between a horse and wings. Similarly, prior to the appearance of agricultural techniques in grafting plant species together along with advanced hybridization techniques, that which human being actually perceived and observed were peaches and plums separately, but this did not stop human being from joining them together in the world of imagination and actually making this image ascend from a possible connection to an actual form of being through the development of agricultural science. While the capacity to imagine a winged horse provides an intrinsic source for artistic creation, the capacity to conjoin a peach and a plum reveals the significance of imagination for science. From artistic creation to scientific research, the role of the imagination is embodied in various facets of the process of living and practicing.

The imagination may produce images in concrete forms, but it is also active in forging relationships between ideas and concepts. Grasping and understanding the world always involves the conceptual level, and similar to the properties of concrete images, there are also different forms of possible connections between concepts. Revealing, discovering, and establishing a variety of possible connections between concepts is the most important aspect of opening up and grasping the world in conceptual form, and imagination plays an indispensible role here. The genesis of new interpretations and explanations as well as the formation of new theories always presupposes discovering and establishing possible connections between different concepts. The history of the scientific understanding of light demonstrates this point. The concept of light based on the image of a wave and the concept of light based on the image of a particle were once mutually opposed for a long period of time, but the more profound and whole-sided contemporary understanding of the phenomenon "light" became possible as soon as the connection between the two concepts was discovered. Establishing a connection between mutually opposed and even mutually exclusive concepts always requires the assistance of imagination. The capacity of imagination unfolds differently in the form of images than in the form of concepts, but these respective levels of unfolding are by no means mutually exclusive. In fact, in the aforementioned understanding of light, the imagistic relationship between "wave" and "particle" and the relationship between the concepts based on it could have only fused together in the imagination. Broadly speaking, this interconnection is also embodied in models of scientific research: the formation of models is inseparable from imagination; as the product of the imagination, a scientific model has the distinctive feature of both being an image and also enveloping conceptual content.

Epistemologically speaking, corresponding to connections between concepts is the synthesizing of different forms in the process of cognizing. At the empirical level, although empirical data can only be obtained through perception and observation, synthesizing diverse empirical data into a meaningful system of knowledge always likewise requires the assistance of the imagination. The formation of a representation, for instance, involves the synthesis of perceptual content, but as opposed to a perception, a representation does not require the presence of an object, and moreover, reorganizing perceptual content under conditions in which the object is not immediately present would be impossible without memory and imagination. Possibility is the basis of imagination here, but possibility here exceeds the limits of the logical dimension of possibility (the non-contradictory), by encompassing the actual dimension of possibility. In a broad sense, the formation of knowledge involves the integration of empirical content and conceptual form, but the basis of this synthesis is not simply a presupposed logical order, for imagination is no less a necessary condition. Kant pointed this out when he argued that empirical content and the categories of understanding were conjoined through the imagination.[23]

Imagining is a way to grasp the world, but, despite the fact that this does not presuppose the presence of the object, imagination still cannot be entirely dissociated from experience. In effect, the imagination of a possible world is always based on specific actual experiences. As for how or in what manner imagination actually works, it is always infused into other forms of consciousness and experience: on the one hand, imagined forms are always already at work in the actual functioning of perception and memory—"to see something as something" in perception already envelops imagined content; on the other hand, any imagining also always includes and makes use of perceptions and memories. In terms of substance, even if some objects do not really exist in the actual world, imagining it always in a way involves already acquired experience. For instance, although it is not actually possible to see a "golden mountain" in the real world, humans still have the concrete experiences of "gold" and "mountains," and a golden mountain in some sense can appear through conjoining "gold" and "mountain" through the imagination. However, while the imagination is based on experience, in a way it simultaneously transcends experience (it does not suffer the limitations of already acquired experiences). In the case of our "golden mountain," it does indeed involve past experiences of gold and mountains, but a relationship between gold and a mountain is already forged anew in the imagination, which could simultaneously be expressed as a breakthrough; that is, breaking through already given relations. While affirming the connection between the imagination and a priori structure (form), Kant also points out that in comparison with the faculty of reason, the imagination is not limited by rules.[24] Whereas requiring determinate experiences as a foundation expresses the rule-abiding character of the imagination, transcending rules and breaking through the limitations of already acquired experiences expresses the free character of the imagination. This dual quality of the imagination has never been sufficiently accounted for in the history of philosophy. A host of philosophers highlighted the power of the imagination to transcend rules. To a large extent, Wittgenstein expressed this tendency when he asserted, "the imagination is subordinate to the will."[25] Being subordinate to the will implies not being constrained by external conditions and laws. In effect, Wittgenstein considered imagining to be a volitional activity but never considered it to provide guidance regarding the external world. Other philosophers, on the other hand, failed to notice that imagining always entails going beyond empirical limitations. Berkeley is undoubtedly a representative of this trend; in his eyes, "my conceiving or imagining power does not extend beyond the possibility of real existence or perception."[26] In brief, one cannot imagine things one has never experienced. It is precisely this outlook that overlooks the power of the imagination to transcend already given experience.

The imagination, by pointing to possible worlds, always forms a kind of distance from the real world, which, along with transcending experience, shows the freedom of the imagination, which simultaneously constitutes the precondition of creatively grasping the world. With the aid of imagination, human being can open up aspects and properties of things as well as connections between things that have never been present, and also use ideas to construct objects that have never existed in reality. The former reveals the imagination's power of discovery, while the latter reveals the significance of the imagination for inventing. Affirming the freedom of the imagination, Wittgenstein thought of imagining as more of a doing rather than a receiving, when he described it as a creative act.[27] This view points out the connection between the freedom and creativity the imagination.

This property of the imagination enables it to interact with reason in a way. With the world of possibility as its free and unhindered space, the imagination is more dynamic than reason, and this dynamic nature always constitutes a motivating force for the act of reasoning: Under the impetus of the imagination, reason may be pushed beyond the limits of logical procedure and become intrinsically vitalized; at the same time, the imagination is always that which pushes reason and reason's contents into a state of movement, which enables thought to expand and extend itself. In ordinary speech, we say "broaden your mind" and "expand your horizon," which means among other things to think up more possibilities. Here, mind and horizon refer to thought, which concerns reasoning, and thinking up more possibilities expresses the very role of the imagination. It is this link between the capacity of reason and the capacity of imagination that concretely reveals the power of the imagination to "expand" and "broaden" reason itself. On the other hand, reason itself also always constrains the imagination, keeping it grounded in actual possibilities as it transcends experience and laws.

Imagination not only constitutes a way to know the world. Broadly speaking, imagination is also embodied in the process of humans mutually understanding one another. Understanding the other always involves putting oneself in the other's shoes. Affirming this, Confucius advocated "the ability to analogize with what is near at hand."[28] By inferring what state the other is in from the state in which one finds oneself, one imagines oneself in the other's position via analogy. When discussing the role of the imagination, Paul Ricoeur once pointed out: "saying I think and perceive like you means: if I were to be in your position, how would I think and perceive."[29] The everyday expression "sympathic understanding" similarly involves this type of imagining: the background of sympathy here is imagining oneself being in the other's position or standing where the other stands. Here, imagining constitutes the precondition of understanding the other. Complementary to putting oneself in the other's shoes is imagining in the process of understanding. Communication between different individuals always unfolds in a behavioral and linguistic way, and there is always some form of distance between the one carrying out the action and the object acted upon, between speaker and listener, and a fortiori, between writer and reader. Understanding requires continuously overcoming the gap in communication generated by such a distance, and imagination constitutes an important link in this process. Whether it is in the case of "listening" or in that of "reading," generating and reconstructing meaning is always involved, but the listener and reader cannot obtain the entire content that is required to generate meaning from what is presently heard and read, and they must use their imagination to compile and link together various kinds of possible resources, which to a greater or lesser extent enables them to overcome those barriers between speaker and listener, writer and reader, which again shows another way in which the imagination conditions the genesis of meaning. At the same time, understanding also involves communicating and integrating the information obtained at one instant with knowledge obtained from past experiences; in this case, one cannot just rely on logical order to understand, one must also make use of imagination. Here, the imagination pervades every facet of communicating and understanding.

In contrast to imagination, intuition has its own characteristics. As I have already shown, the imagination is primarily tied to the world of possibility; by contrast, intuition concerns the relationship between understanding and comprehending the world and oneself and the background and process of knowing. As for the direct nature of the relationship between intuiting and imagining, intuiting seems to be quite like perceiving, but as opposed to perception, intuition is not directed at the external properties that objects present. Insofar as the properties that intuition grasps are intrinsic, intuition seems to be somewhat identical to logical thought. But the properties that intuition grasps do not reveal themselves in a process of deduction that unfolds according to a logical order. In this sense, intuition is also distinct from ordinary logical thought. In brief, as a way of knowing, intuition grasps properties of being that are neither present in perception nor manifest in the ordinary process of thinking logically.

The nature of intuition just discussed makes it such that it demands transcending the limits of logical order and knowledge obtained from past experience. In the history of philosophy, there have been a few philosophers who gave this aspect of intuition an account worth considering. For instance, Zhuangzi proposed "sitting in forgetfulness" (*zuo wang* 坐忘) and "clearing the affective mind" (*xin zhai* 心斋), which concretely consists in "doing away with knowledge and skill" (*qu zhi yu gu* 去知与故) and "undoing the affective mind and releasing [one's] spirit"(*jie xin shi shen* 解心释神).[30] Doing away with knowledge is correlated with negating the prejudiced mentality that has crystallized in one's mind, which is to concretely eliminate pre-established systems of knowledge and ideas. Undoing the affective mind and releasing [one's] spirit demands deconstructing the world of spirit in a broader sense, which further constitutes the condition under which "inner consistency" (*nei tong* 內通) and "spiritual encountering" (*shen yu* 神遇) can occur. At the formal level, "inner consistency" and "spiritual encountering" express the overcoming of the opposition between sensible intuition and rational deduction. The "spiritual" in "spiritual encountering" encompasses the meaning of being unknowable and mysterious (that which is beyond the limits of logic or rational order), and the link between "inner consistency" and "spiritual encountering" manifests itself as the grasping of universal *dao* in an intuitive way. Epistemologically speaking, this means that when a constructed system of knowledge or world of spirit degenerates into a prejudiced mind that is already made up (*cheng xin* 成心), it becomes negative: this negativity is not only exhibited in the trap of dogmatism, but in the tendency of a fixed structure to proceduralize thought as well, which misleads thought into the incapacity of thinking outside of a certain scope; in both cases, thought is restricted and limited. To counter this, deconstructing a preformed system of knowledge and world of spirit expresses itself as inhibiting dogmatic tendencies by means of eliminating the prejudiced mind-set, which also means throwing off the shackles of fixed models of thought. Zhuangzi saw this as the precondition of spontaneously grasping *dao*, and thus noticed the power of intuition to transcend readymade logical orders. Of course, by using "inner consistency" and "spiritual encountering" to express this intuitive act as a wholesale rejection of logical thought, Zhuangzi also seems to have tinged intuition with a shade of mysticism.

As a way to grasp the world and the self, one of the distinctive features of intuition lies precisely in transcending readymade models of thought, as Zhuangzi noticed. Logical thought involves the universal order of logic and pre-established systems of knowledge, and opposed to this, intuition does not suffer the limitations of a pre-established background of knowledge, while remaining grounded in the latter. In an intuition, well-beaten paths of thought are either transformed or suspended, which makes possible the emergence of new horizons. At the same time, via the form of intuition, some links in one's train of thought are foreshortened and even cut out, and the large number of irrelevant or disruptive factors are cleared away and eliminated, which enables thought to become more immediate and direct in nature. In the first book of *The Four Books of the Yellow Emperor*, we find a passage discussing the role of "the illumination of spirit" (*shenming* 神明): "*Dao* is the origin of the illumination of spirit. While dwelling within measures (*du* 度), the illumination of spirit intuits (*jian* 見) that which lies beyond all measures.... Dwelling within measures, [the illumination of spirit] remains tranquil and unmovable; intuiting that which lies beyond all measure, [the illumination of spirit] keeps moving but remains unaffected."[31] As a text with intrinsic theoretical links to Daoist thought, it speaks of spirit as cognitive capacity, including intuition, and speaks of "measures" in connection with *dao* as concerning a definitive order or set of rules. In the view of the writer of the first book of *The Four Books of the Yellow Emperor*, "the illumination of spirit" is grounded in *dao*, and so abides by certain measures (order and rules), and in this sense, the mind is "tranquil and unmovable." On the other hand, the illumination of spirit transcends the limits of measures (order and rules), and thus "keeps moving but remains unaffected." This idea undoubtedly touches upon the distinctive feature of intuition as a way of knowing. In brief, at the level of form, the distinguishing characteristic of intuition is its ability to leap in a direct and unmediated way by means of condensing and foreshortening the links in a thought; at the level of substantial content, intuition is able to bring about a comprehension of the whole object or question under concern by transforming and transcending the tendency to think along well-beaten pathways of thought.

Tied to imagining and intuiting is the capacity of insight. In terms of objective knowledge, while imagination shows possible connections between things, and intuition concerns the modes of being that lie beyond the logical order or off the beaten pathways of thought, insight is directed at the essential determinations of things, or rather, the aspects of things with decisive meaning. In terms of the form of human cognition, imagination enables human being to open up broader horizons, and intuition gives human being the power for new thought and understanding, while insight further enables human being to attain a comprehension of objects and problems as a whole and endow thought with thoroughgoing consistency.

Although insight in the narrow sense is by nature immediate and spontaneous, insight as a whole is also a process. As a process, the starting point of insight is determining what the problem is, and then, reflecting repeatedly upon and thoroughly exploring the problem under consideration so that thought may arrive at a solution. If repeated efforts are still unable to resolve a problem, the problem itself usually reaches a stage where it is suspended or transformed; that is, it must be temporarily set aside as a problem so that one may refocus one's thought, loosen it up, as it were. But to set aside and loosen up is not to abandon thought; to a large extent it is to switch from a state of intensely interested concentration to a more subtle state of latent interest. In such a state, an insight into how to solve the problem is often instantaneously triggered by some other phenomenon or idea. The very beginning of such an insight may just exist in the form of a thought that simply flashes across the mind; and of course, further evaluation and judgment will be required to determine the value and meaning of such flashes of insight, and moreover, the ideas and thoughts contained therein will demand more adequate argumentation and demonstration. Only after undergoing proof, demonstration, and evaluation would such nascent insights be capable of transcending the state of being merely individual, subjective ideas and gain some form of empirical knowledge; but, knowledge in such a shape as this is still incomplete: it still has to enter academic circles or the broader social community, where it is truly put to the test. Here, an insight must prove that it can survive rigorous questioning, intensive debate, and closer evaluation, and finally, to stand up to the test of practical experimentation.

To see the way intuition plays its crucial role, we must first position insight within the multiplicity of problematic relationships it touches upon, the first of which concerns the directionality and lack of directionality of thought. Insight is a process of grasping and understanding the object with which one is concerned, and in this sense, it has a certain directionality: as opposed to aimlessly wandering conscious activity, an insight is always aimed at (directed toward) a determinate object or problem. However, the results at which a thinking process may arrive by no means pre-exist in a readymade form, and so it is hardly possible to concretely direct thought toward some result that does not yet exist at the beginning of a thinking process. Corresponding to this is the relationship between limits and going beyond limits. As stated previously, the starting point of any insight is always a determinate problem, and in a very definite sense the direction of a problem simultaneously determines the limits and scope of thought. Moreover, such limits are necessary: conscious activity without scope or limits would inevitably fall into the empty abyss of vague intentions and would not be able to arrive at any constructive results. On the other hand, looking for insight is a creative thinking process, which also requires one to continuously broaden one's own train of thought and expand one's horizon, so as to free the mind up from narrow limitations and avoid falling into the trap of a one-sided approach. Further examination of this tension between the limited and unlimited reveals another dimension of the process of searching for insight: the relationship between expectation and the unforeseeable. Although an insight is not something that can be obtained right from the start, one needs to have some expectation with regard to the possible cognitive results one is reaching for. Without this necessary expectation, one will inevitably lose confidence and abandon the search altogether; having expectations enables one to hold fast with resolve and persevere so as to maintain the continuity and duration of thought. However, as I already pointed out, the formation of an insight is always distinguished by the feature of "coming out of the blue" as a spontaneous realization, and it will never be possible to precisely specify beforehand the concrete way in which one will eventually arrive at an insight, the specific content of an insight, or even the time it will take to get there. At the same time, excessive expectation usually forces thought into a tight spot—a tense state that inhibits its creativity. How should this relationship be handled? The important point here lies in maintaining a suitable tension between these two opposed aspects, that is, in grasping a certain [intensive] degree. As an expression of human capacities, the intrinsic feature of looking for insight lies in appropriately grasping the "measure" of thought.

As ways of grasping the world, looking for insight, imagining, and intuiting are by no means mutually isolated processes. The world of possibility provided by the imagination always constitutes the background of each insight; intuition gives thought the conditions it needs to switch tracks and adopt other approaches by transcending pre-established models and procedures of thought, since intuitions often directly inspire insights into being. In another respect, the worlds of possibility (including the variety of possible connections) that come to light via imagination and understanding and the realizations that are reached via intuitions always interfuse, which inspires the search for an insight, and consequently fulfills them with concrete meaning. In their actual form then, insight, imagination, and intuition coordinate in an interactive relationship and permeate one another.

From the perspective of human capacities, the point in common between imagination, intuition, and insight consists in revealing the intrinsic powers of human being in different ways from general reasoning and logical thinking. The distinctive feature of imagination lies in being at once based on actual or already established empirical knowledge and also transcending the actual form of being and the empirical knowledge correlated with it through a unique act, which opens up and uncovers the much broader world of possibility (including the possible connections between things and ideas). Thus in pointing to a realm of possibility, the imagination frees up a space to creatively grasp the world. Similarly, by overcoming formalized procedures of thought, foreshortening habitual links of deduction, and transforming thinking patterns, intuition enables human being to move beyond the limits of pre-existing realms and reach new understandings and realizations of the world and the self in a non-deductive way. In connection with imagining and intuiting, insight is based on a creative grasp of the "measure" of thought, and points further to those connections, aspects, and attributes of things with essential or decisive meaning, thereby giving understanding a consistent and holistic character. Thus, in imagining, intuiting, and searching for insight, human capacities achieve an expression with much vaster meaning.

Language and Meaning

Even though imagining, intuiting, and looking for insight differ from a logical mode of thinking, as ways to grasp the world and the self, their roles directly involve the inner mind and consciousness of the individual. Broadly speaking, perception and rational thought are connected to the being of the individual on the basis of the body and the mind. Relative to this, the use of language expresses another facet of human being's intrinsic powers. As the historical sedimentation of social culture, language presents its public and common character. Later, Wittgenstein's critique of private language will point to this characteristic from another angle. Lastly, this distinctive feature of language also reveals the sociohistorical dimension of human capacities.

Chomsky gave a great deal of concern to the human capacity of language. Starting from the concept of universal grammar, Chomsky distinguished between a surface structure and a deep structure of language and considered the latter to be an innate capacity of the human mind.[32] In Chomsky's view, the mission of the future lies in discovering this innate structure of the human mind, but insists that it is entirely mysterious insofar as it is neither a result of natural selection nor a product of evolutionary development.[33] This affirmation of the uniqueness of the capacity of language doubtless attaches a lot of importance to it, but at the same time, examining the capacity of language from the perspective of an innate structure of the human mind and treating such a structure as a mysterious phenomenon that transcends nature hardly bespeaks of a rational approach. It is true that the capacity of language has various connections to the being of the human mind, but these connections are by no means simply innate or just mysterious. As for the individual, what Chomsky called an innate structure could much more rationally be understood as a possible tendency intrinsic to human being; such a tendency would be inseparable from the historical evolution of the species, and its formation as an actual capacity would be gradual through the process of social communication. In brief, as a possible tendency based on the historical evolution of the species, the latent capacity of language is neither a product of the individual's creation nor a result of the individual's activity, and it is in some sense innate, but the transformation of this innate potential into an actual capacity presupposes the process of communicating socially.

The process in which the capacity of language develops and thereby functions involves the activity of thought and contents of thought from the very beginning. The relationship between thought and language is a complex one: in reality, there is no direct identity between thought and language either from the individual's perspective or from that of the species. Relevant anthropological studies have shown that early humans already had consciousness and ideas prior to the formation of language; research in child psychology has shown that consciousness and ideas generally develop in the individual prior to grasping language. Furthermore, some of the thoughts and ideas that people have are often impossible to express entirely by means of language; thus, like an indescribable pain or those thoughts that escape linguistic expression and seem to be unfit for every possible wording, thought and language show their distance from one another in a variety of ways. Mencius once stated, "it is not right to say that what is not attained in words is not to be sought in the mind."[34] From the ethical perspective, this proposition affirms that the mind is not limited by language. In another respect, language is also unable to concretely express thought in every single state. Even though such phenomena could be analyzed according to the theory of the unconscious, unconscious speech is quite different from a self-aware expression of thought, which shows that thought in the broad sense does not absolutely exist within language and moreover that language cannot express thought in any and every situation.

However, at the level of substance, meaningful language always envelops a concrete thought; the consolidation, development, and expression of a self-aware and systematic thought is impossible without language. Davidson once pointed out: "there probably can't be much thought without language."[35] In other words, a rich and systematic thought cannot do without language. When discussing the relationship between thought and language, Quine once asserted: "Our first mental endowment is instinct, thought then arrives later on, and following that there appears language. Due to language, thought is enriched and develops."[36] From the internal perspective, the relationship between thought and language is not meaningfully characterized by assertions concerning which comes first and which follows, neither is it dealt with properly in terms of questions concerning the possibility or impossibility of speech without thought or thought without language. Rather what is important here is that, on the one hand, language is a meaningful system of signs, and since thoughts constitute its concrete content, meaningful language is inseparable from thought. On the other hand, language enriches thought, which enables thought to develop and mature, and thus systematic thought always presupposes a grasp of language. Under the precondition that one's intelligence has adequately developed, even if one fails to find the suitable words and syntax to express some thought, this still presupposes that one has a grasp of language. So, it is evident that although language is often insufficient to fully express meaning, this inability to adequately express meaning is still grounded upon some kind of grasp of language; to say that there is an insufficiency on the part of language to fully express meaning is just to say that a language that has already been grasped has been unable to adequately express some corresponding meaning, which obviously differs from conscious activity under pre-linguistic conditions.

The role language plays in the development of thought first and foremost lies in making conceptual thought possible. One of the distinctive features of thought, which distinguishes thought from sentient emotion and other conscious activity, lies in the fact that the unfolding of thought is intrinsically grounded in a system of concepts. The formation of concepts is itself inseparable from the form of language: the meanings that concepts contain always need language to define and consolidate them. Without language, there would be no foundation for the formation of concepts; and without concepts, conceptual thought would be unimaginable. Language is of course a meaningful system of signs, but language can only have the life intrinsic to it in the process of practical usage. Ogden and Richards noticed this: "Words, as everyone knows, 'mean' nothing by themselves ... It is only when a thinker makes use of them that they stand for anything, or, in one sense, have 'meaning.'"[37] This use of words accompanies the whole process of thinking from beginning to end. In this sense, we can say that thought actualizes language or endows language with actuality.

As for the relation of human being to the world, the use of language both makes possible the recognition of specific objects and also provides the precondition of grasping universal principles or *dao*. In affirming the use of language to point out things (*yi ming zhi wu* 以名指物) and in confirming the use of language to illuminate *dao* (*yi ming yu dao* 以名喻道), classical Chinese philosophy already noticed the role of language in the process of grasping the empirical world and grasping metaphysical *dao*. Using language to point out things means that language is used to describe objects in a determinate space and time, whereas using language to illuminate *dao* refers rather to grasping the world as a whole. What the former reveals is some aspect or level of being; what the latter opens up and sheds light on is the unity and concreteness of being.

As a form through which the world can be grasped, language not only constitutes a condition of object recognition, it also makes the consolidation and accumulation of empirical knowledge possible. It is precisely with the help of language that human beings have become capable of confirming and distilling the achievements of cognition that have been generated under certain specific conditions and thereby prevent them from disappearing along with the transformation of those conditions. Moreover, it is also precisely by virtue of language that humans are able to transmit, inherit, and thereby gradually accumulate experiential knowledge in the historical unfolding of practicing and knowing. Experiential knowledge consolidating in a language could in a sense be expressed as an extension or externalization of human capacities, which in turn enables human capacities to further the development of empirical knowledge. At the same time, as the medium of communication, language acts as the precondition of communication and mutual understanding between different individuals and different communities, which further enables the possibility of sharing the cognitive achievements of knowledge. This characteristic of language both enables human being's grasp of the world to transcend the immediacy of the present moment and also renders it unnecessary for individuals to repeat the cognitive processes of the species; because of this, human being's capacities are grounded in the history of cognition. So, the capacity of language both intrinsically enhances and represents human capacities.

Experience

In lived experience, the capacities of human being are manifested synthetically.[38] Relative to the perception of the external world, experience is also much more intimately tied to the world of spirit internal to the individual. This of course does not mean that lived experience is just an empty affection of the mind without any content; rather, as the manifestation of human capacities, lived experience at once involves both the sensible body and the rational mind (including the achievements of culture that have consolidated in the form of language). Furthermore, insofar as lived experience substantially refers to understanding and comprehending both the meaning of the world and the meaning of one's own being, its content is manifold, pertaining not only to epistemology and ontology but also to aesthetic taste and valued ideals. From thinking about the world of objects to searching for the meaning of being, lived experience unfolds in the process of human being concretely being-in-the-world.

Lived experience encompasses cognition, but isn't limited to it. Whereas objects of cognition in the narrow sense are factual, lived experience always involves the issue of values, which simultaneously involves the subject's desires, attention to values, identification of emotions, and her feeling of being-there. As a way to grasp and get a feeling for the world and oneself, lived experience is tied to the body, that is, it is corporeal and hence impossible to sever from the concrete being of the individual. In the *Huainanzi* we find a particularly relevant passage concerning the relationship between the sage and *dao*:

> Thus, the way (Dao) of the sage is to be tolerant but awesome, to be strict with a gentle touch, to be pliant without becoming crooked, to be severe but humane. The exceedingly rigid snaps and the all-too-supple folds, so the sage is always fixed at the point between supple and rigid and thereby springs from *dao*. Whereas accumulated *yin* leads to sinking and accumulated *yang* to rising, only the communication between *yin* and *yang* generates harmony. A string can act as a measuring devise by bending and stretching it [in different ways]; [one] could bend it [to measure a curve] or stretch it taught and straight [and use it as a sight] to measure one's aim. In harmony with this principle, the sage uses his body to experience things.[39]

Here, "experience" means lived experience or embodied learning, and "body" here refers to the concrete being of the individual; "using one's body to experience" points out that grasping *dao* is always inseparably bound to a lived experience, and this process is also inextricably a concrete experience grounded in one's own body. A common phrase like "to know [something] intimately with one's own body" could figuratively express such a relationship between lived experience and *dao*. Originally, the attributes of "the body" are individuality and sensibility, while experiences of *dao* encompass universal content and rational form; therefore, the inseparability of lived experience from the body makes lived experience the substantial unity of individual and universal, sensible and rational.

In the mode of "experiencing with one's body," experience is always characterized by returning to one's own body. Mencius once stated: "the one who goes to the limit (尽) of the affective mind, knows human nature (*xing* 性); the one who knows human nature knows Nature as such (*tian* 天)."[40] Here, going to the limit of the affective mind points to the self as a process, and Nature (*tian* 天) thus refers to a metaphysical principle, including the transcendent ground of moral principle. For Mencius, grasping the metaphysical Nature is by no means a pursuit that must be directed toward the outside world; rather, one grasps it by realizing and comprehending oneself. Similarly, Zhu Xi affirmed this in returning to one's own body in the practice of learning: "You cannot just grasp [what is to be learned] as a thing in front of you; rather, you must gain an intimate bodily knowledge of it in order to grasp it clearly."[41] In another place when discussing being-humane (*ren* 仁), being-righteous (*yi* 义), being-appropriate (*li* 礼) and being-wise (*zhi* 智) Zhu Xi states, "What is appropriate? What is wise? These are things that can only be learned through one's own bodily experience."[42] What is humane, righteous, appropriate and wise are all moral norms in the broad sense, but according to Zhu Xi's understanding, to concretely grasp their intrinsic content and meaning one cannot abstract them from the lived experience of reflexively pursuing something within oneself. Such a conception reveals experience to be more than just objective cognition insofar as it also inextricably consists in subjectively identifying one's own desires and intentions, one's concern with one's own worth and pursuits in life, etc. What we have called "reflexively pursuing within oneself" (*fan qiu zhu ji* 反求诸己) is also precisely a process of understanding, which can only be pursued in the context of the entirety of the subject's world of spirit, thereby distinguishing it as process that transcends mere objective cognition.

To elaborate further, in his or her reflexive mode, the individual does not simply accept or receive opinions and ideas from the external world or just rely upon the transmission of knowledge coming from outside himself. The reflexivity and self-involvement of experience is actualized in the individual's understandings, realizations, and feelings of him or herself: "reflexively pursuing [x] within oneself" (*fan qiu zhu ji* 反求诸己) always logically entails "actually having [x] within oneself" (*shi you zhu ji* 实有诸己). Experience is a kind of activity that involves the achievements of cognition. When discussing [embodied] learning, Zhu Xi once stated, "Make every effort to perform embodied learning, self-inspection and self-examination. If principles are clearly grasped and learning is achieved, then each thing [learned] constitutes a part of oneself."[43] Here, "each thing [learned] constitutes a part of oneself" (*jianjian shi zijia wushi* 件件是自家

物事) means that through reflexive experience the knowledge under consideration fuses into the spiritual world of the self and becomes an actual part of the being of oneself. The spiritual form of being acquired through the individual's experience simultaneously imparts the internal content of self-consciousness and reflective awareness to lived experience. Self-consciousness is not only directed at the individual's own self; it further encompasses the dimension of self-awareness; reflecting means resisting the tendency to blindly accept something uncritically. With the internal attribute of self-consciousness and reflective awareness, experience at once involves connections to the body but on a much deeper level concerns the critical consciousness of self-awareness.

The interconnection between reflexively pursuing something within and actually having something within oneself distinguishes lived experience from an abstract conceptual or logical system. In fact, the reflexivity and self-involvement of lived experience fuses together the whole life of the individual, which makes experience inseparable from one's living practice. Gadamer noticed this when he stated, "Every experience is taken out of the continuity of life and is at the same time related to the whole of one's life."[44] Insofar as it fuses into living being, our conception of lived experience goes beyond the abstract and external form of experience; connected to the process of living, lived experience has a processual nature and an origin in reality. The ontological background of experience is the unity of the living being and the process of living, which enables it to transcend a static form and unfold as a process of continuously realizing the meaning of being through living and practicing.

As a unique way of grasping the world and oneself, lived experience reveals a characteristic of human capacities in a different way. Under the condition that the mind and body integrate within it, lived experience demonstrates the communication of the individual and the universal: the body is individual by nature and is evidence of a specific living being; that which the body is directed toward and hence faces is also a specific object. However, what "bodily learning" ends up attaining is universal *dao,* which lies beyond the limits of individual properties, and which also reveals some kind of power within the individual to grasp the universal. "The body" is the mode of being of sensibility, but embodied experience directed at understanding and comprehending the meaning of being involves different degrees of rational content, and hence, "learning with the body" also manifests the tendency and capacity to overcome the opposition between sensibility and rationality. As a specific living individual, human being is by nature finite, and moreover, the various situations through which one lives are by nature temporary, and yet within lived experience time often transcends the boundaries and limits of the past, present, and future, and [there are] things within finite situations that can trigger in human being a sense of the infinite; [there are] instantaneous realizations that can give human being a taste of the eternal, and so on. In brief, at the level of understanding the world and the self, embodied experience expresses the intrinsic power of human being to unify the individual and the universal, the rational and the sensible, the finite and the infinite.

The Power of Judgment

Similar to lived experience, the power of judgment is synthetic as well. While lived experience expresses the synthetic capacity of human being as a reflexive self-involvement grounded in the mental world of spirit, the power of judgment reveals the synthesis of human capacities on a broader level. In the actual process of employment, the power of judgment presupposes the synthetic fusion and interaction of rationality, perception, imagination, intuition, insight, and so on, and expresses the active unity of analyzing, comparing, deducing, determining, and deciding all at once. As a synthetic capacity, the power of judgment is grounded in the concreteness of human being's mode of being: the synthetic unity of capacities ontologically presupposes the unity of the mind and the body as well as the unity of individual and social attributes. In terms of the way it is employed, the distinctive characteristic of the power of judgment is primarily to integrate and communicate, which involves fusing the other capacities together and concerns connecting the form of ideas to external objects. In substance, judgment unfolds as a different mode of grasping the world and the power of judgment is expressed as the realization of such a capacity to grasp.

Corresponding to the different domains of cognition and practice are the different forms of judgment. From the perspective of cognition, the power of judgment is mainly concerned with the interconnection between empirical content and universal concepts, categories, and theories: the application of universal concepts and categories to specific objects or empirical contents establishes an intrinsic connection between the former and the latter, and undergirding such a connection is the unity of particular forms of being and the general nature of beings. Furthermore, precisely by means of this connection between empirical content and universal concepts and categories, human being grasps both the intrinsic interconnection between the general nature of beings and particular forms of being along with the interconnection between the different properties of things, and by virtue of this, the individual generates a variety of levels and dimensions of knowledge about things. In effect, to make an epistemologically meaningful judgment always means to form some kind of knowledge. In the moral domain, the power of judgment is expressed through the integration of ethical norms with concrete situations; such activity could be explained as the unity of "one whole principle" (*liyi* 理一) with "numerous partial manifestations" (*fenshu* 分殊) to borrow a pair of categories from the tradition of Chinese philosophy. Whether it is an issue of choosing moral action or evaluating moral action, the issue at hand is always how ethical norms are to be applied to concrete situations. Thus, the power of judgment in the ethical domain reveals the capacity of unifying "one whole principle" with the "numerous partial manifestations." Differing somewhat from the previous modes, the power of judgment in the aesthetic domain is directed at the communication of human purposiveness and forms of presentation of objects: through confirming the purposiveness of a particular object, human being simultaneously forms an aesthetic judgment about the object under consideration.

As a way of grasping the world and one's own being, judgment intrinsically contains a creative dimension: for the concrete individual, making a judgment is always a creative activity. Although a judgment may not provide any new idea from the perspective of society, as long as it transcends the individual's previous understanding of the world and the self and includes a new understanding of being and its meaning, such a judgment has creative significance for the individual. This is to say that the power of judgment in the depths of its own activity expresses the synthetic form of human being's creative capacity. On the external level or in terms of its immediate mode of being, judgment is linked to the imagination: the connections and associations involved in judging always come to light by virtue of imagining. However, if connections emerging in the imagination are not confirmed by the power of judgment, they do not provide one with an actual grasp of the world and one's own being. This is to say that it is the power of judgment that confirms and realizes these connections. In broader terms, the specific circumstance and concrete objects with which a judgment is concerned are always given by perception, while the universal concepts or principles that are related to the former involve reasoning. In summary, employing the power of judgment is not only linked to perception, experience, rational analysis, and logical deduction;[45] it also relies on imagination, intuition, and insight. Whether it is the connection and communication between ideas and objects or a confirmation of the meaning of a corresponding being, even though general rules are involved and must be applied, there is no pre-established or unchanging procedure according to which these rules are to be applied, and it is impossible to just rely on formalized deductive sequences. Here, we must distinguish between rules and the application of rules: rules themselves are formalized, whereas the application of rules is not, and it is the latter that reveals the significance of the power of judgment, while rules themselves only become actual in the process of employing the power of judgment. The form of judgment is exhibited as using the universal to govern the particular and as subsuming the particular under the universal,[46] and the substantial concern and actual content of both lies in opening up the world and elucidating the meaning of being.

The making of a judgment is never based on knowing all the aspects and properties of the object under consideration. In most cases, to judge actually presupposes that one has some knowledge but never a complete knowledge of some thing. In the process of cognizing, when a piece of architecture with a door and some windows comes into view, one will usually make the judgment "this is a building," even though the person at this time sees only a part of the architecture (like one wall with a door and windows) without having seen the whole. So, the judgment in this case involves the application of concepts (by means of the concept "building," the object concerned is subsumed under a certain "kind") and involves some prediction and deduction as well. At the time one forms the judgment "this is a building," even though one has only seen one wall, one simultaneously predicts and deduces that this piece of architecture has three other walls; this prediction and deduction is intrinsically implied in the process and result of the judgment while making the present cognition expand (that is, it enables cognition to transcend the immediate presentation given in a specific space and time), and the judgment itself presupposes [that one has] some background knowledge: on the basis of the experiential knowledge that one already has, a building as a kind of architecture usually has four walls. A judgment is a conscious act that is self-aware and concentrated, but background knowledge is never present to consciousness explicitly, clearly, and distinctly; it is rather present tacitly, as Polanyi described with his concept of "tacit knowing." As a matter of fact, as a form in which human capacities are expressed, a judgment is distinguished by the trait of communicating between an explicit system of knowledge and a tacitly implied background of knowledge, and through this process a judgment appears as a cognitive act of integration that fuses an implicitly underlying prediction and deduction to a self-aware confirmation and decision. In this employment of the power of judgment we see at once both the interaction of such cognitive functions as intuition, association, and the application of concepts as well as the unification of self-aware knowing and tacit knowing.

Through the synthetic employment of different capacities, the power of judgment expresses the intrinsic powers of human being. The employment of the power of judgment involves factual cognition and evaluation. From the perspective of factual cognition, sensible material and conceptual form only provide the conditions and preconditions of knowing, and insofar as they are merely preconditions, they are not sufficient unto themselves to constitute knowledge. But, it is only possible to form knowledge about an object through the making of a judgment upon these grounds. A judgment is intrinsically implied even in simple statements such as "this is a school," and the meaning of such a statement is expressed and confirmed in the act of judging. In the same way, any evaluation in the moral or aesthetic domains will always be realized by virtue of a judgment as well: there are ethical and aesthetic judgments respectively included in statements of the type "I did the right thing" and "this flower is beautiful." Before making a judgment, the various factors involved in a process of evaluating or cognizing are still but mutually unrelated materials and forms; they can only appear as meaningful idea-structures and forms of thought through the act of judging, which concretely consists in grasping human being and the world: the unification of ideas reflects the unification of the form of being. What follows is, the power of judgment allows knowledge and practice to communicate by means of coming to know human being and the world in a different way: a judgment about a concrete object or situation provides human being with a ground upon which choices and decisions can be made, and choosing and deciding leads human being to different forms of practice. In the moral domain for example, having a grasp of one's particular circumstance and universal duty and then making a judgment about the relationship between the two constitutes the precondition of making a moral choice or moral decision in such and such a circumstance, which in turn motivates the movement from "moral knowledge" (knowing what ought to be done) to "moral practice" (doing what ought to be done).

Kant gives a profound and systematic examination of the power of judgment. According to Kant, the power of judgment concerns not only the cognitive realm, but also moral practice and aesthetic processes. In the cognitive realm, the power of judgment aims at the communication between the understanding and the sensibility: "If understanding in general is to be viewed as the faculty of rules, judgment will be the faculty of subsuming under rules; that is, of distinguishing whether something does or does not stand under a given rule (*casus datae legis*)."[47] Here, subsuming consists in linking the particular to the universal (mediating particular empirical content and universal categories). In moral practice, the power of judgment concerns the use of moral concepts,[48] and in the aesthetic domain, the power of judgment involves the judgment of purposiveness, or more specifically, "the power to judge formal purposiveness by the feeling of pleasure or displeasure."[49] When the purposiveness of the object's external form incites a feeling of freedom and pleasure in the aesthetic subject, the subject will form an aesthetic judgment. Through the concept of natural purposiveness, the power of judgment mediates the domain of the concept of freedom and the domain of the concept of nature and makes possible the transition from theoretical reason to practical reason.[50]

Kant's understanding of the power of judgment undoubtedly touches upon the capacities of human being. However, in Kant's philosophy, the power of judgment is primarily linked to a priori form, and "natural purposiveness," as the core concept of aesthetic judgment, is determined to be an "a priori principle."[51] As I have shown, judgment involves subsuming particulars under the universal, and in Kant's view, that which an a priori judgment must do is provide "the a priori condition" of such a subsumption.[52] Connected to this is Kant's understanding of the power of judgment as an innate faculty: "though understanding is capable of being instructed, and of being equipped with rules, judgment is a peculiar talent which can be practiced only, and cannot be taught. It is the specific quality of so-called mother-wit; and its lack no school can make good."[53] As an innate talent, the power of judgment appears to be more of an innate faculty,[54] and not as a real capacity or power. A faculty is similar to a property in that it is readymade and pre-formed, whereas a capacity or power is by nature generative: a capacity or power develops and forms in the actual process of knowing and practicing, wherein it is expressed and deployed. As the intrinsic powers of human being, human capacities constitute the real generative ground conditioning the emergence of cognitive and practical activity. However, when the power of judgment is understood as an a priori and innate (pre-formed) [faculty], we cannot but see the obvious disparity between it and a real capacity. In effect, as an "a priori condition," the power of judgment is already of the same order as the pure concepts of the understanding and other such cognitive forms, where it is predominantly characterized as transcendental and pre-given in contrast to that very characteristic of a capacity, which is to be real. Such a conception of the power of judgment shows yet from another angle that Kant's understanding of human capacities has its own shortcomings.

In summary, reason, perception, imagination, intuition, insight, language, and meaning, as well as lived experience and the power of judgment, express the multiple forms of human capacities. Ontologically conditioned by the unity of such attributes of being as the unity of the body and mind and that of the individual and socio-historical dimensions, human capacities involve both the relationship between rationality and sensibility and in the broad sense the unity of the rational and irrational nature of human being, and shows both its different expressive forms and its synthetic form. On a much broader level, the capacities of human being are there at work in all the different abilities, from technical to artistic, found in the wide variety of human practices and actions that express an embodied "knowing how." In brief, the rich diversity of cognitive and practical processes correspond to the multiple forms of human capacities, and could be examined, understood, and conceptualized from different perspectives. As the conditions of possibility of accomplishing oneself and accomplishing things, human capacities themselves also concretely develop in the formative process of accomplishing oneself and accomplishing things.

Structure and the Fundamental Substance of Being

As the intrinsic powers of human being to accomplish the self and accomplish things, human capacities are structured. From the perspective of knowing the world, the genesis of knowledge is always tied to a problem embedded within a certain background; it is always a problem that motivates multifaceted research based on a pre-existing system of knowledge. Such multifaceted research is directed at concretely understanding and grasping a corresponding object and relationship. From the birth of a problem concerning an object to its eventual solution, the quest unfolds as a continuous deepening of knowledge about the world. As far as the manifestation of human capacities goes, this process dynamically unfolds as the directional structure of spirit or consciousness. In broad terms, employing and unfolding human capacities is always bound to the intrinsic structure of spirit or mind, which links intuitions up to thought, deductions up to judgment, and so forth.[55]

From the perspective of the species, a structure of the mind like the logical form of thought is not an a priori or transcendental being; rather, it develops and takes shape through the long historical evolution of humankind's cognitive and practical [powers]. From the perspective of the individual, the logical structure of consciousness develops and takes shape through the actions of the individual and the reciprocal interaction between the individual and society. As shown, the structure of spirit is not only a psychological being; it is intrinsically connected to the model of logic and the form of concepts. It is true that socially and historically generated logical and conceptual forms are by nature a priori for the individual insofar as they exist prior to individual experience. However, these forms are gradually internalized into the individual's consciousness through education, instruction, and learning as well as his or her interaction with society, and by means of this transmission they acquire the meaning of [being] internal norms: society will only affirm and accept those thoughts (cognitions) and actions (practices) of the individual, which are in harmony with such forms. Through this interaction, universal forms gradually endow individual consciousness with a structured and directed nature. Moreover, the internalization of conceptual forms and ways of thinking is also linked to the activity of individuals themselves. According to research in genetic epistemology, even the earliest and most simple actions of the individual have some structure, and by continuously repeating such actions, a relatively stable structure and form of consciousness is consolidated into memory through understanding. As I already pointed out, the logical and conceptual forms that develop through socio-historical processes are by nature prior to the individual, and so their internalization presupposes that they are by nature pre-formed. But relative to this, the consolidation of the structure of action and the logic of action within individual consciousness unfolds as a generative process. To follow up on this point, even though a universal form is socially constructed, it can only be internalized into the individual's consciousness after the individual has understood and identified it. Thus, this transformation from external form into internal structure, which is realized by means of understanding and identifying is by nature a generative process of becoming for the individual.

Therefore, the construction of the structure of spirit as a whole unfolds as the unity of internalization and generation.

Examining the internalization and genesis of the structure of spirit requires a special consideration of the interaction of the individual with society. In the earliest stages of the individual's life, different modes of active social communication can already be found. With language and demonstrations, the adult members of society work hard to make the individuals who have not yet integrated into society act in ways that satisfy society's wishes and demands. Individuals as babies also make adults act according to their wishes by demonstrating to them in their own unique ways. For example, in circumstances where babies want to grab something but cannot reach it, they will usually point to it, and if adults understand this intention, they can bring them what they desire. This could be seen as effective communication, which includes such links as directionality, understanding, and the realization of an intention, and it is not just an expression [that unfolds in] one direction insofar as it involves mutual understanding and reciprocal communication between individuals. It is precisely in the process of effectively communicating that expressive means like indicative ones gradually establish stable connections with certain intentions and aims, and by undergoing continuous repetitions these connections become more abstract or symbolic and thereby transform into psychological models or spiritual structures. Effective communication is a process of interaction between the individual and society, and at the same time, it involves society's demands upon the individual and the individual's understanding of society; the realization of the individual's aims or intentions usually presupposes, as conditions, grasping and harmonizing with the universal norms and rules that are implied in social demands. Through effective communication, universal norms and forms of thought are gradually understood and accepted by the individual, which is the precondition of these norms and forms internalizing into the individual's consciousness. As the precondition of the formation of the structure of spirit, effective communication determines the structure of spirit to be both social and processual: corresponding to the historical nature of social communication, the structure of spirit is more historical and processual than fixed and pre-formed.

As the embodiment of human capacities, the structure of spirit plays the role of fundamental substance of being (*benti* 本体). What we mean here by the fundamental substance of being is correlated with the conceptual distinction between *benti* (本体) and *gongfu* (功夫) found in classical Chinese philosophy. As is widely known, from the Song and Ming Dynasties onward, the relationship between these two concepts became a core topic in Chinese philosophy. In this theoretical domain, the fundamental substance of being (*benti*) is primarily associated with the being of human consciousness, while the exertion of work (*gongfu*) is associated with cognitive and practical effort.[56] When discussing the relationship between the fundamental substance of being and effort, Wang Yangming states: "that which follows in accordance with the fundamental substance of being (*benti*) is effort (*gongfu*); [one] can only come to know the fundamental substance of being through effort."[57] Here, the fundamental substance of being is the conscience (*liangzhi* 良知), that is, the innate knowledge of the good or a priori consciousness of morality, and effort refers to moral knowing and moral practicing (exemplifying the innate knowledge of the good [*zhi liangzhi* 至良知]). According to Wang Yangming, the fundamental substance of spirit (*jingshen benti* 精神本体) is the foundation from which cognitive and practical exercises (*gongfu* 功夫) stem, and cognitive and practical exercises should be grounded in and harmonize with the fundamental substance of the affective mind. Wang Yangming's doctrine of the affective mind, which insofar as it qualifies the fundamental substance of the affective mind as a priori, is undoubtedly problematic, but not entirely without insight in regard to its affirmation of the fundamental substance of being and its significance.[58] Considered in reality, human being's cognitive and practical activity is socio-historically conditioned and also inseparable from the intrinsic ground of natural human dispositions, and the so-called fundamental substance of spirit could be seen as the internal ground of cognition and practice. In the form of a structured, synthetic unity of consciousness, the fundamental substance of spirit constrains human being's cognitive and practical activity in different ways. From the directional orientation of cognitive and practical activity (i.e., choosing objects, establishing ends, etc.) to the very form of cognitive and practical activity, the fundamental substance of spirit is always at work. Precisely through guiding, prescribing, and giving direction to human being's cognitive and practical activity, the fundamental substance of spirit concretely reveals itself as the intrinsic ground of human capacities.

As the intrinsic ground of human capacities, the fundamental substance of spirit also has its psychological determinations. Whether we are considering the process of its generation, its mode of being or way of being, the fundamental substance of spirit cannot be dissociated from the process of human consciousness; its active constraint upon the process of cognizing and practicing shows that it is always intimately involved in the activity of human consciousness. The mind's original form of being is the synthetic unity of consciousness, but from thinking tendencies to moral character, it presents its psychological nature as well. In linking the fundamental substance of being to the mind, the school of mind already pointed this out. However, we cannot reduce the fundamental substance of spirit purely to a psychological structure because of this. Insofar as the internalization of the universal form of concepts and norms is involved, the fundamental substance of spirit is in the broad sense logical, and is thus beyond and prior to every particular psychological determination. In fact, after the structure of the mind has consolidated, the connections and relations between [the terms that compose it] have stability and thus acquire a logical meaning. In the history of philosophy, there were indeed some philosophers from the school of mind who attempted to mediate the substance of the affective mind (*xinti* 心体) and the substance of natural human tendencies (*xingti* 性体), but when using the substance of the affective mind to define the fundamental substance of being, they always highlighted the empirical and psychological content of the fundamental substance of being without adequately accounting for its universal logical significance. On the other hand, logical behaviorists skew the focal point toward logical form, and thus show the tendency to reduce the psychological to the logical. When discussing the relation between thought and language, Wittgenstein concludes, "thinking is a kind of language."[59] In correlation with his early period's focus on logical form, the language that Wittgenstein speaks of here is mainly the aspects of language that appear when one focuses on the structure and meaning of its form, but reducing thinking to language reveals the tendency to use logic to purify and eliminate psychological determinations. In contrast to such conceptions, the fundamental substance of spirit is distinct from both pure psychological structure and abstract logical form; in reality it is the concrete unity of the psychological and the logical.

The structural and logical dimensions of the fundamental substance of spirit also have formal significance. In effect, from the internalization of the universal form of concepts to the transformation of the logic of behavior into logical thought, the genesis of the fundamental substance of spirit involves the issue of form from beginning to end, and the actual mode of being is such that the logical dimension cannot be clearly separated from the formal. Of course, the fundamental substance of spirit isn't just empty forms; form is always reciprocally tied to some substantial content. The substantial aspect of the fundamental substance of spirit is first linked to the process of knowing the world and the self, and its contents are precisely the accomplishments of this cognitive activity consolidating into a structure of consciousness; interrelated with such contents and yet different in kind are contents of value, which are concretely embodied in moral character and virtues. Grounded in the individual's long practical history, real moral principles, ethical norms, and axiological standards internalize into the moral character and virtues of individuals through their gradual acceptance and recognition of them; the latter go on to constitute an important aspect of the structure of spirit. The fundamental substance of spirit also has another concrete content: aesthetic interest. As an achievement of the internalization and consolidation of both aesthetic ideas and criteria of aesthetic appreciation, aesthetic interest is distinct from instantaneous, coincidental aesthetic feelings; aesthetic interest is rather grounded in the long-term accumulation of aesthetic experiences, which give it a stable and enduring quality. In summary, the fundamental substance of spirit has at once a formal structure and also a concrete form distinguished by the substantial qualities of the true, the good, and the beautiful; in the fundamental substance of spirit, the psychological and logical, form and content are intrinsically unified. As forms with content and contents with form, the fundamental substance of spirit differs from both pure transcendental categories and simple empirical consciousness.

With a concrete form distinguished by the integration of the psychological with the logical and of form with content, the fundamental substance of spirit transcends randomly occurring interest. Wang Yangming once distinguished between interest (*yi* 意) and innate knowledge of the good as the fundamental substance of spirit: "We should clearly distinguish interest from innate knowledge of the good. Every consideration that arises in response to things is interest. Some interests are right others wrong, the capacity to know which interests are right and which are wrong is called innate knowledge of the good. If one does something in accordance with one's innate knowledge of the good, one can do nothing wrong."[60] A consideration of interest is that which arises in response to things; they arise spontaneously, coincidentally, and accidentally. "To arise in response to things" (*ying wu qi* 应物起) is also precisely to be caused by the surroundings (objects) and to change due to the alteration of things; so considerations of interest depend almost entirely upon external objects and lack intrinsic certainty. Innate knowledge of the good is distinguished from considerations of interest, because it is not accidentally generated due to an external state of affairs; the appearance and disappearance of objects do not bear upon its existence. Innate knowledge of the good is consolidated into the unchanging and constant integrity of one's character through the long process of practicing, learning and self-examination. Only this integrity, unchanging and ruling from within, is free from the power of external things and is capable of self-legislating, self-evaluating, and judging the right and wrong involved in considerations of interest. In brief, as the stable structure of consciousness, the fundamental substance of spirit is characterized by transcending the accidental, the situational, and the immediately present.

An important point in the history of philosophy is Zhu Xi's critique of the Buddhists for "solely taking functioning as human nature (*zhuan yi zuoyong wei xing* 专以作用为性),"[61] and explained this critique in the following way: "This is what the Buddhist means when he says 'functioning is human nature.' He doesn't consider right and wrong; he recognizes Dao to be solely the clothing and feeding of oneself, working and resting, seeing and hearing, lifting and moving. He says that the 'this me here speaking, actively functioning, and responding to when called is the mystical effect of spiritual enlightenment,' without considering what a principle is."[62] "The Buddhist" spoken of here mainly refers to Chan Buddhism. Philosophically speaking, "taking functioning as human nature" is to focus merely on drinking, eating, rising, sleeping, walking, standing, sitting, lying down, and the spontaneous considerations of interest that arise as a contingent result; moreover, it is to take this contingent, extrinsic conscious activity to be equivalent to the intrinsic nature of human being. Neo-Confucianism in general and the school of the Cheng Brothers and Zhu Xi in particular did not equate human nature (*xing* 性) with contingently arising considerations of interest but rather with *dao* and principle (*li* 理), thereby giving it the meaning of the fundamental substance of being; "taking functioning as human nature" means denying this universal fundamental substance of being through contingent, spontaneous actions and considerations. It is easy to see that the presupposition of Zhuxi's critique of "solely taking functioning as human nature" is his ontological commitment to the fundamental substance of spirit.

Since the modern age, the tendency "to understand human nature solely as functioning" has expressed itself in different ways. Here, pragmatism is worth mentioning. In correspondence with pragmatism's focus on specific problem-solving situations is its tendency to only focus on human activity in concrete circumstances and the specific workings of behavior involved, while ignoring the universal form of concepts and how they transform into the fundamental substance of spirit. To view the fundamental substance of spirit in this way is also in some sense an expression of "taking human nature to be solely functioning" insofar as it takes the contingent, situational, and immediately present moment to be the entire content of cognitive and practical activity, which does not account for the effect of the sedimentation of the history of civilization upon the process of accomplishing oneself and accomplishing things, and neglects the meaning that the structured and determinate nature of the individual's form of consciousness has for cognition and practice altogether.[63]

Intrinsically grounded in the fundamental substance of spirit, human capacities manifest a disposition. Disposition, here, has ontological meaning. The disposition of objects, for instance, refers to their necessary tendencies like the tendency of water to flow downward and the tendency of sunflowers to turn toward the sun, and the like; from the perspective of the activity of human consciousness or form of consciousness, disposition means a stable psychological tendency. With regard to the human way of thinking, clarifying a thought through analytic distinctions and developing a thought through synthetic integration show divergent expressions of human capacities; different individuals will always present differences of character, but subtleties of character are grounded in the intrinsic structure of the mind, so these differences are different in kind from contingently arising conscious phenomena; rather, they are determinate orientations, which are concretely expressed in the process of the individual thinking about and solving problems. Differences of character in the way humans think are obviously not determined by particular circumstances and situations:

specific circumstances or situations are variable and contingent, and thus cannot be responsible for determinate tendencies of thought. By contrast, the fundamental substance of spirit that has consolidated in the individual is an enduring and stable form, which endows human capacities with a determinate disposition on an intrinsic level.

Human capacities reveal their ontological meaning in the fundamental substance and dispositions of spirit, which in turn constitute their mode of being. As the intrinsic dispositions of human beings, human capacities differ from extrinsic logical rules and conceptual forms: logic and concepts are impersonal; they can be external to or transcendent in relation to specific individuals, and can be neither created nor destroyed due to any alteration of the individual. By contrast, human capacities already transform into the properties of the individual's being, fuse into one with the individual, and are identical to the being of the individual from beginning to end. From the cognitive domain to practical processes, the being of humans is inseparable from human capacities. Using "natural human dispositions" to qualify human capacities is thus first grounded in this ontological nature of human capacities.

That human capacities are equal to the individual makes capacities themselves manifest different characteristics. In effect, corresponding to conceptual forms internalizing into the consciousness of individuals and the manifest diversity of individual modes of being, human capacities are marked with differences in individual character. However, this does not mean that human capacities are only individualistic properties. The fusion of logic into the psyche and the integration of form and content is identical to human capacities coming to possess a universal character. To say that an individual human being has the capacity to solve an algebraic problem means that if you give him one with an appropriate level of difficulty, he will be able to generate a correct solution, and the correctness of the solution itself is by nature universal and common. This connection between universality/commonality and human capacities shows the unity of individuality and universality within the latter.

Knowledge, Wisdom, and Perspective

The structure of spirit gives human capacities an intrinsic ground and the meaning of a determinate disposition in the ontological sense. Complementary to the latter is a perspective. A perspective here means a rather consistent and stable way of seeing the world and attitude [toward the world], which involves both an understanding of the world in the epistemological sense and an approach to the world in the sense of an axiological standpoint. So, a perspective both expresses human capacities and also constitutes the intrinsic background of their deployment.

In the process of accomplishing oneself and accomplishing things, one proceeds from the empirical knowledge one already has and continues to deepen one's understanding of the world by integrating conceptual form with empirical content, thereby generating new empirical knowledge. Empirical knowledge is a grasp of a particular aspect or level of the world; the integration of such a cognitive achievement with its particular content into the system of consciousness not only constitutes the precondition of furthering one's knowledge of objects, it also gradually transforms into the individual's stable perspective. A perspective is an intrinsic tendency, but contents of knowledge also pervade it; so in a sense it could be seen as an angle of inspection that is determined by the contents of knowledge. A continuous accumulation and repeated application of empirical knowledge always endows the individual with a corresponding perspective, which determines the way the individual examines problems and [refines] the particular angle from which the individual understands things and affairs. Individuals with specialized knowledge and individuals without such knowledge have divergent points of view upon the same object. For instance, the average tourist will look at the plants growing atop a mountainside from an aesthetic perspective and appreciate the natural mesh of scenic color the plants present, whereas the botanist will focus on the differences of leaf curvature and examine the relationship between plant shape and altitude, which shows the different perspectives that can be generated out of different accumulations of knowledge. What is ordinarily called a specialized or professional sensitivity is in effect the unique perspective that is correlated with a specific background of knowledge.[64]

One's perspective isn't only grounded in the cognitive domain of knowledge; it also reflects the determinate background of one's being. Considered at the metaphysical level, differences in lived circumstances and differences in the intrinsic properties of human beings will always generate a corresponding influence upon their perspectives. In *Free Movement* (*xiaoyao you* 逍遥游) Zhuangzi analyzed the different perspectives of two birds drastically diverging in size, the mythical giant bird named *peng* and a little quail:

> There lives a bird by the name of *peng*, whose back is as massive as Mount Tai and whose wings shroud the sky like clouds. Taking off, its wings push and pull the air in a cyclonic motion that jets him up to a good 90,000 *li*, beating down the clouds and holding up the blue sky as he heads his way to the south sea. At such a sight a quail could not hold back his laughter: "Where is that bird going? I hop and skip, flit around and dart about here and there, but never higher than a dozen meters before I come down to hover over the reeds. That's the apex of my flight. Where is that bird going?" Such is the difference between the big and the small.[65]

The little quail's laughter at Peng expresses the difference of perspectives and ideas between them; for the little quail, flitting about among the reeds is the entire objective of life; soaring up to above 90,000 *li* is entirely beyond imagination. Ontologically speaking, the difference between the perspectives and ideas of *peng* and the little quail originate from the differences in their respective habitats, living circumstances, and ontological properties: the little quail and *peng* are individuals with different ontological characteristics; this difference in the form in which they exist constrains their ways of being and determines their perspectives and ideas. It is easy to see here that Zhuangzi is using birds analogically to refer to different human beings, which is to say, behind the little quail and *peng* we see the difference between human beings; the disparate worlds that correspond to their divergent perspectives reflect the influence that different conditions of being have upon their ideas.

More specifically with regard to the social domain, as members of an actual society, individuals have differences in status, position, rights, and interests between them, and these differences always transform into diverging points of view and attitudes toward the world, which gradually consolidate into intrinsic perspectives. The viewpoints and biases of individuals, which express their divergent social backgrounds, also go on to influence their understanding of human being and the world after consolidating. Individuals of different social backgrounds and of diverging perspectives often generate divergent opinions about identical objects. In the case of social reform, those groups whose interests will tend to suffer during a specific historical period of reform will tend to develop a skeptical and critical attitude toward such reforms, and vise versa, those who will profit from such reforms will tend to support and identify with those reforms in general. Such differences in standpoint and attitude reflect differences in perspective. Here, a perspective is not only a consolidated form of knowledge; in reality, the content of a perspective is always socio-historical.

As the horizon in which human capacities are employed, a perspective at once constrains one's examination and understanding of specific objects and also influences one's way of viewing the world at a universal level, which concretely bears upon and appears in the philosophical realm. Philosophical positions consolidate into internal perspectives; this is always the general presupposition of philosophical thought, and a philosopher's understanding of the world is always grounded in such a perspective. In terms of Heidegger's philosophy, in opposition to traditional metaphysics, Heidegger raises the notion of fundamental ontology and denies the transcendence of being, while affirming the connection between the being of humans and the being of the world. And yet, Heidegger adopts phenomenology as his perspective, and one of the distinguishing features of phenomenology lies in its concern for the immediate presentation of things in consciousness and its suspension of concern for the evolutionary development of things prior to and posterior to their immediate presentation; such a perspective clearly pervades Heidegger's further understanding of the world. Heidegger's concern for the "being ready-at-hand" character of equipment reveals this point: "being ready-at-hand" reveals the present and readymade character of equipment. Although he clearly affirmed that equipment that is ready-at-hand differs from pure things, the emphasis of "being ready-at-hand" is placed on what already is and readymade. In effect, as a specific form of being, equipment has its own formative process, and this processuality reflects one aspect of the historical and processual nature of being; Heidegger failed to adequately account for this. Although he did indeed affirm the temporality [of being], his philosophical system treats temporality mainly in connection with the existential process of the individual being thrown into the world toward his death, which largely ignores the much broader socio-historical content [of being]. This shows that the perspective of phenomenology pervades Heidegger's conception of the being of the world and the being of humans to a profound degree.

A perspective, which consists in a relatively stable viewpoint or standpoint, constitutes a horizon for the employment of human capacities. At the same time as a perspective constitutes this horizon, it also sets limits upon the employment of human capacities. For instance, those with a specialized field of knowledge mainly pay attention to those aspects or objects related to their field. In other words, they become habituated to considering problems from the perspective correlated with their field along with those objects and aspects pertaining to it; those living in a particular social circumstance tend to look at objects from the social position and circumstance in which they find themselves; those who accept a philosophical idea and standpoint understand the world on the basis of it as presupposition. According to its basic meaning, a perspective is correlated with the broad sense of "viewing" and "seeing," and provides a certain angle from which things can be "viewed" or "seen." Some aspects of things can only be examined or investigated and hence "seen" from a certain perspective or angle. On the other hand, proceeding from just one perspective will always involve having "a view" of this without "seeing" that. At the same time, as soon as a perspective solidifies and is taken to be absolute [and beyond this relative limitation], it can turn into a "prejudice" or a "fixed mind-set." Proceeding from such [a prejudiced mentality], [the mind] naturally tends to become divorced from real being. Proponents of skepticism doubt all possibility of any accurate knowledge of the world due to this [very fact]. Indeed they ask, if human beings always have a prejudiced mind-set in correlation with a certain perspective, then how would it ever be possible to reach the true world?

The chief point in responding to this skeptical position lies in affirming the transformability of perspectives. To reiterate, a perspective has the trait of being relatively stable, but this does not doom the individual to only be able to look at questions from one perspective. The perspective of a concrete individual is neither destined nor unchangeable. Although it is true that investigating an object from a certain perspective will always generate some limited understanding of things, a perspective itself is still transformable and expandable.[66] The common suggestion to "look at your problem from a different perspective" means precisely to overcome the limitations that come with a certain perspective by transforming or broadening it. In the history of philosophy, Zhuangzi once distinguished different perspectives according to which being could be examined: "from the perspective of *dao*, there are no noble or base things; from the perspective of things, self-valuing leads to the comparative devaluation of other things; from the perspective of common values, it is not the self which distinguishes the noble and the base."[67] The *dao* in "from the perspective of *dao*" is determined as the ontological principle of unification and has the epistemological meaning of "being whole-sided;" to view from the perspective of *dao* is to examine the world from a whole-sided and unifying perspective; "things" and "common values" refer to particular forms of being, and to view things "from the perspective of things" or "from the perspective of common values" is to examine the world from perspectives that are based upon such particular forms of being and to form a prejudiced mind-set, a "made-up mind" (*chengxin* 成心) or a one-sided, pre-figured outlook by dint of doing so. Zhuangzi asks us to transcend the latter (the perspective of things and common values) and strive to attain the former (to view from the perspective of *dao*), which undoubtedly implies transforming or broadening one's perspective.

The transformability and expandability of a perspective shows that human capacities have some faculty for self-adjustment. The formation of the mode of being that a perspective becomes is inseparable from the process of human being cognizing and practicing. As the horizon of human capacities, a formed perspective has already sedimented into the deepest levels of consciousness, and has become more or less hidden beneath conscious awareness in a state of being in-itself: proceeding from a certain perspective is never a choice based on the individual's self-awareness; it occurs rather due to a spontaneous tendency. Transforming and broadening a perspective, however, always involves self-awareness. This involves both the relation between determinacy and variability and the difference between spontaneity and self-awareness. The spontaneity, which constrains a perspective, and the self-awareness, by means of which a perspective is transformed, catch sight of the different aspects of the way in which human capacities actualize themselves; the former reveals the intrinsic link between human capacities, the accumulation of knowledge, and the internalization of ideas, whereas the latter forces human capacities to continuously transcend limitations and reach for the authentic, true world.

Transforming and expanding one's perspective is by no means an issue limited to the individual domain insofar as it involves inter-subjective communication. Through different forms of discussion and dialogue, inter-subjective communication can continue to reach mutual understanding and generate a fusion of horizons or overlap of common sense. This understanding or fusion not only refers to the immediately present interaction between subjects, since mutual understanding and a fusion of perspectives can also unfold as a dialogue between subjects crossing historical space-time by means of a text acting as a medium or bridge, as hermeneutics has shown. Reciprocal communication between subjects and the mutual fusion of their horizons provide the condition in which the perspectives of individuals can transform, improve themselves, and expand while motivating the individual at the socio-historical level to transcend the limitations of his or her own horizon in transforming and expanding his or her own perspective.

As for the internal dimension of ideas, in the process of overcoming, dissolving, and transforming the limits of a perspective, we must particularly pay attention to the meaning of metaphysical wisdom. The knowledge we have spoken of thus far has mainly concerned the realm of concrete experience whose concrete object consists in particular factual affairs and things in the world that must be grasped separately through propositions and categories. As opposed to knowledge, wisdom involves the investigation of human nature (*xing* 性) and the way of Nature as a whole (*tiandao* 天道). The *tiandao* spoken of here primarily refers to the whole world and the laws of its being, while *xing* concerns the being of humans and concretely unfolds as an investigation of the relation of human being to the world along with the meaning of one's own being and value ideals. Through the historical unfolding of the process of knowing and practicing, human being gradually acquires and accumulates experiential knowledge and continuously moves toward the attainment of wisdom; both [wisdom and knowledge] transform and consolidate into different perspectives. As already shown, knowledge grasps particular objects in the world of experience, and the perspectives linked to knowledge are by nature limited. By contrast, wisdom reflects an overcoming of limits. In the process of accomplishing oneself and accomplishing things, the domain of wisdom provides a more profound context for the actual employment of human capacities by transforming the individual's perspective and also instigates the transformation and expansion of concrete perspectives by overcoming their limitations.

In contrast to the ontological meaning of the structure of spirit, a perspective has epistemological and axiological meaning at the level of "viewing," "seeing" and of orientations to value, and so on. Empirical knowledge and metaphysical wisdom fuse together in the process of consciousness while simultaneously improving human capacities in different ways, and provide the epistemological precondition and axiological background of the actual employment of human capacities by consolidating into an intrinsic perspective. The interaction and fusion of the fundamental substance of spirit and a cognitive perspective give human capacities and their employment an intrinsic ground and endow them with a form through which they can be really employed at both the epistemological and axiological levels.

In the process of accomplishing oneself and accomplishing things, the capacities of human being constitute both the precondition of knowing the world and changing the world (refining things) and the internal condition of knowing oneself and changing oneself (accomplishing oneself). Capacity as a whole is ontologically grounded in the unity of the mind and body and the unity of the social and individual dimensions in human being, and through the fusion of sensibility and rationality, rationality and irrationality, capacities integrate into the whole being of the human as the internal essence possessing human meaning; the fusion of substance and function, of deep structure and perspective is the basis upon which human capacities reveal concrete ways of acting and modes of being. As the embodiment of the essential powers of human being, human capacities stem from the potential of human being and actualizes in an unfolding process of knowing and practicing; expressing both the stable tendency of being and also the generative nature of becoming, human capacities possess both formal attributes and substantial content, and concern both universal principles and individual minds. Human capacities permeate the entire process of knowing and practicing while consolidating into the internal essence of human being; human capacities thereby in themselves provide accomplishing oneself (knowing oneself and changing oneself) and accomplishing things (knowing the world and changing the world) with an internal defender and upholder.

3 Systems of Norms and the Genesis of Meaning

THE HISTORICAL PROCESS of accomplishing oneself and accomplishing things, as we have seen, is internally conditioned by human capacities, but many forms of normative systems condition it as well. On the one hand, accomplishing oneself and accomplishing things concretely unfolds as a process of knowing and practicing, which involves different senses of normativity. On the other hand, the knowledge and wisdom formed through this process further constrain knowing and practicing by means of externalizing, transforming into universal systems of norms. Directed at knowing the world and the self and changing both the self and the world, norms not only involve questions like "what to do" and "how to do it" but "what to be" as well. In connection with purposiveness, norms encompass an axiological dimension, but insofar as they are based on both reality and what ought to be, norms also have their ontological ground. At the formal level, a norm is similar to a principle (*li* 理) insofar as a norm is external and impersonal.[1] However, the actual role of norms cannot be dissociated from inner consciousness or the affective mind (*xin* 心). So, the relationship between norms, the individual, and his or her conscious activity concretely unfolds as the interaction between the affective mind and principle. As normative principles, which constrain the human process of being and the human mode of being, norms constitute the condition of possibility of humans being-with humans; here, norms grounding the possibility of living-in-common reflects the social universality and commonality of norms and reveals their concrete historicality as well.

Reality, Necessity, and What Ought to Be: the Origin of Norms

Why does human being even have the issue of norms? This is itself a question with original meaning. Logically, with regard to the way of being of humans, the question "Why are there norms?" first of all means "Why do human beings need norms?" One cognizes the world and oneself but also changes oneself and the world. This process not only forces human being to go beyond reality and face the question of what ought to be, it also invests norms with an originality intrinsic to the process of knowing and practicing.[2] In viewing accomplishing oneself and accomplishing things as the very mode of being of humans in the ontological sense, and in tying axiological principles like observing ritual propriety (*li* 禮)

and being-righteous (*yi* 義) to it, Chinese philosophy has already noticed to some extent this relation between norms and the being of humans.

In a broad sense, norms could be understood as the universal standards according to which the human way of doing things and the human mode of being is prescribed and evaluated. The question "what to be" concerns the human form of being, and as I will demonstrate, norms have the meaning of guiding one in one's concern with this question. Doing or acting refers to practicing in the broad sense, but in an extended sense, it also concerns conscious activity (like cognizing, thinking, and so on). Prior to acting as well as during the process of acting, norms regulate activity by guiding and restraining it; after an action occurs, norms furthermore constitute the standards according to which such activity is evaluated. Naturally, regulating is inseparable from evaluating. As far as moral norms are concerned, even when a motive has arisen in the mind of the individual prior to the occurrence of a corresponding action, the conscious individual will also evaluate this motive according to a certain norm or set thereof, and determine whether or not it is appropriate; similarly, the evaluation of an action that has already occurred also constrains and regulates future moral actions.

With regard to the way in which norms function, there is a diversity of modes. As a principle of what ought to be, a norm has "ought" and "should" as one of its meanings, which entails a demand concerning "what to do" and "how to do it." In the form of "ought" or "should," this demand has directive meaning: whereas "what to do" guides human being in terms of the aim and direction of action, "how to do it" guides human being in terms of the way it should be done. Opposed to and yet complementary to guiding is limiting and restricting. To guide is to tell people positively what "should" be done or how it "should" be done, while limiting and restricting stipulates negatively "what shouldn't be done" or "how it shouldn't be done." Directing and limiting then constitute the two sides of the same principle, just as "tell the truth" (direction) and "don't lie" (restriction) are two different expressions of the same principle concerning honesty.[3]

Directive norms also have a convincing quality. In the form of "should," directive norms are not the same as external commands: in the face of a command, it does not matter if one is willing or not, one can only carry it out; the working of directive norms presupposes the agent's acceptance and agreement, and accepting and agreeing involves convincing. Opposed to the convincing is the compulsory. Compulsory norms also entail a certain demand, but a demand that is not simply expressed in the form of a "should" or "ought;" but rather a "must." However, it is essential to notice that the compulsory quality of norms cannot be equated with the restrictive nature of demands. Restrictive norms express a negative demand, but this kind of demand may either come in compulsory form or convincing form. As everyone knows, moral norms and legal norms both encompass restrictive aspects, but moral norms have a convincing quality, whereas legal norms have a compulsory quality.

Norms concern not only what should be done and how it should be done, but also what to be, which concerns the form of one's being. In the moral realm, moral norms do not just restrict human action; they also play a guiding and determining role in relation to whatever form of being humans are aiming to attain. The core of Confucian axiological principles, being-humane (*ren* 仁), is not just a virtue; rather, it has normative meaning as well. Here, the Confucian call to "be humane" (*wei ren* 为仁) demands that one abide by what is humane (*ren* 仁) as a norm in the process of acting, and implies sculpting the self according to what is humane as a principle. In a related sense, a general value ideal also has normative meaning: it serves as a goal that guides one toward such an ideal in the shaping of one's character. Broadly speaking, the norms pertaining to the political, legal, and scientific domains also play this dual role. In the political and legal domains, norms not only prescribe people's behavior, but also demand people to become beings with a political and legal consciousness and with a corresponding character and capacity. What Aristotle called a "political animal" and what we call today a "law-abiding citizen" express different senses of this core meaning. Similarly, scientific norms also restrict and prescribe behavior pertaining to the scientific domain, and furthermore, guide those engaged in such activities as to how to become qualified members of the scientific community.

"What to do" and "what to be" are inseparable. Shaping one's personality and refining one's mode of being is always linked to one's way of doing things. As for being-humane (*ren* 仁), composing oneself according to the standard of what is humane (acquiring a humane character and being-humane) is always inseparably linked to acting in harmony with the norms of humanity (following the norms of humanity in the process of acting). Similarly, the forms of human character pertaining to the political, scientific, economic and legal domains are always consistent with the process of behaving under the constraint of the norms corresponding to those domains. On the other hand, character that has been refined under the guidance of certain norms also needs to gain embodiment and confirmation through concrete actions. So, harmonizing with a set of norms in one's mode of being and way of acting concretely reveals the intrinsic link between being and doing, what to be and what to do.

Norms intrinsically entail purposiveness with the aim of guiding one's actions and refining oneself. At the universal level, norms originate from the historical need of accomplishing oneself and accomplishing things, and their function lies in providing the conditions for knowing and reforming the world and the self. In effect, due to their original form, norms are infused with senses of value, and their meaning lies in attaining "the good" in the broad sense, which constitutes precisely their purposive determination. "The good" tied to the norms in the legal and moral domains first and foremost expresses the legitimacy and lawfulness of behavior, and in domains like that of reforming nature, this "good," as purposive determination, simultaneously concerns the effectiveness of behavior. Some norms, at first glance, do not seem to share a direct link with any purpose. For instance, the respective purposes of the stipulations contained in customs, traditional habits, and game rules are often not very apparent. However, their purposive content can be discovered with closer analysis. Customs are in a sense twofold: insofar as they are phenomena of regularity arising spontaneously, they present traits akin to that of "natural" objects, and it is also precisely on these grounds that the study of customs is often developed in a descriptive manner similar to the way scientific research is conducted. However, customs also constitute the behavioral standards of certain ethnic groups, and are therefore prescriptive. One of the significances of customs, as norms, lies in bringing about community solidarity and cultural identity, which constitute the intrinsic aim of customs. Similarly, purposiveness may also be attributed to game rules. For different forms of competitive activity, rules are purposive insofar as they not only enable actions to make sense (as the conditions of possibility of this type of activity), but also ensure the justified order of activity (like justifiably determining a winner).

As a manifestation of the sense of values, the purposiveness of norms originally concerns human needs. Norms aim at attaining what is good (including the legitimacy and effectiveness of actions), which is itself based on human need. In the domain of moral practice, moral norms constitute the necessary ground of possibility of the integration of individuals, and hence, of social order itself, and the reason these grounds are necessary lies in connection with the production and reproduction of social life: the realization of the production and reproduction of social life would be impossible if the members of society were incapable of rationally managing and positioning their relationships to one another in accordance with basic ethical principles and norms like justice and humane treatment in the formation of a moral order. In the unfolding of life practices, universal ethical ideals, axiological principles, behavioral norms, and standards of evaluation are the intrinsic forces that consolidate the members of a society into a social membership: the members of a society are divided into different roles and positions, which give them each a different status and interest, so their only movement toward community life aside from mutual opposition, reciprocal discrimination, and open confrontation happens under the constraint and influence of the moral ideals and principles they hold in common. Here, the historical needs of social life undoubtedly constitute the intrinsic ground of moral norms. In the same way, the different norms pertaining respectively to the political, economic, legal, and scientific domains of practice are also in a similar sense formed out of the different needs of their corresponding practices.

This connection between purposiveness and need manifests the sense of values; by originating from need, norms show that they are grounded in values. In effect, as what ought to be, norms are the prescriptions and standards pertaining to the axiological domain. However, at the same time, what ought to be in the axiological sense is inseparably linked to reality and necessity in the ontological sense. Chinese philosophy's understanding of *dao* reflects this point. In Chinese philosophy, *dao* is understood to be both the laws of being and the ways of being. As the laws of being, *dao* expresses the objective determination of being, qualified as being in-itself. As the ways of being, *Dao* is interconnected with human being, encompassing the dimension of being for-humans: the ways of being do not only concern how objects exist, but also how human being exists. As the laws of being, *dao* means what necessarily is; as the ways of being in connection with human beings, *dao* means what ought to be. So, in Chinese philosophy, *dao* refers to both what necessarily is and what ought to be; the latter refers to normative systems in the form of ideals, rules, and procedures. So, Chinese philosophy's inquiry into the world does not only aim at revealing the necessary laws of being, but also at discovering and grasping the human way of being. When Mencius stressed that "there is a *dao* to winning the world" and that "there is a *dao* to winning the people,"[4] the *dao* spoken of here both concerns the laws of being of the social domain and also involves the way in which humans *exist* (the way of being of humans).

Wang Fuzhi once gave a concrete explanation of the relationship between what necessarily is and what ought to be at the metaphysical level. When concretely analyzing the meaning of *dao*, Wang Fuzhi pointed out:

> *qi* transforming, that is, the transformation of *qi*. *Yin* and *yang* subsist in their interaction and fusion (*yinyun* 氤氳) in the state of extreme emptiness (*taixu* 太虛): *yin* and *yang* succeed one another, moving and resting, resting and moving, contacting one another and influencing one another, displaying their function in accordance with their proper timing and location; the five phases (*wuxing* 五行) and all things, in melting and congealing, flowing and halting, flying and diving, the birds and fish, the animals and plants—each of them matures in accordance with their own laws without going awry. In this way, there is the *dao* of things for things, the *dao* of man for man, and the *dao* of spirits for spirits. If we know clearly and act properly, then we follow *dao* as the principle of what ought to be: it is in this sense that it is called *dao*."[5]

The *dao* of the succession and flow of *yin* and *yang* initially appears as the necessary laws internal to things, which give the world a universal order (enabling things to follow their respective laws without going awry); and to illuminate the *dao* of necessity so as to grasp the rational way to conduct our actions (to know clearly and act properly) is to provide intrinsic norms for practices, and as the universal principles that prescribe actions, *dao* is simultaneously the principle of what ought to be. So, through the unity of the laws of being and the ways of being, what necessarily is simultaneously constitutes the ontological ground of what ought to be.

In the realm of concrete practice, the formation of norms is always based on actual beings (reality) and the laws that actual beings encompass (necessity); if a norm were to conflict with reality or necessity, then it would never be capable of becoming an actual norm with directive and constrictive significance. For example, traffic rules in modern living conditions regulate the relationship between different vehicles as well as that between vehicles and pedestrians, and the formation of specific rules in this domain requires a consideration of the horizontal and vertical connectivity of the different pathways, highways, and roads as well the density and speed of vehicles, the relationship of the latter to the roads, the characteristics of human behavior, and so on. Even though they are conventional principles of what ought to be (for instance, different countries and regions may have different conventions for driving on the left or right side of the road), their validity and rationality in the end is based on a precise grasp of the various conditions noted above (reality) and the determinate connections between these conditions (necessity). Systems of norms must be adjusted in correspondence with the changes that occur to the real form of being. For instance, as highways appeared, speed limits needed to be adjusted. Thus, with the purposive aim of having traffic circulate safely and fluidly, a normative system of traffic rules, as what ought to be, is simultaneously grounded in reality and necessity.

The connection between norms (what ought to be) and reality (what actually is) is also concretely demonstrated through the concept of "ought entails can." Broadly speaking, "can" logically implies three meanings: first off, having the capacity to do, which mainly involves the agent or whether or not a specific individual has the capacity to complete an action; second, being able to do something involves "possibility," which concerns the broader background and conditions of an action such as in the case of flying a plane, which aside from the capacity of the individual to pilot a plane also depends on other conditions mechanical and meteorological; third, being permitted to do something, which involves the relationship between actions and other normative systems (whether a system of norms with a broad constraining power permits certain actions or not). In the notion "ought entails can," can bears upon the first meaning. In the case of choosing to do something, an "ought" (to do) that is prescribed by a norm presupposes that the individual concerned (the agent) can do what is prescribed, and "can" implies the ability to do something, which is itself a kind of fact (reality): a subject (or agent) having a corresponding ability is by no means based upon an arbitrary, subjective opinion; it is a real mode of being (reality). This connection between ought (norms) and can (capacity) thus reflects the connection between what ought to be and what actually is. Mencius once distinguished between "being unable" (*buneng* 不能) and "being unwilling" (*buwei* 不为):

> When one who upon being asked to jump over the North Sea while holding Mount Tai in one's arms, responds "I can't do it" this is truly an expression of inability (*shi cheng buneng ye* 是诚不能也). When one who upon being asked to break a twig for one's elders, responds "I can't do it," it is not that one is unable to do it (*fei buneng ye* 非不能也), but rather that one is unwilling to do it (*shi buwei ye* 是不为也).[6]

The reason that jumping over the North Sea while holding Mount Tai under one's arms cannot become "what ought to be" (a norm one ought to carry out) is primarily because such an act is truly beyond one's ability; the reason that "breaking a twig for one's elders" "ought" to become a standard of behavior is because it lies within the scope of one's real capacities; the latter is grounded in reality (it is within one's capacity to do it), and it is this ground that is still wanting in the former case.

To elaborate further, norms both spring from the specific needs of concrete practical domains and also concern the specific actions or ways of acting corresponding to such domains; whether it is an actual need or a determinate kind of activity, both have real properties. A need, in contrast to a subjective desire, is the manifestation of an objective tendency determined by an actual relationship. Similarly, different activities respectively possess their own specific order and structure, which are also real. Norms can only effectively guide practical processes on the condition that they are grounded in orders and structures that are themselves real. From the activity of such domains as the economic and the political to legal to technical operations, the rationality and validity of norms always presupposes that they reflect and grasp the specific order, structure, and real needs of the activities of a given domain.

This connection between reality, necessity, and norms in the form of what ought to be has not been accounted for adequately. Some have addressed the issue of the ground of norms, but their accounts are strikingly abstract. The account given by C. M. Korsgaard seems to represent this tendency. In his work, *The Sources of Normativity*, Korsgaard examines the sources of moral norms, and his main conclusion goes as follows: the sources of normativity should first be traced back to the human capacity of reflective scrutiny or the reflective structure of consciousness, which make human beings capable of forming the concept of self-identity, and further, of autonomous self-legislation, by virtue of which laws or norms that provide causes for action are constituted.[7] The sources of normativity concern the foundation, origin, and hence ground of norms; to take the human capacity of reflective scrutiny or the reflective structure of consciousness to be the ultimate source of normativity implies searching for the ground of norms within human consciousness. Although Korsgaard's account here touches upon the relationship between norms and internal consciousness, which I will discuss specifically later on, looking for the source of norms solely within the structure of consciousness is obviously an approach that fails to grasp the actual ground of norms (including moral norms). As for moral norms, investigating their origin first requires a look at the ethical relationships found within actual society. In terms of the ethical relationships found within the family, "taking care of children" and "respecting parents" became basic behavioral norms after humankind evolved up to a certain historical age. As far as humans as concrete individuals go, while it is true that the individual human being's self-conscious understanding and acceptance of norms remains tied to a consciousness of reason, these norms themselves do not directly originate from human being's rational reflection. At a certain stage of social development, when children come into the world, parents, as the life givers of their children, are simultaneously positioned within a certain relationship of responsibility (including the responsibility of nourishing their children); by the same token, as the other party in the relationship, children also have the duty to respect and care for their parents, which is not a simple payback, but rather a demand that is intrinsically entailed by this ethical relationship itself. Moral norms, which constrain family life, are grounded in such ethical relationships. In broader terms, as concrete members of society, humans always exist in multifaceted social relationships, which always determine corresponding duties. As soon as an individual becomes a member of a relationship, he or she simultaneously needs to take on the duties entailed by such a relationship, and follow the rules or norms, which correspond to such duties. The economic activities of the market have their specific market rules; academic groups have their own academic norms; mass media organizations have rules for their media activities; for public discussion, there is a general turn-taking procedure for speaking and responding, and so on. Such rules, norms, and procedures could be seen as the specific forms of expression of corresponding duties, which are themselves determined by the relationships binding the parties of a trade, the members of a group, mass, and media, and so on. Korsgaard overlooks just this fact in taking the reflectivity of consciousness to be the source of normativity.

Norms are rules that constrain the being and doing of humans, but the formation and application of norms remains tied to those practical activities that are repetitive and continuous: a certain rule always exercises directive and restrictive roles in relation to the different actions involved in similar types of practical activity. In the case of soccer competitions, the rules of soccer ought to be followed in every single soccer match. In effect, there are no rules or norms that only apply to isolated actions or activities that occur only once. Whereas being grounded in necessity determines the universal character of norms at the ontological level, that relationship between norms and human activity just mentioned invests norms with universal applicability at the level of social practice. However, on the other hand, norms are not for that matter eternally fixed and unchanging. As already shown, although norms are indeed grounded in reality and necessity, they are also tied to human aims and needs, which qualify them as conventional to some degree. As regards the formation of norms, the time and form in which a norm of a certain practical domain will emerge will always be a contingent phenomenon and not a matter of necessity. This quality of norms in a respect reflects the historical nature of norms. Norms change in response to transformations in the needs, aims, and contexts of the being of humans. In the case of civilian aircrafts, for example, prior to the appearance of wireless electronic devices like mobile phones, there were no stipulations prohibiting their use while riding on airplanes, but after these devices became popular, a norm prohibiting their use emerged as a response to the need of guaranteeing flight safety, that is, in order to avoid the disruption of aircraft traffic and communication signals. From a much broader perspective, the international community has rules that maintain the international economic and political order, and these international rules always need to be readjusted at different historical stages in order to adapt to the new world order. In brief, it is not just the formation of norms that is historical, since norms remain transformable even after they have formed. Here we can see that the universality, transformability, and historicality of norms constitute the properties of norms, which distinguish prescriptive rules from necessary laws.

Considered further, the working of norms always involves the human power to choose: human being can choose to follow a rule or choose to disobey or break it. By contrast, however, human being cannot choose to disobey a law (a natural law) as that which necessarily is. A particular social community may stipulate the rule that "one ought to turn on the heater when the temperature drops below zero," but even with this stipulation, the members of such a community may still choose not to turn on the heater after the temperature drops below zero, and thus break the rule. However, "water transforms from liquid to solid when the temperature of the water drops below zero" is a law of nature, which is a necessary law and hence not something that human beings can disobey: in ordinary conditions, as soon as its temperature drops below zero, a volume of water necessarily transforms into a solid state (ice). This distinction between norms and laws demonstrates in another respect that norms are not equivalent to laws.

However, in the history of philosophy, due to affirming the connection between what ought to be and necessity, there were some philosophers who failed to notice this distinction. The Neo-Confucian philosophers following the Cheng Brothers and Zhu Xi manifest this tendency to some degree. The Cheng Brothers and Zhu Xi saw the principle of Nature (*tianli* 天理) as the first principle, understanding it as both the ground of being and a universal ethical norm. As a universal norm, principle (*li* 理) was often regarded as transcendent:

> "Do not look at anything that violates the observance of ritual propriety."—This is precisely because of what the principle of Nature has donated to our two eyes. In other words, the principle of Nature has never told us to look at anything that violates the observance of ritual propriety. When we look at anything that violates the observance of ritual propriety, there is no principle of Nature [in it]. "Do not listen to anything that violates the observance of ritual propriety."—This is precisely because of what the principle of Nature has donated to our two ears. In other words, the principle of Nature has never told us to listen to something that violates the observance of ritual propriety. When we listen to something that violates the observance of ritual propriety, there is no principle of Nature [in it]. "Do not say anything that violates the observance of ritual propriety."—This is precisely because of what the principle of Nature has donated to our mouths. In other words, the principle of Nature has never told us to say anything that violates the observance of ritual propriety. When we say something that violates the observance of ritual propriety, there is no principle of Nature [in it]. "Do not perform an action that violates the observance of ritual propriety."—This is precisely because of what the principle of Nature has donated to our body and mind. In other words, the principle of Nature has never told us to perform any action that violates the observance of ritual propriety. When we perform an action that violates the observance of ritual propriety, there is no principle of Nature [in it].[8]

"What the principle of Nature has donated" is precisely the given of Nature itself, and when defining the norm of the humane way (*rendao* 仁道), Zhu Xi more precisely pointed out what this means: "The humane way is the principle, which Nature gives me, and which I cannot but carry out."[9] A norm, as that which is given by Nature, is already no longer just a prescription of what ought to be, since it is simultaneously qualified as necessity: to say that one "cannot but do x" already entails that one "must do x." In effect, Zhu Xi tried to transform the prescriptive "ought" into the necessary "must"; we cannot help but see this intention from his discussion of the following: "that which the self is intimately bound by, the constant binding duties—between ruler and minister, father and son, husband and wife, elders and youth, and friends—all necessarily have their prescriptive principle, which the self cannot outstrip."[10] That the self cannot outstrip something means that the self cannot command itself according to its own volition, and the background of such a notion includes an affirmation of a force or tendency beyond one's choice. In the form of an external command that the self cannot disobey, a principle of Nature transcends the self's willing choice: "to fulfill the duty of filial piety is something that Nature commands me to do in such a way that I cannot but do otherwise."[11] For the individual to be unable to do otherwise means that there is no choice but to obey that which Nature mandates. As the objects that one "cannot but" follow, norms like the duty of filial piety are simultaneously invested with necessity: that one's behavior must be like this and not otherwise stems from the necessary compulsion of norms. Logically speaking, understanding prescriptive principles as laws that "outstrip individual choice" and "cannot but be this way" always leads to taking what ought to be for necessity. In the realm of moral practice, taking what ought to be for necessity inevitably makes norms seem like they are forces beyond one's will. From a much broader perspective, confusing the prescriptive with the necessary means weakening or even eliminating the role of human being's autonomous choice in normative systems and thus leads to the other extreme pole of neglecting the objective basis of norms altogether.[12]

In summary, norms are not only grounded in reality and necessity and hence have their actual ground; norms are also infused with human aims and hence contain different senses of value. Simultaneously, as what ought to be, norms are also qualified as conventional and thus differ from natural laws. This property can always be seen in the different ways and forms in which norms emerge. For example, technical rules of procedure first concern the relationship between human being and object (how to effectively manipulate an object so as to make it suit one's needs), and the aspect of norms that is grounded in reality and necessity is often displayed in a variety of ways; in such domains such as the aesthetic, moral, and cultural, norms mainly concern the human self and the relationships between humans (including the variety of activities found in each community), and hence, their purposive and conventional character is more salient. Furthermore, norms, whose object is the constraining of the human self and relations between humans, also have different stresses: compared to aesthetic norms, moral norms more directly display the sense of values, whereas the rules of game play for each community more openly display their conventional quality. But of course, these different stresses are relative: technical rules or procedures may embody an intimate relationship with reality and necessity, but insofar as they also aim at making objects conform to human ends and purposes, they obviously encompass values. Similarly, aesthetic taste and moral norms respectively concern natural forms and actual human ethical relationships, and hence are inseparable from necessity. Although game rules are indeed conventional, as that which ensures the effective unfolding of common activities, they are also infused with values. Considering norms as a whole, even though they have a diversity of expressive forms, they all share something in common insofar as they express the interfusion of what actually is, what necessarily is, and what ought to be as well as the unity of actuality, values, and conventionality.

The Affective Mind *(xin* 心) and Principles (li 理): Norms and Internal Consciousness

Norms, as prescriptive principles, are impersonal and universal: they are by no means internal to or limited to a particular individual; rather, they are external to and transcendent to particular individuals. However, this does not imply that norms may exist in isolation from individuals and individual consciousness. Regardless of whether we are considering the actual effect of external norms or considering the process of internal conscious activity, we can see the reciprocal checking and balancing of the two. From the perspective of Chinese philosophy, norms could be seen as the concrete form of principles (*li* 理), and human consciousness could be considered as belonging to the realm of the affective mind (*xin* 心); thus, the interaction between norms and internal consciousness simultaneously involves the reciprocal interaction between the affective mind and principles.

Normative systems, their birth and their existence, are inseparable from humans, and their functioning is based on human being's acceptance of them, identification with them, and choosing of them. In connection with this standpoint, one's attitude and willingness, one's acceptance of, identification with, and choice of norms intrinsically involves one's conscious processes and mental activity or spiritual state. Accepting and identifying with a norm presupposes understanding it, which not only refers to understanding what it concretely stipulates and demands; it also includes a judgment concerning its necessity and legitimacy. Choice arises from the human will, and when a norm conflicts with one's will, even if one adequately understands its meaning, one will not actually follow it in practice. Here, understanding, accepting, identifying with, and choosing all unfold simultaneously in the process of mental activity, which also includes the conscious activity of what Korsgaard called reflective rationality and rational scrutiny: viewing rational scrutiny as the source of norms is undoubtedly abstract, but this type of internal consciousness is indeed involved in the process of applying norms.

Wittgenstein once examined the following of rules and especially affirmed their universality and publicity: "It is not possible that there should have been only one occasion on which someone obeyed a rule. It is not possible that there should have been only one occasion on which a report was made, an order given or understood; and so on.—To obey a rule, to make a report, to give an order, to play a game of chess, are *customs* (uses, institutions)."[13] Rules thus, as behavioral norms, are not limited to particular individuals or specific situations, and in connection with customs, uses, and institutions, they have universality and publicity. For Wittgenstein, customs are always expressed through concrete actions: "And hence also 'obeying a rule' is a practice. And to *think* one is obeying a rule is not to obey a rule."[14] From emphasizing the extra-individual and practical nature of rule-following, Wittgenstein proceeded to separate the following of rules from internal consciousness and mental processes. The distinction between following rules and "to think" that one is following rules in fact implies such a separation. As for the actual form of a rule, although "to think" one is obeying a rule is indeed different from obeying a rule, it is impossible to entirely exclude the individual's self-awareness from the process of obeying rules. Yet, while affirming the former ("to think" one is obeying the rules is different from obeying the rules), Wittgenstein seems to have neglected the latter (the impossibility of disconnecting the individual's self-awareness from the process of obeying rules); from the following statement, we cannot help but see this: "When I obey a rule, I do not choose. I obey the rule blindly."[15] As I have already shown, choice is based on self-awareness and internal volition, but "blindly obeying rules" and "not choosing" is different from naturally according with principles without either needing to think or self-consciously exert oneself to do it: the latter involves transcending self-awareness through self-awareness (reaching a higher state of spontaneous awareness), whereas to blindly obey the rules and to not choose is a way of behaving that has never undergone such a process of self-aware willing, and hence, this means that it is to some degree disengaged from self-awareness and one's willingness. As a whole, Wittgenstein actually tended to understand the following of rules as an external mode of behavior that has nothing to do with internal consciousness, which overemphasizes the public and practical nature of the process of employing norms and neglects the connection between norms and internal consciousness. Here, it is not hard to see some sort of behavioralist perspective in Wittgenstein.

As compared with Wittgenstein, Mencius expressed a different tendency of thought. According to the book *Mencius*, there is the following record of a dispute between Mencius and his contemporary Gaozi, which unfolded around the problem of being-humane (*ren* 仁) and being-righteous (*yi* 义):

> Gaozi states: "To eat, drink and copulate; such is human nature. Being-humane is internal and not external, whereas being-righteous is external and not internal." Mencius asks: "Why do you say being-humane is internal and being-righteous external?" Gaozi responds, "Let's say the other standing before me is an elder and so I respect him as an elder (*wo zhang zhi* 我长之), this would have nothing to do with anything elderly in myself (*fei you zhang yu wo ye* 非有长于我也). Here it is as if there were an object standing before me that was white, and so I regarded it as white; this would be due to the white color of it being external, and so I say that being-righteous is external." Mencius retorts: "Indeed there is no difference between regarding the white color of a white horse and the white color of a white man. But would recognizing the old age of an old horse be the same as respecting the elderly nature of an elderly man? And

then would we say of the elderly man here that he is the one who is being-righteous? Or wouldn't we rather say of the one who is respecting the elder that he is being-righteous?"[16]

Being-humane and being-righteous both have the broad sense of virtue and norm, and in the context of this dispute, being-righteous refers more to external norms, including showing respect for elders. Gaozi initially equates respect for an elder in the axiological sense (let's say the other before me is an elder and I respect him as an elder) with a regard for white things as being white in the factual sense (let's say the object before me is white and I regard it as white). The white color of the thing is an external factual property, and to regard the white color as white is grounded upon this external property. In the same way, for Gaozi, the old age of the elderly person is also external, and Gaozi deduces from this that respect for the elderly person is also external in nature: "let's say the other before me is older and I respect him as an elder" is merely grounded upon the old age of an object, this external property. Opposed to this, Mencius distinguished between the recognition of facts and the recognition of norms, which pertain to values, through a comparison of humans and horses: one affirms that a horse is old on the grounds that it has aged many years, but one shows respect for an aged human being; the former is attributed to what is actual (fact), while the latter is attributed to what is righteous (what ought to be). Mencius opposes merely investing what is righteous with the attribute of externality on the grounds that the functioning of norms (the manifestation of what is righteous in such forms as respecting the elderly) is inseparable from internal consciousness. Mencius clearly expresses this through rebuttals like "Would we say of the elderly man here that he is the one who is being-righteous? Or wouldn't we rather say of the one who is respecting the elder that he is being-righteous?" The old age of the elder is an objective property, but treating an elder as elderly is a way of behaving (respecting elders); as an attitude and way of treating elders, its distinctive feature lies in emerging from an internal sense of respect. For Mencius, only the latter can be a manifestation of "being-righteous." When discussing filial conduct, Confucius once pointed out: "Those today who are filial are considered to be so because they are able to provide for their parents. But even dogs and horses are given that much care. If you do not respect your parents, what is the difference?"[17] Filial piety embodies the moral norm of behavior between relatives, and "respect" here is the expression of internal consciousness, including sincere respect and care for parents. For Confucius, lacking this internal moral consciousness, even if one were to display different kinds of external expressivity like "providing for," one's behavior would still not qualify as following or according with the norm of filial conduct. The emphasis that Mencius placed on the internality of appropriate conduct could be seen as a further development of this train of thought in the Analects of Confucius. As opposed to Gaozi's reduction of norms (what is righteous) to external properties, Mencius's conception certainly reveals a much more profound grasp of the distinctive feature of actual norms.

Of course, to say the functioning of norms is linked to internal consciousness does not mean that following a norm could be simply expressed as intending to do something and then doing it. In the actual process of living, people do not first think of some norm or first make the decision that they ought to follow a norm and then act in accordance with it. Actions that accord with norms often unfold as habitual processes that do not involve thinking. Taking traffic rules as an example, for drivers in a modern society, to see a red light and then stop, and to see the light turn green and then go has become a series of almost instinctual reflexes. This habitual following of norms presupposes the internalization of norms. Here, the internalization of a norm refers to the process of undergoing a repetitive series of practical exercises over a long period of time, through which the agent gradually comes to understand, accept, and identify with a norm as it fuses gradually into the agent's consciousness or structure of spirit, after which it becomes a kind of tacit consciousness and internal mental disposition. Thereby, as soon as a situation linked to a norm arises, one will act in accordance with this norm in a nearly spontaneous way. Here, the link between following norms and internal conscious processes has not changed in any fundamental way; what has changed is only the way in which consciousness functions: the conscious acceptance, identification with, and choosing of norms gradually transforms into the internal constraint of a tacit consciousness and fixed mental disposition.

This link between following norms and internal conscious activity reveals the influence of the affective mind upon principle. From a much broader perspective, as the affective mind acts upon principles (norms), the affective mind becomes constrained by principles in many ways. In the process of cognizing, one can see the different influences and regulative effects universal norms have upon perception and thought. The general principle pertaining to the realm of perception is the objectivity of observation, and although objectivity may be understood in different ways and observation may often involve theories, to grasp the external world as it is doubtless involves this general principle guiding the act of perception. Similarly, different norms also constrain thought. At the level of form, thinking presupposes the following of logical rules. Even though people do not in fact think of logical rules at every moment in the process of thinking and although just following logical rules will not ensure that one will arrive at a creative thought, to think according to logic undoubtedly constitutes one of the conditions of accurate knowledge of the world.

The influence and constraint of principles (norms) upon the affective mind likewise appears in the moral realm. An important mode of moral consciousness is moral sentiments. At first glance, moral norms seem primarily to be external social demands, while moral sentiments are internal to the individual's consciousness, which seems to suggest that there is no intrinsic connection between them. However, further analysis will reveal that this is not actually the case. Moral norms directly or indirectly influence the formation and cultivation of moral sentiments, as concrete embodiments of moral consciousness. Engendering a sense of guilt, for example, involves the pervasive functioning of moral norms: guilt often follows a self-accusation of some kind, which springs from the inconsistency of one's behavior with moral norms, and logically speaking, this includes both measuring behavior with moral norms as well as the emotional response that arises from this measuring. Similarly, dissatisfaction with immoral phenomena or immoral deeds is also linked to evaluations based on moral norms: immoral deeds incite discontent due to their disharmony with the moral norms the agent affirms and accepts.

In a more universal sense, moral norms also constrain the cultivation of virtue. Virtue, as the unified structure of spirit, envelops universality insofar as it is inseparable from the self-conscious acceptance of norms. In effect, the formation of virtue is always tied to the process of molding oneself in accordance with norms; a normative system that occupies a dominant position for a definite period of time at once both constrains people's behavior while also influencing the orientation of human character in terms of social values. In *The Book of Rites* (*liji* 礼记), it is said: "Without observing ritual propriety, morality, humanity and righteousness does not mature [in human character]."[18] In broad terms, there is a universal aspect to the humanity and righteousness of morality and an internal one as well. When opposed to "observing ritual propriety," being moral, humane, and righteous appear as having more to do with the internal determination of human virtue and character. Here, ritual propriety (*li* 礼) refers to the institution and general normative system of the rites. This whole statement in *The Book of Rites* means that the growth and formation of inner character is inseparable from the constraint of the universal rules of ritual practice. Li Gou gave a more concrete affirmation of this, when he stated: "lead the people with learning, regulate the people with ritual propriety and human nature will mature."[19] Here, human nature (*xing* 性) mainly refers to the second nature of virtue as opposed to the first nature of what is instinctual or innate, and to "lead the people with learning and regulate the people with ritual propriety" means to lead people to self-consciously accept and identify with universal norms and consequently constrain themselves with them: "human nature will mature" means that first nature will be raised through cultivation into the second nature of virtue. Zhang Zai also had a similar idea, emphasizing that "human nature that is still pending refinement depends on ritual propriety for support" and "moral right grows out of knowing ritual propriety in the refining of human nature."[20] Here, Zhang Zai confirms the unity of knowing ritual propriety (grasping a system of norms) and refining human nature (transforming first nature into the second nature of virtue). In broader terms, norms also guide the sculpting of spirit by influencing one's virtue.

In connection with scientific knowledge and ethical virtue we find an aesthetic consciousness. The aesthetic sphere also has its own standards or norms, which influence many facets of aesthetic consciousness, including aesthetic taste. What distinguishes an aesthetic experience is its difference from a pure sensible pleasure. One of the fundamental differences between a feeling of beauty and a feeling of sensible pleasure lies in the connection between aesthetic standards or norms and the cultivation of aesthetic experiences. In *The Analects*, we find the following statement: "When at the kingdom of Qi, hearing the imperial music of Shao, Confucius didn't even notice the taste of meat for three months. He stated, 'I never imagined that music could have ever reached such perfection!' "[21] To "not even notice the taste of meat for three months" due to "listening to the imperial music of Shao" means that enjoyment in the aesthetic sense enables human being to transcend the feeling of pleasure at the level of sensibility; such a raising of spirit is linked to the application of aesthetic norms. *The Analects* also records the comparison Confucius made between the music of Shao and that of Wu: "Confucius said of the music of Shao: 'completely refined both in terms of beauty and in terms of good,' and of the music of Wu: 'completely refined in terms of beauty, but incompletely refined in terms of good.' "[22] The aesthetic standard of perfection for Confucius is thus the unity of the beautiful and the good. The reason Confucius appreciated the music of Shao is due to its attainment of this standard of perfection.[23] On the other hand, it is precisely with the music of Shun in mind as the standard of an aesthetic judgment of the unity of the good and the beautiful that Confucius weighs in favor of listening to the music of Shun while ignoring the taste of meat. Opposed to appreciation in the positive sense is repulsion in the negative sense. Confucius once insisted on "banishing the music of Zheng;"[24] the reason it called for rejection is due to the discordance it evoked in relation to the aesthetic standards Confucius upheld—"I detest the sounds of Zheng for corrupting our classical court music."[25] Here, his "detest" includes a feeling of repulsion in him, which contrasted perfectly with that aesthetic enjoyment inspired in him by the music of Shao. In brief, the difference between the music of Shao and that of Zheng as well as the different emotional responses to which they give rise are all linked to the application and influence of aesthetic norms.

Evidently, norms emerge in a diversity of forms, which correspond to the diversity of human being's practical activities and ways of being-in-the-world. Moreover, this diversity of norms also constrains human being's conscious activity in many ways. Of course, by guiding and influencing, norms condition the rational and effective unfolding of conscious activity, but certainly without rejecting or limiting human creativity. In effect, norms always entail creative space.

For instance, to play chess or some other competitive activity, following a defined set of rules is the basic precondition of joining the activity concerned, but to become the winner, just following the rules alone is obviously not enough; to win, the participants of the activity are simultaneously required to use norms creatively. A similar case could be made for the process of knowing. To follow logical rules while thinking is the necessary precondition of arriving at precise knowledge, but just following logical rules alone cannot ensure the attainment of any genuine, profound knowledge of the world. As norms guide and restrain thought in the process of thinking, they also provide creative thought with the vast world around us and thus present an openness. But, norms are unable to predict how a creative thought will concretely unfold.

In the domain of moral practice, we can likewise see the reciprocal interaction between universal norms and individual consciousness. Moral practices always unfold in specific circumstances. Analyzing concrete situations demands the application of norms and involves the flexible modification of principles. In Chinese philosophy, this issue emerged very early in debates concerning the distinction between *jing* (经) and *quan* (权).[26] *Jing* primarily refers to the universality and determinateness of rules, while *quan* refers to the flexible bending of rules. Chinese philosophers insisted on returning to the rules (*fanjing* 返经) but also opposed upholding rules inflexibly (*wuquan* 无权),[27] which concerns the relationship between applying norms and considering concrete circumstances. But what is worth more attention is that in Chinese philosophy the interaction between *jing* and *quan* is always intertwined with the individual and inner consciousness. Here, the following quote from Wang Fuzhi is certainly representative of Chinese philosophy in this regard:

> Only by knowing in advance the principles that connects things together consistently (*xiangtong zhi li* 相通之理) and by keeping those principles in mind will it be the case that a step here will not prevent a step there. When things change, one must keep in mind their consistent connections; when things are consistent, one needs to keep in mind their transformability—when the great functioning of such a practical actualization harmonizes with what one fully wills, this is called miraculous."[28]

Wang Fuzhi here touches upon "the way of Nature" (*tiandao* 天道) and "the way of humans" (*rendao* 人道). According to the way of humans, those so-called "principles of consistency" include universal norms, and to know principles of consistency and to maintain them means transforming universal norms into an internal conceptual structure. The unity of consistency and change includes the interaction of *jing* (the constraint of universal rules) and *quan* (the bending of rules based upon an analysis of circumstances). As Wang Fuzhi sees it, this unity and interaction is rooted in an internal conceptual structure by harmonizing with what the whole affective mind maintains. This connection between the unity of the consistency and transformability of principles and what the whole affective mind maintains also reveals the role of the individual's conscious activity in the process of applying universal norms and analyzing circumstances.

Norms work through the individual's understanding, accepting, identifying with and choosing of norms, and the individual's conscious activity is also constrained by norms in many ways; linked to this is the reciprocal interaction between according with norms and creative thought. In one respect, this relationship between norms and the individual's internal consciousness concretely reveals the unity of the affective mind (*xin* 心) and principles (*li* 理).

Form, Procedure, and Norms: the Actual Conditions of a World of Meaning

The interaction of general norms with the individual's conscious activity reveals the internal attribute of norms in terms of the relation between norms and the individual. But, as principles prescribing what ought to be, norms play a role that is by no means limited to the individual domain. In effect, norms are both universal and public in both reality and history. The concrete role of norms can be seen everywhere from the process of humans being-with humans to the founding of social institutions.

Human being is a social being who is incapable of living in isolation from others or a group. This being-with of human being with humans is at once a mode of being in the ontological sense and also a fact to which history attests. A correlated problem is: how is this being-with possible? Here, norms are indispensible. Considered historically, the tribes of prehistoric ages selected different animals or plants to serve as totems, which in a corresponding sense served as important signs that reciprocally differentiated tribes from one another and also constituted the ground of collective identity of the members of each tribe; the consolidation and group solidarity of a tribe was intrinsically tied to it. At the level of form, totems were a cultural sign; At the level of content, totems also contained norms, expressed in such forms as prohibitions (like the prohibitions against injuring or eating the animal or plant constituting the tribe's totem). Here, the relationship between the formation of social groups and norms in the broad sense shows itself quite clearly: the influence and constraint that totems exercised upon the formation of social groups involved the functioning of norms.

In Chinese philosophy, the being-with of human being with humans was always understood "to be a group" as opposed to "being an individual." According to Confucianism, the capacity "to group" is the fundamental feature that distinguishes humans from animals and enables them to transcend animals. When comparing humans and other beings, Xunzi once stated:

Water and fire have energy (*qi* 气) but no life; plants and trees have life but no awareness (*zhi* 知); beasts and birds have awareness but no sense of what is righteous (*yi* 义); humans possess energy, life, awareness, and also a sense of what is righteous, and therefore rank of the highest nobility among beings in nature. Human strength does not compare to that of the bull; human mobility does not compare to that of the horse, but humans use the bull and horse as tools; how is this possible? The answer: humans can group, the others cannot. How is it that humans can group? The answer: differentiation. How is it that humans can carry out this differentiation? The answer: with a sense of what is righteous. Thus, with a sense of what is righteous humans can differentiate and then combine harmonically, to combine harmonically is to combine into a whole, to combine into a whole is to multiply strengths, to multiply strengths is to become powerful, to become powerful is to conquer other creatures; thus, a center of control can be attained and fixed. Thus, according to the order of the four seasons, all creatures are measured and conjoined to benefit the unified world; there is no other way through which or principle according to which the world could be unified other than through differentiation in accordance with what is righteous.[29]

The concepts of energy, life, awareness, and righteousness fall on the side of ontology and axiology, while the concept of "grouping" has sociological meaning; aside from having energy, life, and awareness, that humans also have a sense of what is righteous distinguishes humans from other beings at the ontological and axiological level. "The capacity to group" enables humans to transcend animals in terms of form of social organization. What is worth attention here is that Xunzi also advances from this point to raise the question "How is it that humans can group?" In Xunzi's view, to group (*qun* 群) presupposes differentiation (*fen* 分). Differentiation here is the division of social roles into a hierarchical structure. In this way, the question concerning how grouping is possible concretely transforms into how it is that this "differentiation" can be carried out, and what is righteous (*yi* 义) derives from this question.[30] Etymologically, *yi* (義) is closely connected with its homonym *yi* (宜) which broadly means "suitable, appropriate," and by extension "what ought to be." So, to differentiate according to what is righteous means to separately position the component members of society into a determinate social structure in harmony with a defined principle, and thereby establish a hierarchically ordered social organization (to group).

Being righteous (*yi* 義) in the sense just mentioned is directly connected to the previously mentioned concept of observing ritual propriety (*li* 禮). Thus, to divide [roles] according to what is righteous is also to divide [roles] in harmony with ritual propriety and what is righteous. When discussing the origin of ritual propriety, Xunzi concretely elucidated this:

> What is the origin of the rites? The answer: one is born and has desires; one desires, but when one does not attain [what one desires], one cannot help but

> seek it; so, one seeks it, but does not do so within the measure of boundaries, so one cannot help but conflict with others; they conflict, so there is disorder, and due to this disorder, poverty. Past kings were disgusted with this chaos, so they instituted a code of rites determining what is appropriate and just so as to measure boundaries and divide them, that is, in order to cultivate their desires and give them what they seek; by making desires such that they do not come up poor over material things, and by making things such that they do not suffer under the reign of desires, so that both things and desires raise each other and grow; this is the very origin of the rites."[31]

As I have already shown, the rites refer to both an ethical-political institution and a corresponding system of social norms. Here in the same way Xunzi analyzed the origin and function of the rites from the perspective of how to establish and protect "the group." For Xunzi, the distinctive feature of the rites lies in prescribing specific "rights" and "duties" for each member of society, which simultaneously establishes the limits or boundaries of the activity of each member; within the measured boundaries distributed to each, the behavior of each member is reasonable and permitted (including their striving for their own benefit), but if any such boundary is overstepped, one's activity will be checked. This so-called measuring of boundaries effectively implies a conception of order; it is precisely the different limits placed on their rights and activity that enable the members of a society to harmoniously co-exist in "group" fashion, thereby preventing internal strife and disputes. We can see that the rites (li 禮) and what is righteous (yi 義) as universal norms are understood as protecting the possibility of ordered co-existence (grouping).[32]

Being-with or the co-existence of humans involves multiple factors. In actuality, human being is always first a being in some relationship; from everyday life to economic and political practices, the being-with of humans essentially unfolds in relationships. A relationship is in some sense transcendent to the individual self; from the static perspective, the individual's being constitutes the background of the other's being, and vise versa; from the dynamic perspective, a relationship leads to inter-subjective communication. As the background and form of being-with, the relationships in which one lives come in different forms, but harmony and conflict are the basic forms. Harmony is grounded in identity and unity, while conflict stems from difference. Considered in its actual form, there is both unity and multiple senses of difference between humans, and how one leads from unity to harmony in the positive sense and how one prevents difference from developing into conflict in the negative sense constitute the preconditions of being-with, and the formation of this condition is inseparably bound to social norms. As the principles of what ought to be, universal norms make the members of a society communicate, coordinate, and cooperate with one another in life practices by guiding and demanding in the positive sense, while preventing the members of society from overstepping their own rights and duties by means of limiting them in the negative sense, thereby preventing the movement from difference to conflict or from conflict to disorder. As Xunzi recognized, these two functions of norms make them become the conditions of possibility of humans being-with humans.

In the social or public sphere, norms have a regulative function, but also a constitutive one as well. A social structure does not just emerge directly through the relationships between humans, for institutions are needed as well. The formation of an institution involves different conditions and preconditions, and an important facet among them is universal value principles. Value principles involve general ideals, present normative meaning, and pervade a particular social institution in different ways. The system of the rites in the Shang and Zhou dynasties, for instance, suited the historical needs of the Shang and Zhou societies, and also embodied the value principles and value ideals based on the blood ties and kinship relations of that age. As a concretization of value principles and value ideals, the formation of the rites system was founded on those value principles and value ideals. Similarly, modern political institutions embody the value principles and value ideals of the enlightenment age, such as democracy, equality, and freedom. The latter (modern value principles and value ideals) constrain and guide the construction of modern political institutions. Broadly speaking, certain norms participate in the constituting of certain social organizations and communities: norms for scientific research drive the formation of the scientific community. Different industrial norms construct corresponding business organizations; while involving a specific form of activity, various game rules motivate the establishment of different groups and organizations such as baseball teams and chess associations. Of course, while catalyzing the formation of different institutions and groups, norms themselves are also constrained by institutions. After a particular organization or institution is formed, the institution will demand that a system of norms suit it, and thereby adjust whatever norms were originally in place. In this way, norms create institutions, and institutions demand those norms to undergo adjustments in harmony with their own form. So, norms and institutions interact and fuse together. In the course of social evolution, norms and institutions are not strictly separable. As has been repeatedly mentioned, the rites of ancient China are a typical expression of this: they are at once a politico-ethical institution and also universal principles and norms; the rites (*li* 礼) as an institution was intrinsically based on ritual propriety (*li* 礼) as principles and norms, but the latter also had to adapt to the former.

As the conditions of possibility of social life, norms are characterized by universality. If the norms of a specific community of a given age are effectively valid, they always have a constraining or regulative effect upon all the different individuals within that community. Wittgenstein's rejection of the possibility of private language on the basis of following rules simultaneously entails an affirmation of the public nature of norms or rules. However, some philosophers fail to give an adequate account of this universality of norms. The philosopher J. Raz is an example worth mentioning. When considering the different forms of norms, Raz made a distinction between a personal rule and a social rule.[33] The presupposition of this distinction is accepting the existence of personal rules. In fact, these so-called rules, which are merely valid for a specific individual, can be nothing but individual self-determination, like demanding oneself "to wake up everyday at 6 o'clock" and "to go for a half-hour walk every morning." Although these types of demands have some sort of normative relation to the individual's own activity, they are neither public nor universal, since they only have validity in the sphere of the self; thus, they can only be seen as personal plans or a self-determination as regards working and resting hours, and do not belong to the list of norms.

Individual plans and demands in the aforementioned sense also differ from what Kant called self-legislation. In the moral domain, Kant saw the good will or practical reason of human being as the legislator of moral laws, but those laws which practical reason issues are not solely valid for the self; rather, they must be valid for all individuals. One of the basic moral laws Kant affirms is: "Act only according to that maxim whereby you can at the same time will that it should become a universal law."[34] According to Kant, "the ground of all practical legislation lies objectively in the rule and in the form of universality."[35] In brief, self-legislation differs entirely from individualistic demands; the precondition of moral self-legislation lies precisely in a confirmation of the universality of moral laws. Even though Kant's view here shows a tendency to mistake what ought to be for necessity, he does notice the universality of norms from the perspective of moral practice.

The universality of norms also intrinsically influences human practice. As explained previously, norms guide and constrain human activity through demands such as "ought" and "ought not," and it is just such demands that constitute the ground or cause of action in different senses: "ought" implies that there is a reason to do something, while "ought not" provides the basis for inhibiting some action. These grounds or reasons that norms contain are not only founded on reality and necessity; they are also the consolidation of the historical experience of the species, which have come to express social demands that relieve the individual not only of the need to discover anew before each action whether or not it ought to be executed but also of the need to repeatedly examine how it should be concretely done after the action is chosen. Similar to general propositions in epistemology, the universality of norms transcends both the individual and the particular, and covers different aspects of the practical sphere. When based on norms, the individual's choice of action and way of acting is awarded legitimacy, and at the same time unnecessary repetitions are avoided. In some sense, then, norms embody an economic principle of action.

Directed at practices, norms are also systematic. The norms of the different practical spheres do not appear in singular isolated form, but rather, as a systematic set. From moral and legal norms to rules of game play, this characteristic is present in each case. To take chess-like games as an example, there are systematic sets of rules for how to move the pieces and how to strike the opponent. With regard to the social realm as a whole, there are differences in authoritativeness between different systems of norms. Generally speaking, norms of law have a much higher authoritative status: if other norms in society clash with legal norms, they will not be awarded legitimacy. Of course, there are cases of mutual toleration between different systems of norms. Under the condition that they do not conflict with legal norms, it may be the case that other norms such as moral norms and trading or industrial norms are tolerated by norms of law. The systematicity of norms and the relationship between norms reveal their publicity and universal sociality.

Here it seems we may distinguish between norms and normativity. In contrast to norms, normativity is broader in meaning. To take language as an example, to understand the connotations of a word means that one can accurately use the given word; in this case then, the meaning or connotation of a word entails "how" (how to use a word). Thus, to grasp the meaning of a word implies that one has grasped its normativity. In a similar sense, in the process of organizing empirical data, categories and concepts also present normativity. Kant expressed this point clearly when he said: "A concept is always, as regards its form, something universal which serves as a rule."[36] Aside from this, commands, permissions, promises, demands, prescriptions, and threats (of the type "if not, then I'll . . .") all contain different degrees of normativity. Of course, normativity cannot be simply equated with norms. Generally speaking, norms have a universal character. However, although the commands, permissions, promises, demands, and prescriptions found in particular contexts have normativity, insofar as they concern specific people and singular affairs, they lack universality. At the same time, norms are characterized by systematicity, and therefore, although commands, permissions, promises, demands, and prescriptions have a normative form of expressivity, they unfold as singular mutually distinct demands and thus differ quite clearly from the systematic nature of norms.

At the level of form, a norm involves the relationship between a categorical judgment and a hypothetical judgment. Kant made a distinction between the two from the perspective of moral practice, emphasizing that a moral law is categorical rather than hypothetical. Hypothetical judgments include in logical terms a relationship of conditional implication (if x, then y), whereas categorical judgments are not constrained by conditions, and thus appear in the form of unconditional commands. For Kant, hypothetical judgments involve ends of utility. So, the actions they concern are based entirely on some external aim. The distinctive feature of moral actions on the other hand consists entirely in having duty as their basis. So, they do not involve either a concrete end result or concern any notion of utility. Thus, moral laws can only be given in the form of categorical judgments. On this basis, Kant distinguishes between moral actions and actions based on utility and rejects the empiricist and utilitarian understanding of moral action. This distinction is undoubtedly significant. But whether or not moral laws can be seen as unconditional categorical judgments or absolute commands remains an open question.

Moral laws concern both action and agent. As a concrete being, the agent always finds himself embedded in a set of actual social relationships, so it is evident that moral laws cannot just be understood as categorical judgments. In actuality, moral laws take the following form: if you find yourself in this or that type of social relationship, then you ought to fulfill the duty that such a relationship prescribes and follow the norm that corresponds to it. Here, moral maxims also present a hypothetical dimension. In effect, it is precisely this hypothetical form of judgment (if-then) that at the logical level enables substantial social relationships to communicate with formalized (universalized) moral laws; and it is this logical relationship that reflects the actual connection between the two.[37]

In broader terms, the role of norms outside of the moral realm similarly involves actual relationships and a specific background, and thereby entails some sort of hypothetical nature. In everyday life situations where the maxim "when in Rome do as the Romans do" applies, the Chinese use the proverb "follow the customs of the village you enter." The term "customs" here points to behavioral norms in reference to how to do something and whether or not it can be done; the term "village" here could be seen as a certain state of being or setting of being; "to follow the customs of that village" means following the behavioral norms that such a set of customs entails. And this following of norms presupposes being embedded in a certain social situation whose logical form could be expressed as follows: if you arrive at or exist in a certain social situation, then you ought to follow the behavioral norms that such a situation demands. A similar case could be made for other activities where norms reign, like following traffic laws and the operational procedures of a production process or abiding by academic standards. Here, the functioning of a norm is always premised by a certain background setting of actual relationships, which issues a demand expressed in the following forms: if you drive or walk in some state then you ought to follow the local traffic laws; if you work on a particular assembly line then you ought to follow the corresponding operational procedures; if you engage in research in some academic community, then you ought to abide by the academic standards of that community. Here, behind each (if-then) logical form we see the substantial meaning of an actual social relation and a certain background setting of being. That which the hypothetical form of norms reflects, therefore, is the sociality of the being of humans and the historicality and concreteness of norms themselves.

Norms at the formal level not only involve logical relations; they also have different ways of expressing themselves. Firstly, there is the linguistic way. Generally speaking, norms that are fabricated in a self-conscious way like laws, regulations, prescriptions of different forms, and technological procedures (like instructions for how to operate machinery) more straightforwardly express themselves in linguistic form; in fact, the norms expressed in the form of prescriptions could also be seen as speech acts. But, norms may also be expressed in the form of rituals and other ways of behaving. In the course of the historical evolution of society, the norms that took shape spontaneously like customs exist mainly in non-linguistic form, and they function more through the setting of examples and the imitating of those examples. There are still other norms, whose manner of being and manner of expression show even more complex characteristics. Character appraisals and written criticisms of certain social figures played a normative role in traditional Chinese society; their content consisted in evaluations of certain political affairs and the political figures involved at some specified period of time. These criticisms played an extremely important role in influencing and constraining the words and deeds of the political officials and those occupying prestigious positions in the social group at the time. Although these criticisms concerned concrete affairs and particular persons, they also entailed some kind of universal principle of values; and in the process of evaluating these characters and affairs, the principles entailed were certainly expressed through language, but not in the form of a clear and distinct judgment or concept. To a large extent, such principles existed in the form of beliefs that were held in common by the community, and were expressed in a narrative style quite distinct from the form of a logical deduction. While language expresses the universality of norms at the level of form, common beliefs embody the sociality of norms at the level of substance.

Human Capacities and Universal Norms

Directed at accomplishing oneself and accomplishing things, the function of norms is inseparable from the capacities of human nature. In effect, the interconnection between human capacities and systems of norms is shown through the interaction of the affective mind (*xin* 心) or internal consciousness with principles (*li* 理) or external norms. The process of accomplishing oneself and accomplishing things is grounded in human capacities and is constrained by systems of norms. Human capacities intertwine with systems of norms, constituting at different levels the actual conditions of the genesis of a world of meaning.

Tied to the genesis of meaning, accomplishing oneself and accomplishing things concretely unfolds as the historical process of knowing and practicing. With the substantial content of knowing oneself and refining oneself and of knowing the world and reforming the world, the process of knowing and practicing opens up being and transforms both oneself and the world, while continuously driving the development and formation of knowledge and wisdom. Human capacities and systems of norms constitute the conditions of possibility of cognition and practice, whose unfolding in turn influences and constrains human capacities and systems of norms by developing wisdom and knowledge. Concretely speaking, presupposing the multifaceted unfolding of the individual's understanding, comprehension, recognition, and practical action, the knowledge and wisdom that takes shape in the process of knowing and practicing gradually integrates into the individual's perspective, thinking tendencies, and inner virtue, and are thereby gradually internalized as human capacities. On the other hand, knowledge and wisdom also take shape as universal systems of ideas and systems of norms through the historical unfolding of practices, and thereby take on a social and public form. By integrating into the process of human cognition and practice and by guiding and influencing human activity both at the level of ideas and at the level of practice, universal knowledge and systems of wisdom acquire normative meaning and externalize as normative systems of different forms.

With the wisdom and knowledge formed through knowing and practicing as their common source, human capacities and systems of norms present their intrinsic unity at their origin. As the internalized form of knowledge and wisdom, human capacities constitute the internal conditions of accomplishing oneself and accomplishing things, whereas by contrast, systems of norms, as the externalization of knowledge and wisdom constitute the external conditions of the same process. As mentioned, the genesis of a world of meaning is the content of accomplishing oneself and accomplishing things, and by correspondence, human capacities and systems of norms constrain the process of generating a world of meaning in different ways.

As the internal conditions of accomplishing oneself and accomplishing things, human capacities endow this process with creativity. With respect to accomplishing oneself (refining oneself), the individual's character is by no means simply designed according to a fixed procedure: the formation of virtue is not a proceduralized process. Developing free character always involves the individual interacting with society. In this process, it is not the case that the individual passively accepts the external mold of society; rather, always and everywhere the individual is expressing autonomous choice, concrete flexibility, a diversity of responses and the like. It is this choice, flexibility, and capacity to respond that reveals the creativity characterizing the process of accomplishing oneself. Similarly, the process of accomplishing things, whose aim is reforming the world, is not entirely the unfolding of a predictable procedure. Whether it is transforming things in-themselves into humanized beings or constructing a world that harmonizes with human nature in the social sphere, the inner creativity of human beings is always at play. Objects in-themselves will not by themselves suit human needs, so transforming things in-themselves into humanized beings is also a process of overcoming the being in-itself of objects by making them become things for-us. Social reality likewise unfolds as a continuous process of moving toward an ideal form, but meanwhile this reforming, as well as the resulting gains and losses made, always involve the creative activity of human being. This creativity of accomplishing oneself and accomplishing things undoubtedly involves multiple facets, among which human capacities constitute one, as the internal conditions of this creativity: as stated previously, the degree to which human being has refined itself and reformed the world marks the depth and breadth to which human being's knowing and practicing has reached, which in turn corresponds to the degree of development of human capacities.

However, even though accomplishing oneself and accomplishing things is not limited to external procedures, aspects of form are still involved. One of the meanings of human being refining itself is moving toward the ideal form of human character, which concerns both the goal of character development (what to become) and the way in which it is be accomplished (how to become it). From establishing the goal to seeking out a way to realize that goal, there is no way to ignore aspects of form and procedure. While advocating that one must accomplish oneself, Confucianism repeatedly demanded that one ought to "take one's stand in ritual propriety" (*li yu li* 立于礼).[38] Here, the aim of taking one's stand is to accomplish oneself, but not without ritual propriety, which refers to formal prescriptions and demands. The connection between accomplishing oneself (taking one's stand) and ritual propriety shows the relation between form, procedure, and the process of accomplishing oneself. As opposed to establishing oneself, the process of accomplishing things unfolds as a practical activity, but the rationality and effectiveness of practical action is also inseparably bound to formal prescriptions and procedure. In the case of reforming nature, there are always technical procedures involved, from working and producing to undertaking scientific research. Similarly, activities in the social domain—political, legal, and moral—also need to accord with different forms of procedure. Modern society tends to use the rule of law to overcome the rule of man, and the rule of law is immersed in procedural demands. This procedural dimension of the process of accomplishing oneself and accomplishing things is first of all tied to systems of norms: it is precisely different forms of norms or rules that qualify the process of knowing and practicing as procedural. Although human capacities internally ground the creativity of accomplishing oneself and accomplishing things, if they, as the intrinsic properties of the individual, were unbounded from the constraint of norms, the process of accomplishing oneself and accomplishing things would never cease to harbor the possibility of becoming subjective and whimsical. Accomplishing oneself and accomplishing things demands that the creative tendencies of human capacities overcome the restrictions placed upon them by formalization and routinization, but also demands that one conquer the arbitrariness and subjectivity that human capacities may harbor with the guidance and direction of norms. So, from a broader perspective, the mutual constraining of human capacities and systems of norms undoubtedly protects the possibility of accomplishing oneself and accomplishing things.

Now, creativity is inseparable from individuality. Whether it is the goal or the concrete process one has in mind, in both cases the process of accomplishing oneself and accomplishing things is characterized as a process of individualization and diversification. What human development aspires to accomplish is by no means a world of uniformity where everyone has the same personality, and similarly, there is no single model for the humanization of Nature into social reality. As human capacities make accomplishing oneself and accomplishing things a creative process, they also condition the unfolding of the individualization of knowledge and practice. On the other hand, however, there is also a universal dimension to the process of accomplishing oneself and accomplishing things in connection with procedural serialization. The common aim of ideal human character is the movement toward the realm of freedom, and so the goal of humanized reality is bringing nature into harmony with human need and into a shape that befits human nature. Even though the implications of accomplishing oneself and accomplishing things may be quite particular in correspondence with different stages of social development, from the perspective of the historical direction of social evolution, this ideal goal is unquestionably present in all the different forms of accomplishment and thereby constitutes the universal tendency of accomplishing oneself and accomplishing things. This universal dimension of accomplishing oneself and accomplishing things is obviously linked to the universality of systems of norms in an intrinsic way. In the historical process of cognitive and practical development, norms that embody universal ideals always involve a rather constant viewpoint upon the being of the world and the being of humans; such a viewpoint is linked to a universal principle of values and a universal orientation of values, and so as a whole determines the goal and direction of accomplishing oneself and accomplishing things. At the same time, norms are also general rules for action, rules that guide in a stable way the actions correlated with each situation; such stability in guidance protects the universality of cognitive and practical norms. Whereas human capacities give individuality and diversity to the process of accomplishing oneself and accomplishing things so that the tendency toward uniformity may be overcome, systems of norms give this process universal guidance through a supply of value-oriented ideals and principles, along with behavioral rules, thereby helping it to ward off the degenerating whim of randomness and relativity.

Accomplishing oneself and accomplishing things, whose agent is human being, is directed at human being and the human world. As the internal properties of human being, human capacities also constitute the real efficient cause behind the unfolding of the process of accomplishing oneself and accomplishing things. If the process of refining oneself were to be divorced from the actual employment of human capacities, it would stop at the ideal level; similarly, the world only unfolds as an actual process of reform when it enters the actual sphere of employment of human capacities. Furthermore, prior to integrating with human capacities, systems of norms remain abstract, that is, the only possible way for norms to come into possession of actual life is through the actual employment of human capacities. From this perspective, human capacities are precisely what make the process of accomplishing oneself and accomplishing things real and actual. On the other hand, however, the efficient cause can never be entirely separated from the formal cause. Therefore, human capacities are indeed the real efficient cause of the process of accomplishing oneself and accomplishing things, but their actualization is always constrained by systems of norms, whose guidance over cognition and practice constrains the manner of employment of human capacities on the formal level. In brief, divorced from human capacities, systems of norms degrade into abstractions, and likewise, unconstrained by systems of norms, human capacities run the risk of going blind. So, human capacities give the process of accomplishing oneself and accomplishing things actual properties from the inside, while systems of norms give it self-awareness from the outside.

To reiterate the argument of this book, accomplishing oneself and accomplishing things is the generative process of producing meaning, which first concerns the realm of ideas. In the world of ideas, the genesis of meaning is rooted in human capacities and is tied to a variety of systems of norms. The formation of knowledge, for instance, is based on the interaction between human being and object, whose concrete unfolding is inseparable from human capacities and systems of norms. From perceiving to thinking, from imagining to experiencing, and from intuiting to deducing, human capacities can be seen at work in each phase of the genesis of knowledge. On the other hand, for knowledge to be a meaningful system, it must be constrained by different norms. A perception needs to abide by the principle of the objectivity of observation, a thought may not disobey the rules of logic, and so on. Though imagination should not stick to what is fixed and settled, it must still stay grounded in the determination of possible worlds (it cannot involve logical contradictions). Moreover, as Jin Yuelin demonstrated, the concepts and categories connected to systems of knowledge also have the dual function of being both descriptive and prescriptive, and the so-called prescriptive function of concepts involves guiding and restraining cognition. While human capacities make the formation of knowledge creative and actual, the systems of norms constituted out of logic and concepts ground the universal validity of such formations of meaning.

The reciprocal interaction between human capacities and systems of norms can likewise be seen in a world of meaning infused with senses of value. When considering the process of accomplishing oneself, what must first be taken into account is the meaning that emerges in the form of a spiritual world. As discussed later, in the process of cognizing, the world first emerges as an understandable world-picture; through evaluating, the world shows human being what significances of value are there for human being. Proceeding from the being of the world to one's own being, questioning the meaning of objects leads one further into a concern for the meaning of one's own being, connected to which are different worlds of spirit or states of mind. As a manifestation of the refinement of one's own being at the level of ideas, a state of mind not only springs internally from the creative employment of human capacities, it is also inseparably bound to the guidance and constraint of systems of norms such as ideals and principles of evaluation. Whether human being is transforming facts into significances of value or forming a consciousness of an ideal and becoming conscious of a mission, human being remains rooted in human capacities and dependent on universal principles of evaluation.

Turning from meaning in the form of ideas toward the actualized form of meaning involves humanizing reality in the broad sense. Presupposing that human beings transform things in-themselves into things for-us, a world of meaning in actualized form is linked more directly to the process of accomplishing things (refining the world). The movement from being in-itself toward humanized being involves multiple facets, including grasping reality, necessity, and actual possibilities; the forming of ends and ideals; the making of plans and blueprints, and so on. Furthermore, the genesis of a world of meaning at this level is always inseparably bound to practice: transforming things in-themselves into humanized beings presupposes the historical unfolding of practice. This process of generating a world of meaning involves the reciprocal interaction of human capacities with systems of norms from the very beginning. Grasping reality, necessity, and actual possibilities involves knowing, which is internally conditioned by human capacities, but which can never come about without the constraint of cognitive and logical norms; on the foundation of first having a grasp of reality, necessity, and actual possibilities, one integrates the ends that one values into a whole and thereby forms the blueprint of an ideal, which also involves the creative employment of human capacities and the guidance of principles; the unfolding of practice must therefore be rooted in practical wisdom that expresses human capacities, but must also follow concrete rules and procedures for action. This interaction of human capacities with systems of norms also develops in the process of generating social reality. As the actual form of a world of meaning, the formation of social reality (including various kinds of institutions) is likewise conditioned by human capacities and universal norms. From social institutions to a system of civilization, the emergence and development of social reality is always immersed in the actualization of human capacities and the functioning of universal norms.

Aiming at the genesis of a world of meaning, the process of accomplishing oneself and accomplishing things is at once internally grounded in human capacities and also rooted externally in universal norms. As the conditions of possibility of accomplishing oneself and accomplishing things, human capacities and universal norms are intrinsically interconnected. Severed from human capacities, systems of norms are doomed to abstraction and formalization and drained of actual vitality; unguided by systems of norms, human capacity as a whole would be doomed to the whim of arbitrariness and random chance, and would quite possibly due to this lose consciousness of itself. It is precisely through the interaction of human capacities with systems of norms that the process of accomplishing oneself and accomplishing things brings about the union of creativity, individuality, actuality, procedurality, universality, and self-consciousness, the union of which concretely ensures the genesis of a world of meaning.

4 Meaning in the World of Spirit

Conditioned by the interrelation of human capacities with systems of norms, accomplishing oneself and accomplishing things constitutes human being's basic way of being and mode of being. In the historical unfolding of accomplishing oneself and accomplishing things, the presentation of things and the directionality of intentions reciprocally interact; the world enters the realm of ideas through this interaction and henceforth becomes being with meaning. As noted earlier, the problem of meaning does not occur to the world in-itself; rather, the source of meaning lies in the historical process of one coming to know the world and oneself while transforming both oneself and the world. Originating from the being of humans and the being of the world, meaning is within and unfolds within humanized reality, but also emerges in the form of ideas. The former (humanizing reality) means that humans transform "Nature in-itself" into "Nature for-humans" through practical action, by means of which the world in-itself becomes being, which is impressed with the mark of human, and which embodies the ideal of human values. The latter (meaning in the form of ideas) is not only being that is known or understood, insofar as it also unfolds into different forms of the world of spirit in the process of being evaluated and being invested with senses of value.

World-Picture: Understanding and Meaning

As far as the form of ideas is concerned, a world of meaning first shows the understandability of being. As objects of cognition and understanding, things in the realm of ideas differ from chaotic and contradictory things without understandability; they are, rather, beings with meaning. Here, in opposition to meaningless absurdity, the meaningfulness of being is first of all the understandable and comprehensible nature of being.

With understandability, a world of meaning first emerges in the form of common sense. In broad terms, common sense could be seen as the various ideas and beliefs that take shape through common everyday activities; such ideas and beliefs gradually accumulated and took shape over the course of hundreds of thousands of years of human history, and they were passed down from one generation to the next. The ideas or beliefs constituting common sense consist of human being's understanding of the world and the being of humans, but this kind of understanding is not established through theoretical argumentation or reflection; it establishes itself rather in the form of being accepted spontaneously as self-evident without undergoing any proof, and its acceptance usually presupposes social influences and the practices of everyday life. The distinction between common sense and uncommon sense is relative. In the case of the relationship between the earth and the sun, ideas like "the sun rises in the east" and "the earth doesn't revolve, the sun does" were common sense for a rather long historical period, and moreover, even up to the present moment, these ideas still have meaning as common sense in the domain of everyday life. However, in today's world, that "the earth revolves around the sun and rotates on its own axis" and that "the sun's rising and setting is actually due to the earth rotating around its own axis" has also become a matter of common sense among human beings with at least a middle school degree of education. Although this latter kind of common sense includes astronomical knowledge, as a popular idea, it does not require any argument or reflection; it is rather a common belief that is universally accepted by certain groups of people.

As a system of ideas, common sense involves a grasp and understanding of the world. In the form of common beliefs, common sense enfolds the world into an ordered framework, making it capable of being understood and accepted by human beings, which henceforth provides a basis for the unfolding of everyday life. In the horizon of common sense, the world is not a fictional being or an illusion; rather, it presents reality. Philosophical speculations may understand the world as a construction of the mind, but common sense still firmly believes without a doubt in the reality of the various objects it faces in the living world; everyday life practices, including everything from eating, drinking, and communicating to waking up and going to sleep, are all based on these beliefs. Things not only actually exist in the living world, they are also connected to each other in different ways, and for common sense, these connections between things are of a fixed and constant nature. In terms of temporal relations, the different things existing in the past, present, and future always emerge in consecutive order; nothing can ever emerge counter to this order of succession. In terms of the growth of things, planting a melon will not yield a bean, and planting a bean will never yield a melon. Such a determinate belief in the fixed constancy of connections between things constitutes a condition of the very possibility of everyday life and labor.

We can see that in the world of common sense, in spite of the infinite variety and ceaseless transformation of objects and things, there is still the structure of succession between them. To a degree, the distinctive feature of common sense consists in arranging things in an order of succession so that the intangibility of the world and the estrangement of human being from the world can be overcome, enabling a routine form of regular life practices to become possible. This orderliness of succession that common sense reveals makes the world understandable and endows it with intrinsic meaning. Consisting of perceptions, understandings, and identifications of the world, the world of common sense simultaneously appears as the world in the eyes of human being or the world for everyday consciousness. Here, common sense shows a world of meaning in the form of ideas.

Opposed to common sense is science. As is widely known, science has reached a relative maturity in the modern era. As a way of grasping the world, the distinctive feature of modern science lies in its emphasis on mathematical methods and empirical means. To experiment in general is to observe an object under a set of ideal conditions of human selection or arrangement, and to use experiments as a means of research entails grasping the world with idealized means; idealized means always bring to light some aspects of a thing while suspending or ignoring others, which thereby reveals a different world-picture. As for its goal, modern science aims at grasping the world in a mathematical way. As the very complement of the tendency to idealize, which experimental means entail, mathematization has gradually become the objective that science pursues; whether or not an understanding of the world can be summarized in mathematical terms has become the very standard of judgment for whether or not such an understanding is scientific in the strict sense. The mathematized understanding of the world in a sense started with Galileo. As Husserl states: "Through Galileo's *mathematization of nature, nature itself* is idealized under the guidance of the new mathematics; nature itself becomes—to express it in a modern way—a mathematical manifold [Mannigfaltigkeit]."[1] To mathematize nature means to grasp nature with greater exactitude in terms of quantitative relations and formal structures, which endows the scientific world-picture with another distinctive characteristic.

In contrast to the world in the view of common sense, the scientific view undoubtedly presents a different kind of meaning. As ideas spontaneously accepted and recognized by certain social groups of certain historical periods, common sense grasps the world in a predominantly non-reflective way. In the realm of common sense, the orderly succession and understandability of the world is first based on the repetitive cycles and routine nature of everyday life: Having taken in and arranged the world by means of everyday beliefs presupposes the orderliness and regularity of things themselves and their relation to one another in everyday life practices (it is not without reason and therefore incalculable); the non-irregularity of the world (like the sun rising at dawn and setting at dusk) and the routine nature of everyday life practices (like working when the sun is out and resting after the sun sets) are one and the same thing. Science's understanding of the world differs from a simple and direct perception of phenomenon by virtue of presenting the means of experimental verification and theoretical argumentation. Science also reveals a world order distinct from that regularity and routine found in everyday experience; rather, it is a framework whose demonstration makes use of theory and logic. Through mathematical models and structures of mathematical symbols, the order of the world gains a unique form of expression in the scientific view as it is verified with rational arguments, mathematical operators, and the like.

As a picture of the world shaped through such means as idealization and mathematization, science is undoubtedly abstract; in contrast to common sense, such a world-picture is already distantly detached from the concreteness of sensibility to a considerable degree. However, in the framework of scientific concepts, mathematical models, and the like, science also reveals the order of the world at a more profound, intrinsic level. Although the scientific picture of the world differs from the concrete sensible world, it endows the world with an understandable form and makes it reveal a specific meaning at the cognitive level by illuminating the properties and necessary laws intrinsic to things. Similar to the form of being presented through the horizon of common sense, the scientific view also presents a world of human understanding or a world that has entered the human sphere of ideas. Even though both pictures of the world refer of course to the same objects at the ontological level, the world as it is understood through common sense and the world as it is grasped by scientific means present different kinds of meaning to human being at the epistemological level: as worlds of meaning differing in form, the cognitive content contained in the world of common sense and that provided by the scientific world differ both in breadth and depth.

While the scientific view of the world generally refers to objects in the empirical realm, the metaphysical view of the world has its own focus. In contrast to science's way of grasping the world by means of empirical verification, the metaphysical horizon takes a more speculative approach. However, in terms of understanding the world as an ordered system, there also seem to be zones of consistency between them.

Differing from the scientific picture of the world, the metaphysical horizon does not focus on particular domains or specific objects; it is concerned rather with being itself or the world as a whole. Does being as a whole have one origin? By tracing the world back to its basic constitution or by determining the origin of being, whether the source of all things is thought to be water or atoms as it was in the West, or whether it is thought to be the five phases (*wuxing* 五行) of *qi* as it was in the East, the metaphysical horizon enfolds the world into a unified system through perspectives of a different focus. When water, atoms, or *qi* is thought of as the ultimate constitution or origin of being, all things come into possession of an attribute that unifies them, and the links between them cease to be a confusing mess that confounds all attempts at understanding. *The Book of Changes* assures that it "simulates the heavens and the earth and that is why it can encapsulate the natural way of change (*dao* 道) of the heavens and the earth." To encapsulate the natural way of change of the heavens and the earth means to grasp the world as a whole, whose precondition is thinking of the world itself as a being of immanent unity.

Linked to the origin of being is the way of being, which concerns how the world exists. When discussing the connection between all things, *Zhongyong* (Doctrine of Mean) mentions the following concept: "All things nourish each other (*bingyu* 并育) and do not harm one another, their paths are parallel and do not conflict." Everything in the world co-exists, despite the lack of identity between them; they tolerate one another and develop forms of being that are mutually consistent, rather than mutually exclusive. For those philosophers who propounded the theory of *qi* monism, such a beneficial and consistent relationship between things is thought of as occurring due to the immanent principle contained in the transformative movement of *qi*: "Although the *qi* of the heavens and the earth is condensing and dissolving, aggressing and accepting in its innumerable ways, its principles are reasonable and not absurd."[2] All things arise from *qi*, The congealing and dissolving of which follows necessary principles; such a process reveals "the order of Nature" (*tianxu* 天序 or *tianzhi* 天秩) of everything that is happening and co-existing: "In generative growth there is preceding and succeeding, so there is *tianxu*;[3] the big and small, high and low abut up next to one another and shape one another, so there is *tianzhi*. There is order (*tianxu*) in Nature's generation of things, just as there is order (*tianzhi*) in the generated form of things."[4] In the form of *tianzhi* and *tianxu*, the being of things overcomes chaos and becomes understandable. In contrast to the picture of the world that a unified origin would provide, the formation of being expressed through the order of Nature seems to show the metaphysical meaning of the world in a more immanent way.

While seeking transcendence, religions also try to render the world into an ordered system, and so constitute metaphysical perspectives in the broad sense. For instance, although Buddhism does not accept the reality of the actual world, it still attempts to give order to the world under the premise that it is accepted as the state of suchness in contradistinction to the state of illusion. When discussing the phenomenal world (*se* 色), *The Awakening of Faith in the Mahayana* states: "There is no differentiation or sameness in the manifested phenomena of suchness, which can manifest itself freely in the ten quarters of the universe as an infinite number of Bodhisattvas, an infinite number of Buddhas of enjoyment-body, and infinite sublimities, but each variation is neither different from nor the same as the others, so they do not interfere with one another. But to become aware of this is beyond the capacity of the deluded mind who thinks it knows things by consciously separating them, for the reason that these [manifestations] are the effect of suchness freely being in-itself."[5] The things populating the phenomenal world are multitudinous and manifold, but whether they are different or identical, they are mutually co-existing (without interfering with one another) within the horizon of suchness. Hua Yan (Flower Garland) Buddhism's doctrine of "a world without mutual obstruction between phenomena" further summarizes this relationship of mutual non-interference. Leaving aside their presupposition of a distinction between true and false worlds, their understanding of the world undoubtedly shares something in common with the philosophical view that "all things nourish each other and do not harm one another, their paths are complementary and do not conflict."

Similar to the world-pictures confirmed by common sense and science respectively, being as it is revealed through the metaphysical horizon is not the same as the form of being as it is originally in-itself; it is rather being as it is understood or being in the realm of ideas. While explaining the perspective of true emptiness, Fa Zang, the great proponent of Hua Yan Buddhism in China, once remarked: "The external world emerges from the mind (*you xin xian jing* 由心现境), the mind emerges from the external world (*you jing xian xin* 由境现心), but the mind does not enter the [external] world and the [external] world does not enter the mind. Continuously attaining this perspective, wisdom deepens in profundity, and so it is called the perspective of true emptiness absorbing the world in returning to the mind."[6] The perspective of true emptiness expresses Hua Yan Buddhism's understanding of being. Such an understanding affirms a world-picture that is primarily that of the mind, thereby differing from a factual world. When he states that "the mind does not enter the [external] world and the [external] world does not enter the mind," he emphasizes that the world in the realm of ideas is not actually within the external world, and similarly that the external world does not directly enter the realm of ideas. Of course, Hua Yan Buddhism's perspective of true emptiness does not go beyond the position that the world is created and destroyed with the mind, but it undoubtedly shows that the world-picture found within the metaphysical horizon is primarily characterized by ideas. By explaining the world and apprehending objects through such concepts as "the order of Nature" and "a world without mutual obstruction between phenomena," metaphysical horizons endow being with understandability and show the meaning of the world at the level of ideas.

The world-pictures belonging to the horizons of common sense, science, and metaphysics respectively express human being's understanding of the multiple dimensions of being and reveal different facets of the not unreasonable order that being follows. As stated previously, understandability and order enable the world to become being with meaning, but the meaning of the being of things will differ in correspondence with the differences between the world-pictures presenting it. Taking water for example, according to the world-picture of common sense, water is primarily seen as a transparent, colorless liquid that humans may use for drinking, for the purposes of irrigation, and so on. But according to the scientific picture of the world, water is understood as a form of being constituted out of the bonding of two hydrogen atoms and one oxygen atom; furthermore, from the metaphysical perspective, water could be determined as the origin (Thales) or one of the origins (one of the five elements) of all things. We can see that the same object (water) presents different meanings through different pictures of the world. This difference in meaning reveals the different relationships that pictures of the world formed out of ideas may have with actual beings, while displaying the different forms and dimensions through which human being may grasp the world.

From the perspective of common sense to that of science and metaphysics, as being from the perspective of human understanding, world-pictures involve the relationship between consciousness and conceptual form. The world presented in the form of ideas could also be seen as the world of spirit, whose being is inseparable from the consciousness and mental processes of humans. But at the same time, the formation of world-pictures is always accompanied by an ordering of the world through different conceptual forms. The common sense view that the sun moves while the earth stays still, that the sun rises in the east and goes down in the west not only uses such concepts as "the sun" and "the earth," it also implies a determination of the relationship between the sun and the earth with such concepts as "to move" and "to be still." The scientific world-picture more specifically presents an ordering of the multitude of things and events found within the empirical realm with the use of physical and mathematical concepts. Metaphysical horizons, in turn, adopt a speculative system of concepts as a way to understand being, and their pictures of the world are thus founded upon such conceptual systems. In the process of shaping a picture of the world, concepts become an actual form of understanding the world by integrating with conscious activity, and the latter simultaneously overcomes simple psychological affections and sensations through the usage of concepts. So, the integration of concepts with conscious activity informs pictures of the world with ideas, and simultaneously differentiates world-pictures from the individual's ideas by giving them universal meaning. Now, the substance out of which the formation of a world-picture occurs is the affective mind: On the one hand, a world-picture, as being as it is understood, is not a physical object; it is rather a world that exists in the mental domain in the form of ideas. On the other, a world-picture takes shape through such mental acts as understanding, integrating, and determining being. When explaining Zhang Zai's proposition that "by enlarging one's affective mind, one can become the substance of the things in the world," Wang Fuzhi remarked: "Everything in the world is all function, while the principles of my affective mind are their substance (*wu xin zhi li qi ti ye* 吾心之理其体也); if one fully exerts the affective mind to the limit (*jin xin* 尽心) in order to follow these principles without disobeying them, then substance establishes itself and naturally functions in an infinite way."[7] To make the affective mind "become the substance" of everything in the world is precisely to grasp everything through conscious activity; in this way, "everything in the world" does not refer to physical beings in the original sense of beings in-themselves; it refers rather to things as they are grasped by ideas or things as they are experienced by the substance of the affective mind. Here, "the principles of my affective mind" could be seen as a conceptual system or conceptual knowledge internalized into consciousness, which goes on to constitute the ground upon which the substance of the affective mind experiences things. As for things as they are grasped by ideas, the affective mind evidently constitutes their "substance," for without the affective mind as the substance of things, things would neither have a way to enter the realm of ideas nor to acquire the form of being that ideas have. This understanding of the affective mind as substance, and of the thing as function, shows the role of "the affective mind" consisting of "principles" in the formation of a picture of the world. As for its actuality, consciousness as well as its active connection with conceptual systems constitutes the internal ground of possibility of a world of meaning in the form of ideas.

The substance of a world-picture is the affective mind, which doesn't mean that pictures of the world exist merely in the private domain or psychological world of the individual. As being in the form of ideas, world-pictures possess meaning, which is indeed relative to human being, and moreover, in correspondence with the different ways of grasping the world, that is, via common sense, science or metaphysics, the meaning of a world-picture also appears differently to different individuals; that said, these meanings certainly bear no similarity to the alleged meaning of a so-called private language, which would reside solely within the consciousness of a particular individual.[8] The meaning of a world-picture has an actual form of existence, which not only presupposes the understandability of the world, but also the inter-subjective understandability of meaning itself, which is grounded in the union of "the affective mind" and "principle." As explained previously, "the affective mind" as the "substance" of a world of meaning does not refer simply to individual ideas, for by virtue of fusing together with a system of concepts, it contains principles that are universal. Here, principles involve the universality of logic at the level of form and the universal attributes of being at the level of content; both in different senses make the inter-subjective understandability of world-pictures possible.

The inter-subjective understandability of world-pictures also reveals the openness of the latter. This openness then in a much broader sense reveals the interconnectivity between world-pictures. Considering their concrete form, those different world-pictures mentioned previously actually envelop different senses, but this does not mean that those views are entirely unrelated or that there are unbridgeable gaps between them. In fact, even though different world-pictures express different relationships of human being to reality, in terms of their origin, they are rooted in the same world: in the historical process of accomplishing the self and accomplishing things, what human being faces is the same actual world that has transcended the form of being in-itself; "actual" here at once refers to reality and the overcoming of original being in-itself. With the affective mind as the substance of world-pictures, the latter develop and take shape as the different ways human being grasps the world. However, as we have already analyzed, as the internal "substance" that shapes world-pictures, the affective mind contains universal principles (including conceptual content and logical form) by virtue of fusing together with systems of concepts; this universal dimension of ideas simultaneously makes possible the communication between different systems of ideas. While having the same actual world as an origin provides the ontological ground for the interconnection between different world-pictures, the universal principles contained in ideas (the affective mind) intrinsically protects their interconnection as ways of grasping the world.

The Domain of Values

A world-picture reveals human being's understanding of being. Through different world-pictures, being is presented in meaningful forms in the event of understanding. In terms of ways of grasping the world, the meanings presented through world-pictures are first linked to the question "What is it?" Although world-pictures envelop many aspects of meaning, as human being's understanding of being, they are what the world presents to human being from different perspectives, and so most immediately correspond to the question "What is it?" In effect, what human being understands the world to be is precisely to say, from another perspective, "what" the world "is" from human being's perspective. But interconnected to the question "What is it?" is "What does it mean?" which directs a world of meaning in the form of ideas into the domain of values.

Directed at understanding, the question "What is it?" is primarily linked to cognition; relative to this, the question "What does it mean?" primarily concerns evaluation, which is specifically directed at what relationship of value there is between human being and beings. As for its actual form, a world of meaning is not just the form of being of that which human being understands; it also has the meaning of confirming the relationship of value that stands between human being and this form of being. While explaining the meaning of the term *jue* [awareness—trans.], Fa Zang put forward the following interpretation in his commentary on *The Huayan Sutra*: There are two kinds of *jue*, one is awareness as enlightenment (*juewu* 觉悟), which refers to non-discriminating wisdom (*lizhi* 理智) illuminating truth; the second is awareness as observing, which refers to discriminating wisdom (*liangzhi* 良知) observing conventional phenomena. The term "*jue*" here first expresses a form of consciousness in the context of Buddhism. However, we also see a general view upon a world of meaning already infused in it: so-called awareness as observation focuses more on the aspect of understanding the world, whereas awareness as enlightenment refers more to an instantaneous comprehension and realization at the level of values. Suspending the horizon and standpoint of Buddhism pervading it, as the dual meaning of the form of consciousness (*jue*), this union of awareness as observation and awareness as enlightenment reflects the interconnection between the questions "What is it?" and "What does it mean?" in a world of meaning.

Wang Fuzhi deals with this issue from another perspective. While analyzing and defining the affective mind (*xin* 心), he remarks:

> We must say that only the affective mind-set of being humane and righteous can be the conscience. If we only say "affective mind," then it is only awareness of things and affairs; it must be humane and righteous for it to be conscientious. For the affective mind to be virtuous, it must simply be empty, aware and not confused so as to be the bearer of all principles and the responder to all affairs, but as such it is merely not wicked and only capable of corresponding to the good, while not necessarily being good as such. One must cultivate one's moral tendencies in order for the affective mind to maintain and ensure that the principle of what is humane and righteous is not lost.[9]

Here, Wang Fuzhi distinguishes between two forms of the affective mind, that is, the affective mind-set of being humane and righteous and the affective mind of awareness: the affective mind-set of being humane and righteous shows an axiological orientation or conception of value that contains "the principle of the ultimate good."[10] Awareness is then the capacity to know and understand, but simply grounded in the affective mind of awareness, although one may still be able to grasp principles and cope with affairs, one still has no way of making the affective mind ensure the development of what is good at the level of values. This is to say that the world of spirit can only acquire senses of value when it is also grounded in the affective mind-set of being humane and righteous. Wang Fuzhi's opinion undoubtedly takes notice of the link between a world of meaning and consciousness of values, and in some sense, it could also be seen as an extension of the theory of the affective mind as fundamental substance and of the world of spirit (the things that have entered the realm of ideas) as function.

To reiterate, a world of meaning has senses of value, which are inseparably tied to evaluating. Values express the relations things have to human needs, ideals, and ends, and such relations are concretely determined and confirmed in the act of evaluating. In the process of cognizing, the world presents itself as an understandable scene, and in the process of evaluating, the world shows what is of significant value for human being. So, a world of meaning at the level of values could also be seen as the world of valuable interest or a world-picture invested with senses of value.

At the theoretical level, though the questions "What is it?" and "What does it mean?" differ in terms of content, they both concern a being that differs from a form of being in-itself. When one poses such questions, the being one places oneself within or faces is already humanized. Humanized being is also concrete being, and one of the meanings of this concreteness goes as follows: the object does not only contain those properties and qualities concerned with the question "What is it?" but also the properties investigated by the question "What does it mean?" A pure fact does not include all of the properties of the thing: it leaves out the multitude of relationships in which the thing is involved as well as the multitude of properties these relationships invest in the thing, and so remains abstract. In the form of humanized being, things are not only identical to themselves, they are also related to human being, and so contain different meanings for human being. As for the relationship of the thing to human needs, this relationship and its meaning are characterized by possessing a value, which is not an external or subjective addition: as the determination of humanized being, relationships of value and properties of value are both actual. In actual being, factual properties are inseparable from properties of value; the true and concrete nature of things themselves consists in the union of the two.[11] This union of facts and values also constitutes the ontological ground of the interconnectedness of world-pictures both at the level of cognition and at the level of evaluation in the world of valuable interest.

There are different cases of evaluation confirming a relationship of value. When the thing's properties already fulfill human needs or when the identity between the thing's properties and human needs already becomes apparent at the practical level, evaluation unfolds as a real affirmation of this relationship of value or properties of value; when the thing's properties merely *could* suit human needs or when the thing's properties are only potentially of value, then evaluation confirms this value in the form of an expectation. Before the thing is evaluated, the possible properties of value that a thing may contain are only the properties of the thing in-itself. It is precisely through the act of evaluating that such properties are finally confirmed as properties with value. In this act of evaluating, forming a consciousness of values and investing a world of meaning with values constitute two sides of the same process. Therefore, a world-picture, as being that is understood, presents things in the form of ideas, but a world of meaning, which human being forms in the act of evaluating and investing things with value presents things in the form of ideas as well.

With the aim of confirming the value of some thing, evaluation is first rooted in the relationship between the thing and human being's needs, and among the variety of human being's needs, the need to survive is the most fundamental:

". . . mankind must first of all eat, drink, have shelter and clothing, before it can pursue politics, science, art, religion, etc."[12] In other words, satisfying the needs of survival is the precondition of satisfying other needs, and what is of significant value emerges in correlation with this precondition. As far as the natural objects of the world-pictures pertaining to cognition and understanding go, as things, they first present the different meanings corresponding to the question "What is it?" but starting with the relationship of value between object and human being, the thing presents meaning in correlation with the question "What does it mean?" When defining water, fire, and other such things, *the shangshu* states: "Water and fire are what the people need to drink and eat; metal and wood are what the people need to stimulate productivity; earth is the resource which nourishes the lives of all things. These are for human use." Here, the expression "for human use" mainly emphasizes the meaning that things like water and fire have for human survival, while eating and drinking, stimulating productivity, nourishing the lives of all things, and the like are different expressions of this "use." Taking water as an example, as opposed to understanding the meaning of water through its molecular structure (H_2O), water in the aforementioned case is defined from the perspective of needing to eat and drink, which invests the meaning of water with a sense of value. Broadly speaking, when people affirm the meaning that minerals and forests have for human beings, the meaning here is likewise grounded in such a relationship of value.

Of course, the confirmation that the act of evaluating gives to a relationship of value happens mainly at the level of ideas: in the act of evaluating, the senses of value that beings have are presented at the level of ideas. From the realization of such ideas to their actual verification, the meaning of values is always inseparable from living practice and work. The meaning water and fire have for human thirst and human appetite, for instance, can only be actualized through such activities as using water to steam rice and using fire to cook food; the "use" of minerals for human beings can only be actualized through mining, smelting, and other forms of labor. So, the realization of the meaning of values at the level of ideas is different from the actualization of this meaning at the level of practice, which reveals the difference between the ideal form and the actual form of a world of meaning.

The meaning of values at the level of ideas is rooted in the needs of human being, but is also based on the ends, ideals, and values of human being as well. What kind of value a thing will present to human being remains inseparably bound to what kind of ends, ideals, and axiological principles human being finds worthy to accept. Taking social reality for example, evaluations of its reform and transformation always correspond to the values that humans uphold. In the last years of the Spring and Autumn period (*chunqiu* 春秋) in China, society underwent intense vicissitudes, and in the eyes of the main thinker of this time, Confucius, this transformation first of all meant "the collapse of ritual propriety and the fall of literate culture," that is, it presented a negative meaning and a destructive value. The evaluation Confucius makes of social transformation here is founded upon his affirmation and appraisal of the system of rites and ritual, which shows his ideal of value and valuing orientation. The reason the social transformation of the Spring and Autumn period presented such a negative meaning to Confucius as representing "the collapse of ritual propriety and the fall of literate culture" lies in the conflict it engendered with the valuing orientation he upheld (in protecting the ritual system). Here, the meaning that being presents to humans is consistent with the values humans uphold.

The connection just noted between the meaning of being and human being's consciousness of value is demonstrated much more concretely in the domain of ethics. As the very being of the social sphere, the relationships between moral subjects are first of all actual ethical relationships. As a social relationship, an actual ethical relationship transcends individual consciousness. However, whether the ethical nature of such a relationship or of the subjects involved is or is not confirmed depends entirely on the existence or non-existence of moral consciousness. When discussing the relationship between intentions and things, Wang Yangming states this:

> What issues from the affective mind is intention (*yi* 意). The fundamental substance of intention is cognizance (*zhi* 知), and wherever intention is directed is a thing. For example, when intention is directed at serving one's parents, then serving one's parents is a "thing." When intention is directed at serving one's ruler, then serving one's ruler is a "thing." When intention is directed at being-humane to all people and feeling love toward things, then being-humane to all people and feeling love toward things are "things," and likewise, when intention is directed toward seeing, hearing, speaking, and acting, then each of these is a "thing."[13]

As that which "emanates from the affective mind," "intention" belongs to the individual's inner consciousness. Cognizance (*zhi* 知) for Wang Yangming here refers to conscientiousness (*liangzhi* 良知), which when taken to be the fundamental substance of intention stresses the ethical connotation of "intention." With cognizance as its fundamental substance, intention differs from psychological ideating as a moral consciousness with a sense of values. Moreover, "a thing" here differs from a being in-itself. A being in-itself is always beyond human consciousness (never having entered the sphere of human cognition and practice). A thing, as that at which "intention is directed," has already been affected by consciousness and thus has already entered the sphere of consciousness. That "intention is directed at a thing" is the very process of intention focusing on an object as the object's meaning is presented to human being. For humans who lack a moral and political consciousness, parents, rulers, and people are merely beings in the biological sense. Only when intentions with a sense of morality affect such objects do parents, rulers, and people appear to the subject as parents, rulers, and people in ethical and political relationships, and hence gain ethical and political meaning. By presenting ethical meaning, objects overcome their externality in relation to ethical consciousness and are brought into the realm of ideas, the concrete form of which is a world of meaning. As physical objects, the being of things does not depend on human being's consciousness of values, but as beings in a world of meaning, their presence is inseparably tied to human values. As Wang Yangming points out, for individuals who lack moral consciousness, the relationship between parents and offspring does not have any moral meaning.

A world of meaning emerging in the form of a world-picture first concerns human being's understanding of being: through such a picture, the world is mainly understood as some form of being. By comparison, a world of meaning in the form of values is more closely tied to the life practices of human beings. As a form of ideas infused with senses of value, the ethical world of meaning is intrinsically related to ethical life. To give objects ethical meaning simultaneously means to act upon things in an ethical way. The flip side of this is that an ethical way of practicing or doing stems from an ethical consciousness of values. It is precisely in this sense that Wang Fuzhi insists: "Filial piety is not an affair that could be qualified in simple terms (*wu ke zhi yan zhi shi* 孝无可质言之事), rather what motivates it is solely the affective mind."[14] As a concrete form of moral practice, the practical activity of "filial piety" itself has no fixed model or mechanism; its motivating force comes from the inner mind's recognition of moral meaning. In other words, ethical practice (filial piety) is tied to the ethical mind. When, furthermore, Wang Yangming determines the nature of "intention" he expresses a similar idea from another perspective: "Intention is never suspended in a vacuum (*yi wei you xuan kong de* 意未有悬空的). It is always connected with some thing or affair. Therefore if one wants to make one's intentions sincere, one should rectify it right in the thing or affair at which one's intentions are directed."[15] Here, what is to be rectified (*ge zhi* 各之) refers to the embodied practice of moral action. Intentions focus on objects and thereby give beings in-themselves ethical meaning (parents and offspring in a natural blood bond become objects in the ethical sense). This ethical meaning of objects is then corroborated by moral practices like serving one's parents and respecting one's elders. Here, ethical consciousness fuses together with ethical life. These viewpoints notice from different angles that in the world of value the genesis and formation of a world of meaning is inseparably bound to the practical life embodying this meaning.

The value and meaning found in the ethical realm are concerned more with what is good, and aesthetic activity also pursues what is good, but in a different sense of the value "good." Here, the axiological dimension of a world of meaning is also effectively embodied in aesthetic processes. In another respect, similar to the ethical world, the aesthetic world intrinsically involves the genesis of meaning as well, but in the latter, this concerns the production of works of art and the appreciation of beauty. Whether or not a being presents a sense of beauty and what sense of beauty it presents does not just depend on the physical properties of the object. In reality, what answers such questions may hold depend on one's aesthetic capacity, aesthetic ideals, aesthetic taste, and aesthetic standards. An aesthetic object is not a being in-itself; it only presents a sense of beauty to subjects with an aesthetic capacity and aesthetic consciousness. As Marx aptly remarked: "the most beautiful music has *no* sense for the unmusical ear."[16] Here, the metaphor of the unmusical ear refers to a lack of aesthetic capacity. For those who exist in this condition of being, the genesis of aesthetic meaning is inconceivable. Now, aesthetic capacity is linked to aesthetic consciousness, which opens up a broader horizon. Aesthetic consciousness more specifically constrains the presentation of aesthetic meaning in terms of whether or not things will present aesthetic meaning at all and what kind of aesthetic meaning things can present. In the poem "Birdcalls Echo in the Ravine," Wang Wei writes:

> Man idles, Osmanthus flowers fall,
> The night is still, the spring hills empty.
> The moon comes out, startles the hillside birds,
> Whose calls echo and echo in the spring ravine.

In this poem, Wang Wei mentions several things—flowers, the moon, hills, a ravine. These things could be viewed from different perspectives: one could view the flowers from the perspective of botany; one could look at hills and the ravine from the geological perspective or observe the birds from the zoological perspective. Much simpler still, one could just see these things as the familiar things they are in everyday life. Viewing, looking, and observing through such perspectives, objects mainly present the attributes and properties, which correspond to such perspectives. However, in the eyes of the poet, man idling and the drifting fall of the flowers, the stillness of the night and the emptiness of the hillside, the moon coming out and the startled flight of the birds, the trickling of the ravine and the startled birdcalls all intertwine, constructing a poetic picture that differs both from the scientific view and the scene of everyday life. Here, objects of the scientific and everyday perspectives present a different sort of aesthetic world: the same mountain, moon, flowers, and birds transform into another world of meaning (the poetic world) in the human mind (the world of ideas). As the precondition of this transformation, the aesthetic eye itself is grounded in the inner aesthetic consciousness and aesthetic ideas of the poet.

Rooted in aesthetic consciousness and aesthetic ideas, the genesis of meaning is directly linked to human being's imagination, affects, and experiences. In his "On the Absence of Sentiments in Music," Ji Kang makes a distinction between the sound of music and the sentiments of grief and joy: "Hurrying up and calming down (*caojingzhe* 躁静者) is the work of sound; sorrow and joy is subject to one's emotional state."[17] Sound generates the difference of calming down and hurrying up; an emotional state generates the difference of sorrow and joy. There is no distinction between sorrow and joy in sound itself. That sound may give human being a sense of sorrow or joy springs chiefly from the workings of human being's inner emotional state:

> A sorrowful heart is hiding within, and only emerges after confronting an agreeable sound (*yu he sheng er hou fa* 遇和声而后发); an agreeable sound bears no likeness to it, so the sorrowful heart is the agent (*zhu* 主). So, a heart of sorrow, which has agency, emerges to the level of awareness because of an agreeable sound, which bears no likeness to it—this is only due to sorrow itself.[18]

In brief, music acquiring the meaning of being either sorrowful or joyful is inseparable from one's own emotional experience; emotion attaches to music, and then sorrow or joy emerges. Ji Kang's viewpoint here takes notice of the link between the aesthetic meaning of music on the one hand and the emotional passion and aesthetic experience of human being on the other. Of course, Ji Kang goes too far in believing that "the affective mind and sound are clearly two distinct things,"[19] which without a doubt overemphasizes the division between the affective mind and things. In fact, the genesis of meaning implies the intrinsic unity of the presentation of things and the directionality of the intentional will. So, while affirming the directionality of intentional states, Ji Kang fails to give an adequate account of the presentation of things.

In the aesthetic dimension, humans may construct different aesthetic worlds through varying compositions of scenery and things, by means of meshing scenery and emotional states. In the poem "A Journey in Jiankang after Dismissal from Prefect of Hezhou," Liu Yuxi writes:

> Autumn rivers so clear, and forceless,
> Cold Mountain at dusk, heart sunk in thoughts.
> From official duties unbound, gauging not the journey's length,
> On pilgrimage to every temple built in the age of Southern Dynasties.

As physical phenomena, "clearness" and "force" are two different properties, but they mesh together within the autumn river through the poet's imagination. The clearness and forcelessness of the autumn rivers illustrate the autumn scenery of the river flowing unhurriedly, lagging against the rocks, making one associate this with the idle free time of the official's life, which hints further at the snags and potholes impeding the ascent of the official's career. The cold mountain at dusk gives one a sense of frigid stillness. In contrast to the complicated noise of the bustling human world, the poem provides more of a contemplative space, but the "heart sinking" into the mountain shrouded in dusk intrinsically suggests that this idleness is not true idleness: it shows that here to journey along mountains and autumn rivers is not to recede from the world and forget human affairs. Even though the temples dating back to the Southern Dynasties seem to stand for something far removed from the human world, as a figure for Confucians, the poet is still preoccupied with the idea of benefiting the world. In this aesthetic imagery, humans, things, and scenery are recomposed through the imagination, which constructs a world of meaning that expresses the poet's unique experience and feelings. A similar view could be seen in the following poem by Wang Wei:

> The spring's gush chokes the shaky hold of rock.
> The sun shines through the cold green pines.

The water springing forth against the bank of precariously layered rocks emits a choking bellow; the sun glares through the pine forest, casting a cool hue upon the scene. Springs and rocks themselves are not living, but they are linked to a choking bellow with emotional implications; sunlight originally symbolizes warmth, but here it appears in a cool color with a depressing emotional hue. Through anthropomorphic associations, the lonely silence, the frigid mountains, and one's own thoughts fuse together, by virtue of which the external scenery of water and mountains acquires internal aesthetic meaning.

As forms of meaning infused with values, the aesthetic and the ethical constitute inseparable worlds. The aesthetic form of meaning is not only embodied in the outpouring and expression of the individual's emotion, it also plays a role in other aspects of life. Confucianism found the link between aesthetic activity and "cultivating human being" (the cultivation of ideal character). According to Confucius, "to civilize [human being] through ritual and music" is the way to cultivate human being (chengren 成人).[20] This implies cultivating one's sentiments and one's temperament through aesthetic activity. Confucius stresses very much the role of aesthetic activity in the process of cultivating human being, advocating: "to stimulate [yourself] in the Odes (xing yu shi 兴于诗), take your stand in ritual propriety (li yu li 立于礼), and refine yourself in music (cheng yu yue 成于乐)."[21] That is to say, virtuous character is cultivated through education in ritual propriety and music. Confucius himself, upon hearing the music of Shao, "did not notice the taste of meat for three months,"[22] by which he meant that his spirit had transcended natural desires (the pleasing of the organism through food and drink) and was cathartically purified in the aesthetic realm that the music evoked, thereby heightening the inner strength of his character. Xun Zi also observes the particular role played by artistic aesthetic activity in the process of refining one's character. According to Xun Zi, by correcting behavior, music plays an important role in the process of transforming human nature: "The depth to which music touches the human soul and the celerity with which it transforms human being is profound." "Music is that which the sages enjoy and it is capable of refining the hearts of the people. It [music] affects humans profoundly, its movement changes the spirit and current of society."²³ As a form of art, music can reverberate and resonate in the soul and purify the spirit, and is thereby capable of reforming the moral constitution of human beings. Here, the interest of the beautiful and the intention of the good embody distinct but interrelated worlds of meaning, whose concrete form is the unity or mutual enjoyment of the beautiful and the good.

The pursuit of the good and the beautiful is directed toward ideals based on actuality. Differing somewhat from this pursuit in spiritual tendency is the ultimate concern, which is closely related to the religious domain. Religions presuppose the transcendence of beings such as gods or God and undoubtedly have external forms of expression, as in religious organizations, religious rituals, and religious architecture. However, from the internal perspective, religion is substantially tied to the human world of ideas. When discussing religion in his later years, Kant once stated "religion is conscientiousness." "To have religion, the concept of God is not required."²⁴ Conscientiousness primarily involves the immanent world of the human spirit, whereas God is transcendent in relation to human being. For Kant, only the former constitutes the substance of religion. The actual form of the religious world of spirit also unfolds as a world of meaning possessing senses of value. Affirmatively speaking, religious ideas always imply a yearning and hope for a transcendent realm; negatively speaking, this implies a rejection of the being of reality or the being of the common human world. To this attitude or standpoint correspond the different meanings this world presents: within the religious horizon, the being of reality and the common human world chiefly present negative meaning, while the transcendent realm seems to present a positive, eternal meaning; and it is out of this contrast between the two that religion develops its own world of meaning.

Of course, in some forms of religion, the boundary between this world and the other transcendent world is not so clearly demarcated. Worthy of mention here is Chan Buddhism. As the sinosized form of Buddhism, the Chan tradition does not make a dichotomy between this world and a world beyond. This of course is not to say that Chan Buddhism sees the world to be the same always and everywhere. For Chan Buddhism, the distinction between a Buddha and all living beings lies in the difference between being enlightened (*wu* 悟) and being caught up in an illusion (*mi* 迷): "To hold on to a previous deluded thought (*qian nian mi* 前念迷) makes one ordinary (*fan* 凡), but the next thought if enlightened (*hou nian wu* 后念悟) makes one a Buddha."²⁵ "Hence we know that without enlightenment, a Buddha is no different from other living beings. With enlightenment, even in a single instant of thought, all living beings become the same as a Buddha."²⁶ Consistent with this is the distinction between the being of this world and that of the other world, which requires the enlightenment of the mind [as the substance of the world]. If one realizes that one's mind is Buddha, one can reach the Western Region (Pure Land, Paradise): "If the mind is absolutely pure, the Western

Region is not far away."²⁷ As different forms of the internal world of ideas, "deluded" and "enlightened" express different understandings of the being of humans and the being of the world, and also contain different value orientations; "a Buddha" and "the Western Region" thus express the different meanings that the world presents to the human being after enlightenment. Attaining enlightenment also involves the use of wisdom as its precondition: "Using wisdom to see things, neither holding onto nor rejecting anything, this is the way of realizing human nature and becoming Buddha."²⁸ "Wisdom" here expresses the perspective of Buddhist teachings. In this way, according to Chan Buddhism, the difference between the transcendent realm and actual beings as well as that between this world and the other world is relative to the different perspective of those human beings. By changing the world of ideas, including certain concepts of value, and "using wisdom to see things," human being makes the same being present different meanings: as soon as one has awakened from the deluded state, one can experience oneself as Buddha; as for the mundane world, as soon as it is seen from the perspective of the detached mind, it may appear as the pure land of the West. Here, this transformation of how being is presented in the Buddhist horizon corresponds to a change of values and unfolds substantially as the reconstruction of a world of meaning.

From ethics and aesthetics to religion, a world of meaning is invested with many senses of value. In connection with the active role of a valuing consciousness, the genesis of a world of meaning involves the agent's meaning-giving activity and has as content the presentation of the meaning of objects: the object presenting some kind of meaning to the subject and the subject giving this object meaning is one and the same process. In the ethical domain, an object appearing not simply as an ordinary biological entity but as a being that is given ethical meaning is always inseparable from the subject simultaneously seeing the object as a being that should be treated with ethical principles rather than with biological ideas. There is a similar relationship to be found between the aesthetic object and the aesthetic subject and between the object of belief and the believer. This union of presenting meaning and giving meaning is identical to the fusion of presentation and intention into one.²⁹ Internal consciousness focusing upon things makes the presentation of the thing's meaning become possible, while the presence of the thing enables intentional activity to gain actual content. The union of the presenting of meaning and the giving of meaning could be seen as a further demonstration of this interaction.³⁰

Similar to the nature of a world-picture, although a world of meaning infused with senses of value remains tied to human being's experience and perspective, it is not just limited to the realm of individual consciousness. As one of the preconditions of the genesis of a world of meaning, there is also a universal dimension to values and to a consciousness of values, of which Mencius gave an account early on. For Mencius, the affective mind always possesses "what is common" (*tongran* 同然), which includes "principle" (*li* 理), and "what is righteous" (*yi* 义). "What is it that all affective minds have in common? It is a sense of principle and what is righteous. The sage is the first to come into possession of what is common to all affective minds. Therefore moral principles please our affective minds as beef and mutton and pork please our mouths."[31] "Principle" and "righteousness" here pertain to values. As what is common to all affective minds, they are intrinsic to the human mind as human being's consciousness of values, and commonality here means universality. This universality of a consciousness of values enables the world of meaning, which it permeates, to possess an inter-subjective openness. To say that principle and righteousness "please our minds" is to emphasize that this consciousness of values with universal content can be commonly understood and accepted by different subjects. Of course, as an actual process, this accepting presupposes that this consciousness of values itself embodies the common historical needs of a specific age, and moreover implies the background of inter-subjective communication and interaction between subjects in the process of practical life.

As the forms through which a world of meaning emerges, pictures of the world and interests of value present inseparable worlds. Although a world-picture mainly refers to the question "What is it?" it is still always invested with different degrees of value regardless of whether it is scientific, metaphysical, or a form of common sense. In fact, "the truth" linked to "What is it?" still expresses a value in the broad sense. Likewise, although an interest of value is first of all tied to the question "What does it mean?" it also implies some understanding of "What is it?" From the moral domain to the aesthetic sphere, from the actual pursuit of what is good and beautiful to the ultimate hope of the transcendent plane, values are always inseparable from some understanding of the world. This interrelation of pictures of the world and interests of value presupposes that their foundation is originally the same actual world and demonstrates that the two questions concerning meaning, "What is it?" and "What does it mean?" are by no means strictly separable.

The World of Spirit and the Human State of Mind

As the union of presenting meaning and giving meaning, the meaning of both pictures of being and values of being more directly involve the domain of the object: whether we are considering what it is that a thing presents itself as being to humans (What is it?) or what a thing means for humans (What does it mean?), both questions concern the meaning possessed by the object. Now, returning to one's own being from the being of things, the investigation of the meaning of objects leads one further into the concern for the meaning of one's own being.

When one reflects upon why in the end one exists, one's concern focuses on precisely the meaning of one's own being, and linked to the self-investigation of the meaning of being are different forms of the world of spirit or states of mind (*jingjie* 境界).

As the history of thought shows, the term *jingjie* used in the previous context first came from translations and interpretations of Buddhist canons.[32] In the Buddhist discourse, a state has a division between inside and outside, and thus it is said that external and internal states are of the mind's acting.[33] The external state of being refers to the world of phenomena arising out of causation. In Buddhism, this sense of a state originates from the mind and lacks reality: "The state is non-being (*jingjie shi wu* 境界是無); it is only an appearing from one's own mind (*wei zixin jian* 惟自心見). I say that unenlightened here is only the affective mind itself: in seeing various external things, the affective mind clings to them as being or non-being. Therefore, the wise do not see the state."[34] Because the external state arises from the affective mind but is unreal, it is impossible to enter the Buddhist realm of wisdom. Master Wu Ye of the Chan tradition also remarks: "Every state is originally of itself empty and null. There is no phenomenon that is obtainable. The deluded do not get this and are confused by the state. Once confused by the state, he remains in the endless circle of samsara."[35] The state here also refers to external being. For Chan Buddhism, clinging to this external world means being lost in confusion, in an unenlightened state. The internal state opposed to the external state concerns a certain state of mind or level of spiritual attainment, which the mind achieves by transcending worldly consciousness. In the conclusion of the *Huayan yicheng jiaoyi fenqi zhang,* Fa Zang specifically points out the difference between this state and "states of affairs" (*shi* 事): "Only the state of wisdom is not a consciousness of states of affairs, which serves merely as an expedient means to understand the single vehicle."[36] "A state of affairs" is an empirical phenomenon, and although the state of wisdom, which transcends worldly consciousness, cannot be grasped through empirical phenomena, illustrating "a state of affairs" to explain the state of wisdom is a convenient form of explanation for the unenlightened. This differentiation of the state of wisdom from "a state of affairs" shows the internality of such a state, and furthermore, confirms the meaning of this state of mind as a positive mentality.[37] On this note, Hui Neng concludes: "Those who understand the method of absence-of-thought will experience the states of all Buddhas."[38]

Accompanying historical evolution, using the word "state" to express a world of spirit gradually spread beyond the bounds of Buddhist discourse. In "Occasional Verses at the Hall," Bai Juyi writes that "the leisurely state in which I lived my whole life could be exhaustively expressed in five characters." Here, "state" has the meaning of a state of mind. In the poem "Remembrance of Bygone Days," Lu You mentions the concept of state:

> Happenstance to live among humans, a stretch ages long;
> Only afterthoughts spot the madness of being young.
> Out in public saying things, seeding these regretful pangs;
> Verses welling up from drink, lost in fog by dint of sleep.
> The tortoise swallows countless fish and becomes the whale;
> Immeasurable earth fills the valley and flattens the hill.
> This state of getting old leaves no trace of youthful days;
> Looking at ropes of incense smoke bending around the curtain.

Here what is expressed is the thoughts and consciousness of the poet's august years. At this time, the poet lacks the sharpness of his youth. He is aged, now with no shortage of weariness toward the world; by "this state of getting old" he means a condition of spirit quite different from that of youth. The concept of "state of mind" developed even broader connotations through the writings of philosophers living during and after the Song and Ming dynasties. When discussing the substance of the mind, Zhu Xi ties the vacuity of the fundamental substance of being to a state: "Although the fundamental substance of the affective mind is inherently always empty, how could one even see such a state now that it has been covered over by one's selfish desires for such a long time? Thus, the sage must propose rectifying the affective mind, but in order to correct the affective mind, one's intention must first become sincere, and to become sincere, one must first extend one's knowledge. One must first put one's efforts to uses following this order, and then one may acquire the uprightness of the affective mind and recover the emptiness of the fundamental substance of being, which is of course not a day's labor."[39] As the specific way of being of the fundamental substance of the affective mind, state of mind here is also meant in the sense of a mentality. For Zhu Xi, to attain such a mentality, the substance of the affective mind must put in the effort of extending knowledge, of becoming sincere in each intention, and of rectifying the affective mind, which unfolds as a long process (it is not a day's labor).

Wang Fuzhi analyzes this term "state" from the perspective of perfecting virtue: "'Resting content with humanity (*an ren* 安仁)' and 'performing humanity without obstruction (*li ren* 利人)' are always states of perfected virtue."[40] In *The Analects*, Confucius claims: "The humane rest content with humanity, while the wise perform humanity without obstruction."[41] For Wang Fuzhi, these two constitute states in the cultivation of virtue. Of course, from the perspective of perfecting virtue, a state of mind can be expressed in different modes; as long as one has merely the distinction of the high honor of wealth from the poverty of low stature on one's mind, one's state never surpasses the limits of this realm: "Therefore, solely exercising one's efforts with the intention to distinguish oneself in wealth and honor against the lowliness of base stature, one merely struggles to

separate states (*duan jingjie* 段境界), and as the latter marks the extreme limit of one's reach, one never passes to the limit of heavenly principles and natural laws."[42] On the contrary, if one perseveres in upholding the humane way (*rendao* 仁道) without at any time going contrary to what is humane, one may enter another state: "having reached the state of 'the superior one who betrays humanity not even for the interval of a meal,' whose state naturally distinguishes itself, remarkably harmonizing with heavenly principle."[43] Here, the distinction between states involves the distinction between high and low in terms of virtue, but also the difference between forms of inner spirit.

As we move from Zhu Xi to Wang Fuzhi, the concept of "state" comes to focus more upon the level of spirit and ideas. As the being of ideas, a state of mind could in the broad sense be seen as a world of spirit concerning a much broader horizon of consideration. Mencius makes the following statement: "Everything is already completely there within oneself (*wanwu jie bei yu wo* 万物皆备于我). To examine oneself and be sincere, there is simply no greater joy."[44] What Mencius means here by "everything is already completely there within oneself" is not that the external world is already inside the individual in physical form, but rather that it exists as a world of meaning at the level of ideas: in the expanding of horizons, the imagining of reasons, and the deepening of internal experiences, "I" grasp the world as a whole and realize its meaning, by virtue of which everything enters "my" world of ideas. The relationship between the two is like that between the world "truthfully being" and the human being "sincerely thinking": "to be truthful is the way of Nature; to think sincerely is the way of humans."[45] Here, the world opening up "to me myself" and the openness of "I myself" toward the world, the world presenting meaning "to me" and "I" comprehending the meaning of the world blend into one, and the genuine affective experience of this state of spirit is accompanied by an internal spiritual joy that goes beyond that pleasure of the senses—this is what Mencius means when he states: "To examine oneself and be sincere, there is simply no greater joy." This "joy" that is reached by means of taking the world in through an open perspective such that its meaning is deeply comprehended is precisely what is meant by a state of mind. On this note, Wang Fuzhi stresses: "Mencius, under the pretext that 'everything is already completely there within oneself,' states that 'to examine oneself and be sincere, there is simply no greater joy;' how outstanding is this state indeed!"[46]

This consistency between a state of mind and the world of spirit can also be discovered in Zhang Zai's theory of "the greater mind." When discussing the relationship between the internal mind and external things, Zhang Zai points out:

> If one expands the affective mind, one can grasp the substance of things under the rule of nature; things are without substance, so the affective mind reaches outside (*xin wei you wai* 心为有外). The affective mind of the average human

does not expand beyond the narrow limits of what is perceived or heard. The sage fully exercises the capacity of human nature to the limit without letting what is perceived and heard exhaust the affective mind; in the sage's view of the world, there is not a single thing that has nothing to do with oneself (*wu yi wu fei wo* 无一物非我). This is what Mencius meant when he said that fully exercising the affective mind to the limit is to know human nature, and to know Nature itself. Nature itself is so infinitely great there is nothing beyond or outside of it; so, an affective mind, which has an outside beyond its limits (*you wai zhi xin* 有外之心), is unable to converge with the affective mind of Nature itself.[47]

To "expand the affective mind" is to expand the horizon of spirit; this horizon differs from what is perceived and heard at the level of the senses. The object of perception at the level of the senses is the external form of particular things, whereas the object of the spiritual horizon is the meaning of the world. Thus, to grasp the substance of things under the rule of nature is precisely to transcend particular things or a finite form of being so that one may grasp and experience the meaning of the world as a whole. The statement "there is not a single thing that has nothing to do with oneself" is thus similar to the previous proposition made by Mencius that "everything is completely there within oneself." Here, that which envelops everything under the rule of Nature is the affective mind that expands to the point where nothing is outside of it. This mind unfolds as the world of spirit transcending the finite in pursuit of the infinite.

As the being of ideas, a state of mind or the world of spirit exhibits different forms. In fact, Mencius, Zhang Zai, Zhu Xi, and Wang Fuzhi each confirm the difference between higher and lower states of spirit in their respective understandings of the world of spirit. Feng Youlan affirms this in a much clearer fashion. For Feng Youlan, since people have different understandings of the universe and human life, their states of mind diverge as well: "People can have different degrees of awareness of the universe and human life. Because of this, the meaning of the universe and human life is not the same for all human beings. All humans have some degree of understanding of the universe and human life, and because of this, the different kinds of meaning the universe and human life has for humans, constitute the kinds of states of mind that humans may have."[48] As a world of meaning in the form of ideas, state of mind or the broader world of spirit encompasses different senses and distinct levels; different senses correspond to the differences between the ethical world, the aesthetic world and the religious world; different levels correspond to the different degrees to which spirit can rise and develop. In ordinary speech, we say that a state of mind is either high or low, which expresses different levels of the world of spirit. These differences in the world of spirit not only concern the different depths of understandings of the world in the cognitive dimension but also the different standpoints of evaluation of the world in the evaluative dimension. Feng Youlan's term "awareness" seems to envelop both dimensions.

In the process of being-in-the-world, the different senses of the world of spirit, which correspond to the different modes of being humans may attain, show human beings different meanings of what it is to be. In actuality, human being undergoes different stages of development, and so human life is a multifaceted process. In the different facets of these different developmental stages of human life and of different lives, the world of spirit encompasses different contents, both normative and adaptive. Normative here means guiding human being's way of being-in-the-world and improving one's state of being. To be adaptive is to arrange a process through which to survive, which is manifested in everyday practices. As the form through which the production and reproduction of life is realized, everyday life constitutes an important facet of the being of humans, and although the mentality that suits everyday life emerges spontaneously, it still has its own meaning. Confucianism's proposition that *dao* is to be found in everydayness (*riyong ji dao* 日用即道) affirms this. At the same time, different individuals value and pursue a great diversity of life goals, and behind this diversity of orientations are different mentalities. If these different mentalities do not happen to substantially conflict with the axiological principles manifesting the broader tendency of historical development, they all show their respective meaning for the being of humans. In brief, in the process of growing, one should both affirm the development and cultivation of one's mentality and also respect the diversity of mentalities.

At a deeper level of value, what the world of spirit points to is the meaning of the being of humans qua human. In effect, from the joy Mencius finds in sincere reflection and from what Zhang Zai finds in the expansion of the affective mind to Wang Fuzhi's state of perfected virtue, in the world of spirit, understanding and grasping meaning leads one further to think about and comprehend the intrinsic meaning of one's own being. As this book argued in chapter 1, from within the horizon of self-reflection upon the meaning of being, the core of a state of mind or the world of spirit is concentrated within the pursuit of an ideal and the consciousness of a mission. While the pursuit of an ideal corresponds to the question "What can one hope for?" or "What ought one hope for?", becoming conscious of a mission corresponds to the question "What ought one take responsibility for?" which are both intimately connected to the self-reflective inquiry "What does one exist for?" which shows a deepening concern for the meaning of one's own being.

While demanding human being to expand the affective mind, Zhang Zai also advocates: "Establish an affective mind for the heavens and the earth, establish a way (*li dao* 立道) for the livelihood of the people, continue the line of learning that leads to sagehood, and start a world of peace for all generations to come."[49]

This imperative statement expresses the pursuit of an ideal and the inner consciousness of a mission. For Zhang Zai, human being is the affective mind of the heavens and the earth, and the people are the root of society, while the path of learning leading to sagehood embodies the spiritual lifeline of culture, and a secure and peaceful world constitutes the goal of history; the pursuit of an ideal consists in establishing the true value and role of human being in nature, in responding to the aspirations of the people, in prolonging the lifeline of culture, and in realizing enduring peace in the world; human being's historical mission lies in transforming these ideals into social reality. For Zhang Zai, the expansion of one's mind is the internal precondition of the world of spirit, and this unity of pursuing an ideal and being conscious of a mission expresses the core sense of "expanding one's mind."

The pursuit of an ideal corresponding to the question "What ought one hope for?" also responds to the self-reflective inquiry "What does one exist for?" by providing a worthy purpose. At a broader level, the question "What ought one hope for?" is directed toward accomplishing oneself and accomplishing things: to accomplish oneself means to move toward a more perfect state of freedom through one's own multifaceted development; to accomplish things means to make things become beings that harmonize with the needs of human nature by means of reforming the world. In the process of accomplishing oneself and accomplishing things, one gives substance to hopes and ideals and gives intrinsic meaning to one's own being. Here, the meaning of being is intrinsic first of all because accomplishing oneself and accomplishing things is directed at the complete refinement of both oneself and the human world. In other words, this process manifests and confirms the purposiveness of human being.

Relative to the pursuit of an ideal through the question "What ought one hope for?" is the consciousness of a mission, which is a response to the meaning of the question "What ought one take responsibility for?" Here, one responds by taking up a concern for the meaning of one's own being in terms of responsibility and duty. As the stipulation and demand of the species or society, responsibility and duty makes human being transcend the finite ends of survival and manifest the essence of humans qua human at the level of social history. Kant states: "Man, as animal, belongs to the world, but, as person, also to the beings who are capable of rights—and, consequently, have *freedom* of the will. Which ability [*hanilitaet*] essentially differentiates him from all other beings; *men's* is innate to him."[50] "The world" here is attributed to nature in the broad sense; as animal, [human being] is also a natural being. For Kant, the main thing that makes human being transcend nature and distinct from other beings consists in human being's possession of both rights and free will. In substance, the confirmation of rights presupposes the recognition of the value of human beings, while the intrinsic form of value involves purposiveness: that human being possesses intrinsic value means that human being is an end in itself; in a complimentary sense, affirming that humans possess rights implies seeing humans as purposive beings. This understanding of human being is consistent with Kant's ethical demand that human being always be seen as an end and not as a mere means. Furthermore, tied to rights is free will. For Kant, free will always involves duties and responsibilities: "How is the concept of freedom possible? Only through the imperative of duty which commands categorically."[51] "The concept of freedom is founded on a fact: categorical imperative."[52] Evidently for Kant, the premise of free will is responsibility and duty; logically speaking, this relation between rights and free will also corresponds to the relation between rights and duties. In summary, as the intrinsic property of human being, which distinguishes humans from other beings, the purposive dimension entailed by rights and the duties and responsibilities entailed by free will express the essence of humans qua human.

Similar to Kant, Mencius also focuses on the attribute of humans qua human: "There is merely a nuance that distinguishes humans from beasts. Commoners do away with it, whereas the superior one preserves it."[53] What is the main thing, which, in the end, distinguishes humans from animals? What in the end is this nuance that the commoner does away with and the superior preserves? When discussing the main characteristic of the superior human being (*junzi* 君子), Mencius gives us the following explanation: "What distinguishes the superior from the common is that the superior human being is mindful (*cunxin* 存心). The superior human being is mindful in being-humane and observing ritual propriety."[54] For Mencius, the superior one is human being's completely refined form of being, the one who is the concentrated manifestation of the essential characteristic of humans qua human. The concrete nuance of the superior human being is mindfulness. The content of what the affective mind is mindful of is precisely the inner world of spirit's reserve of "humanity" and "propriety." The latter two have the meaning of virtue and express "what ought to be" (the norms that ought to be followed). As a being distinguished from animals, human being ought "to be" in harmony with what is humane and behave in accordance with ritual propriety. What is expressed here is a moral ideal (establishing a world of spirit with moral consciousness) and a consciousness of moral responsibility (that one ought to uphold what is humane in harmony with ritual propriety means that one has the responsibility to abide by moral norms). To be mindful by being-humane and observing ritual propriety is precisely to establish and protect the world of spirit of moral ideals and moral responsibilities. For Mencius, it is precisely this inner spiritual world that distinguishes humans from beasts and makes humans become human in the true sense.

In broader terms, the state of mind of human beings whose core is melded out of the consciousness of an ideal that embodies "What one ought to hope for?" and the consciousness of a mission that embodies "What one ought to take responsibility for?" shows the essential attribute of human being qua human at the level of ideas. As it embodies the essential attribute of human being, one's state of mind in this sense could also be understood as the human state of mind. From within the horizon of the human state of mind, the meaning of the very being of humans becomes the focus of concern and is manifested in different ways. As far as the dimension of ideals goes, insofar as one is directed at accomplishing oneself and accomplishing things, human being affirms itself as an end in itself and one establishes the direction of one's own being, which invests the being one is with intrinsic meaning; as far as a mission goes, human being transcends the finite end of survival by taking on responsibilities and duties. This reveals the essential attribute that distinguishes humans from other beings, and furthermore, shows the meaning of one's being from the perspective of one's way of being and mode of being. These two aspects of the human state of mind are inseparable; this dual sense of the human state of mind can be seen in Zhang Zai's imperative to "establish an affective mind for the heavens and the earth, establish a way (*lidao* 立道) for the livelihood of the people, continue the line of learning that leads to sagehood, and start a world of peace for all generations to come." On an even broader level, the movement of human being toward a state of freedom through the multifaceted development of the self (accomplishing oneself) and human being's transformation of the original state of being in-itself into a world that suits human development (accomplishing things) is simultaneously human being's long sought ideal and unavoidable historical mission.

With the essential attribute of human being qua human as its concern, the human state of mind is the manifestation of the self-awareness of being in a twofold sense: with regard to what kind of being human being is, it means affirming that human being is different from natural beings in correspondence with the distinction between human and animal; with regard to why one exists, it means aiming at accomplishing oneself and accomplishing things as the intrinsic goal of being, which entails the in-depth realization of the meaning of one's own being. This sense of the human state of mind reveals both the depth of the world of spirit as well as its universality, which transcends the individual. Of course, as a world of meaning in the form of ideas, the world of spirit also encompasses differences of individual character and presents a diversity of forms, but in substance, there is no mutually exclusive relationship pitting the universality of the human state of mind against the individuality and diversity of forms of the world of spirit, that is, an affirmation of the universal determination of the human state of mind does not entail a denial of the diversity and individuality of the world of spirit. In effect, accomplishing oneself and accomplishing things, as the concrete aim of the human state of mind, entails that one demands the multifaceted development of oneself, and to develop in a multifaceted way means to overcome the one-sided and undifferentiated nature of the world of spirit and to shape the world of spirit with nuances of individual character and diverse tendencies.

The Human State of Mind and Human Capacities

The actual form of the world of spirit cannot be divorced from the process of accomplishing oneself and accomplishing things. This is not only because accomplishing oneself and accomplishing things is the very aim of the world of spirit but also because the world of spirit itself takes shape in the process of accomplishing oneself and accomplishing things. From the perspective of accomplishing oneself and accomplishing things, the world of spirit not only involves the human state of mind but also human capacities. Whereas the human state of mind confirms the meaning of one's being by directing one toward accomplishing oneself and accomplishing things, human capacities provide one with the conditions of possibility of accomplishing oneself in the process of accomplishing things.

As explained in the previous section, the human state of mind first shows the human nature of the world of spirit through the consciousness of an ideal and the consciousness of a mission (duty). Relative to this, human capacities show the actual powers [at work in] knowing and reforming the self and the world. As the conditions of possibility of accomplishing oneself and accomplishing things, human capacities are not abstract logical forms, nor are they reducible to functions of pure consciousness or simple psychological functions. In the form of the unity of sensibility and rationality, of rationality and irrationality, human capacities are synthetic and concrete, acting upon one's knowing and practicing from within, and the depth and extent to which knowing and practicing can reach always corresponds to human being's different capacities. Insofar as they differ from external means by expressing the human being's essential powers, and differ from abstract logical forms by integrally fusing into the human process of being such that they are the same as the being of humans, they have the meaning of being natural human tendencies.[55]

However, though human capacities do show human being's essential powers as intrinsic, this does not imply that their being and actual employment necessarily accord with the direction of human development. Just as the alienation of labor during a certain historical age results in human being's self-estrangement, human capacities still carry the possibility of alienating themselves into external means or instruments. Since the modern age, accompanying the triumphant song of scientific progress, the horizon of adopting scientific technology to guide development has increasingly pervaded every level and corner of society. In the scientific domain, nature and other beings are first of all dealt with as objects. As science reached maturity in its modern form, this characteristic became increasingly obvious. Heidegger analyzed modern technology in this vein, designating the term "enframing" (Gestell) to express the essence of technology. He states, "Enframing means the gathering together of that setting-upon which sets upon man, i.e., challenges him forth, to reveal the real, in the mode of ordering, as standing-reserve."[56] Enframing means to limit, to fix; it limits and fixes the relationship between man and nature into a relationship between knower and known, user and used, and nature (that is, being in the broad sense) becomes a calculable object because of it. Science and technology are of course not the same, but in no way can the former exist in isolation from the latter; the tendency of technology to objectify being is in a way the mark of the objectivizing characteristic of scientific thinking. In fact, as Heidegger illuminates technology's objectification of nature, he simultaneously points out the same characteristic of science: "Theory makes secure at any given time a region of the real as its object-area. The area-character of objectness is shown in the fact that it specifically maps out in advance the possibilities for the posing of questions. Every new phenomenon emerging within an area of science is refined to such a point that it fits into the normative objective coherence of the theory."[57] Associated with the tendency to objectify is science's inclination to question and structure the world in a one-sided way, which leads to the forgetting of the very meaning of the being of humans. For the being of humans, of course science proves itself to be more than just negative. In fact, as science opens up the world, it simultaneously provides the process of accomplishing oneself and accomplishing things with a much vaster space. However, when the objectifying tendency of thought is directed toward understanding human being, the axiological principle that human being is an end in itself becomes obscured, and as human being is objectified human being also faces the threat of turning itself into a thing. In connection with this is the tendency of the human capacities to be degraded into instruments or tools: as human being gradually objectifies itself, human being's capacities gradually lose meaning as the intrinsic ground of accomplishing the self and accomplishing things, and are viewed either as being just instruments directed toward some scientific object or as means to reach some scientific or technological goal.

From a broader perspective, under historical conditions in which there are still "relations of personal dependence" and "objective [*sachlicher*] dependence" as Marx put it, extrinsic fame and gain at odds with the direction of human development become the objects human being seeks; compared to the movement toward freedom, which is a goal of intrinsic value, fame and gain are in essence "things extrinsic to the self." Zhuangzi once distinguished between "things" and "human nature," putting forward the following critique, he states: "There is no one in the world who doesn't alienate human nature through things. Commoners sacrifice themselves for gain, while the knight sacrifices himself for fame."[58] Here, "human nature" refers to the intrinsic attribute of human being qua human, the "things" opposed to this are the objects that are extrinsic to human being;

"fame" and "gain" fall under this type. That one alienates one's human nature through things means that one substitutes the pursuit of things extrinsic to oneself for the pursuit of the intrinsic attribute and intrinsic meaning of one's own being. As soon as one's capacities are used mainly just to gain these "things extrinsic to oneself," human capacities necessarily alienate themselves into extrinsic instruments and means.

To prevent human capacities from degrading into instruments and means concerns not only the dimension of social history but also the dimension of ideas. At the level of social history, it means overcoming the alienation of labor and the self-estrangement of human being by overcoming relations of personal dependence and objective-dependence, and quelling science and technology's usurpation [of being] in the aspects of guiding values and practice; with regard to internal ideas and the world of spirit, necessary attention must be allotted to the human state of mind. As stated previously, as the concrete form of the world of spirit, the deepest level of the human state of mind is the concern for why one exists (the purpose of life) and of what kind of being one is (the distinction between human and animal), which involves the essential attribute of human being qua human and the meaning of one's own being. From the doctrine that "there is merely a nuance that distinguishes humans from beasts. The commoner does away with it, whereas the superior one preserves it" to the imperative "to establish an affective mind for the heavens and the earth, establish a way for the livelihood of the people, continue the line of learning that leads toward sagehood, and start a world of peace for all generations to come," the human state of mind confirms the essential attribute of human being, which distinguishes human being from other beings and affirms the meaning of being in the dimension of human being as an end in itself. With this as its intension, the human state of mind determines human capacities to value the intrinsic dimension of the world of spirit while guiding one in the expression of one's essential powers in the process of accomplishing oneself and accomplishing things, so as to prevent their alienation into extrinsic means or tools.

Another aspect is that although the human state of mind includes values, if separated from the human capacities and their concrete manifestation in the process of knowing and practicing, the human state of mind remains merely at the level of ideas, and is easily reduced to an abstract, mysterious, and empty spiritual enjoyment. Historically speaking, Neo-Confucianism expressed this tendency by focusing mainly on the affective mind and natural human tendencies. Although some Neo-Confucians did speak of accomplishing oneself and accomplishing things, they limited this process to the ethical domain of cultivating virtue, wherein the human capacities are restricted to developing ethical knowledge of what is virtuous, which inhibits the expression of the entirety of human being's essential powers. Orientated in this way, the human state of mind cannot avoid appearing speculative and mystical. Mentioned previously, although "establishing an affective mind for the heavens and the earth" and other such ideas express the pursuit of a grand spiritual end, when they are severed from the historical process of actually practicing, they remain empty. Huang Zongxi once wrote a critique of the later decadent schools of Neo-Confucianism for abandoning the real activity of managing the warp and woof of the heavens and the earth: they "merely choke the world with a broad theory of establishing a principle for the people, an affective mind for the heavens and the earth and peace for the world. When the time comes to take the responsibility of a minister and serve the country, they blindly open their mouths like their heads are lost in some cloud or mist."[59] This criticism is not without its basis. Neo-Confucians repeatedly defined the so-called pure Confucian scholar as the ideal human character, but the focus of this character is to grasp principles and eliminate selfish desires within the world of spirit, driving the multifaceted development of human being and the actual process of reforming the real world out of the equation. In this abstract world, state of mind is understood to be the individual's spiritual "enjoyment" (*shouyong* 受用). Some figures of the school of mind in the late Ming dynasty associated "the substance of the affective mind" with "returning to silence," which is a perfectly typical expression of this. Nie Bao, for instance, saw the fundamental substance of the inner mind to be silence, thinking that as soon as the silent foundation is reached one enters the state of essential meaning borne in spirit (*jingyi ru shen* 精义入神): "Fully cultivated in the silent substance of empty alertness without letting a single desire to cover it up is called the state of essential meaning borne in spirit and function is within it."[60] "Fully cultivated in the silent substance of empty alertness" here means developing an inner spiritual state. "Function" here expresses an abstract functioning of spirit severed from the actual process of knowing and practicing, where it is reduced to cultivating the affective mind to reflect inwardly upon itself in some speculative experience. Unfolding the pursuit of meaning solely in a moral realm in total disconnection from the broader sense of the human capacities and their actualization drives the human state of mind into a closed, mystical, and empty space.

    A similar tendency is also inherent in Heidegger's understanding of human being. At the philosophical level, Heidegger's skepticism concerning the propensity of development of modern science and technology is related to his criticism of traditional metaphysics. As is widely known, in Heidegger, the negative tendency of traditional metaphysics lies in merely focusing on beings and forgetting Being itself. The substantial sense of Being, according to Heidegger, lies in Dasein, that is, the human's "being there." This focus on the being of humans undoubtedly includes a concern for the meaning of one's own being. In effect, accusing science and technology's tendency to objectify actually echoes his theoretical critique of the forgetting of Being; both do indeed presuppose a self-affirmation of the meaning of Being. However, Heidegger's pursuit of the meaning of Being is directed toward the authentic self. For Heidegger, after the individual is thrown into the world the individual cannot avoid being-with-others, and this process of being-with makes one continuously discover oneself in existential states and experiences such as care and anxiety but also makes one fall into "the they" (das Man) and lose one's authentic self. Only in the process of being-towards-death (Sein zum Tod) through the experience of anticipating the arrival of death can one truly become conscious of one's individuality, singularity, and irreplaceability and thereby return to the authentic self and realize the meaning of human life. This understanding of the being of humans and the meaning of one's being not only fails to go beyond the realm of individual existence, it is also limited to the experience of the individual mind. In this spiritual experience of existence, human capacities and their actualization are likewise placed outside of the process of being. This direction of thought is in a sense correlated with this accusation of modern science and technology: doubting modern technology logically leads to ignoring the human capacities inside of them; and the abstract, speculative quality of this direction of thought also seems to echo the traditional Chinese theory of the affective mind and human nature.

As far as the realm of spirit or ideas goes, if human capacities were severed from the human state of mind, they would end up with a lack of commitment to intrinsic values and ideals to guide them, which would doom them to become externalized as instruments and means; on the other hand, if severed from human capacities and the actual historical process of employing them, the human state of mind would turn into a mystifying abstraction. Considered from within the horizon of accomplishing oneself and accomplishing things, the human state of mind and human capacities not only take shape through the process of knowing and reforming the world and the self, but are also directed toward this process in different respects and constitute the internal conditions of its unfolding. Presupposing the unification of human capacities with the human state of mind, human capacities overcome their externalized form and show their intrinsic sense of value by expressing the essential attribute of human being as an end in itself; on the other hand, by fusing into the actual creative act of accomplishing oneself and accomplishing things, the human state of mind transcends the state of abstract agreement and mystical spiritual enjoyment. With regard to the being of humans, while the formation of the human state of mind enables humans to become moral agents in the sense of coming into possession of a worthy purpose, the development of human capacities enables humans to become practical agents in the sense of becoming creators of values, and free character has the historical meaning of concretely integrating the two together. As the concrete unity of human capacities and the human state of mind, this free character gives a deepened sense of value to a world of meaning through one's own being.

5   Meaning and Reality

IN THE PROCESS of accomplishing oneself and accomplishing things, meaning is not only presented at the level of ideas in the act of cognizing and evaluating; when grounded in practical activity, meaning is also externalized as the world of actual beings or the real world. As the externalization or actualization of meaning, this domain of being, which is generated through the process of knowing and practicing could also be seen as the actual or external formation of a world of meaning, whose actual content is the Nature for-humans or things-for-us as social reality or the living world.

Transforming Nature in-Itself into Nature for-Humans

A world of meaning, as actual being, is first of all said in opposition to being in-itself. Being in-itself is what has not entered the human sphere of cognition and practice, and whose meaning therefore is still concealed for human being. A world of meaning, on the other hand, is already imprinted with the mark of human and presents the different levels of things for-us. In Chinese philosophy, Nature in-itself (*tian zhi tian* 天之天) refers to things in-themselves. As the form of being beyond the domain of cognition and practice, Nature in-itself has never formed an actual connection with human being; so, it does not constitute an object with meaning at the level of ideas and has no actual meaning in the practical realm. Abstractly speaking, "being" is attributed to both human being and Nature in-itself, so they are not absolutely divided from one another, but while Nature in-itself still lies beyond the domain of practice and cognition, they are presented more as two worlds divided apart rather than as a world integrally whole.

To overcome the division separating human being from Nature in-itself presupposes human being actively reforming the world. Being in-itself will not spontaneously suit human beings, no more than it will fulfill human needs by itself. Even in the primitive age of humankind, that of hunting and gathering, the being of humans did not by any means passively rely on the gifts of nature. In effect, hunting and gathering itself also falls under the category of productive labor in the broad sense. It is precisely by means of this practical activity that humans moved out of nature on the one hand and moved toward nature on the other. To move toward nature means to continuously open up being at the epistemological level and to transform being in-itself into human being's world at the ontological level. By means of turning toward and reforming nature, human being makes nature suit human needs, and meanwhile, imprints the mark of human upon the world in-itself, thereby giving it various kinds of meaning.

Under the precondition that human being is opening up and reforming the primordial form of being in-itself, being emerges as actuality. Here, from the perspective of the relationship between humans and being, a distinction must be made between "actual" and "real": being in-itself is undoubtedly real, but this does not mean that it is actual for human being. Here, actuality means entering the domain of cognition and practice, becoming an object of cognition and practice, and consequently obtaining actual meaning.[1] When the light of cognition has yet to shed upon them, things remain concealed in the state of being in-themselves. A metaphor alluding to this point can be found in the following saying: "If Nature had not created Confucius, history would be, as it were, a long night." "Confucius" should of course be understood here in the sense of human being as species. Similarly, while things in-themselves lie beyond the practical domain, there is nowhere from which their form of being and concrete properties could be presented. But, one confirms human being's essential powers in the process of "participating in the developmental growth of the Heavens and the Earth," in the process forming the actual world, and meanwhile the world in-itself presents its actual qualities by merging into human being's cognitive and practical processes. In fact, it is precisely their internal identity and unity that led Marx to connect the actuality of objects to the objectification of human being's own essential powers:[2] "On the one hand, therefore, it is only when the objective world becomes everywhere for man in society the world of man's essential powers—human reality, and for that reason the reality of his *own* essential powers—that all *objects* become for him the *objectification of himself*, become objects which confirm and realize *his* individuality, become *his* objects: that is, *man himself* becomes the object."[3] Here we can see that objects obtaining actuality and objects obtaining a humanized form (objects becoming man's own objectification of himself) are two aspects of the same process, which manifests human being's unique way of being through the objectification of its own essential powers, and meanwhile transforms the being of the objective world: after Nature in-itself (*tian zhi tian*) transforms into Nature for-humans (*ren zhi tian*) it simultaneously forms substantial connections with the being of humans and is thereby determined as actual.

In correspondence with the dimension of actuality, being also presents the quality of being "true." Here, "true" refers simultaneously to the grasping of being as it really is in the epistemological sense and also to reality in the ontological sense. Though things in-themselves "exist," for human being, this kind of "existence" has never been confirmed, so it is as if they are not there even though they do exist. Yet, in the process of knowing and practicing, being is presented as being that is confirmed, and its true reality is concretely manifested; this true reality expresses the "truth" of the world at an original level. This "truth," whose content is reality, therefore constitutes the ontological precondition of the attainment of "true" knowledge.

The humanized world confirms the truth of being, which is identical to human being reforming the object out of its being in-itself. This is to say that cognizing and practicing not only opens up the world, but also transforms it. Historically speaking, from the basic process of existing (maintaining life functions) to the development of society and culture, the being of humans is always faced with a multiplicity of needs. However, the world will neither harmonize with humans on its own initiative nor spontaneously fulfill human needs; only by acting upon the world in different ways will humans make objects qualify as being "for-humans." In effect, transforming being out of its original state into humanized being essentially means making the world in the original sense become "things for-us," which suit human needs. "That which is desirable is called good;"[4] at an original level, "desirable" here could be understood as harmonizing with human needs; when being in-itself is acted upon by human being and becomes identical to human needs, it is presented as possessing the value of "good."

Aside from displaying value for the being of humans, the humanized world is also linked to human aesthetic activity. As the beings that have not entered the process of knowing and practicing, things in-themselves simultaneously lie beyond the realm of beauty, and do not present any sense of beauty. Zhuangzi states that "the heavens and the earth have a great beauty that is without words."[5] Here, "the heavens and the earth" are no longer purely things in-themselves; they have already formed some kind of connection with human being: here, "great beauty" refers to the beauty of nature or a natural beauty differing in kind from a humanized form, which although differs from the kind of beauty that human beings intentionally cut out and assigns to nature, its aesthetic meaning still remains relative to humans. In fact, the very reason the beauty of the heavens and the earth is "great" here is because it agrees with Zhuangzi's aesthetic standards. It is precisely during the unfolding of aesthetic activity and in the consequent germination of aesthetic consciousness that a sense of beauty finally emerges, which presupposes the transformation of things in-themselves into things for-us.

As the external form of a world of meaning, humanized beings or things for-us first emerge through overcoming the form of being in-itself. It is precisely in the movement from "Nature in-itself" into "Nature for-humans" that the concrete actuality of the world emerges out of abstract being. So, the formation of actuality is the precondition of reality in-itself transforming into the human world, whose constituents are the only beings that truly have actual meaning for human beings. This actuality of being is by no means formless. From the very outset, it is tied to human being's multifaceted needs and envelops the substantial sense of such values as the true, the beautiful, and the good. In brief, transforming things out of their being in-themselves into being for-humans means impressing the mark of human upon the world of objects, and its profound significance lies in endowing being in-itself with senses of value.

The actuality of being and the significance of values it presents take shape through human being's cognizing and practicing, which in essence is to say that "Nature in-itself" is gradually freed from the primal state of being in-itself while obtaining humanized form through human being's active opening up and re-forming of the world. As regards the humanization of objects, human being's most original mode of activity is labor. Labor is at once the direct medium that connects human being to nature and also the basic way in which human being acts upon the world. From the earliest stages of hunting and gathering to modern production with technological means, labor transforms both the world and human being itself. Through the "metabolic interaction [stoffvechsel] between human being and nature"[6] labor not only creates values in the narrow economic sense, it also invests the world with meanings and values in vaster dimensions and at deeper levels. Humankind's activity through the original mode of labor simultaneously expresses human being's intrinsic creativity and essential powers. In effect, giving objects meaning and value is the very process by which human being objectifies its own creativity and essential powers. So, the creativity and essential powers of human being as such could be seen as the source of meaning. As the actualization of being which consolidates human being's creativity and essential powers, the humanization of the world expresses its deepest level of meaning as the historical confirmation of human being's creativity and essential powers.[7]

As the source of the meaning of the humanized world, human being's creativity and essential powers first emerge in the form of human capacities. As discussed previously, the relationship between human capacities and human being's cognizing and practicing is interactive. The historical unfolding of cognitive and practical activity constitutes the precondition of the development and formation of human capacities, but cognizing and practicing as such is likewise inseparable from the condition of human capacities of a specific historical stage, which shows their unity with the actual process of opening up and reforming the world. As the precondition of knowing and practicing, human capacities also constitute the internal conditions of possibility of a world of meaning. The achievement of man recognizing and reforming the world is always conditioned by a specific historical background, which involves different stages of development of human capacities. The degree to which things have been humanized out of the mode of being in-themselves is also identical to the degree to which human capacities have developed. The world belonging to human being was born in the true sense when human being first transcended its instinctual adaptation to the external world and formed its first capacities to reform the world. What differentiates the hunting behavior of humankind from the carnivorous behavior of animals under "the law of the jungle" is human being's knowledge and understanding of the world, which is concretely grounded in human capacities, and further, concretely integrates with them. In connection with the continuous development of human capacities, the breadth and depth of human being's transformation of the world is also ceaselessly expanding.

The movement from the Nature in-Itself into Nature for-Humans also stems from human being's different ideals. Similar to human capacities, ideals are formed in the process of opening up and reforming the world; they embody human being's ends and demands and are also based on the possibilities provided by the actual world; as still unrealized but hoped to be realized ends, ideals possess the quality of "what ought to be." After its formation, an end proceeds to continuously guide and constrain cognition and practice, and thus presents a normative function. Directed at reforming the world and creating values, transforming things in-themselves into things for-us also unfolds as a process of realizing ideals, the historical product of which is a world of meaning.

As already mentioned, conscious processes and psychological dispositions manifest human capacities. In this sense, there is a strong relationship between human capacities and the concept of the affective mind (*xin* 心) in Chinese philosophy. As an end, an ideal gives direction to cognition and practice, and meanwhile, by concretizing into projects and plans, an ideal also guides and constrains the process of cognizing and practicing. Thus, ideals are similar to principles (*li* 理) in the sense of what ought to be. As opposed to ideals and human capacities, the world in-itself could be seen as things (*wu* 物) in the broad sense. In the historical unfolding of the unified process of knowing and practicing, the affective mind, principles, and things reciprocally interact, which catalyzes the transformation of things in-themselves into things for-us. Things for-us could be seen as the actual form of a world of meaning. In this sense, the interplay of the affective mind, things, and principles on the basis of practice also constitutes the precondition of the formation of a world of meaning.

As the external form of a world of meaning, things for-us are undoubtedly an overcoming of things in-themselves, but the distinction between the two is not absolute. Although things in-themselves have not yet opened up to human being, this does not mean that they will be concealed in-themselves for eternity. Ontologically speaking, things in-themselves always contain the possibility of transforming into things for-us. So in a sense, they could be seen as potential things for-us. On the other hand, things for-us, as beings that have entered the domain of practice and cognition, have already overcome the state of being in-themselves, but to open them up and reform them does not mean to alter their reality. While obtaining an actual form and significance, a thing for-us still remains in possession of its physical and chemical properties, which do not depend upon human being's consciousness and activity. These properties that do not rely upon human being obviously qualify as being in-themselves. But, there is no insurmountable gap between things in-themselves and things for-us; rather, there is as it were, an alterable boundary between the two. In the historical unfolding of the process of knowing and practicing, the humanized domain is ceaselessly expanding into the domain of being in-itself. This link between things in-themselves and things for-us unfolds as the continuity between the two. Hegel once stated that "Spirit is presaged in Nature."[8] For Hegel, Nature is the externalization of the absolute idea and constitutes the medium out of which the absolute idea develops toward Spirit. Though this logical deduction is speculative and abstract, if Spirit is tied to the being of humans and the world of things for-us, then the saying that Spirit is presaged in Nature seems also to mean that there is a concrete continuity between Nature and human being, between Nature being in-itself and Nature being for-ourselves. Considered historically, as the subject of meaning, the being of humans ontologically presupposes the being of Nature in-itself. This fact at once determines that human being cannot break the link between what is human and what is natural while emerging out of nature, and moreover, that being for-ourselves is inseparably linked to being in-itself.

In the history of philosophy, we can see different understandings of this relationship between things for-us and things in-themselves. Here, the thought of Immanuel Kant presents an important view. As is widely known, Kant makes a distinction between phenomena and the thing in-itself: the former is tied to human being's sensible intuition and thus has the character of being for-us; the latter (the thing in-itself) is a rather complex notion. Insofar as it is beyond the phenomenal world, the thing-in-itself qualifies as being in-itself; but on the other hand, in the cognitive domain it is also understood as the origin of sensible phenomena, while in the practical domain, it is supposed to be the metaphysical ground of moral practice, and in this regard, it undoubtedly possesses an aspect of being for-us. With this in mind, Kant seems to have noticed the connection between being in-itself and being for-us. However, at the same time, Kant emphasizes that the phenomenon is different from the true form of the thing in-itself, while holding that the latter is the origin of the former, and in this sense, phenomena are in substance determined principally as things "for-us;" although the thing in-itself is the source of phenomena, it is determined as the object that human being can never reach, so in substance, the whole of its being is determined as "being in-itself." This dichotomy between phenomenon and the thing in-itself thus separates the dimension of being in-itself from that of being for-us.

Relative to this duality in Kant's philosophy, is the emphasis of other philosophers, who stress the being for-itself dimension of the humanized world. Here, Wang Yangming's theory of mind is representative. As far as the relation between mind and things goes, Wang Yangming famously remarks "wherever intention is directed is a thing."⁹ Things here are not beings in-themselves. Beings in-themselves are always beyond human consciousness (unaffected by the subject). A thing, as wherever intention is directed at, is already a being, whose being is affected by consciousness and thus has been brought into the conscious domain. "Wherever intention is directed is a thing" does not mean that consciousness constructs a physical world in external space-time, it means rather that the substance of the affective mind invests a being with meaning through its own externalization (the act of intending), thereby constituting the agent's world of meaning. Wang Yangming insists that the constitution of a world of meaning is always inseparably of human being's doing, and because of this, he proposes that "there are no things outside of the affective mind,"¹⁰ which obviously does not give needed commitment to the being in-itself of the world.

A similar tendency can be found in pragmatism. One of the basic features of pragmatism is the tendency to understand beings in connection with values. This standpoint undoubtedly notices that an account of an actual being cannot omit specifications of value, and in a sense, the ontological meaning of pragmatism lies first of all in underscoring that the actual form of things cannot be severed from their significance of value. However, while pragmatism affirms that concrete things envelop determinations of value, it simultaneously diminishes if not neglects entirely the independence of things or the being in-itself of things due to the strength of its commitment to the connection between human being and things (the humanized dimension of things). The following point made by James clearly demonstrates this: "When we talk of reality 'independent' of human thinking, then, it seems a thing very hard to find . . . It is what is absolutely dumb and evanescent, the merely ideal limit of our minds."¹¹ Here we can see in pragmatism a sort of mutually exclusive relationship between the being in-itself dimension of things and the being for-us dimension of a world of meaning. So, this standpoint obviously stands before the impossibility of truly reaching the actual form of being.¹²

In modern philosophy, this understanding has emerged repeatedly, cloaked in different forms. Heidegger's fundamental ontology, for instance, which he takes to be the origination of all other ontologies,¹³ is another. Fundamental ontology focuses on Dasein; as opposed to the first cause or the ultimate whole, Dasein is first of all the being-there of human being. For Heidegger, opening up being presupposes an elucidation of the being, who human being is. As human being's mode of being, Dasein exists for the sake of the being, which in each case is its very own, and any understanding of being is itself a determination of being of Da-sein.¹⁴ Heidegger attempts to overcome traditional metaphysics and its forgetting of being through analyzing Dasein as the process of being-in-the-world. The so-called forgetting of being at once refers to both the neglecting of the historical process of the being of humans and one's slinking away from one's own being-there in transcendent speculations about being. Heidegger's standpoint here shows that the question of being is essentially tied to the conditional setting of one's own being. Compared to the tendency of traditional metaphysics to determine being either through the reduction of being to its first cause or through seeking the ultimate being, the approach of Heidegger's fundamental ontology is undoubtedly different. However, while affirming that the meaning of being is undiscoverable when separated from the being of humans, Heidegger seems to unfittingly overemphasize the nature of the world as being for-us: he attempts to construct the entire architecture of a world of meaning upon Dasein, understood as the conscious agent tied to such affects of spirit as care and anxiety, which more or less restricts the domain of meaning to experiences of individuality. To determine a world of meaning in such a way as this fails quite evidently in terms of concretely ascertaining the nature of being in-itself. A similar tendency can be found in Jaspers. As an existentialist, Jaspers likewise prioritizes the question of being. However, for Jaspers, being is equated with consciousness, which the following statement shows: "To analyze existence is to analyze consciousness."[15] Even though existence here is first linked to the being of humans, the meaning of the world for Jaspers is only given by humans. Therefore, behind his equating of existence with consciousness is his equating of a world of meaning with consciousness as well.

Although contemporary analytic philosophy differs from the speculative philosophy of Heidegger and Jaspers in terms of philosophical form in a variety of ways, there is no shortage of aspects in common that the latter share with some representatives of the former. Differing somewhat from early positivism's rejection of metaphysics altogether, later developments of analytic philosophy show the germination of a concern for the question of being. When Goodman discusses the problem of the being of the world for instance, he proposes the view that "what there is consists of what we make.'"[16] For Goodman, we make versions, and true versions make worlds."[17] This making of which he speaks here is not a reforming of objects in a practical way; it is rather tied to consciousness and symbolic activity. To use his own words, "The worldmaking mainly in question here is making not with hands but with minds, or rather with languages or other symbol systems."[18] It is clear that making in this context is never anything but the making of a world of meaning out of the consciousness and symbolic activity of human beings. The world or form of being made thereby is therefore solely being for-us.

As opposed to the previous tendency, naïve realism is concerned with the being in-itself of the world. In Chinese philosophy, the thought of Wang Chong is representative of this tendency. In terms of the relation between humans and nature, Wang Chong establishes his theory on the side of nature. "Nature" in his philosophical theory is again said in opposition to human being, where nature means being in-itself. According to Wang Chong, the Cosmos has its own operational laws and human activity cannot have any substantial influence upon this process: "The Heavens and the Earth combine energies (*tiandi heqi* 天地合气), and things are contingently born out of it. Thus, plowing, weeding, sowing, and planting is undertaken intentionally, but the growing or failing to mature of the plants is a contingent result of Nature."[19] Here, plowing, weeding, sowing, and planting are originally human being's way of acting upon and transforming nature with the intrinsic aim of making things in-themselves accord with human needs (to provide humans with the resources they need to survive), which simultaneously implies endowing objects with the nature of being for-us. However, for Wang Chong, whether or not things grow does not depend on the "intentional undertaking" of plowing, sowing, and so forth; it unfolds rather as a natural process, and in this sense, whether or not things mature, it still is a matter of being in-itself. As opposed to human activity, the transformation of objects in-themselves is always a matter of nature: "Thus the way of Nature is spontaneous, spontaneous and not deliberate, the two [*yin* and *yang*] are ordered to couple, they meet together and suit one another, such that when human affairs are initiated, the energies (*qi* 气) of Nature are already there."[20] Prior to human effort, nature already operates according to its own means. In other words, human activity has in no true way impressed the mark of human upon objects in-themselves; even though the world enters the domain of practice and cognition, it still does not qualify as being for-us. Similarly, the condition of one's own being is also exhibited as a process of being in-itself: "That a human life has become rich and noble—this is the cultivation and maturation of the initial gift of the spontaneous energies of nature that make such a rich and noble life so powerful."[21] Based on the spontaneous energies of nature, that is, the properties of being in-itself, whatever state one might happen to find oneself in, one never finds oneself beyond the unfolding of the determination of being in-itself. According to this view, human being is also presented to oneself as being in-itself.

These viewpoints just mentioned present different aspects of the two one-sided understandings of a world of meaning, from the side of being in-itself and from that of being for-us. Overcoming the skew of each side presupposes an affirmation of the double-sidedness of the world of meaning (simultaneously being for-us and being in-itself), but also concerns human being's different attitudes toward the world. With regard to the relation of human being to the world, Hegel distinguishes between the practical and theoretical attitudes with which human being treats nature: "In man's *practical* approach to Nature, the latter is, for him, something immediate and external."[22] Understanding Nature as something external determines "the practical attitude toward Nature . . . to use Nature for our own advantage, to wear her out, to wear her down, in short, to annihilate her."[23] As for the relation between being in-itself and being for-us, the practical attitude is expressed as making the object be of use for human being, that is, as overcoming the primordial being in-itself of the object, endowing it with the nature of being "for-us." By contrast, "[i]n the theoretical attitude toward Nature (a) the first point is that we stand back from natural objects, leaving them as they are and adjusting ourselves to them."[24] In general, although grasping the object in a theoretical way also involves "the human perspective," proceeding from the human perspective in the process of knowing always demands continuously overcoming the limitations that come along with this perspective, so as to represent the object as it is. The human perspective expresses the "for-us" dimension of objects in the theoretical relation, whereas "letting them be as they are" includes a confirmation of their being as it is in-itself.

In contrast to the practical attitude's overcoming of the being in-itself of things, the theoretical attitude proves to be an overcoming of the "for-us" dimension, which humans give things. In an extended sense, it seems that we may be able to distinguish the mode of being in the practical relation from the mode of being in the theoretical relation: although both involve the relation between being in-itself and being for-us, the focuses and tendencies of the two are actually not the same. Directed at the unity of being in-itself and being for-us, a world of meaning is in some sense the union of the mode of being in the practical relation and the mode of being in the theoretical relation.[25]

As the actual mode of being, a world of meaning is not only constrained by both the practical and theoretical attitudes as it is also linked to many concrete factors and relations as well. If we were to use Aristotle's theory of four causes here, the formation of a world of meaning involves a formal cause, a material cause, a final cause, and an efficient cause. The formal cause here could be extended to include conceptual and theoretical forms, including the theoretical systems and frameworks through which and in which we explain and reform the world as well as the plans and projects that they lead to; the material cause includes the world of things or objects used; the final cause includes ideals of diverse forms; the efficient cause may be understood concretely as human practical activity. Directed at the humanization of being in-itself, opening up and reforming the world prove to be two sides of the same process. At the conceptual level, opening up the world involves explaining and understanding, which is expressed in different conceptual and theoretical systems; this explaining of the world is at once grounded in practice and also constitutes the precondition of reforming the world further. As the unity of being in-itself and being for-us, a world of meaning is not "being" generated out of "nothing"; it is essentially the world of objects affected and reformed by human beings. Without the material cause (the world of things or objects), a world of meaning would be merely the prospect of abstract ideas. At the same time, transforming Nature in-itself into Nature for-humans unfolds concretely as the process of transforming ideals into actuality. Ideals that are actually possible and that embody human ends have an intrinsic guiding effect upon the process of humanizing the world out of the primordial state of being in-itself. While the conceptual mode of explaining the world involves principles in the sense of "necessary" reasons, human ideals are principles of "what ought to be"; the two are interconnected and regulate the process of reforming the world in different ways. As for its actuality, affecting and reforming the world is always inseparable from human practical activity: whether it is explanations of the world transforming into reformations of the world or ideals transforming into actuality, humans acting practically is always the actual efficient cause.

What is of particular interest here is practical action, which constitutes the efficient cause of the genesis of a world of meaning and exhibits an originative nature and synthetic function overall. The latter (its original and synthetic nature) is shown first of all in making communication between the world of objects (material) and conceptual systems (form) possible, and furthermore overcomes the contingency of the link between them. Considered purely at the material level, a humanized form is somewhat contingent in relation to materials. For instance, the form "table" is by no means a necessary determination of the material "wood," since "wood" could be used to make a table, but it could just as well take on other forms such as doors and windows or others still (it could be burned in a forest fire or rot and decay naturally). However, through human practical action, an intrinsic link is slowly established between "wood" and "table": in the process of refining wood with the form of "table" as an end, the relationship between "wood" and "table" is already no longer contingent. At the same time, human practical activity links human being's idealization (final cause) and human being's actualization (efficient cause) together: it is through the medium of practice that purposes and ends surpass the realm of ideas and merge into the actual process of reforming objects. We can see that the practical action of human beings both constitutes the internal efficient force driving the formation of a world of meaning, and in a deeper sense, provides the intrinsic precondition for the unity of the formal cause and material cause as well as the efficient cause and final cause.

In the history of philosophy, those philosophers who were mainly concerned with reason and universals tended to emphasize the importance of conceptual form (formal cause) while neglecting or forgetting the actual world of objects (material cause). Plato determined ideas as the true beings. For him, the world of ideas is the world that truly has meaning. However, while affirming the authenticity of ideas, Plato isolated ideas from the world of objects, seeing the world of objects as so many copies of ideas. The world of ideas from this perspective is obviously an abstract form of ideas, lacking actuality. Other philosophers gave being in-itself ultimate meaning, thereby eliminating the humanized form of being from "Nature for-humans." Wang Chong shows this tendency in his understanding of the relation between humans and nature. He saw nature and the mode of being of the social sphere as the unfolding of the determinations of objects in-themselves, which omits human being's reforming and acting upon the world. As far as actual form goes, when a thing in-itself enters the process of cognizing and practicing, it is always marked in different ways by some kind of human impression, and this "humanizing" of the object is simultaneously the process through which human being invests the object with forms of meaning (including conceptual and theoretical forms of explaining the world); to neglect this would be to one-sidedly emphasize the role of the material cause and turn a blind eye to the concrete role the formal cause plays in reforming the world.

There are similar tendencies to skew the issue in terms of the relationship between the final cause and efficient cause. Those philosophers who stress the meaning of one's own being give more consideration to the purposive determination of human being. Early Confucians, for instance, claimed: "Human being is the affective mind of the Heavens and the Earth."[26] The essential meaning of this proposition lies in highlighting the axiological status human being has in the cosmos, implying that human being is simultaneously an end in-itself. However, in later medieval Confucianism, the specifications of human being's worth was one-sidedly reduced to the dimensions of the affective mind and human nature: while emphasizing that human being is the affective mind of the Heavens and the Earth, they gave axiological priority to the attainment of inner sagehood in the sense of consummating the spirit of the Confucian scholar. Here, the internal end of refining oneself and becoming sincere gradually inhibited the historical end of "adding nourishment to the cultivation of the Heavens and the Earth," so the practice of reforming objects was repeatedly suspended. In modern philosophy, existentialism in some sense shows a similar tendency. From Heidegger's authentic being to Sartre's being for-itself, the meaning and purpose of the being of humans was repeatedly underscored. However, regardless of whether it is an issue of recovering authentic being from a fallen state of being in the case of Heidegger or an issue of moving toward being for-itself from the state of being in-itself in the case of Sartre, the realization of the meaning of being is still divorced from the historical practice of transforming the world and is understood predominantly as a transformation of consciousness or ideas. While the traditional school of affective mind and human nature focused on the axiological goal of cultivating morality while neglecting the actual deed of acting upon the object, existentialism seeks either the authentic mode of being or the mode of being for-itself but under the pretext that human being's reforming of the world is suspended. Both schools weaken the efficient cause (concrete historical practice) with the final cause in different ways.

In contrast to these approaches, modern scientism shows yet another tendency. Following the triumphant march of progress in scientific technology, scientism is filled with an optimistic belief in the ability of science to reform the world. The power of science is exhibited concretely in the process of humans conquering Nature. The propagation and approbation of technology is always accompanied by the demand to transform and conquer Nature, which is identical to what Hegel deemed the practical attitude of treating Nature, and affirming that technology can conquer Nature entails a commitment to practice. Now, technology originally presents the being of humans with a form of means, the meaning of which lies in providing the development of human freedom with more extensive conditions and possibilities; however, while believing in the power of technology to transform the world, scientism is often unclear concerning the intrinsically valued end of this process, and to varying degrees sees the development of technology itself as the sole end. As far as the relationship between human being and science goes, this tendency cannot prevent scientific alienation: the loss of balance between humans and Nature in the modern age and the increasingly obvious ecological crisis we face demonstrate this; as for the process of transforming Nature in-itself into the Nature for-humans, this implies dispelling the final cause by praising the worth of the efficient cause.

In brief, in the process of humans opening up the world and reforming the world, the externality of objects is gradually overcome, and things in-themselves start to become actual. Connected to this is the transformation of Nature in-itself (*tian zhi tian* 天之天) into Nature for human being (*ren zhi tian* 人之天) whose deepest implication is the genesis of meaning and value. By giving Nature in-itself actuality and value, human being simultaneously transforms Nature in-itself into a world of meaning. Conditioned by human being's cognitive and practical activity, this process unfolds as the interplay of the affective mind with things and principles and the reciprocal interaction of the four causes—formal, material, efficient, and final. In actual fact, these two interactions themselves interlace and fuse together as well: the material cause is akin to things, whereas the formal and final causes are similar to principles or reasons and the efficient cause, which includes cognitive and practical activity, not only concerns things and principles but also the affective mind, whose contents are human capacities. As different phases of the historical process of transforming Nature in-itself into Nature for human being, these aspects themselves present an intrinsic unity, and this unity not only exhibits and confirms the nature of a world of meaning as being for-us by endowing being with actuality and value it also overcomes the abstract form of a world of meaning by affirming the in-itself dimension pertaining to it.

The Meaning of the World of Everyday Life

A world of meaning does not concern external objects divorced from the "being" of humans. As far as the being of humans goes, the primary point of concern should be the world of everyday life. Similar to being in the world of objects, the world of life also has the facet of being in-itself or being natural. This can be deduced from the following facts: as individuals with life, human beings must undergo metabolism, which is a natural process. However, human being is not just a biological entity in the natural sense. While transforming Nature in-itself into Nature for-humans, human being continuously gives human life a civilized or humanized mode of being, which makes a world of meaning take shape at the level of everyday life.

From the philosophical perspective, everyday life is first of all tied to the reproduction of the individual's own being,[27] the basic form of which is the unfolding of ordinary practices or daily routines. Daily routines are primarily directed at maintaining and prolonging life, such eating, drinking, and having sex. Eating and drinking broadly refer to those everyday activities that satisfy the needs of the organism, which are the basic conditions of possibility of the individual's life; sex is an everyday activity based on the relation between the sexes, which constitutes the precondition of prolonging individual life. Of course, the everyday activities that maintain life are not limited to eating, drinking, and sexual intercourse, but they are a typical display of the relationship between everyday life and the being of individual life.

As the conditions of possibility of the continuity and being of individual life, activities or relations such as eating, drinking, and fornicating undoubtedly have a primordial quality of being natural or being in-itself, which belongs to "the wild" (*ye* 野) as opposed to "the civilized" (*wen* 文); here, humans share something in common with animals. However, in the process of realizing the humanization of Nature, humans continuously civilize these kinds of activities or relationships out of the wild state. Eating and drinking, for instance, have the direct function of eliminating thirst and hunger, but there is however a substantial difference pertaining to the concrete way in which these functions are realized. In earlier stages of history, humans mainly used their own hands, nails, and teeth to grind raw flesh as means to slake thirst and eliminate hunger, which is a way of eating and drinking that does not fundamentally differ in kind from that of animals. However, as humans learned how to use fire, and design tools such as knives, forks, and chopsticks as means for eating and drinking, the everyday way of being of humans was radically altered in an important way. As Marx put it: "Hunger is hunger, but the hunger gratified by cooked meat eaten with a knife and fork is a different hunger from that which bolts down raw meat with the aid of hand, nail and tooth."[28] This difference is first of all the distinction between cultured or civilized (*wen* 文) and natural or prehistorical (*ye* 野). To use one's hands, nails, and teeth to tear up and grind up raw meat in order to eliminate hunger is still akin to the instinctual behavior of animals, but to use such means as knives, forks, and chopsticks to eat cooked food is an expression of the evolution of civilization.

With the aim of human survival, eating and drinking blends in with a much broader social life, and the different ways of eating and drinking mark the different degrees of civilization of ways of life. Confucians noticed the importance of this early on. The Confucians repeatedly affirmed the rites (*li* 礼) to be the social, political, and ethical institution of norms, and for Confucians, the rites most directly concern eating and drinking: "The emergence of rites (*li* 礼) starts with eating and drinking."[29] The rites involve the order of society, a civilized way of behaving, and eating and drinking in accordance with a ritual code concretely expresses the order of society and the civilized way of life. Precisely because of this, the Confucians determined eating and drinking in a variety of ways:

> When a youth is in the attendance of an elder at a meal, if the host gives anything to him with his own hand, he should bow to him before eating it. . . .[30] If a youth is in the attendance of and drinks with an elder, when the cup of spirits is brought to him, he rises, bows, and goes to receive it at the place where the spirit-vase is kept. . . .[31] And (the bridegroom) should make a feast, and invite his friends in the district and neighborhood, and his fellow officers—thus giving its due importance to the separate positions (of male and female) . . .[32] He regulated (also) the observances for the collateral branches of his cousins; associating all their members in the feasting. He defined their places according to their order of descent; and differentiated them in accordance with what was proper and right . . .[33] When (the Master) was eating by the side of one who had mourning rites in hand, he never ate to the full.[34]

These examples illustrate that the activity of eating and drinking already involved the whole order of descent from elders to youth, the friendships binding a village, and the communication of emotion between relatives within a clan and between other clans, which already transcends the simple act of filling the stomach and eliminating thirst and hunger. It was understood as the form through which the wild was converted into the civilized. For Confucians, the main point that makes *wen* (culture/civilization) differ from *ye* (the wild and barbaric) lies in the former's embodiment of the way of humans (*rendao* 人道). *The Book of Rites* traces eating manners back to ancient times, when, it claims, people did not yet understand how to use fire to cook food: "They knew not yet the transformative power of fire, but ate the fruits of plants and trees, and the flesh of birds and beasts, drinking their blood, and swallowing [also] the hair and feathers."[35] From the perspective of the way of humans, this way of consuming obviously has negative meaning. By contrast, "the [way of] eating in today's world is due to the way of humans being well refined."[36] Here, "the way of humans" is said in opposition to the "the way of Nature" (*tiandao* 天道) in that it differs from the natural or primordial form of being; this difference is linked to the way in which being is humanized through the defining of places in accordance with the order of descent and differentiating persons in accordance with what is proper and right. To be "due to the way of humans being well refined" here means that the human way of eating transcends the natural (*ye* 野) form and expresses a form in harmony with civilization (*wen* 文).

The mode of being that harmonizes with the way of humans is exhibited at a more intrinsic level as living with dignity. Eating is originally a means of maintaining life, but if food is obtained in such a way that involves losing or damaging the dignity of human character, then one may reject this food. *The Book of Rites* preserves the following record:

> During a great dearth in Qi, Qian Ao had food prepared on the roads, to await the approach of hungry people and give it to them. [One day], there came a famished man, looking as if he could hardly see, his face covered with his sleeve, and dragging his feet together. Qian Ao, carrying with his left hand some rice, and holding some drink with the other, said to him, "Poor man! Come and eat!" The man, opening his eyes with a stare, and looking at him, said, "It was because I would not eat food given [to me] with the words 'Poor man! Come and eat!' that I have come to this state." Qian Ao immediately apologized for his words, but the man after all would not take the food and died.[37]

The phrase "Poor man!" here expresses the pitiful address of the high to the lowly; the offering of food linked to this form of address comes with the intention of a generous hand-out, which obviously shows a lack of adequate respect for human character. To reject the food handed out implies linking the act of eating food to maintaining the dignity of human character. Here, eating is no longer simply the instinctual activity of maintaining life; it is now linked to the confirmation of the intrinsic dignity of the human being as human; in order to maintain one's own dignity one must even be willing "to die rather than eat." As far as the relationship between the being of life and the dignity of human character goes, the old man's position first expresses a concern for the dignity of human character; this is a tendency, that, if not suitably enforced, could lead to the inability to adequately affirm the intrinsic value of living beings. However, with regard to grading the status of everyday life, eating, as one of its most basic forms, acquires another humanist meaning by transcending the natural or primal form of life.

As stated previously, at the level of everyday life, there is a link between the maintenance of life and the continuation of life, and in correlation with this, eating is consistent with the sexual relationship between man and woman. The difference between the sexes is first a natural difference, and the relationship between the two sexes has a primordial or natural quality from the very beginning. The practice of having multiple spouses in primitive ages shows that the relationship between men and women was akin to that between animals of different sexes. However, consistent with moving from an instinctual way of eating to eating in a human way in accordance with the way of humans is the relationship between the sexes transforming from "barbaric" to "civilized." In the state of nature, man and woman communed sexually without order, that is, it was consummated chaotically and without refined distinctions. By establishing the institution of marriage, however, distinction and order between man and woman gradually prevailed. *The Book of Rites* explains this in the following way: "Those rites of marriage are to exhibit the separation that should be maintained between males and females. Generally speaking, rites are to prevent the rise of disorder and confusion, and are like the embankments which prevent the overflow of water."[38] The rites of marriage embodying the form of civilization permeates into everyday life, which enables intercourse between male and female to move out the natural state of disorder and indifference into the state of social order, by virtue of which everyday life transcends its natural significance through the acquisition of humanized (civilized) meaning.

In the form of marriage, the relationship between man and woman is no longer restricted to having biological meaning at the level of the way of Nature; rather, it simultaneously presents social meaning at the level of the way of humans. The tradition of Confucianism found great importance in this. When discussing the rites of marriage, *The Book of Rites* asserts: "The ceremony of marriage is to be a bond of love between two families of different surnames, securing services in the ancestral temple and the continuance of the family line. Therefore, the exemplary human being sets a great value upon it."[39] Here, the "two surnames" no longer merely refer to the two sexes; rather, it involves different families and members of society, while "the ancestral temple" and "the family line" manifests the historical connection between prior and posterior generations. Here, the integration of man and woman is nested into a background of social interaction and historical transmission, which invests it with broader socio-historical meaning as the relationship between the sexes transcends the natural meaning of simple erotic feeling.

As one of the basic relationships embedded in everyday life, the relationship between man and woman in a more profound sense represents the degree to which human being has removed itself from being in-itself (Nature in-itself) in the movement toward being for-us (being humanized). Marx once illustrated this process concretely:

> The direct, natural, and necessary relation of person to person is the *relation of man to woman*. In this *natural* relationship of the sexes man's relation to nature is immediately his relation to man, just as his relation to man is immediately his relation to nature—his own *natural* function. In this relationship, therefore, is *sensuously manifested,* reduced to an observable *fact,* the extent to which the human essence has become nature to man, or to which nature has to him become the human essence of man.[40]

When the relationship between man and woman is still based on instinctual desires or drives, in effect, it possesses no dimension that truly transcends nature. By extension, when a wife is merely taken to be an object of commerce or possession, the relationship between man and woman remains stuck at that level opposed to human nature, that of objectification in the form of being natural. Marx speaks of this as the human essence becoming nature to man. The relationship between the two can only truly manifest the "human essence" and transcend the natural dimension, when this relationship has acquired a civilized and egalitarian form.

In correspondence with civilization pervading everyday life, the latter simultaneously possesses the meaning of linking and communicating nature to society. Everyday life, linked to the means of satisfying natural needs metabolic and sexual, is also not limited to Nature, since it is given a humanized form of being; as this double nature makes everyday life transcend Nature in-itself, to some degree it also enables nature and society to communicate. As far as the being of humans goes, this communicating and linking is the ontological precondition of the unification of human being's inborn nature and moral nature and of human being's vital sensibility and rational essence. It is precisely this original linking of nature and humans in everyday life that grounds the capacity of inborn nature to develop into a moral nature, and as human being's moral nature overcomes inborn human nature, hostility toward the latter is also avoided, so as to prevent the alienation of human nature. At the same time, the humanized dimension of everyday life is also expressed in many ways through learning customs, conventions, and traditions as well as acquiring common sense; from procuring food and dwelling space to engaging in social interactions, the effect of customs, common sense, conventions, and traditions can always be seen. According to their substance, even though customs and common sense differ in terms of their intrinsic content, they are both the consolidation of human being's understanding and grasp of the world in the course of the historical development of the species (transcending individuals); furthermore, they are also the accumulation of the accomplishments of culture and civilization. When discussing the origin and function of rituals and rites, Xunzi remarks:

> Therefore ritual propriety is cultivation. The superior human being achieves the cultivation of ritual propriety and enjoys the distinctions in rites. What is meant here by distinction? That the noble and the base are ranked (*guijian you deng* 贵贱有等), that elders and youth are differentiated (*zhangyou you cha* 长幼有差), that poor and rich, unimportant and important may be weighed (*you cheng zhe* 有称者).[41]

Here, so-called "cultivation" points to the fulfillment of everyday human needs, that is, "to cultivate human desires, and provide for human needs."[42] A code of rites originally belongs to institutionalized and standardized forms of civilization, but for Xunzi, a code of rites is inseparably linked to the fulfillment of everyday human needs from the outset; the function of rites—to establish an ethical social order—arises from the aforesaid link (to be good at distinguishing rites presupposes accomplishing the cultivation of ritual propriety); this expresses the link between what is natural and what is human. Historically speaking, with customs, traditions, and common sense as regulative principles, everyday life continues itself while also enabling the previous accomplishments of civilization that have consolidated and accumulated in customs, common sense, conventions, and traditions to be transmitted to posterior generations. Therefore, while ensuring the historical succession and transmission of culture, everyday life also transcends Nature in-itself and more concretely connects the natural and the human.

Based on the communication of the natural and humanized dimensions of being in everyday life, human being's separation from this world is overcome to some extent. As the enactor of the world, human being exhibits a different tendency in opposition to the world of objects, and social differentiation, which the division of labor engenders, furthermore entails the possibility of the separation of human being from human being. Both the separation of human being from the world of objects as well as interpersonal distance give human being a sense of estrangement and alienation in relation to this world. So, the relationship between human being and the world could be quite distant. By comparison, in everyday life human activity involves external objects but also involves imprinting the mark of humanization and society everywhere, and the two are by no means mutually exclusive. Similarly, even though the relationships found among humans are never lacking in tensions and conflicts, everyday life as a whole—from living together with family members to affiliating with friends and neighbors—never ceases to demonstrate the affinity between humans. The integration of human being with the world of objects and interpersonal harmony enables humans "to be" in the world as if they were at home. This sense of being at home cancels out and overcomes the distance and estrangement between human being and the world, while simultaneously providing individuals with the ontological ground to identify with this world and accept it.

At the metaphysical level, to identify with this world not only means accepting and blending into this world, it also means affirming the true reality of this world. For the individual, objects in the world of everyday life are the most immediate and real beings. As far as consumption goes, the everyday actions of clothing oneself, eating, and procuring dwelling space do not involve virtual things, but real objects, which each fulfillment of a human need confirms. Philosophers who have fallen into speculative fantasies may deny the reality of the world in a mystical state, but as soon as they return to the world of everyday life, they will be constantly reminded that the various resources human beings need to survive are not ideal beings. Granted, this verification of life is different from the verifications provided by rational arguments, but it gives one grounds to confirm the reality of the world in an experiential or common sense way. Similarly, in the everyday world of communication, the agent of communication and the process of communicating really do exist in this world; with language as well as the body, tools, and behavior as mediums, inter-subjective relationships, though easily concealed, present their reality time and again; even virtual connections in the internet age ultimately require real subjects and inter-subjective relationships as their foundation and actual support. Although the individual's grasp of being in everyday life is spontaneous and pre-reflective in nature, life in its everydayness, with its immediate authenticity, provides the individual with the initial grounds upon which a vivid sense of reality concerning this world can be formed.

This real sense of the world could also be seen as ontological evidence, which simultaneously constitutes the basic precondition of the individual being-in-the-world. Now, the mode of being of everyday life is relative to the process of producing and reproducing the stuff of material life. Even though everyday life in earlier historical ages was tightly intertwined with laboring, in later stages of development, the distinction between everyday life and non-everyday life has become relative. Yet, with the production and reproduction of life as its content, everyday life undoubtedly encompasses features that differ from productive labor. The production and reproduction of life is directly tied to maintaining and continuing biological life, including the revival and conservation of bodily forces, the fulfillment of vital needs, the development of vital capacities, and so on, and important ways and paths through which these goals are realized include leisure and play. As ways of everyday life, leisure and play presuppose a foreshortening of work time. When labor time occupies the majority of human existence, everyday life and labor nearly coincide in terms of time, and so there is no way for leisure and play to become a substantial part of life. In accompaniment with the foreshortening of labor time, humans gradually came into the possession of an increase in surplus time aside from labor, and leisure began to enter the process of human life. In contrast to labor, leisure and play in everyday life present the characteristic of being free. Throughout a rather long historical period, laboring exhibited a two-fold quality: insofar as it exhibits human being's power to affect and reform the world of objects, it undoubtedly presents the aspect of freedom; yet insofar as it is still pressed with the demands of survival (constrained by the necessities of survival) or suffers under forms of alienation, it has not truly reached a free state. By contrast, insofar as leisure and play presuppose the possession of time that one can control according to one's own will, they imply some liberation from compulsory survival activity and to a rather large extent transcend direct ends of utility; both exhibit the character of freedom in different ways. As the forms in which it is linked to everyday being, such kinds of freedom differ from liberty in the socio-political realm, and exhibit a more direct and original relationship to the being of humans. When discussing the relationship between human being and play, Schiller once remarked that, "to declare it once and for all, Man plays only when he is in the full sense of the word a man, and *he is only wholly Man when he is playing.*"[43] Whether or not a human being is human "in the full sense of the word" only while playing is of course open to debate, but if "in the full sense of the word a man" is understood as the human being who has developed free character, then there is certainly a correlation between human being and play. At the same time, leisure and play are also not just simple diversions insofar as they make possible the cultivation of various interests, the development of character and many other capacities. The cave paintings of early humankind could be seen in the broad sense as active play in the surplus time of leisure beyond labor. As an early form of artistic creation, cave painting also shows human being's interest in artistic creation, which furthermore exhibits a corresponding capacity. What is important here is that play alludes to the free use and control of time, which is not the same as wallowing around in diversions: when human being is caught up in some amusing activity and cannot pull itself out, human being substantially is controlled by this activity and is incapable of truly entering into free play. According to their original sense, play and leisure, as forms of everyday life, endow the world of everyday life with intrinsic meaning from the perspective of the free state of being of humans and the possibility of the individual's multi-faceted development.

We can see that similar to the conversion of things in-themselves into things for-us, everyday life taking on the form of a world of meaning is tied to the humanization of nature: this implies that the production and reproduction of life in the natural sense transcends nature and acquires a socialized and civilized form of being. Transcending nature does not, however, entail human being's total separation from nature. As the concrete form of being, which conjointly involves nature and human being, everyday life simultaneously integrates both the way of nature and the way of humans and enables them to communicate, which grounds the unity of inborn human nature and human being's moral nature and of human being's sensible life and rational essence. In the form of leisure and play on the basis of free time, everyday life provides space for the development of human being's multiple facets and freedom. While things for-us confirm human being's essential powers by bearing the mark of human impressions, everyday life more directly represents the transformation and elevation of human being's very mode of being, which is precisely what makes everyday life become yet another form of a world of meaning.

A World of Meaning and Social Reality

As opposed to the world of objects, everyday life shares a closer connection with the social sphere. In fact, some philosophers understand the world of everyday life as the predominant form of social reality.[44] However, from a broader perspective, social reality is not limited to the world of everyday life, and possesses much richer and more diverse content. When we transform Nature in-itself into Nature for-humans, overcome the being in-itself of everyday life, and more closely consider the actual form of a world of meaning, social reality becomes an object of the utmost importance.

As the mode of being of the social sphere, the characteristic that distinguishes social reality from natural objects lies first in the formation of the social sphere and its activity, which is always tied to the being of humans. Before natural objects enter the domain of meaning, their determination as being in-itself is their original state: whether we consider them from the logical or historical perspective, in the natural world objects may "exist" beyond the domain of cognition and practice without presenting their meaning to human being; in other words, their being and their meaning may not coincide. Being in-itself, on the other hand, may not be said of social reality: things in the social sphere take shape through and exist within the human sphere of practice and cognition, and therefore, their being and their meaning are inseparable.

In a broad sense, social reality includes everyday life, but if considered at a more substantial level, social reality exists in the form of institutions, organizations, and interacting communities and in their associated activities and modes of being. Everyday life, as the conditions of the production and reproduction of individual life, contains a natural dimension and possesses a diffuse nature of sorts: by contrast, in the form of institutions and organizations, social reality presents socio-historical meaning and is characterized by stability. In regard to its concrete mode of being, social reality in the latter sense (institutions and organizations) involves the economic, political, and legal domains as well as those of the military, education, and culture. In the economic sphere of modern society, we find many kinds of economic organizations such as factories, companies, markets, and banks—from production and transportation to trade and finance. In the political and legal domains, there are states, political parties, and governments as well as their legislative and judicial organs. In the domain of education, we find many classes of education from universities and high schools to middle schools and elementary schools, and even training organizations. In the cultural domain, there are publishing houses, journals, the media, and theatre companies as well as other organizations and institutions such as literary arts associations; in the domain of scientific research there are multiple forms of organizations such as research institutes, peer review journals, and academies.

In the form of institutions and social organizations, social reality is intimately related to the ideals, ideas, and practical activities of human beings. From the macroscopic perspective of social history, there are different understandings of how to locate the ontological status of individuals, groups, ideals, ideas, and material forces; that is, one may stress the role of the individual or highlight the function of the group while another may emphasize the role of ideals and ideas or focus on the function of economic and political activities. But, all confirm the role of human beings in the process of forming and transforming social reality, even if in different senses. This connection between social reality and human being shows a kind of constructivism of social reality, which different theories of society have demonstrated. Social contract theory is worthy of mention here. As a theory of social politics, contract theory first aims at explaining the origin of the state. Taking Rousseau's contract theory, for example, based on the supposition that human rights are inborn or innate, the origin of the state is understood as the result of the individual transferring his or her rights: a person transfers his or her own right to a political organization that represents the common interest, which then generates the state. Evidently here, the state as social reality is mainly seen to be the product of a compromise (enveloped only in this transferring) and agreement among humans, which as a process entails a certain constructivism.

The contemporary philosopher John Searle gives a more concrete analysis of the constructivist nature of social reality. Searle distinguishes two varieties of facts, that is, facts that are independent of human beings and facts that are dependent upon them: social reality is of the latter variety. As a fact that relies on human beings, the formation of social reality is tied to the act of humans assigning functions. To assign a function is precisely to attach a function to an object, which gives it a corresponding status function. For instance, to give some specific piece of paper a general function such as possessing value, it becomes currency or money, and currency or money is a kind of social reality. Correlated with assigning functions is collective intentionality, which is exhibited concretely in the common acceptance or mutual agreement of individuals in a community. In the case of currency, if some kind of "paper" is assigned the function of serving as money, and this function is collectively recognized and accepted, then it actually becomes money. Searle sees this process as the formation of social reality or institutional facts and emphasizes the constructed nature of social reality.[45]

Compared to social contract theory, which primarily refers to the macroscopic dimension of society, Searle's function assignment theory concerns a diversity of institutional facts; but, not withstanding the difference of stress between them, both undoubtedly share much in common insofar as they understand social reality as a human construction. In the form of constructs or constructions, what is mainly emphasized is the role of consciousness or the dimension of self-awareness in the process of forming social reality. Whether it is persons transferring rights or persons assigning functions, both unfold as self-aware and intentionally undertaken activities; and this self-awareness of action is first of all tied to conscious processes: while making a contract presupposes the willing agreement of all parties, assigning a function more directly involves collective intentionality.

As objects of the domain of cognition and practice, the formation of social reality is inseparably bound to man's self-aware actions. Identical to the broader sense of humanized things, social reality also embodies different human ideals, the formative process of which is always pervaded by human ends, intentions, rational thought, and planning. From political institutions like the state, to concrete objects like money production and efficacy always involve these aspects. This connection between human activity and social reality makes the latter not only exist in the mode of being "for-us" in the general sense, but also endows it with the mode of being self-aware. In this respect, neither social contract theory nor function assignment theory is without due insight.

However, seeing social reality merely as the intentional construction of human beings or as the product of human being's self-conscious construction obviously fails to grasp the whole substance of the issue. Although humans indeed undertake activities and creations self-consciously in and throughout social history, such activities are never completely isolatable from the unconscious realm of nature. For example, labor, as the basic form of practical activity, presupposes that "He [man] opposes himself to Nature as one of her own forces."[46] As the interaction of humans and nature, labor is obviously steeped in the dimension of Nature in-itself. At the same time, human creations are also based on certain conditions, which arise from the free choices of human beings. Marx once remarked on this: "Men make their own history, but they do not make it as they please; they do not make it under circumstances chosen by themselves, but under circumstances directly encountered, given and transmitted from the past."[47] These pre-existing conditions of creativity that cannot be chosen do not just constitute the limitations of creative activity in the negative sense; at a more profound level they reveal another aspect of the creativity that is opposed to constructing self-consciously: these aspects of the conditions of creativity show that social reality is always constituted by a dimension of being in-itself, which makes social reality also manifest itself as a process of natural history.

Historically speaking, although social reality embodies human ideals and human ends, it also reflects the objective needs of the evolution of society. The state, for instance, is such that its formation is not based on the will of the individual or that of the group, nor does the state arise merely out of the rational planning of the few; rather, at a more primary level, its formation is linked to the development of the economy, the transformation of the system of ownership (first, the emergence of the system of private property), society's differentiation (including the formation of classes), and so on; it is, moreover, the social disparities and conflicts accompanying these formations and transformations that generate the historical need to produce a state. In the same way, the emergence of currency, as an institutional fact, stems from the objective needs of the development of commodity trade relations. The earliest forms of currency did not exist in the form of assigning some "paper" with the function of currency. As a matter of fact, as opposed to some conscious assignment of a function, the emergence of currency was rather spontaneous from the very beginning: when trading things for things no longer suited the needs of the development of trade relations, people spontaneously took some kind of thing or several kinds of things as a universal equivalent, and money developed upon this basis. This spontaneity in the process of historical development reveals the being in-itself of social reality in yet another way.

As mentioned previously, highlighting the self-consciousness of social reality demands emphasizing the function of consciousness or intentionality. From the agreement between the members of society (social contract theory) to the acceptance of collective intentionality (function assignment theory), conscious or intentional action has been given an important role in social reality; in a sense this role appears as intentional recognition. As regarding its external form, intentional recognition is linked to "seeing as." In Rousseau's social contract theory, the state is "seen as" the public will or the representative of the General Will, and in Searle's assignment function theory, some object (such as a specific kind of paper) is "seen as" money or currency through intentional recognition. This "seeing as" based on intentional recognition involves action at the level of ideas; and placing emphasis on this ideal activity means giving it priority.

Relative to intentional recognition is practical recognition. The external form of intentional recognition is "to see as," whereas practical recognition refers to accepting in practice or to practically "use as." Although the formation and operating of social reality involves agreement at the level of ideas, it is likewise inseparable from "using as" in practice. As mentioned previously, from the perspective of history, social reality originates from spontaneously "using as," the actual mode of which is inseparable from practically "using as." Institutions and institutional facts do not have vital forces in themselves; they only gain intrinsic vitality and actuality when they are in "practical use." So, in the formation and operating of social reality, intentional recognition and practical recognition are not strictly separable.

We can see that social reality, as the being of the cognitive and practical domain of humans, is on the one hand constructed, but on the other hand, it is also the product of natural history, and thus encompasses the dimension of being in-itself; the formation and operating of social reality simultaneously intertwines intentional and practical recognition. Insofar as it is inseparable from the being of humans, social reality differs from the world of objects; insofar as it confirms itself through practical recognition, it also differs from the world of ideas. In terms of its actuality, social reality at once takes shape through the process of humans cognizing and practicing without ceasing to constitute the conditions of possibility of human cognitive and practical activity.

Corresponding to its actuality, social reality also has its external aspects of form, which are physical. Governments have offices, buildings, and other material means of guaranteeing that orders are carried out; industrial enterprises have their factories, machines, and equipment, which are undoubtedly physical; they distinguish social reality from the world of ideas while endowing the former with the nature of being in-itself. However, the determination of social reality as social reality does not consist in merely encompassing a physical form; at a more substantial level, social reality reveals its intrinsic determination through the being of humans and the human activity of cognizing and practicing. Physical forms are themselves lifeless; they may only acquire vitality through human activity. When we form connections to different forms of social reality, we interact with more than just things without human character, we interact with the humans who give institutions their living vitality. In the actual operating of social reality, there is everywhere and always human participation; human activity is the very precondition of the actualization of their concrete roles. Without physical form social reality would be unable to present its actual external form, whereas without the internal meaning of humanization, social reality would lose its internal life. In its substance, the meaning of social reality springs from the being and acting of humans; in this sense, one could say that the core of social reality is human. When Searle ties social reality to the assigning of functions he undoubtedly grasps this point.

In the form of the unity of physical formations and the humanized contents filling them, social reality presents consistency with things for-us. However, things for-us presupposes the humanization of the natural world and appears as reformed or modified objects; as objective being, things for-us more precisely exhibit the mode of being "instruments." Social reality differs from the world of objects insofar as it is always immanent to the process of humans interacting and their connections, and human being always constitutes its core. Confucianism once insisted that "the superior human being is no instrument,"[48] which is an idea with multiple dimensions; its intrinsic sense lies in transcending the domain of "instruments." Transcending the domain of instruments first shows that social reality cannot rest simply on things or the world of objects, and means that we must overcome the mere external form that things like instruments present through a grasp of their internal humanized substance.

As for the way in which rituals function, You Zi once laid out a famous argument: "The most valuable function of rituals lies in harmonizing."[49] As argued previously, the "rituals or rites" that Confucians speak of refer to the systematic body of universal norms, including the socio-political institution, which belongs to social reality; "harmonizing" appears as an ethical principle that is manifested in human interactions; considering it negatively, harmonizing demands that tensions and conflicts between humans be assuaged and subdued through mutual understanding and communication; as regards its positive aspect, to harmonize means to strike a concord of mind and power between humans, integrating forces and cooperating. Rites primarily concern the operating of institutions (including the holding of ordinary rituals, the stipulations of hierarchical structure, the carrying out of political orders, and the symbiosis of the rulers and ministers, along with the higher and lower strata), but Confucians linked this operating of institutions to the ethical principle of "harmonizing," stressing the functions of rituals, the most valuable of which consists in following the principle of harmony and embodying it; here, we can see their understanding of the background of social reality in general and institutional organizations in particular as a relationship of humans, which entails overcoming the external mode of instrumental things by grasping the substantial meaning of the human principle of ritual propriety. "When one says 'The rites, the rites,' is it enough to mean by this only presents of jade and silk?"[50]—such statements explicate this point aptly: jade and silk are external in form, belonging to the world of "instruments;" rituals are not limited to gifts of jade and silk, and mean to move from instruments to human being. This understanding takes notice of the fact that the core of rituals, as social reality, is human being.

It is precisely this human core that contains the meaning of social reality. Things "for-us" at the level of objects are also tied to human being, but as reformed and modified objects, their roles and functions are first grounded in their physical form. By comparison, social reality, the substantial content of which is the being and practicing of humans, is immediately the human world. While things for-us require the cognitive and practical activity of humans as a medium for them to constitute a world of meaning, social reality, as a world of meaning, is internal to this cognitive and practical activity itself, which embodies it. At the same time, the value of things "for-us" lies first of all in serving as means for the fulfillment of rational human needs. Differing somewhat from this, the dimension of ends and the dimension of means fuse together in social reality. So, social reality, as a world of meaning, presents the very characteristic of the world as the human world.

The human world of course is not just the embodiment of human impressions or the manifestation of human actions; at a much more intrinsic level, it consists in according with human nature. In broad terms, according with human nature means expressing the universal essence of human being, which distinguishes humans from all other beings, and social reality thus constitutes a representation or concrete measure of whether things accord with human nature or not or to what degree things are fitting with human nature. In Confucianism's discussion about the relationship between rituals and humans, we find this remark: "Although a human who doesn't observe ritual propriety can still speak, doesn't he or she still have the mind and sensibility of a beast?"[51] "The reason a human is therefore human is due to observing ritual propriety and being righteous."[52] Here, the observance of ritual propriety as a social reality is seen as the intrinsic determination of human being, which distinguishes humans from animals (beasts). In other words, whether or not something accords with ritual propriety becomes the scale that measures whether or not something accords with human nature.

Daoism touches upon this issue from another angle. Here, Zhuangzi's perspective is worth mentioning. In the debate concerning the distinction between humans and Nature, Zhuangzi gave central status to the existential condition of humans. Proceeding from this, Zhuangzi opposes the equating of human being with a thing or "burying oneself in things": "Those who have buried themselves in things and who have lost their human nature in social customs are called the people who have been inverted (*daozhi zhi min* 倒置之民)."[53] "Self" here expresses the mode of the individual person, while "human nature" is the intrinsic determination or essence of human being qua human. For Zhuangzi, as the individual form of human being, the self has priority in relation to things; similarly, as the intrinsic determination of human being, human nature also has a higher value than the customary values of recognition and wealth; as soon as the self dissolves into things or the intrinsic determination of human being is lost in the pursuit of fame and gain, this means the relationship between human being and things as well as that between nature and custom have been overturned or inverted. On the basis of the same premises, Zhuangzi repeatedly insisted that one must "not destroy oneself with things,"[54] and "not alienate oneself with things."[55]

For Zhuangzi, social reality in the humanized form is not necessarily constituted by beings that accord with human nature. As for rites, music, and morals, although their form carries a humanized nature, the process from which they were derived was not congruous with the mode of being of human-naturalization:

> To make humans bow to rites and bend to music, to propagate the principles of humanity and justice in order to allay the affective mind of the world—this is to undo the natural state of the affective mind and the world. There is a natural state of things. To arise from the natural state is to draw a curve or circle without a compass, to draw a straight line or square without ruler or carpenter's square, to attach things without glue or lacquer or to bind things without strings or ropes ... Thus, to put it into words, for three generations there hasn't been a single human being who hasn't used things to alienate the natural human tendency (*xing* 性). The petty man sacrifices himself for wealth, the man of office sacrifices himself for prestige, the higher official sacrifices himself for family, and the sage sacrifices himself for the world.[56]

The natural state spoken of here refers to the original form that was never refined or reformed, like squares and circles that are shaped without the help of ruler or compass; the "natural state" of human being is what is fitting with the original form of human nature. According to Zhuangzi's view, ritual codes and music, moral codes and justice are external standards; to place human being under the yoke of such standards leads to the replacement of the natural human tendency with extrinsic standards, thereby forcing humans to lose the "natural state" of human nature. Zhuangzi's mistaking the original form of being for the humanized form of being shows a failure to genuinely grasp the substantial sense of humanization, and his critique of rites and music connects social reality to humanized being in the form of a negation: to be grounded in rites and music is necessarily to fall into the inhuman and so is rejected. The logical premise of such a deduction is that social reality ought to harmonize with human nature. While Confucianism distinctly and positively sees harmonizing with human nature as the intrinsic attribute of social reality, Daoism expresses a similar viewpoint in an obscure way by means of negation; of course, there is still an important difference between both viewpoints concerning how to harmonize with human nature in the true sense.[57]

With regard to the being of humans, the meaning of social reality is inseparable from whether or not something accords with human nature. While the main characteristic that distinguishes social reality from the world of objects lies in its human core, according with human nature endows social reality with the meaning of being at a more intrinsic level. As the intrinsic attribute of a world of meaning, according with human nature could be understood on different levels. Considered in broad terms, humanity and sociality share something in common insofar as harmonizing with human nature means acquiring social characteristics or social properties. But the more substantial and intrinsic expression of human nature lies in human freedom and the multi-faceted development of human potential. As Hegel states, "Nature exhibits no freedom in its existence, but only *necessity* and *contingency*."[58] Only with humans is there the demand and capacity for freedom; the development of human nature and the realization of freedom are in terms of content two sides of the same process. Historically speaking, it is precisely in the process of moving toward freedom that human being gradually distinguishes itself from the world of objects, and it is also precisely within this process that human being gradually acquires the essential determination that distinguishes human being from things and natural objects. So, to accord with human nature implies the demand to move toward freedom: whether or not and to what extent social reality accords with human nature is identical to whether or not and to what extent social reality manifests the historical process of moving toward freedom.

Furthermore, as the concrete form of a world of meaning, social reality not only constitutes the representation of humanized nature, it also ensures the movement toward harmonizing with human nature. When discussing the role of rites, *The Book of Rites* points out: "To value holding to one's word, cultivating peaceful relationships, and to show kind consideration and courteous compliance so as to do away with quarrelling and plundering: how could this practice possibly reign without observing ritual propriety?"⁵⁹ Here, "to value holding to one's word and cultivating peaceful relationships" expresses the positive sense of human beings fostering harmonious relationships among themselves, while "doing away with quarrelling and plundering" expresses the negative sense of eliminating conflicts; both manifest the order of society, and as a social reality, the code of rites is seen as the conditions of possibility of this form of being. Concretely speaking, how do rituals embody this role? *The Book of Rites* elucidates this further:

> The rituals at the court audiences of the different seasons were intended to illustrate the righteous relationship between ruler and subject; those of friendly messages and inquiries, to secure mutual honor and respect between the feudal princes; those of mourning and sacrifice, to illustrate the kindly feelings of ministers and sons; those of social meetings in the country districts, to show the order that should prevail between the young and the elderly; and those of marriage, to exhibit the separation that should be maintained between males and females. Those rituals inhibit the cause of disorder and confusion.⁶⁰

This passage touches upon different social relationships—between ruler and minister, between dukes, between townspeople, between husband and wife, and so forth—behind these relationships we find such social fields as the political, diplomatic, familial, and so on. For Confucians, each kind of relationship marking the social field needs a specific ritual to regulate it; it is this normative and regulative role of rituals that enable society to avoid falling into disorder. Generally speaking, conflict, opposition, and chaos present negative meaning to humans just as harmonious order better suits the needs of human development; by undoing conflicts and oppositions in the negative sense and by upholding social order in the positive sense, "rituals" provide the conditions for the attainment of a form of being that accords with human nature.

Of course, the movement toward a form of being that accords with human nature unfolds as a historical process, and so the meaning of social reality presents a corresponding historicality and complexity. Considering its actual form of being, social reality itself may manifest the tendency of history and the demands of human development, but may be at odds with the former as well; the Daoist critique of alienating human nature with things and the postmodernist critique of modernity both show different senses of this conflict of social reality with the demands of human development.⁶¹ In essence, only a social reality that is consistent with the tendency of historical evolution of and the demands of human development can ensure the advance toward a form of being that accords with human nature. Here it seems some sort of circle is implied: only a social reality that suits the development of human nature is historically rational, while attaining a form of being that suits human nature presupposes the preexistence of this kind of a social reality. However, this circle is not only that of mutual presupposition in the logical sense; it is also a historical interaction in the substantial sense.

With the historical evolution of knowing and practicing as its precondition, a world of meaning takes shape and unfolds into concrete forms of being in different dimensions. Through the transformation of Nature in-itself (the primordial state of being) into Nature for-humans (things for-us), the world of objects overcomes its primordial state and acquires the form of being actual, which is the union of being in-itself and being for-us, the intrinsic attribute of which is suiting human needs; by confirming the creative powers of human beings, social reality exhibits its multi-faceted meaning; the sphere of meaning further infuses the world of everyday life by going beyond the natural form of being of biological survival and reproduction and by endowing the individual with her social and civilized form of being; aiming at a form of being that accords with human nature, social reality is the representation of humanization and ensures the movement toward the humanized form of being. In this formation of a world of meaning the intrinsic union of the actual nature of objects, the essential powers of human beings and the value of being itself are thoroughly manifested.

6 Meaning and the Individual

GROUNDED IN THE historical process of accomplishing oneself and accomplishing things, a world of meaning may take shape into different forms. Whether it is exhibited internally in the form of ideas or unfolds externally into humanized reality, a world of meaning is always inseparable from the being of humans. Now, when considering the relation between the being of humans and a world of meaning, the individual or the person is an important aspect that cannot be ignored, because a world of meaning is first opened up and presented to the concrete individual or person. At a much broader level, the being of the individual possesses some sort of ontological priority: accomplishing oneself in the social sphere is likewise the concern of a specific individual. As a historical process, accomplishing things and accomplishing oneself and the consequent genesis of a world of meaning concerns the being of the individual at both the metaphysical and social level. Therefore, it is impossible to dodge the problem of the individual in a concrete consideration of a world of meaning.

The Individual from the Metaphysical Perspective

The Chinese term for "individual" (*geti* 个体), is composed of two characters. The character *ge* (个), which means "a unit of," expresses precisely that the individual is first of all a singular mode of being, and the pronoun "this" is usually used to express this singularity. The singularity linked to the pronoun "this" has bounded meaning: "this" individual is not "that" individual; in this sense, the individual is distinct from another. The other character composing this compound word *geti* is *ti* (体), which could be translated as "body" or "substance." The individual is at once "this" or "a unit of" "body" or "substance"; the body or substance not only gives the individual its reality, it also makes it become the bearer of different properties or determinations. As the bearer of diverse attributes and determinations, the individual is a concrete unity: the diverse attributes a specific individual possesses are always unified and interrelated in this "substance." As for the latter aspect, the individual has at once singularity and specific unity. Philosopher Francoise Suárez (1548–1617) already noticed this link between "this" and "substance" when he called the individual an "individual unity," even though his understanding of the individual pertains more to the theoretical trend of nominalism.[1]

As a unity, the individual contains its own system and structure; as soon as the original structure of the individual is fundamentally altered, the said individual no longer exists. If a piece of chalk crumbles, transforming into powder, it is no longer the individual piece of chalk it originally was, since the way it held together originally as a structured unity has been entirely altered. This touches upon the irreducible nature of the individual as well: the unity possessed by the individual is the individual's basic form of being. If an individual disintegrates or is reduced to a more primary set of parts, the said individual correspondingly disappears. A piece of wooden furniture is made out of wood, but if a specific piece of furniture like a bookshelf is entirely disassembled it becomes nothing more than just wood and no longer exists as an individual piece of furniture; an animal consists of a skeleton, muscles, blood, and so on, but if a specific animal like a cow disintegrates into bones, flesh, blood, and so on, and is thereby reduced to those [more primary] parts, it ceases to be the individual it originally was. This irreducibility in a sense makes the individual the primary unity or the basic unit of being.[2]

As the primary unity or basic unit of being, the individual, although belonging to a definite species, cannot itself be further exemplified. For instance, human being as a species can be divided into such different individuals as Socrates and Confucius, but under Socrates and Confucius no further individual specimens of the human species can be differentiated. In connection with this fact, the fundamental characteristic of the individual is at times understood to be its "noninstantiability."[3] In terms of the relationship between name and object, noninstantiability is first linked to a proper name like Confucius or a qualified name such as "the current president of Peking University." This link between the noninstantiability of individuals and proper or qualified names shows the uniqueness and singularity of individuals. Uniqueness means that each individual possesses attributes other individuals do not have, and singularity means there are no two completely identical individuals.

In the process of being, the individual continuously faces the issue of particularization. Individuals and particulars are often seen as the same type of phenomenon. According to this understanding, there is no substantial distinction between the individual and the particular.[4] But in fact, the two cannot be simply equated. As stated previously, at the metaphysical level, the individual is first of all a specific unity, while particulars correspond to different positions of space and time: so concretely speaking, so-called particulars are the different positions of the individual in space and time. When considering the individual's particularization, Jin Yuelin states: "The particularization of the individual is precisely the individual's temporalization and spatialization."[5] The being of the individual unavoidably involves different relations of space and time. While growing, the human being, for instance, undergoes different stages of life, and ontologically speaking, such differences are presented through reciprocally distinguished relations of space and time (an individual human being respectively occupies different positions of space and time from youth to old age). The same individual always obtains particular form of being according to the different positions of space and time he or she occupies. This particularization of the individual in relation to space and time actualizes and concretizes the uniqueness of the individual.

Corresponding to the individual's particularization in space and time is the problem pertaining to the changing and unchanging aspects of the individual. That the individual passes through different positions of space and time means that the individual is always experiencing alterations, due to which the question naturally arises: In what sense is the individual the same in the process of changing? This question concerns both the relationship between the individual and the universal, and that between the particular and the general. The individual's alteration in space and time is the individual's ceaseless formation of specific particulars; the individual's particularization thus emerges through particulars, and so-called change is first and foremost the altering of particulars. However, the individual is simultaneously an individual belonging to a certain species; this belongingness of an individual to a corresponding species or that an individual is attributed to a species, presupposes that the individual possesses whatever is attributed to the species universally in common. That Confucius is subsumed under the species "human being" is due to the fact that he possesses the universal attributes of human being qua human, which includes possessing rationality, sociality, and so on. However, while universal or common attributes are within the individual, they always blend together into the specific being of the individual in the obtaining of a concrete form, which could be seen as the concretization of universals or concrete universals. On the one hand, a concrete universal is one of the universal attributes of a species; on the other hand, a concrete universal and an individual also integrally combine, emerging as one concrete form of being. In correspondence with this fact, we can also make a distinction between universal, concrete universal, and particular. The universal "human being" distinguishes such individuals as Confucius and Socrates from all other non-human beings (including living and non-living things). Concrete universals, in turn, distinguish different individuals within the species "human": the same universal attribute of human being is manifested differently in the sociality that Confucius presented in his social relations and social activities on the one hand and in the sociality that Socrates presented in his social interactions on the other. Here, the concrete form of the universal "social" constitutes the key factor that reciprocally distinguishes individuals within the same species "human." Furthermore, each and every individual undergoes a variety of particular transformations throughout the process of being: the Confucius who took up an official post in the State of Lu is different from the Confucius who traveled from state to state; young Socrates is not the same as elderly Socrates. However, regardless of how the particulars of Socrates and Confucius in space and time may change, Socrates remains Socrates and Confucius Confucius. Is this phenomenon understandable, and if so, how? Once again, we need to focus on concrete universals: the particulars of the individual change while the individual stays the same; the reason for this is that the concrete universals that the individual possesses never change. Although the position Confucius had in space and time altered from the Kingdom of Lu to different kingdoms, and although Socrates transformed from youth to old age, as the unity of universal attributes and the individual's being, concrete universals do not fundamentally change in the meantime. The latter determines individuals to remain the same individuals. Here, concrete universals seem to have a double meaning: on the one hand, a concrete universal reciprocally differentiates distinct individuals belonging to the same species, while on the other hand, it provides the intrinsic ground for the individual to maintain self-identity throughout the transformation of his or her particularity.

We can now see that beneath the changing and unchanging aspects of the individual is the relationship between particulars and universals and that between individuality and universality. In the history of philosophy, it is Leibniz who is celebrated for his thorough treatment of the individual. While focusing on the individual and denying that two substances may completely resemble each other and differ only in quantity, Leibniz also insists that "every substance is like a complete world and like a mirror of God or of the whole universe, which each one expresses in its own way."[6] "Expressing the whole universe" and being "like a mirror of the whole universe" here relates to the reciprocal connections between individuals and the universal dimension implicated in each individual. The expression "mirror of God" illustrates this point figuratively: For Leibniz, God is the most universal being. What we find in Leibniz here is a certain grasp of the link between individuals and universality.

B. Bosanquet perhaps gained an even more distinct awareness of this. In his view, the individual is inseparable from the universal. Precisely with this in mind, he defined the individual as "the concrete universal."[7] Even though as a neo-Hegelian Bosanquet also stressed that, in the ultimate sense, there is only one individual, which is the absolute,[8] what he called the concrete universal is undoubtedly similar to what we have thus far called "a concrete universal," which includes the unity of what Dons Scotus called "thisness" and "common nature."[9] This link between the individual and the universal or particulars and universals enables the alteration and enduring identity of the individual to coincide without contradiction.

This connection between the individual and the universal just mentioned does not, of course, imply that the individual only exists within the whole. Here, a distinction could be made between the individual's being and relations of internality. A representative figure of the theory of relations of internality is Francis

Bradley. According to this theory, each thing is related to all other things, and in relations of internality, if one of the terms within a relation is separated from the other term(s) in the relation, it loses its identity and ceases to be the thing it originally was. Arthur Pap once summarized the characteristic of internal relations at the logical level: "An internal relation is a relation which forms part of the *description* of a particular, such that the particular would, as it were, lose its identity if it ceased to stand in this relation."[10] In ontology, internal relations exhibit the connection between the individual and the whole; however, a determination of the individual merely on the basis of internal relations harbors the tendency to dissolve the individual into the whole. In effect, the individual's properties are not simply reducible to relations; although the individual stands in a relationship to the universal, individuals always possess facets that cannot be assimilated by or reduced to such relations, which is to say that an individual's properties and unique characteristics cannot be totally qualified by relations. There is always some boundary between individuals: "this" is not "that," and "that" is also not "this." This boundary is not only exhibited in relationships of space and time, but also in the different properties found among individuals. This kind of difference and differentiation demonstrates that there is also an externality that pertains to the individual's relation to other things.

External relations between things ontologically presuppose the being of individuals and also show the relative independence of individuals and the diversity of beings through individual properties that transcend those relations. The individual's actual form of being is such that the relations between individuals have both internal and external dimensions. The internality of relations demonstrates that the individual is not an isolated, abstract being; the externality of relations demonstrates that the individual possesses some being in-itself that no relation can diminish to nothing. Whereas Bradley fails to adequately account for the being in-itself and relative independence of individuals and reveals the tendency to dissolve the individual into the whole when highlighting the internality of relations, Russell and Moore gravitate to the opposite pole in their quest to refute Bradley's absolute idealism, and fail to adequately account for the individual's connection to the whole and the unity of being due to their affirmation of the exteriority of relations between things and their focus on the multiplicity of being. This shows that Bradley, Russell, and Moore all produce one-sided understandings of the individual, which distort the issue in different ways. So, only a twofold overcoming of the theory of internal relations and that of external relations can grasp the concrete characteristic of the individual.

Considering the internality of relations, the individual is by no means an isolated being; rather, the individual exists in a certain system or whole and belongs to a certain species, just as Confucius and Socrates, as individuals, belong to the species "human being." This relationship between individual and species is the intrinsic precondition of the connection between individuals in the same species: the common attribution of individuals to the same species simultaneously makes them interconnected. But on the other hand, the belonging of individuals to a species does not dissolve them into a melting pot; there are always differences and boundaries between a specific individual, as a concrete being, and the other individuals in the system; such differences and boundaries reveal the self-identity and uniqueness of individuals while reciprocally differentiating them from one another. This "integration" and "differentiation" of the individual into and from the species shows the diversity and complexity characterizing the relations in which the individual stands.

When considering the externality of relations, the being and alteration of the individual always involves the issue of contingency. The emergence of a specific individual still depends on a variety of conditions; whether or not and how these conditions arise and take form is contingent upon the constraint of a variety of factors; this contingency stipulates that there is no way to completely write off either the emergence of individuals or their transformations as necessary processes. For human being this means that there is no specific person that could be seen as a necessary link in the evolutionary derivation of the human species. On the contrary, that an individual person comes into this world is a matter of contingency. Moreover, a specific person as a finite being inevitably dies, but the time of his or her death and the manner in which he or she dies cannot be determined in a necessary way. In brief, considering the universal connections between things and the internality of relations between individuals, there is necessity in principle; but considering the indeterminacy of a specific individual's alteration and the externality of relations between individuals, what has the potential to happen does not necessarily occur.[11]

Individuals and Persons

At the metaphysical level, individuals are first presented as things. However, from the philosophical perspective, questioning about things cannot be disengaged from a meditation upon human being. In the book *What Is a Thing?* Heidegger writes: "The question 'What is a thing?' is the question 'Who is man?'"[12] This link between things and human being consists in the following: the meaning of things is always open for human being, and questioning about things always leads back to the being of humans, and the form of being of humans that concerns the individual is first of all that of the person.

In the dimension of the individual, the mark of a person is first of all a body. A "body" not only has physical attributes but also properties in the biological sense as well; these properties give a person real being to the extent that they distinguish the person from an abstract idea, making the person a concrete being with flesh and blood. As the substance of sensibility, the body has a bounded meaning: "this body" is not "that body," and it is bodies that reciprocally distinguish persons at the level of substance, and that makes them unique individuals. The body of sensibility involves different aspects at the same time: from the physical body in the broad sense to the sense organs with their different functions, all of these belong to the body of the individual, and it is in the formation of the body that these different parts and aspects intrinsically unite. We can safely say that this unity exhibited by the body constitutes the ontological precondition of the person becoming an actual individual.

As the ontological mark of the person, the body is the direct medium linking the person to the world. In terms of the most basic relationship of human being to the world, the spatial one, the body is the main reference for whether an external object is either above or below, in front or behind, east or west, north or south, and so on. Likewise, directly intuiting the world from the human perspective always starts with the body. The body determines the angle from which the human being inspects an object, which furthermore constrains the manner of presentation of an object. In the social sphere, the basis of the communication and connections between individuals is the body as well; the body is the foundation of the most basic familial relations, but also of economic and political interests. For the person, the body simultaneously constitutes a social sign and an extra-linguistic form of expression. On the other hand, the body is also the ultimate bearer of every social identity and social role: without bodies, social identities and social roles have no real meaning.

Social life is essentially practical; human being exists in the world and participates in various forms of social activities and social practices, and is therefore a practical agent. The basic mode of action or practice is such that it contains the dimension of sensibility, which determines that practical action is inseparable from the body. Gilles Deleuze states: "The event results from bodies, their mixtures, their actions, and their passions."[13] Here, "the event" refers to the result of human activity, which is based on human actions, passes through a certain duration, and has a relatively independent sense. To affirm the connection between the event and the body means in substance to confirm the link between the body and practical activity; Deleuze undoubtedly notices this when he links the event to the actions of bodies.

In the dimension of history, a body or sensible being who envelops social meaning (including practical meaning) is formed through a historical process and is the consolidation of achievements of historical development. Marx vividly illustrates this point: "The *forming* of the five senses is a labour of the entire history of the world down to the present."[14] The link between the body and practical activity should also be understood in accordance with this historical dimension. Although practice as activity of the sensibility is inseparable from the body, the body simultaneously acquires a social characteristic through the historical unfolding of practical activity. Marx once analyzed this in detail: "Thus, the objectification of the human essence both in its theoretical and practical aspects is required to make man's *sense human,* as well as to create the *human sense* corresponding to the entire wealth of human and natural substance."[15] To "objectify the human essence" is precisely to make objects express human being's essential powers and become humanized beings through the historical practice of humans acting upon objects, and it is precisely through this process that sense organs in the natural sense and the senses linked to them are gradually endowed with a humanized nature.

Related to the body is the affective mind (*xin* 心). As the being of spirit and ideas, the affective mind envelops different facets, from rationality, emotion, and will to intuition, imagination, understanding, and spirit. These different capacities exhibit the affective mind's different ways of being. Dynamically speaking, the affective mind unfolds in a variety of modes of activity, from intuiting, deducing, analyzing, synthesizing, and judging to choosing and deliberating, just to name a few. Yet, however many forms of spirit and capacities the individual may have, and however the individual's conscious acts may unfold in time, they are all united in the person as a whole; they are the different forms of expression of the same individual's world of spirit and mental activity. Even if the individual encounters internal tensions at the level of ideas, like the conflict between reason and emotion in the making of moral choices or the clashing of different ideals, all of these discordances are still interrelated modes of the same world of spirit. This unity of the world of spirit and mental activity exhibits a different aspect of the unity of the individual.

The corporeal body of sensibility and the affective mind of ideas are not only intrinsically unified; they are also involved with one another. As interrelated facets of the individual, the corporeal body and the affective mind are inseparable. The individual form of being possesses both sensibility and corporeality as well as consciousness and spirit; without the former (body), the individual would be nothing but an illusory specter; without the latter (the affective mind), the individual would be a walking corpse. In both cases, the true individual is nowhere to be found. Now, classical Chinese philosophy stresses the inseparability of the affective mind and the corporeal body, and so speaks of the concrete form of the individual as the unity of the affective mind and the corporeal body. By contrast, dualistic theories put the mind and body on two parallel tracks, which entails a commitment to a "mind without body" and a "body without mind." In this way, dualism ontologically dispels the true individual.

The individual is also a practical agent. So, the unification of body and the affective mind within the individual unfolds in the process of practicing and acting. As we have seen, Deleuze notes that the event arises from bodies. Actually, to be more precise, the event, which corresponds to human activity, arises from both the body and the affective mind. From the everyday practical activities of eating and dwelling to economic, political, and cultural activities, the affective mind and the corporeal body interact and fuse together in different ways. Even in unconscious activity we can see the reciprocal interaction of the affective mind and the corporeal body: as activity, it not only unfolds as the actions of the body, for it also includes consciousness. Even though activity in an unconscious or subconscious state seems not to involve the self-aware participation of consciousness, it does involve the unfolding of conscious acts in a tacit or implicit form. So, we can see that the interaction between the affective mind and the body in action and practice gives the unity of the individual person a dynamic form.

The unity of the person not only involves the relationship between body and mind. In a broader sense, it also concerns the question of personal identity. In the dimension of accomplishing oneself, the self-identity of the person is obviously an issue of considerable importance. As for the being of the individual, the basic condition of accomplishing oneself is the enduring identity of the individual through time: if the "I" of yesterday weren't the "I" of today, or if the "I" of tomorrow were to differ from the "I" of yesterday and today, then one would have no ground upon which to refine oneself. Ontologically speaking, if the individual were to dissolve into mutually unrelated forms of being at different spaces and times, the unified agent who refines himself would cease to exist. Considering the individual from the perspective of values, accomplishing oneself is different from an extrinsic duty; rather, it is the very responsibility one takes on for oneself. However, this relationship of responsibility of one to oneself only has meaning under the condition that the subject remains the same throughout different succeeding times: if the "I" of yesterday, today, and tomorrow were to separately belong to three different subjects, it would be impossible not only to confirm the one "who" is responsible but also to clarify "the one for whom" one is responsible. So, refining oneself essentially unfolds as a process, which is based on the enduring identity of the individual, but if the individual were to break up into different fragments, there would only be the birth and death of each instant and no continuous process of self-maturation (taking steps to the ideal form of being).

In connection with the question of "whether or not the individual stays the same in the process of changing," there is the problem of personal identity, which concerns the alteration and identity of the person. How could we confirm that a person undergoing a variety of transformations in space and time is still the same person? For this, Searle once summarized the following criteria. First, there is the spatio-temporal continuity of the body. Even though the corresponding parts of the body are continuously replaced at the molecular level, the person's body has its continuity from youth to old age. Even though many different kinds of things happen to change in a person's body throughout this time, like the maturation of certain organs, the growth of limbs and overall height of the body, and so on, the basic structure of the body usually remains relatively stable. Second, as for the physical body, in ordinary cases the human body will not become as large as an African elephant nor become as tall as a giraffe. Third, there is memory. The first and second criteria deal with the third person, whereas the third involves the first person singular; it concerns the order of before and after between conscious states. The fourth is the continuity of personality, which concerns the continuity of such facets of the person as character and temperament.[16] The first two criteria belong to the "physical" stratum, whereas the third (memory) belongs to the psychological stratum or the stratum of consciousness. Locke was in fact one of the first to confirm the identity of the person from the perspective of memory, and directly called it "consciousness."[17] The fourth criterion is much more complex; it is linked to the mind and consciousness, but also differs from phenomena of conscious activity like memory. However, Searle never analyzed or explained this fourth criterion in sufficient depth.

On the physical and psychological stratum, there is no fundamental difference between the identity of the person and the identity of the individual in the metaphysical domain; both involve the continuity of physical things in time. The identity of the person based on memory mainly points to the conscious realm; as the ground of personal identity, what must be emphasized is the continuity of consciousness. The spiritual world of the person in the process of existing always undergoes a variety of transformations, but this does not mean that a succeeding mental state will be isolated from the preceding, parts-extra-parts. On the contrary, as the conscious activity of the same individual, it contains internal continuity, and the individual's memory is the condition of possibility of this continuity. But, even this continuity depending on consciousness is not enough to account for the identity of the person, as the thought experiment of brain transplantation shows. Yet, speaking in negative terms, if there were no such continuity of consciousness, the identity of the person would be similarly unimaginable. So, beginning with the unity of the affective mind and the corporeal body, the identity of the person is obviously inseparable from the continuity of consciousness.

The continuous duration of consciousness involves temporality. In actual fact, the identity of the person concerns the problem of time from the very beginning. In the social sphere, the meaning of time consists in historicity; it is precisely the historical unfolding of society that distinguishes time from an abstract and empty passage of succeeding moments. For persons, the meaning of time is similarly expressed through their actual lives and practices. According to its substance, the continuation of preceding and succeeding states in the temporal sense has as its actual content the continuity of the person's life and practices; this continuity of life and practice makes the unity of the person's self-recognition and understanding of him or herself possible while providing others with the grounds to grasp the identity of the person through preceding and succeeding states. Although the duration of consciousness also involves time, this kind of time only emerges in the process of one practicing and living; abstracted from the latter, the conscious subject would amount to Putnam's hypothesized "brain in a vat," in which the duration of consciousness is not so much temporal as it is logical.

Personal identity is not of course just limited to the mind, the body, and the continuity of both in time; it also concerns values, which are embodied in such facets as character and virtues. Searle touched upon these facets concerning the continuity of human character in some sense, but his analysis seems to focus on the psychological dimension of character and temperament. In actual fact, relative stability can be seen in other facets too, from the everyday issue of being a person to the much broader social issue of directed action, and this stability is based on the stability of virtues and character. Despite the specificity of situations and the diversity and variability of actions, the person's character and virtues remain relatively continuous and stable; even though there is some variability pertaining to character and morals themselves such that they are not absolutely unchanging, as the ontological attribute of personal identity, their transformation and development are intrinsically interconnected; the latter differs from the continuity of consciousness attained through memory. In a more profound sense, they consist in the duration of values and value orientations. In contrast to the conscious mind and the physical body, the identity and duration of virtues and character have a much more intrinsic characteristic.

In regard to the broader sense of meaning, the self-identity of the person cannot be restricted to the individual dimension. As an actual being, the individual always lives in society. Consequently, the self-identity of the individual is inseparable from this ontological circumstance. Every individual forms unique relationships with other people, society, and other conditions in the process of existing. Such relationships not only constitute a by–no-means inessential facet of the individual's being; they also constrain the character of the individual being and his or her practice of life. From the very moment the individual arrives in the world, he or she forms an inseparable connection with the parents that have given him or her life; such bonds are natural (blood line) as well as social. Regardless of how the individual transforms later on, this relationship between him/her and his/her parents will remain unchanged and unchangeable: there may be differences between the "I" of yesterday and the "I" of today, but it is always the same parents who gave the individual his or her life. In broader terms, the variety of political, economic, and cultural relationships the individual forms in social life not only have aspects that change, they also encompass enduring facets that do not disappear fleetingly as soon as they arise. This enduring nature of social relations is at once based on the enduring nature of social life while also ensuring that social life endures with continuity as well. In regard to the individual's form of being and way of being, this continuity of social life and social relations both determines and exhibits his or her enduring identity.

In the context of accomplishing oneself and accomplishing things, the meaning of the self-identity of the individual at the ontological and axiological levels lies first in providing one with the precondition of refining oneself in the individual domain. When the individual maintains his or her enduring identity and remains the same "I" with regard to one's mind, body, social relationships, and practice of life despite the changes one undergoes in time, not only does the unity of the subject of the individual domain gain confirmation, but the problem of "who" is responsible and "whom" one is responsible "for" in this domain gains a basis for solution as well.

At the level of ideas, personal identity also involves the person's self-confirmation, which is reflexive. "Reflexive" here means that the object of the person is himself or herself, which is inseparable from the individual's self-consciousness and reflective consciousness. Charles Taylor once compared humans and animals when considering the intrinsic characteristic of persons. Taylor discovers that which distinguishes humans from animals not in simply having desires, but in the capacity to make one's own desires objects of one's own evaluation, which constitutes the characteristic of the person and self.[18] This process of evaluating that Taylor analyzes reveals in another way the reflexivity of the person or the directedness of the person toward himself or herself. As for the person's external form, there seems to be a mutually exclusive relationship between the objectifying characteristic of being directed toward oneself and the self-recognition of the individual, since objectification tends to eliminate agency. Natorp mainly grounds his critique of phenomenology upon this. For him, the reflective method that phenomenology adopts involves objectifying, which leads to the following dilemma: how can agency be reached through consciousness's objectification of itself?[19] We will temporarily leave aside the critique of phenomenology here and show what needs to be pointed out at the theoretical level: Natorp's argument ignores that the individual possesses a twofold characteristic in self-consciousness or one's reflexive consciousness of oneself: the individual is at once both object and agent, and it is precisely this twofold nature that makes the person's reflexive consciousness or reflective consciousness become the mark of the person's individuality.

Tied to the person's self-confirmation is the distinction between the self as individual and the other as individual, which logically presupposes the uniqueness of the individual's self-confirmation. At the metaphysical level, the uniqueness of the individual lies first of all in his or her noninstantiability. For the person, this uniqueness not only consists in the unrepeatable and irreducible nature of the individual or the fact that there are no two identical individuals, but also in the irreplaceable nature of the individual in the axiological sense. As an individual, the human being is ontologically speaking an unrepeatable being and axiologically speaking a one-and-only irreplaceable being. Perhaps a person's concrete social role could be replaced, but the concrete being of a person cannot be replaced by other beings. So, it is precisely in the person that the uniqueness of the individual is most profoundly expressed.

Of course, the unique character of the person is not just limited to the unrepeatable ontological nature and irreplaceable value of the person. At a much more intrinsic level, the person is inseparable from character or individuality. Once again at the metaphysical level, individuals show their respective particularities through particular relations of space and time (at different positions in space and time, the individual exhibits different forms); the person's concreteness, on the other hand, is expressed through diversity of character. Individuality is a synthetic form of being, including not only the person's temperament and mental disposition, but also his or her reason, emotion, and will; individuality not only concerns one's intrinsic capacities, but also one's character and virtues, so as a whole, individuality expresses the synthetic unity of temperament, disposition, reason, emotion, will, capacities, and character. The spiritual form of this unity is the feature within every specific individual that reciprocally differentiates individuals from one another. As a synthetic spiritual attribute, individuality is not just a mental tendency; it also expresses the human being's character in a holistic way. In contrast to the variability of particulars in specific positions of space and time, individuality has both the characteristics of unity and stability, which enables individuality to be beyond pure and simple relations of space and time and possess an internal form of presentation.

As a unique manifestation of human being's individual character, individuality also concretely reveals the intrinsic link between individuality and the being of humans. This link is exhibited at a deeper level in the relationship between individuality and purpose. When discussing the relationship between individuality and purpose, Bosanquet states that purpose is secondary to individuality.[20] As a neo-Hegelian, Bosanquet speaks of the individual in terms of the absolute, but we could produce a broader understanding of his statement. In an extended sense, purpose entails value. So, to say that purpose is secondary to individuality is to emphasize the ontological priority of the individual, which entails that purpose originates from the individual; in contrast to saying that the individual entails purpose, to say that purpose originates from the individual is to emphasize the original value of the individual's being.

Persons differ from things at the level of purpose. Heidegger once examined things within the scientific horizon. For Heidegger, science concerns itself with universality, and science understands particular things merely as examples.[21] By extension, an individual as a thing is presented merely as a specimen of a species. However, the individual as human being cannot be simply reduced to a specimen or example. Specimens of a species are merely contingent beings, which are mutually replaceable in the dimension of values, possessing no unique intrinsic value in and of themselves. A person on the other hand constitutes the source of a purpose, and so the meaning of the person's being is irreplaceable. In terms of physical structure and physical nature, there are no fundamental differences between different specimens of the same species, but persons are not simply beings at the physical level; the difference between a person's individuality and that of another's encompasses the purpose of being and values that cannot be substituted for one another. Viewed as things, the birth, transformation, and death of a specimen of a species has no substantial influence upon the being of the species itself. Viewed as human beings, every single person possesses facets that are neither dismissible nor ignorable.

That a person has individuality of course does not mean that a person is an isolated individual. At the metaphysical level, individuals are original unities in systems of different forms, and in each case are involved in a diversity of relationships. Similarly, a person is likewise a being within relationships, which are not only physical, but also in a more substantial sense social. When one arrives in this world, one immediately finds oneself within relationships corresponding to the ethical norms of family and kinship ties. Huang Zongxi once pointed out: "Human being is born and falls to the earth tied only to parents and siblings, the inextricable feelings of this stage emerge with birth and are truly real, and so begin to bear the prestige of being-humane and righteous."[22] Although between parents and offspring, brother and brother there is the natural dimension of blood ties, but as the origin of social ethical principles, filial relations are more social than natural. Moving from everyday family life to the broader social sphere, more economic, political, and cultural activities are involved, and so the person finds himself or herself in social relationships of diverse forms. From the external perspective, the other seems to transcend the person: others external to the individual in this sense constitute the other and are opposed to the person. However, as stated previously, ontologically speaking, the relations between individuals and those between the individual and the system and whole are marked by internality, which is similarly the case for those between persons. In metaphysics, it is precisely these relationships marked by internality that sublate this transcendence of the Other over and against the individual.

At the same time, as beings in social relationships, every person possesses certain rights and must fulfill corresponding duties. Now, the content of these rights and duties is always specified in correspondence with the concrete position a person occupies in a social system. In the previous case of familial relations, whether one is a father or a mother, one has the duty to care for one's adolescent sons or daughters, and has the right to demand care from one's sons or daughters at old age. Similarly, whether one is a son or daughter, one has the right to demand care and support from one's parents while still dependent, and has the duty to care for one's parents when they need it. Here, son and daughter, father and mother are all concrete beings, and the duties and rights corresponding to them are no less unique: my responsibilities and duties in relation to my own mother and father differ from those responsibilities and duties other people have in relation to their mothers and fathers. Similarly, other people cannot substitute for a particular child in his or her fulfillment of the rights and duties he or she has in relation to his or her parents. In this sense, the person could be seen as the bearer of specific rights and duties. Of course, the content of the rights and duties that a person takes on will differ in accordance with different historical ages and different social backgrounds. Moreover, there are also differences between the duties and rights that different individuals of the same historical age take on, but as a human being, the individual always possesses the most basic rights (including one's own right to live) and the basic duties corresponding to them (including the duty to respect and honor the same rights in others). Even though this right and duty may suffer a variety of restrictions under certain historical conditions and for that reason remain unrealized, that they are the essential property of humans as social beings is something that never changes. This most basic right to live and this most basic duty to respect and honor the same right of others to live are intrinsically connected to the irreplaceable nature of the being of the individual in ontological terms. Each person is a singular being, so the rights and duties he or she has are singular as well. The unique rights and duties that a person has gives him or her the ontological attribute of individuality at the social level and manifest the social characteristic of the person as well.

Marx analyzed the connection between the person and society in greater detail from the perspective of interest:

> Each pursues his private interest and only his private interest; and thereby serves the private interests of all, the general interest, without willing or knowing it . . . private interest is itself already a socially determined interest, which can be achieved only within the conditions laid down by society and with the means provided by society; hence it is bound to the reproduction of these conditions and means. It is the interest of private persons; but its content, as well as the form and means of its realization, is given by social conditions independent of all.[23]

Private interest is tightly bound to the person as a prominent marker of the person's individuality. However, something social still proves to be seen even within this individualizing aspect. Although the initial motivation of a particular producer to make a product may be the seeking of his own interest, to truly realize the worth of the product, the producer must fulfill the needs of others, and it is the social or general interest that is realized in the process of fulfilling such needs. In brief, from the concrete content of private interest to the mode and means of its realization, from the sought goal of individual interest to the objective result of seeking such an interest, the individual always remains just as tied to others as to society as a whole. After entering the modern age accompanying the development of economic interactions was the tightening of the bond between the person and the other: "In the case of the *world market,* the connection of the *individual with all,* but at the same time also the *independence of this connection from the individual.*"[24]

Does the aforementioned social characteristic of the person result in the dissolution of individual character? Does sociality contradict individuality and vice versa? Could they possibly be mutually inclusive? From a broader perspective, these question touch on the relationship between individuality, sociality, and natural disposition. Natural disposition is precisely the first nature of what is most natural, including the biological determination of human beings in the concrete acts of eating, drinking, and fornicating. Human being is such that the natural dispositions of different individuals do not differ at the fundamental level: one is hungry and desires food; one is thirsty and desires drink; one is cold and desires clothing to keep warm. Individuals are more similar than different as far as the intentions behind such instinct-based activities go. In other words we would be hard pressed to deduce unique individual characteristics merely from these actions and intentions alone. However, the case is not the same at the social level. When satiating hunger and quenching thirst in the natural sense transforms into eating and drinking as a cultural affair in the social sense, differences in character can then be seen to mark eating and drinking (the differentiation of taste at the culinary level). Similarly, when materials that serve the natural function of providing warmth become symbols differentiating identity, status, and taste, so many individualizing distinctions begin to take shape between individuals in terms of what they wear (fashion culture). Essentially, individuality is itself a social characteristic, and individuality can only truly develop in a social context. Ways of thinking, for example, involve the capacity of human beings to understand and reform the world. In contrast to aesthetic taste, which is tied to natural dispositions in relation to food and clothing, ways of thinking express the social attribute of human being in a much more intrinsic sense, and differences in character at this level presuppose the adequate development of this social attribute in human beings. The difference between Hume's empiricist way of thinking and Hegel's speculative way of philosophizing expresses the difference between English character and German character much more profoundly than what's on tap at this English pub compared to that German bar, which demonstrates the interconnection between the social attribute of human being and the diversification of character.

As the internal manifestation of individuality, human character is neither pre-formed nor readymade; rather, it is generative; although the genesis of character is not entirely separable from the natural disposition of human being, it still requires social guidance and education. From the perspective of external form, this seems to imply some sort of contradiction: character is ordinarily tied to uniqueness, diversity, and difference, while social guidance and education is directed at realizing the socialization of the individual, and the socialization of the individual here means bringing the ideas and actions of the individual into the general guidelines of society and making them exist in the world in harmony with the demands and permission of society, which undoubtedly entails the aim of conformity. However, in a much more substantial sense, the guidance and influence of society does not exclude the formation of individual character. In fact, guidance and education do not only involve universal norms; they are also rooted in individual differences as well. The individualization of education that we see everywhere today and the tailoring of education to the unique talents of each individual demonstrates this point. At the pre-social (natural) level, differences between individuals are always relatively limited; the cultivation and formation of individual character and the socialization of the individual exhibit two sides of one and the same process, and education and guidance dealing directly with the individual is undoubtedly indispensible in this process. The actual form in which society influences and guides does not resemble anything like a one-way indoctrination of the individual; the relationship between the influence and guidance of society and the individual's own understanding and acceptance is interactive. This interaction determines the socialization of the individual to be complementary with the diversification of individual character.

In summary, human being's concrete form of being is the being of the individual person. A person is a union of the affective mind and corporeal body, showing an enduring identity unfolding in time, an enduring identity of a body (the physical and physiological) and spirit (the affective mind and consciousness) whose content is the continuous duration of virtue and character. This enduring identity of the person is the ontological precondition of accomplishing oneself and accomplishing things. As a concrete being, the person has a unique character; this uniqueness is expressed in ontology as non-repeatable singularity and in axiology as irreplaceable non-substitutability. As a thing an individual may be understood as a specimen of a species; as a human being, however, the individual person possesses the intrinsic attributes of purposiveness and unique character. So, character is the ontological uniqueness of the person, but in combination with the axiological purposiveness of the person, character is the orientation of the person's being. The genesis of character and the process of developing character involve the historical content of the individual (person) interacting with society. Synthetically speaking, this content intrinsic to the person is concretely expressed as the union of individuality and totality, which Marx concretely elucidated as follows: "Man, much as he may therefore be a *particular* individual (and it is precisely his particularity which makes him an individual, and a real *individual* social being), is just as much the *totality*, the ideal totality—the subjective existence of thought and experienced society present for itself—just as he exists also in the real world as the awareness and the real enjoyment of social existence, and as a totality of human life-activity."[25] Tied to the "particular individual" is the irreducible, unrepeatable, and irreplaceable characteristics of the person, and "totality" here expresses the unity of the person's intrinsic attributes and the multiplicity of relationships in which he or she is involved; both constitute interrelated aspects of an actual person.

Accomplishing Oneself and the Development of Character

From a much broader historical perspective, the interaction between the individual person and society is not only shown in the fact that society's guidance of and influence upon the individual can only be accomplished through the individual's own understanding and acceptance; it may also be seen in the intrinsic link between the derivation of society itself and the transformation of the individual's mode of being. When discussing the transformation of society, Marx once pointed out:

> Relations of personal dependence (entirely spontaneous at the outset) are the first social forms, in which human productive capacity develops only to a slight extent and at isolated points. Personal independence founded on *objective [sachlicher]* dependence is the second great form, in which a system of general social metabolism, of universal relations, of all-round needs and universal capacities is formed for the first time. Free individuality, based on the universal development of individuals and on their subordination of their communal, social productivity as their social wealth, is the third stage. The second stage creates the conditions for the third.[26]

What is analyzed here is the historical derivation of society. According to Marx, changes in the form of society correspond to changes in the form of the individual's being: the first form of society corresponds to the person's dependence upon the other; the second great form of society is characterized by objective dependence or the person's dependence upon things; the third stage of social development is based upon the whole-sided development of the person and free individuality. The meaning of the individual's being comes into view through this historical development of society: the person's mode of being constitutes one of the most important grounds upon which historical stages are distinguished.

This historical role the person plays in the development of society also highlights the meaning of the person's own development. Historically speaking, personal development and self-accomplishment have constituted the motif of philosophical concern for a very long time, but different philosophical positions and schools have formed very different understandings of personal development and self-accomplishment. As far as Chinese philosophy goes, Confucianism found "cultivating human being" (*cheng ren* 成人) or "accomplishing oneself" (*cheng ji* 成己) to be of the highest priority since the pre-Qin period. Confucius himself once distinguished between "for-oneself" (*wei ji* 为己) and "for-others" (*wei ren* 为人); the former is directed at the complete realization of the self, whereas the latter is directed at working for others. The basic orientation of Confucius was to deny "being-for-others" on the basis of "being-for-oneself." With a stress on "learning for-oneself" (*wei ji zhi xue* 为己之学), "cultivating human being" (*cheng ren* 成人) is also precisely the refining of human being or perfecting the ideal human character. In this sense, there is no substantial difference in the senses of "cultivating human being" and "accomplishing oneself." Confucianism aside, there is also Daoism. Although differing in philosophical standpoint, the former and the latter still share a common concern for the person. Zhuangzi's affirmation that "the fully singular person (*du you zhi ren* 独有之人) is the height of nobility,"[27] and his warning not to "alienate oneself with things,"[28] while succeeding in "complying with others without losing oneself,"[29] all manifest a confirmation of the value of the person (the self).

However, that one affirms the value of the individual (person's) being does not imply that one has truly grasped the meaning of the individual's being or the mode of being one ought to have. Confucianism places great emphasis on self-refinement or self-realization, but it has its own slant on the issue of how to understand the self and the individual. For Confucianism, cultivating human being or accomplishing oneself is primarily directed at the attainment of sagehood. We can see a simple summary of this point in the following passage by Zhang Zai: "The way of the superior human being is to work toward accomplishing oneself and refining human nature, but until sagehood is reached, all practical activity remains incomplete."[30] To attain sagehood means to take the sage as a universal model of ideal human character and to sculpt oneself according to it as the criterion. So, although accomplishing oneself in the sense above prioritizes the person and the self, in terms of content, the "self" or person here refers to a universally valued goal, and the aim of accomplishing oneself is the attainment of the same form of character (sagehood). In this way, the diversity and individuality of human beings is more or less covered up by this universal and uniform orientation of personality. Similarly, although Daoism's opposition to "alienating oneself with things" shows a concern for the individual, Daoism continues to understand the ideal form of "the self" or individual as an "authentic person" (*zhen ren* 真人) or "natural human being" (*tian ren* 天人);[31] so corresponding to Daoism's idealization of the natural condition, in terms of the distinction between what is natural and what is human, to be authentic and natural is just to harmonize with nature or blend in with nature. Daoism's appraisal of nature is simultaneously tied to overcoming the determination of purposiveness. The statement, "acting without effort is what is called natural" demonstrates this point.³² Here, "acting without effort" (*wuwei wei zhi* 无为为之) is first of all said in opposition to the effort of pursuing a purpose, so its distinguishing feature is acting without intentional projects; defining "nature" as "acting without effort" implies a disengagement from purposeful action. This mutual exclusion between nature and purpose simultaneously distances the natural person from the determination of purposiveness. Whereas Confucianism's theory of cultivating human being entails diminishing individuality through a universal orientation of human character, Daoism's theory of "the authentic person" and "natural human being" logically leads to the elimination of purposiveness.

The Confucian and Daoist understandings of the individual or self mentioned earlier reflect the existential condition of human being under natural economic conditions, albeit from different perspectives. According to Marx's understanding, human being finds itself in the first form of society when "human productive capacity develops only to a slight extent and at isolated points"; the relations of personal dependence he speaks of in connection with this is exhibited both in the dependence of particular individuals who live in lower social classes upon other particular individuals who live in higher social classes. Such a relation also unfolds as the dependence of the individual upon the group or social class system itself. Under conditions "in which human productive capacity develops only to a slight extent and at isolated points," one's being is inseparably tied to the group; in this vein, Confucianism affirms that "human life cannot be sustained without the group"³³ and that if one were to "leave the group and not depend on others one would face nothing but predicaments,"³⁴ which both point out, to different degrees, the existential condition of human being. The importance Confucianism places on the universal attribute and social content of human character seems to reflect this relationship between the individual and the group or society. By contrast, Daoism's appraisal and appreciation for the pre-civilized form of nature reveals another tendency. For Daoism, social systems and systems of norms exercise nothing but constraints and restrictions upon human being, which is in a sense a reflection of relations of personal dependence; so, returning to nature here, means overcoming these limitations and restrictions, which seems to express dissatisfaction with relations of personal dependence in a unique fashion.

Moving from the first form of society toward the modern age, "personal independence" gradually replaces "personal dependence." In contrast to the various forms of "personal dependence" (including the subordination of the individual to the species, group, and social system), "personal independence" provides human being with more possibilities for multi-faceted development. However, on the other hand, accompanying the universal unfolding of material trade relations, the development of individuality gradually comes to suffer restrictions in another sense. Since the modern age, the market economy tied to the capitalist mode of production raises the "general social metabolism" to a higher level. At the economic level, the core of a general social metabolism is the trading of commodities, whose basic principle is the exchange of equivalents. According to its original form, the exchange of equivalents presupposes disregarding the differences of commodities in terms of their physical properties and use-value. Furthermore, distinctions between the persons participating in the trade become increasingly irrelevant. In effect, under the same principle of exchanging equivalents, the particularity of individuals does not enter the exchange equation; on the contrary, these particular characteristics are flattened out and equalized:

> Activity, regardless of its individual manifestation, and the product of activity, regardless of its particular make-up, are always *exchange value*, and exchange value is a generality, in which all individuality and peculiarity are negated and extinguished.[35] ... The subjects in exchange exist for one another only through these equivalents, as of equal worth, and prove themselves to be such through the exchange of the objectivity in which the one exists for the other. Since they only exist for one another in exchange in this way, as equally worthy persons, possessors of equivalent things, who thereby prove their equivalence, they are, as equals, at the same time also indifferent to one another; whatever other individual distinction there may be does not concern them; they are indifferent to all their other individual peculiarities.[36]

In brief, the exchange of commodities affirms not the uniqueness and difference of individuals, but rather their equivalence and homogeneity; with the exchange of equivalents as a universal principle, human individuality is never truly manifested. Accompanying the commodification of labor, human being itself starts to enter the market of exchange, and under the same principle of equal exchange, the characteristic of human individuality is further concealed underneath general equivalents.

The eliminating of individuality through the exchange of commodities itself presupposes the abstract form of labor. The use-value of commodities takes shape in concrete labor, while the exchange-value of commodities originates from abstract labor. Differences in use-value correspond to the diversity of concrete labor, but exchange-value is linked to abstract labor. In order to make the exchange value of commodities become comparable, quantitatively speaking, the concrete form of labor needs to be canceled and reduced to abstract general labor:

> Just as labor, which creates exchange value, is indifferent to the material of use-values, so it is to the special form of labor itself. Furthermore, the different use-values are the products of the work of different individuals, consequently the result of various kinds of labor differing individually from one to another. But as exchange values, they represent the same homogenous labor, that is,

labor from which the individuality of the workers is eliminated. Labor creating exchange value is, therefore, *abstract general labor*.[37]

At the level of abstract labor, not only are the differences of the objects of labor ignored, but also the concrete characteristics of the laborer and his or her productive activity. This essential homogeneity of labor makes the individual differences of the laborer seem to lose all substantial meaning.

The concealing of individual character by abstract labor and the relation of exchange associated with it makes the intrinsic value of the individual encounter the threat of dissolution. As stated previously, associated with the unrepeatable nature of the individual in the metaphysical domain is the irreplaceable nature of the individual at the level of value. However, the process of exchange and circulation based on abstract labor not only renders individuals homogeneous and equivalent, it also renders them replaceable: "At a definite moment circulation posits each not only as being equal to the other, but also as the same, and its movement consists in each alternately taking the place of the other from the standpoint of the social function."[38] When the individual is seen as a largely replaceable object, the intrinsic value of the individual's being diminishes.

This diminishing of the individual's value appears as an objectification and equipmentification of human being at an intrinsic level. When abstract labor equalizes the individual characters of the laborers, there is no more substantial difference between the individual and other beings, and the commodification of labor power further reduces the laborer to a thing that could be weighed with the same measure as used to measure things. In a relation of general social metabolism, the relation between human being and human being is implied to be a relation between thing and thing and the value of human being is reduced to some equivalent object, to which one is tied in one's objective dependence upon things.

A further development of the commodification and objectification of human being is the subordination of the inner self to external things. In modern society, this has become increasingly obvious. The omnipresent constraint of institutions and the process of routinization tied to it renders the individual's creativity irrelevant: the individual's action then consists in nothing more than the completion of institutional procedures or the carrying out of institutional functions, and the inflation of mass culture also makes individuals become increasingly uniform, gradually losing their capacity of judgment in the realms of aesthetic taste and manner of behavior. In connection with the gradual formation of technical guidance, experts and authorities in each specialized field continue to push upon people criteria for each kind of choice and behavior through their respective paths and ways, thereby engendering habitual submission: aside from accepting and following the opinions of experts and authorities, people seem to have no other choice. As an extension of human being's objective dependence upon things, these processes prevent the actual individual from manifesting his own value.

How is it possible for the individual to truly actualize his intrinsic value? From the perspective of ideal human character, particular attention must be paid to the idea of "free individuality." Marx saw "free individuality" as the main characteristic of the third stage of social development and shows its meaning in the dimension of history. The initial form of social development is that of personal dependence; in relations of personal dependence individuals are subsumed under other persons or an external social system (including hierarchical structures), and lack genuine individuality and freedom. As the manifestation of this relation of personal dependence in terms of form of human character, the goal of ideal character is universalized and uniformized, which the determination of accomplishing oneself with "the attainment of sagehood" demonstrates. Attaining human freedom and independence by means of overcoming relationships of personal dependence constitutes the most important aspect of developing free individuality. Interconnected with personal dependence is objective [sachlicher] dependence. While personal dependence implies the elimination of human individuality and autonomy, objective dependence implies concealing the intrinsic value and purposive determination of human being through the objectification and equipmentification of human being itself. While overcoming personal dependence, free individuality also demands overcoming objective dependence. In positive terms, the actual meaning of the latter lies in confirming the intrinsic value of human being and affirming human being's purposive determination.

The double overcoming of personal dependence and objective dependence exhibits the negative characteristic of free individuality. At the positive or affirmative level, free individuality is concretely expressed in terms of the whole-sided development of the individual person. Marx in fact links free individuality to the "whole-sided development of the individual." From a broader perspective, the whole-sided development of the individual first of all concerns the relationship between mind and body. Here, "body" includes the being of sensibility and the capacity of sensation tied to it. "Mind" then points broadly to consciousness and the world of spirit. In this sense, "whole-sided development" means combining and integrating the two. The body as sensible being is also linked to "Nature" (innate or natural properties), while the mind as the world of spirit envelops human being's cultural content. So, the whole-sided development of the individual person also involves the relationship between humans and Nature. Historically speaking, Confucianism stressed the way of humans (*rendao* 人道), and Daoism the way of Nature (*tiandao* 天道). Sublating these two opposed ways implies simultaneously grasping both primordial nature (Nature in-itself) and civilized or humanized nature (Nature for-humans).

The humanized dimension, as the historical sedimentation of cultural development, is predominantly the manifestation of human being's sociality; the natural disposition of human nature, by contrast, is internal to every concrete individual and is predominantly the manifestation of human being's individuality. Individuals whose development is whole-sided are in a way individuals whose social relations are their own communal relations,[39] and whose social potentials have been adequately realized to the point that they express their unique individuality. So, the "whole-sided development" of the individual consists in this double-sided unfolding of sociality and individuality.

Broadly speaking, free individuality implies overcoming the one-sided nature of being. For consciousness, this demands overcoming the mutually restricting boundaries between reason, the passions, and the will, so that the individual adequately develops rationality and sensibility; as for the determination of human character, it is directed at the unity of being truthful, beautiful, and good; as for the world of spirit, it is directed at the ideal goal of integrating one's real capacities with one's inner state of mind. This development of individuality implies overcoming the uniformity of human character. From the integration of reason, passions, and will to the attainment of the unity of being truthful, beautiful, and good, from the development of capacities to the elevation of one's state of mind, the actual forms of individual perfection are rich and diverse, and there is neither universal model nor single path among them.

The whole-sided development of human being is the content of free individuality, which is also manifested in the process of creating values. The free form of individuality does not exist purely in the form of ideas and mentality as it also involves human being's creation of values and is concretely expressed in the process. Creating values is directed at reforming the world and refining oneself: the unity of reason, passions, and will in the interfusion of being truthful, beautiful, and good takes shape in the process of reforming the world and refining the self, where it is manifested. For the individual, the process of creating values not only constitutes the actual source of development of free individuality; it also provides free individuality with rich, concrete content. Therefore, creativity is the very essence of free individuality.

Free individuality expresses the individual's concrete way of being, and unfolds as the overcoming of different limitations. When human being is still constrained by personal dependence and objective dependence, human being's capacities, interests, and ways of engaging activities subsist in a variety of limiting forms. Under historical conditions in which personal dependence is predominant, the person is anchored to a solidified and unchanging social role; in relations of objective dependence, persons are reduced to bearers of objectified functions, the typical manifestation of which can be found in large-scale industrialized production: On a massive industrial assembly line, the individual is reduced to a link in this material production process. As regards human being's way of being and mode of being, the historical precondition of developing free individuality is overcoming such limitations and restrictions, which furthermore demands the multifaceted realization of the individual's potentials and the multifaceted unfolding of the individual's activity in both breadth and depth. When discussing the individual's ideal way of being, Marx once illustrated this in a figurative fashion; that is, in the ideal society still to come:

> Nobody has one exclusive sphere of activity but each can become accomplished in any branch he wishes, society regulates the general production and thus makes it possible for me to do one thing today and another tomorrow, to hunt in the morning, fish in the afternoon, rear cattle in the evening, criticize after dinner, just as I have a mind, without ever becoming hunter, fisherman, herdsman or critic.[40]

Of importance here is that the person will not "always be" a particular individual, which implies transcending the limitations that external roles and functions exercise upon the person, enabling the person to genuinely attain multifaceted development.

Diverse formations of individuality intrinsically involve the relation between the directionality of individual development and different possibilities of development. At the processual level, later stages of development start out from prior stages which condition them, but prior stages of development do not necessarily lead to certain later stages, which reveals a certain dissymmetry. The relatively mature and relatively stable form of being that a person has attained in character and capacity can always be traced back to some sources or seeds that can be found in the person's earlier environment, education background, and prior efforts, but this does not mean that the person's earlier development necessarily determined the formation of later phases. Due to changes in the individual and in the individual's social circumstances and by virtue of the consequent effect of such changes, one's individuality always implies different possibilities of development; so the direction of individual development is never absolutely unchanging. Based on this fact, it seems we could make a distinction between the actualization of potentiality and the realization of possibility. The actualization of potentiality to some degree presupposes the determinate direction of a tendency: the resultant phase of development corresponds to the direction of development that was already implicitly contained in the point of departure. The realization of possibility, on the other hand, does not presuppose a pre-determined direction, but rather implies different possible tendencies, and provides the individual's own creativity with necessary space to develop. Evident here is the interweaving of necessity, possibility, contingency, directionality, and self-creativity in the process of developing individuality. The development and formation of individuality does undoubtedly have its internal ground, and this ground does determine a tendency of development, but to understand this development as a necessary and predetermined process because of this would be an error. The process of developing individuality is always influenced by factors and conditions both social and individual, among which we find contingent constraints tied to varying circumstances and the individual's own inner creative activity. Viewing the development of free individuality purely as the actualization of a potentiality or reducing it to the mere realization of a possibility show two one-sided approaches. The determinate direction implied by potentiality and the creativity implied by possibility exhibit modes of interaction in the process of developing free individuality.

The realization of possibility and the actualization of potentiality both unfold as different aspects of the same process. In broad terms, the development of individuality intrinsically entails historicity and processuality. At the processual level, the whole-sidedness of individuality has different historical meanings. In earlier stages of social development, the individual seems to present a whole form, but this is the primordial "wholeness" found in those historical stages where the differentiation of social relations and the division of labor had not yet adequately developed. The latter can neither be seen on the same level as nor equated with the whole-sided development found in the theory of free individuality. Marx once wrote in his *Grundrisse*, "In earlier stages of development the single individual seems to be developed more fully, because he has not yet worked out his relationships in their fullness, or erected them as independent social powers and relations opposite to himself. It is as ridiculous to yearn for a return to that original fullness as it is to believe that with this complete emptiness history has come to a standstill."[41] Whole-sided development, manifested by free individuality, on the other hand, is the mode of being human being attains after overcoming both objective dependence and personal dependence, which in contrast to the primordial wholeness and primitive abundance is grounded in a much higher stage of social development and contains a deeper historical meaning. It is precisely in this sense that Marx claims that "[u]niversally developed individuals, whose social relations, as their own communal relations, are hence also subordinated to their own communal control, are no product of nature, but of history.[42]

As a product of history, free individuality and the whole-sided development of human being have their actual preconditions; aside from overcoming both personal dependence and objective dependence at the level of social history, particular attention must also be paid to what is called free time. Free time is first of all said in contrast to the necessary time of labor. From the perspective of society, production in the intellectual sphere only becomes possible once the labor time used to produce means of livelihood and the means of production has been reduced to a definite degree. The less time invested in the former, the more time can be spent on the latter: "The less time society requires to produce wheat, cattle, etc., the more time it wins for other production, material and mental."⁴³ Similarly for the individual, under conditions in which the individual's entire time is occupied by necessary labor, the development of his other facets and capacities remain but empty ideals; only after obtaining time that he can freely control does the schedule open up for the individual to develop multiple facets. The meaning of increasing the individual's free time through the saving of his labor time consists in creating the conditions for the individual's full development: "The saving of labour time [is] equal to an increase in free time, i.e., time for the full development of the individual."⁴⁴ The intrinsic link between the reduction of the person's labor time, an increase in his free time, and his full development is obvious. The free development of individuality will become actual as soon as each person is allotted free time through a decrease in the labor time of all: "The free development of individualities, and hence not the reduction of necessary labour time so as to posit surplus labour, but rather the general reduction of the necessary labour of society to a minimum, which then corresponds to the artistic, scientific etc. development of the individuals in the time set free, and with the means created, for all of them."⁴⁵ There is a consistent unity between the free development of individualities and the multifaceted development of the person in different fields, and the common precondition of both is coming into possession of free time. Evidently, free individuality shows its actual character on the basis of free time.

Turning from the prior condition and ground of the free development individuality to the internal process of this development, we encroach upon a different form of freedom. In positive form, the free development of individuality means realizing a concrete diversity of worthy ideals through creative activities. The realization of such ideals is exhibited at the individual level as the person's self-realization or self-refinement. In negative form, the free development of individuality aims at liberating the person from various forms of subjugation, disturbances and restrictions; at the historical level, this "liberation" is manifested as the double-sided overcoming of personal dependence and objective dependence.⁴⁶

In regard to its primitive and abstract form, freedom in the positive sense originates from such desires as that for self-determination and to be the master of one's own will, which could be more generally formulated as "freedom to."⁴⁷ The latter exhibits the tendency to start out from a certain set of values, and to uphold an idea and standpoint in order to struggle for the thoroughgoing realization of the ideal that corresponds while reforming the world and refining oneself. If this approach is excessively and one-sidedly developed the individual readily falls into influencing if not dominating others with his own will power, ideas, and ideals; at the level of society, this leads to the molding of human beings on the basis of a one-sided and universal model, which results in dogmatic ways of thinking and despotic ways of behaving. At the same time, the pushing of ideas is often linked to a rational design; when both are integrated with indoctrination of thought and the modification of practices, the despotic enforcement of rationality readily results. Here there seems to be a paradox: the "positive" aspiration toward freedom readily leads humans to the opposite of freedom. A historical consideration reveals that under the one-sided implementation and carrying out of ideas like democracy, rationality, equality, and revolution, some sort of deposit quality was engendered within each of them. In the form of positively realizing an idea, this idea becomes alienated from itself while degenerating into a tool for the repression, control, and violation of people's thoughts and actions. The ideological maintenance of a pre-established form of being and the utopian pursuit of illusory plans show different aspects of this tendency. Here, the positive approach to freedom undoubtedly expresses its negative meaning as well.

Relative to the positive form of freedom is the negative form of freedom, which aims at shaking off restrictions and forms of control issuing from outside, or in other words, "freedom from."[48] However, while demanding to break free from restrictions, the negative mode of freedom seems to entail a tendency to eliminate already fashioned ideals and goals. Whereas the positive mode of freedom embodies the internal demand of "What ought to be done?" the negative mode of freedom entails a doubt and denial of all such demands. If this negative and skeptical standpoint is excessively developed it could run the risk of abandoning all worthy commitments on the substantial or universal level. When he ties "absolute values" to "our primitive past" and views the demand to transcend the relative validity of individual beliefs as an "incurable metaphysical need,"[49] Berlin shows his rejection of dogmatism but also reveals his accusation of and distance from universal values. Logically speaking, when shaking off and destroying becomes the main let alone only choice and approach, any agreement about or commitment to values loses its essential ground, thereby leading inevitably to the nihilistic orientation toward the destruction of all values. So-called post-modernism manifests an aspect of the negative ideal of freedom. Post-modernism aims at deconstructing pre-existing worlds of meaning (including value principles), but while transcending, destroying, and negating pre-existing systems of meaning, post-modernism neither commits to nor opens up any new world of meaning. After shaking off and eliminating everything, what remains is a sense of nothingness and meaninglessness.

At the same time, the process of developing individuality involves the constraint of norms. Norms include purposes on the level of substance and have the dual function of guiding and restraining. Guiding expresses the positive sense of directing and restraining expresses the negative sense of limiting. In direct correspondence with the role of ordinary ideas in the process of reforming the world and refining the self, freedom in its positive form essentially involves agreeing with and affirming the meaning of universal norms. By contrast, with shaking off, transcending, and negating as its approach, freedom in its negative form logically entails some estrangement from norms, which corresponds to the dispelling of valued goals, and which makes the guiding role of value principles impossible to actualize in the process of reforming the world and molding the self.

Evidently, each of these two forms of freedom has its own limitations. So, the ideal of freedom linked to the whole-sided development of the individual (free individuality) cannot be simply equated with them. Even though the positive orientation of freedom affirms human creativity and confirms the meaning to which values lead, excessively emphasizing this aspect of freedom skews it along the path of dogmatism and despotism; even though the negative mode of freedom may assist in inhibiting the dogmatism and despotism to which positive freedom may inevitably lead, because it has its own deficiency in a commitment to values and ignores the guidance of norms it logically leads just as easily to nihilism. Confucius once mentioned the principle of being loyal (*zhong* 忠) and empathic (*shu* 恕). Being loyal means "helping others take their stand insofar as you wishes to take your stand, and get others there insofar as you wish to get there,"[50] the essential tendency of which is to extend oneself to others, to influence and effect the other with one's own value ideals, so as to make such ideals become the aim pursued in common by the self and the other. Being empathic then refers to the principle of "not doing unto others what you yourself do not desire."[51] Although this principle cannot entirely extricate itself from a certain kind of solipsism, it still envelops the will to avoid violating the other and a willingness to respect the other. The former is positive, but with this as the sole principle there is always the risk of forcing one's own values upon others and falling prey to dogmatism; the latter is negative, which obviously harbors the negative tendency to inhibit and suppress the former ("helping others take their stand insofar as you yourself wish to take your stand, and getting others there insofar as you yourself wishes to get there"); yet, holding too strongly to the latter may also lead to the suspension of all worthy ideals. Confucius saw the unification of the two as the way to realize moral principles while avoiding the one-sided intentions harbored respectively by the positive and negative approaches. Even though Confucius was unable to go beyond the model of thought that determines accomplishing oneself with the attainment of sagehood, in responding to the issue of determining a moral way of being, his viewpoint is most certainly profound. Concretely understanding the free development of individuality through the unification and mutual supplementing of being contentious and being empathic we can notice further that this process is inseparable from the guidance of worthy ideals and the intention to create values on the one hand and also that adequate respect should be paid to the internal characteristics of the individual so as to avoid the dogmatic and coercive tendency to destroy the diversity and concreteness of individual beings. Furthermore, while affirming the valuing of ideals and the creation of values, we must avoid absolutizing them and abstracting them from their position in the process of history. Entailed here is some way of combining negative freedom and positive freedom or the twofold sublation of their opposed aspects.

The process of accomplishing oneself whose aim is free individuality, concretely expresses the meaning of the individual's being as regards the transformation of history and the significance of values. While the fact that the individual precedes purpose reveals the meaning of the individual's value at the level of ontology, the free individuality linked to the whole-sided development of human being gives concrete substance to this meaning. With the overcoming of personal dependence and objective dependence as a prior condition, free individuality reveals the purposive determination of human being and reflects the transformations and developments undergone by the form of society, from which the meaning of the individual's being gains deeper senses of value and broader historical implications. This very process of generating meaning shows furthermore the historical and axiological dimensions of a world of meaning at the level of individual existence.

7   Accomplishing Oneself and Accomplishing Things

Value in a World of Meaning

FREE INDIVIDUALITY, HUMAN capacities, and inner state of mind most directly involve the personal space of the self but also in a broader sense the distinction and interaction between the individual domain and the public sphere. As interrelated aspects of the social world, the individual domain and its connection to the public sphere also sets the concrete background for the historical process of accomplishing oneself and accomplishing things. As the actual mode of being, accomplishing oneself and accomplishing things is never separable from diverse social resources, and the acquisition, possession, and distribution of resources involves the issue of social justice. Since accomplishing oneself and accomplishing things is one unified process, the individual domain is inseparable from the public sphere as self-realization is from social justice. Involving the transformation of society, justice is itself historical, that is, it will be overcome in the course of historical evolution. With the elevated growth of resources and material wealth as its historical precondition, the genuine realization of the value of the being of humans is concretely exhibited in human being freely developing itself with the aim of refining itself and refining the world. Through the interaction of the free development of each with the free development of all, accomplishing oneself and accomplishing things possesses deeper significance as the historical genesis of a world of meaning.

The Individual Sphere and Accomplishing Oneself

History shows an understanding of the private domain as a sphere of society opposed to the political domain. According to Habermas, modern Scottish philosophers saw civil society as the genuine domain of private autonomy standing in opposition to the power of public authority.[1] In still other perspectives, the private domain was seen as fastened to private life, which involved receding from the public world and staying out of the public eye: "The distinction between the private and public realms ... equals the distinction between things that should be shown and the things that should be hidden."[2] The public sphere standing opposed to the private domain has therefore either been seen as a political domain distinguished from the domain of social life[3] or as a "common world" that appears outside and that gathers us together[4]; or even as "a sphere which mediates between state and society,"[5] in which public opinion is formed and that is accessible to all citizens. The private and public spheres, which this chapter discusses, may indeed share something in common with the private and public spheres as discussed in such modern social politics, but at the same time, they do not entirely coincide. Roughly speaking, this book focuses more upon the distinction between the personal and social domains when examining the individual and public domains. The individual or private domain in this context concerns the variety of facets related to the person; such facets neither directly appear nor unfold within society, nor can they be entirely controlled or dominated by society. The public sphere, by contrast, is established upon social communication and the reciprocal interaction between humans, and is marked by openness, externality, and public accessibility.[6] While I connect the individual to the private domain mainly to show that the person's form of being contains aspects that cannot be swallowed up by or reduced to society, understanding society from the standpoint of the public sphere has the advantage of pointing out that the facets of communication, common life, and public participation constitute society's form of being. As I will show later on, the individual domain is inseparable from the public sphere, and the distinction between them is somewhat relative. For the individual human being, of course, self-recognition and self-accomplishment involves many facets of the personal or private domain in the sense just mentioned. In regard to the actual mode of being, intellectual and practical activities related to private space constitute important aspects of self-accomplishment.

As mentioned, the public or social sphere is external, while the distinctive feature of the individual or private domain first appears at the level of the inner mind. As for the internal dimension of ideas, character undoubtedly has unique meaning in the individual or private domain. Here, character is said in the broad sense, encapsulating both the ethical dimension of virtues and the diverse individualities and degrees of intelligence found among human beings. The different forms of character have different senses or meanings: in connection with the good, being virtuous as ethical character exhibits a positive sense of value, while the powers of insight and understanding and other such mental characteristics, on the other hand, have more neutral senses of value. Yet, regardless of what their concrete sense of value may be, character is never separable from the being of the self, and thus pertains to the individual dimension.

Here it seems a distinction could be made between virtue as internal ethical character and external ethical norms. Ethical norms, as universal social standards, are by nature public. By contrast, virtues, as the internal properties of individuals, are by nature private. What are ordinarily called public virtues concern the objects of virtue or the background of virtuous action. As to their way of being, public virtues act upon external social objects and social relations, but are still internal to the self and the individual. Linked to this distinction is the difference between reforming society and refining oneself. Reforming society consists of refining institutions and shifting the shape of society, which involves external social objects; refining oneself, considered at the ethical level, aims at cultivating virtue, which involves the development of individual spirit and the raising of character. Naturally, refining oneself is inseparable from reforming society. In effect, there is always interaction between social reform and self-refinement. Yet, with the aim of reforming institutions, the transformation of society more directly concerns the public sphere; by contrast, self-refinement is based upon the efforts and demands of the individual self, and unfolds as the cultivation of inner virtue, which obviously is not a public process. This difference between reforming society and refining oneself proves that the two cannot be simply equated. As soon as refining the self is thought of as society reforming human being from the outside, the private domain falls entirely into the public sphere, which leads to such consequences as the disregard for private space and even the elimination of individuality, along with the self. In ancient China, it was recorded that an individual "opposing in his gut" (*fu fei* 腹诽) and "disagreeing in his heart" (*xin bang* 心谤) were enough grounds to punish him.[7] Opposing in one's gut and disagreeing in one's heart involve the individual's inner conscious activity; condemning someone on these grounds not only entails trying to take control of the individual's inner conscious activity; it also denies the individual the right to have an inner self with the capacity to think autonomously. Under the influence of an extreme leftist trend of thought in modern China, social reform was accompanied by demands for "thought reform" (*sixiang gaizao* 思想改造) and "the revolution of the soul" (*linghun geming* 灵魂革命), which resulted in the coercive control of individuals from the outside, which led logically to inhibiting and stomping out individuality, or in a word, to self-annihilation.

The individual's character is of course not limited to just virtue in the ethical domain. Corresponding to the diversity of modes of being and practical activities of human beings, individual character also takes a diversity of shapes. From emotion to will, from reason to intuition, and from bodily experience to the capacity to be affected as well as in aspects of individuality, capacity, mental disposition, and degree of intelligence, selves exhibit different characteristics. The shaping of individual character at this level undoubtedly involves the interaction of the individual with society, which includes the communication of emotions between individuals and the cultivation and improvement of reasoning capacities by means of recognizing and grasping the knowledge that society has generated. However, this interaction is always based on the individual's own affective experience and understanding. Whether it is individuality or other characteristics of spirit, the process of their formation and form of being is always distinctive, and can never be entirely universalized, publicized, or enfolded into an external uniform model. Though it is true that the internal character of spirit is manifested in different ways in the process of knowing and doing in the broad sense and thereby enters the public sphere of practice through real actions, the practical process of acting upon and participating in the public sphere does not imply that spiritual character only has a public form of being; while acting upon the outside, spiritual character is still within a concrete self. With regard to the emotional world, respecting oneself and respecting others respectively involves an attitude toward oneself and an attitude toward others. As experiences of sincere emotion, such attitudes are individual affections existing within the self and so differ from public criticisms or public opinions of the public sphere. As soon as these affections are intentionally "shown" to the public, they immediately degenerate into forms of external "posturing," usually with some scent of pretention, and hence cease to be the self's genuine emotions and true feelings. The inseparability of spiritual character and emotional experience from the internality of the self distinguishes them from external institutions and universal norms through their individual mode of being, which is not public. This characteristic in a broader sense constitutes the ground conditioning the diversity and richness of the spiritual character and individuality of human beings.

As social beings, individuals not only have diverse spiritual characteristics but different values as well. The latter concretely unfold in moral ideals, political beliefs, directions of life, ultimate concerns, religious beliefs, and so on. Spiritual character mainly presents the internality of the being of humans. Values, by contrast, involve the pursuit of meaning and the hope of an ideal form of being. Of course, spiritual character is not strictly separable from values. Ethical virtues, for example, are fused together with moral ideals: ethical virtues refer to moral ideals as to their core, and the formation of moral ideals within individuals is based upon the ethical virtues they possess. This interconnection on the internal level is grounded in the fact that both concern the being of the individual: even though ethical virtues and moral ideals do encompass universal social content, they are also individual attributes or individual pursuits, and only obtain an actual form of being within a concrete individual.

Similarly, the political domain, including its institutional organs and their performance, is undoubtedly public, but political beliefs that reflect certain value orientations are, however, tied to specific individuals, and remain the pursuits and hopes of those individuals. What sort of political ideas an individual will accept and what sort of political ideals she will choose of course depends on multiple influences, but this acceptance and choice can only ultimately actualize within the individual self. As the practical agent of the political domain, the self must indeed comply with certain norms in order to invest one's actions with legitimacy, but the political role an individual plays does not entirely coincide with his political consciousness: that an individual carries out some political duty in the public sphere also does not mean that her internal political consciousness is consistent with it. For example, a political figure in a monarchical political system may participate in the wide variety of political activities found within the monarchical system, while also accepting some constitutional ideals that would pertain to a republic. At the level of ideas, even an agent of political practice can still have her own private space. In contrast to the public character of political organizations and their functioning, values whose form of being is internal, such as political beliefs, are individual and private in character. Neglecting the latter leads to blurring the distinction between institutional facts and political consciousness, and readily results in a simplistic understanding of the practical processes of the political domain.

A more internal manifestation of the individual dimension of values can be seen in religious beliefs. Religion is a cultural phenomenon with its external aspects of form, including religious organizations, religious rituals, religious architecture, religious prohibitions and laws, and other religious activities; these aspects show the different senses of the public and social character of religion. However, at the same time, as the manifestation of an ultimate concern, religion also has its internal aspects, specifically, the beliefs and hopes of the self. In contrast to organizations (like churches), rituals, laws, and other externalities, beliefs concern the individual's emotional experience and acceptance of something; whether or not one should follow a religion and to what extent one should believe in a transcendent being show some of the different choices a self may have in the spiritual realm. While a religion in the form of a social organization has a public character, the individual's religious beliefs remain private. Equating belief with an action conducted in the public sphere will result in the outside interfering with the private domain and may even lead to the persecution of individuals. In the European Middle Ages, the tendency to publicize the beliefs of individuals took hold in accompaniment with multiple invasions of private space, not to mention religious persecution as well.

In contrast to the metaphysical character of an ultimate concern, there are other modes of being of the individual domain related to the world of everyday life. At the level of ideas, we could first mention personal interests, hobbies, and habits, to name a few. From personal taste in the case of food and drink to preferences in fashion and dress, from spare time interests to leisure time plans; from personal habits in resting, working, waking, and sleeping to educational and physical hobbies, personal spaces of life emerge in different forms. As forms through which the production and reproduction of life is realized, everyday life constitutes an important facet of humans being-in-the-world, and the interests, habits, and hobbies tied to it invest everyday life with an individualizing and diversifying characteristic. In the context of the actual unfolding of everyday life, interests, customs, and hobbies also exhibit the self's individual way of being and mode of being; ignoring this mode of being of the self not only makes it impossible to derive a true understanding of everyday life, it also leads to an abstraction of the individual himself.

Interests, habits, and so forth mainly concern the aspect of intentionality in the process of everyday being. In a more actual way, human being's everyday being also involves private activities of diverse forms. Family life, for example, unfolds at different levels: from the employment and income of family members to family budget and spending; from educating the children to caring for the elderly; from everyday consumption to leisure activities. Such activities are predominantly private affairs, which can be seen through such distinctions as the one between the family budget and the government budget, raising children and schooling, nursing one's parents and caring for the elders in one's community. As private affairs, these issues within family life cannot be entirely up to society to resolve, and are also not issues society may arbitrarily meddle with. Likewise, although the person exists within society, his opinions and actions also have a confidential or private aspect, that is, some may not be suitable to disclose and may best be kept unpublicized. Even the life of a so-called public figure still has sides that are not always for the public to know of. What is ordinarily called the right to privacy is but the respect for and affirmation of the private nature of individual life. In broader terms, communication between humans is not just a public phenomenon, containing as it does a private and individual dimension, which is not just limited to such private relationships as friendly feelings and emotional connections between persons or intimate conversations between friends; at a broader level, it also concerns cooperation between the political and economic domains and international relations, wherein personal relationships, including private friendships, are also involved. This individual dimension of communication shows both the interlaced nature and complexity of the public and private domains, and also shows the individual dimension in the process of being human.

The individual dimension of the being of humans stems from the externality of the relations between humans. At the ontological level, relations between humans are marked by both internality and externality. The individual cannot exist in isolation from his relations with others, and indeed can only exist in those relations, but he always contains facets that cannot be assimilated to those relations. There is always some boundary between individuals: "I" am not "you," nor "you" "me." This boundary is not only exhibited in space-time; it is also concretized as psychological distance, differences of interest, and so on. As already mentioned, although other people may act as substitutes for some social roles "I" am taking on, "my" individual being, however, is irreplaceable. The difference between being (or existence) and role therefore demonstrates that the individual or self cannot be entirely reduced to relations.

Individuals in a relation have their internal worlds. Although the mutual understanding and communication between humans requires their internal worlds to open up to one another, within this opening up there is always a non-disclosure. The undisclosed aspect within "me" not only cannot be assimilated by the relation, it also constitutes one of the conditions of possibility of understanding and communicating: When "I" entirely open myself up in object form, "I" as understanding subject also cease to exist. Communication between individuals at least encompasses the two aspects of understanding the other and being understood by the other; if "I" only consider the dimension of being understood by the other, "I" am merely a being-for-others, the property of which is an adaptation to and affirmation of the other, and meanwhile, I am evacuated of the subjective characteristics of choosing, evaluating, denying, and so on. On the other hand, communicating and understanding are both directed at coordinating interactions between individuals and ordering the inner world of the self; so, with only the former as a focus, "I" estranging myself into equipment is unavoidable.

Historically speaking, autocratic political systems usually ignored the individual or private domain. In pre-modern traditional societies, everything pertaining to people, including their way of life, thoughts, and ideas, fell under the scope of the monarch's right to control, and thought suppression was the corresponding result; when theocratic systems assumed the highest authority, personal beliefs fell under the scope of their control. In modern totalitarian conditions like the reign of Nazism, the person's political beliefs, religious beliefs, ethical ideas, and so on, were all objects of control, and the person's whole life had to unconditionally submit to the extreme authority of the so-called benefit of the nation. The confiscation of personal diaries, the monitoring of private messages, and so on, which occurred during the reign of extreme leftist thought in modern China show another example of an outrageous invasion of the individual or private domains. All of these forms reflect expansions of the public sphere into the private domain, and behind these expansions followed the invasion if not all-out elimination of the individual domain.

In actuality, there are many sides to the being of humans. Now, although the externality of relations between human beings and the private life tied to this externality make one in a certain sense exist outside the public sphere, private life gives one's being concreteness and actuality. Human being evacuated of individuality and privacy is but abstract being, and human being's self-refinement or self-realization could not be initiated in an abstract individual. So, respecting and approving the individual or private domain constitutes an important content of accomplishing oneself and accomplishing things, and entails overcoming the abstractness of this process. Here, confirming the concreteness of being and affirming the actuality of the process of accomplishing oneself constitutes two sides of the same process. Furthermore, the goal of refining the self is the multisided development of the individual, which concerns both the sociality and the individuality of human being. From inner virtue, capacity, and degree of intelligence to political beliefs, orientation of life, and ultimate concern; from personal taste to everyday habits; from the private space of the person to the emotional attunement between individuals, this variety of sides to the self's state of being are also the very topics of self-refinement and self-improvement. By ignoring the contents related to the individual or private domains, the self cannot avoid a partial or one-sided development. In the history of philosophy, Dong Zhongshu once equated "the self" with "what is righteous" (*yi* 义), thinking that "what is righteous is the term used to speak of the self."[8] Here, "what is righteous" is tied to "what ought to be," which merely exhibits universal social norms, and reducing the self to "what is righteous" here as universal norms means dispelling the individual character of the self and universalizing it. Starting from this point, the process of accomplishing oneself will obviously fail to attain the true form of one's being.

Refining oneself also unfolds as a process of seeking meaning, and realizing the meaning of one's own being is inseparably linked to the genesis of a world of meaning. Regardless of whether we are considering the ideal form of being or the actual form of being, the individual's world of meaning is based on neither a one-sided self-recognition nor a universalized "I," but upon one's whole being, and requires the all-around recognition of the whole of human being. As one of the sides this all-sided recognition cannot neglect, the properties of the individual sphere of one's being also pervade one's world of meaning and constitute its true and concrete content. In brief, in the process of refining oneself and producing a world of meaning, confirming the individual sphere of being means affirming the concreteness of individual being and giving a world of meaning both actuality and multiple sides and facets.

Social Justice

Directed at one's own perfection, the actual process of accomplishing oneself is inseparable from the individual or private domain. However, recognizing and respecting the private domain is not the whole content of the process of refining oneself. One's self-realization and perfection is neither limited to the level of ideas nor to individual self-identification. As a concrete process that unfolds into many sides, cultivating the self is also based on economic, political, educational, and cultural conditions. Such conditions are the actual resources of the process of accomplishing oneself.

As the actual conditions of the process of accomplishing oneself, resources are by nature social. When discussing the structuration of society, Anthony Giddens specifically pointed out two elements, that is, rules and resources. Rules co-ordinate the activity of human agents, and resources involve the control of material products or of aspects of the material world.[9] Here, the term "resources" is said in reference to the construction of the whole of society, and in an extended sense, resources could be understood as one of the social preconditions of refining oneself and reforming the world. As the conditions of the being and development of human being, resources express meaning in the process of human practice. Minerals only constitute actual production resources once they enter the metallurgical process of mining. Similarly, education opportunities only effectively appear as developmental resources when a degree of education directly impacts the development of one's potential and position within society. In this sense, the relationship between resources and human development is interactive: there is no way for human beings to develop and realize their potential without actual resources, and resources would possess no concrete meaning outside of the process of human practice. This relationship between resources and human beings also determines the historicity of resources themselves. If we consider basic forms of survival activities in the primitive age of human development such as procuring clothing, food, and shelter, only those things that could satisfy needs such as protection from wind and rain and satisfying hunger constituted resources for human survival and development. However, in modern societies, "clothing" is no longer just a thing that protects the human body; it is now also made for the purposes of fashion, serving the function of representing one's social identity. Similarly the meaning of food no longer consists in simply killing hunger, as it is now tied to the needs of taste, nutrition, and health. So, only those things that also serve the latter functions constitute actual resources for the satisfaction of needs in clothing and food. By extension, accompanying the evolution of society, economic wealth, political status, education opportunities, and conditions for obtaining information have all come to constitute diverse resources intimately tied to one's being and development.

Human development and individual accomplishment is clearly not just a matter of elevating one's state of mind; it is inseparable from a certain background of social being and actual resources from the economic, political, cultural, and educational spheres. Such resources are the historical conditions of accomplishing oneself and accomplishing things, and in a way make this process transcend the stage of ideas internal to the mind, giving it concrete content. So, as the expression of human being's essential powers, human capacities constitute the internal conditions of possibility of accomplishing oneself (refining the self) and accomplishing things (reforming the world), while universal norms, as the unity of what actually is, what necessarily is, and what ought to be, provide the process of accomplishing oneself and accomplishing things with rules of guidance constitutive and regulative, but these conditions are still ineffectual without social resources, which are the actual foundation and material conditions of accomplishing oneself and accomplishing things. So, human capacities, universal norms, and social resources interact in the process of accomplishing oneself and accomplishing things.

As the actual conditions of accomplishing oneself and accomplishing things, resources are social. The social character of resources is not only manifested in the fact that their actualization and meaning take shape through the historical process of cognizing and practicing, but also in the fact that the acquisition, possession, and distribution of resources are all achievements of the social sphere. Individuals inherently need different social resources to develop, but this does not mean that every individual may naturally acquire needed resources. How do we distribute resources rationally and fairly? Under historical conditions in which resources are relatively limited, we necessarily confront the problem of justice. Now, the problem of justice permits a diversity of understandings, and there have indeed been many different readings of the meaning of justice in history. But at the level of content, the core of the problem lies in the reasonable occupation and fair distribution of social resources.[10]

As for the relationship between resources and individuals, the acquisition, possession, and distribution of resources first concerns individual rights. Resources that can be reasonably and legitimately acquired and possessed are precisely resources that are acquired and possessed by right. In this sense, justice directly relates to human rights, that is, justice clearly implies acknowledging and respecting rights. In fact, when Plato and Aristotle understand justice as getting what is deserved, they also seem to have this first in mind: To get what one deserves is precisely to acquire what one has the right to acquire.[11] In this context, right has both positive and negative aspects. The positive aspect of rights expresses rights as demands grounded in legitimate reasons; in this sense, having the so-called right to acquire something is, in other terms, having legitimate reasons to demand acquiring it. The negative aspect of right denies others or society the permission to interfere with, disregard, or restrict such a demand so long as it is based on the individual's own right.

In contemporary philosophy, John Rawls, whose approach to the problem of justice is rather systematic, focuses mainly on human rights. For Rawls, utilitarianism starts with the desires of human sensibility, and so is unable to arrive at a universal principle of justice. At the same time the target for utilitarianism is arriving at the greatest good for the majority or greatest number of people, which logically implies disregarding the rights of the minority. Differing from utilitarianism, Rawls first sees human beings as rational beings and links justice to human rationality, thinking that "[t]he desire to express our nature as a free and equal rational being can be fulfilled only by acting on the principles of right and justice as having first priority."[12] Under the pretext of a presupposed veil of ignorance and original position, Rawls raises the two basic principles of justice: the first is that "[e]ach person is to have an equal right to the most extensive system of equal basic liberties compatible with a similar system of liberty for all."[13] The second holds that "social and economic inequalities are to be arranged so that they are both (a) reasonably expected to be to everyone's advantage, and (b) attached to positions and offices open to all."[14] This slightly repetitive formulation is ordinarily summarized as the principle of liberty and the difference principle; while the former points out the connection between justice and equal rights, the latter stresses that economic and social inequalities are just under the condition that those living in the least advantaged position within a social system receive the greatest possible benefit and that equal opportunities can be guaranteed.

Rawls see equal rights as the core of justice, which in theoretical terms stresses the dimension of equality pertaining to rights. In contrast to this, Robert Nozick turns his focus toward the dimension of individuality pertaining to rights. The principle of liberty and the difference principle, which Rawls mentions, logically entail affirming the redistribution of benefits between individuals, but for Nozick, just acquisition and just ownership are of primary significance. He specifically lays out the following principle:

1. A person who acquires a holding in accordance with the principle of justice in acquisition is entitled to that holding.
2. A person who acquires a holding in accordance with the principle of justice in transfer, from someone else entitled to the holding, is entitled to the holding.
3. No one is entitled to a holding except by (repeated) applications of 1 and 2.[15]

Ownership in harmony with this principle is entitled ownership as well as just ownership. Entitlement here is consistent with right. In other words, to be entitled to own something is to have the right to own it; but, in this understanding of rights, priority is given to the right to own or possess. Logically speaking, just ownership is the owning of something in accordance with the principle of just acquisition or the principle of just transfer; this formulation may seem like circular reasoning, but its intrinsic meaning lies in stressing the rights of the person (the right of the person to own).

According to Nozick, this entitlement theory of justice is also tied to a historical principle, which demands tracing back the past historical conditions of acquisition or ownership: "*historical principles* of justice hold that past circumstances or actions of people can create differential entitlements or differential deserts to things."[16] Even though Nozick does not actually give concrete consideration as to how initial ownership relations emerge from the historical perspective, a historical principle does entail such a demand to trace back ownership relations to their origin. For Nozick, the most original right of ownership is "self-ownership;" the infringement upon the most basic right of the human being is the seizure of the human being's labor or forcing someone to do something without reward, because this would mean that the party who is violated or forced to work is "partially owned" by some other party: "This process whereby they take this decision from you makes them a *part-owner* of you; it gives them a property right in you."[17] As the most basic and original right, self-ownership includes the person's ownership of his own body, time, and capacities. According to Nozick, it is precisely this property right that provides the historical and logical starting point for justice based on rights.

Rawls and Nozick undoubtedly present us with different perspectives. Even though his criticism enables us to get beyond utilitarianism's disregard for the rights of the minority or individual rights, as a whole, Rawls determines justice in a formalistic and procedural manner: whether he proceeds by emphasizing that humans are rational beings, or by presupposing a veil of ignorance and an original condition, or even by determining the principle of justice by means of contracts, in each case he is concerned with universal form and procedure. By contrast, Nozick is able to reach the substance of justice by approaching it as an issue concerning the being of humans (primarily the individual human being) with his emphasis upon "self-ownership." However, the self-ownership that Nozick speaks of is still abstract. In actuality, the individual is never an isolated being, and that which he "possesses" or "owns" is by no means a simple individual object or individual property. With regard to the most fundamental things the individual "owns," his life and body, the acquisition and growth of these do not simply originate from "the self" by itself. As Confucianism puts it: "We dare not hurt our body, hair or skin, since all of these things are derived from our parents."[18] Here, what is stressed are the aspects of the individual's life and body, which transcend the individual. In regard to the individual capacities that the self possesses, their formation is also not just conditioned by natural inheritance; their formation also involves the influence and education of society and those historically formed achievements of knowledge. That aside, the very "owning" that "self-ownership" entails does not imply that the self may arbitrarily "use" itself. I may "own" two legs, but under conditions where I am not permitted, I cannot arbitrarily "use" my two legs, for instance, to enter the private domicile of another; one's use of one's own body (practicing in the broad sense) is always constrained by a variety of social conditions. In this respect, self-ownership only has relative meaning. Even though Nozick's account concerns historicality, establishing individual rights upon such an abstract concept of "self-ownership" evidently shows little consciousness of actual social history.[19]

Justice at the substantial level concerns the fair acquisition and possession of resources for individual development, and the fair acquisition and possession of resources is a concrete display of an affirmation of, respect for, and actualization of individual rights. But where in the end is the intrinsic ground of justice in this horizon? Here what is of primary importance is the principle of individual autonomy. The individual autonomy spoken of here includes choosing and determining the goals of one's own multifaceted development and realizing different goals through the legitimate application of one's own capacities (including one's own physical force and intellectual powers); these facets present the concrete right of the individual to freely develop. Insofar as Rawls chooses the equality of liberty among individuals as the first principle of justice and insofar as Nozick selects self-ownership as the starting point of justice, they both indeed take notice of this; even though there are discrepancies between them in terms of how individual rights are to be understood, they do coincide in affirming that individuals possess the right of free development. Early Enlightenment thinkers such as Locke did also stress this in a sense. The right of the person to develop freely concerns many domains not only economic and political but also cultural and educational.

As actual beings, however, individuals exhibit all kinds of fundamental differences at the level of what Nozick termed "self-ownership." As for capacities, whether in terms of physical force or intellectual power, no two individuals are entirely the same. Marx points this out in the following way: "it [this equal right] tacitly recognizes unequal individual endowment, and thus productive capacity, as natural privileges."[20] In the socio-economic circumstances of individual beings, we see all kinds of disparities not only in social relations such as family backgrounds and class origins but also in social resources that may be accessed and used. These natural and social differences not only make individuals differ in terms of the starting point of their free development; they also make individuals exhibit a variety of differences with regard to their actual choice of worthy goals and the use of their capacities in the realization of those goals. The inevitable result is inequality between individuals in their possession of developmental resources. The unrewarded seizure of the labor of one group of people by another in the economic domain demonstrates this point concretely. We can see that the free development of individuals based on the right of autonomy logically results in actual inequality, which makes those individuals standing in weaker positions fail to acquire the resources they need for their own development.

This result, which individual autonomy entails, prevents us from establishing social justice upon individual autonomy alone. How is it possible to overcome this negative tendency that may arise from the simple principle of individual autonomy? Here, it seems we could refer to another principle of social justice, that is, the principle of the equality of human nature. Here, human nature refers to the essential value of the human being as such, so the equality of human nature consists precisely in an affirmation and recognition of the equality of human beings at the level of value. Confucianism pointed this out rather early on. Mencius elaborates a theory that human nature is good, and that the nature of every human being is good means that there is no essential difference between human beings. From here, Mencius goes further, proclaiming that "the sage is my equal,"[21] and that "the people are equal to the Yao and Shun emperors."[22] Here the important point lies in understanding the relationship between human and human (including the sage and the ordinary human being) from the perspective of "equality." If we overcome its abstract understanding of the human being, we may find in it a principle of the equality of human nature. Considering actual individuals, granted there are manifold differences between them in terms of their natural endowments, capacities, social backgrounds, and much more, at the level of value where human being is essentially an end in itself, there is an essential equality between human beings. This equality of human beings at the level of value would provide individuals with an intrinsic ground to equally acquire developmental resources; at the social level, this equality constitutes the precondition of society fairly distributing the resources needed for individual development. As stated previously, the principle of individual autonomy confirms the right of individuals to freely develop. Relative to this, the equality of human nature affirms the right of individuals to obtain developmental resources. The former entails that limiting and denying the free development of individuals is unjust, because it strips individuals of the right of individual autonomy; the latter entails that leading individuals to lose developmental resources is likewise unjust, because it fails to ensure the right of individual acquisition based upon the equality of human nature (equal value).

The right of individual acquisition based upon the equality of human nature (the equality of human beings in terms of value) undoubtedly concerns the distribution and redistribution of developmental resources. The difference principle that Rawls suggests in a sense also concerns such a distribution. However, Rawls simultaneously proclaims: "The difference principle represents, in effect, an agreement to regard the distribution of natural talents as in some respects a common asset and to share in the greater social and economic benefits made possible by the complementarities of this distribution."[23] For Nozick, the difference principle in this sense implies an illegitimate expropriation of the individual from himself. Theoretically speaking, the understanding Rawls has of social distribution obviously misses the substance of the problem. The precondition that must be fulfilled here is distinguishing between "natural talents" and the actual capacities of human beings. Although so-called natural talents constitute the beginning of individual development, they themselves are still not actual capacities, which I analyzed when discussing Nozick's "self-ownership." The formation of the actual capacities of human beings is always grounded in a multifaceted social background and is inseparable from society's concrete constraint and influence. From the historical accumulation of cognitive achievements (knowledge) to cultural education and social practice, these socio-historical factors are always at work in different ways in the process of the individual forming actual capacities. In this sense, differences between individuals in terms of capacities are not entirely determined by their natural talents, and involve the participation of society and the working of society from the very beginning. Furthermore, the application of individual capacities and the extension of the self's abilities is also constrained in a multifaceted way by social conditions. So, with regard to an individual who is socially advantaged and thus in possession of more resources throughout his free development, the achievements he reaches do not only belong to him, but to society as well (constituting a "common property" of society); it is precisely this which provides social redistribution and social regulation with an intrinsic ground. It is evident that as "common property," what enters the process of social distribution and social regulation is not "natural talent," as Rawls put it, but rather social resources produced by actual capacities that are no less social, and it is precisely this fact which makes distribution and regulation as such differ from what Nozick called the expropriation of the individual.

Justice at the substantial level is evidently inseparable from rights. Individual autonomy and the equality of human nature in different ways constitute the fundamental ground of rights. Without individual autonomy, the right of the individual to freely develop is not a practical option; if the equality of human nature is disregarded, there is no way to protect the right of the individual to acquire developmental resources. In this sense, the principle of individual autonomy and the principle of the equality of human nature undoubtedly constitute the twofold precondition of social justice.

Historically speaking, under the pretext of natural law and innate human rights, early Enlightenment thinkers gave increased priority to personal freedom and individual rights.[24] The personal rights that Locke acknowledges include the right to live, the right to enjoy freedom, and the right to own property. One of the key points to this idea of rights is the free development of the person, and later the market economy will gradually offer an actual space for the concrete application of this right. However, although the market economy formally paves a way for the forward gallop of personal freedom, the result of formal personal freedom ends up being substantial injustice due to the individual differences and social limitations mentioned previously. The labor movements and broader socialist movements of the nineteenth and twentieth centuries could be seen as historical responses to this idea of rights and its consequences. Tied to these movements was an emphasis upon the rights of the individual to be protected by society, which included the right of the individual to acquire from society resources for survival and development: it demands that society give those individuals of weaker social standing who are exploited in the market-orientation of free development the resources they deserve. This derivation of the idea of rights since the modern age reflects an actual transformation of society, and also involves the two principles of social justice at the historical level, that of individual autonomy and that of the equality of human nature.

From the theoretical perspective, social justice in this context concerns the relationship between rights, legitimacy, and the good. At the formal level, legitimacy is usually linked to universal principles and norms. Legitimacy in this sense is mainly understood as norms that accord with universal principles. Legitimacy is simultaneously tied to rights as well. In this sense, legitimacy appears as the recognition and protection of the rights humans deserve to have. The word "right" in the context of Western philosophy expresses both the sense of "legitimate" and "right," which seems to show the connection between the two. Similarly, in Chinese philosophy, the concept of ritual propriety or rites (*li* 礼) and the concept of what is right or righteous (*yi* 义), as universal norms, determine the boundaries of the rights of persons. In another respect, what accords with ritual propriety and what is right is also a legitimate action, which again entails the unity of what is right and what is legitimate. The good, as positive value, is not limited to the moral domain; its scope is much broader, including all forms of being, which have positive value for the being of humans (benefiting the being and development of humans). In confirming and protecting the legitimate rights of human beings, justice simultaneously reflects what is good at the substantial level, and resources for the being and development of humans are concrete expressions of what is good in the broader sense just mentioned. Although the theory of justice over which Rawls elaborates also includes a notion of the good, he also claims "the concept of legitimacy has priority over the concept of the good."[25] This idea, however, seems incapable of grasping the unity of legitimacy and the good. The logical trend of this thought is obviously determined by its focus on the formal dimension of justice (procedural justice): When form and procedure become the most important dimensions, the status of the good in the substantial sense, though equally important, is underestimated. However, with the unification of substance and form as a precondition, what is right, legitimate, and good constitutes the essential meaning of justice. Therefore, an affirmation of what is right and legitimate cannot be isolated from a consideration of what is actually good.

In brief, human existence, individual development, and self-refinement would be impossible without necessary social resources from the economic, political, and cultural spheres; the rational acquisition and distribution of social resources constitutes the substantial intension of social justice. Acquisition and possession of social resources is also tied to individual rights from the very beginning: the fair distribution of resources expresses the legitimate right of individuals, and the confirmation of and respect for the rights of the individual is the essence of social justice. As a whole, the right of individuals is expressed as free development, whose content is the equal acquisition of resources; the two are grounded in the principle of autonomy and the principle of the equality of human nature respectively. As the origin of individual rights, individual autonomy and the equality of human nature simultaneously constitute the intrinsic ground of social justice.

Individual and Society

Pointing to the fair distribution of social resources, social justice ensures the process of accomplishing oneself and accomplishing things with a reasonable allotment of developmental resources. In a much broader sense, social justice could also be seen as the mark of a legitimate social order: the social form of justice expresses the orderliness of society not only at the formal level, but also at the level of values. As a form of being, society's orderliness concerns both the process of accomplishing things and the relationship between the individual and the public sphere.

Although the individual domain and public sphere have different properties and contents, they are not for that matter unrelated. The capacities of individuals are tied to their natural talents, which are the ontological properties of individual beings, and hence inseparable from individuals. However, as stated previously, the formation and employment of capacities is always based on a certain social background and set of social conditions, and is thus inseparable from the public sphere. In broad terms, ideas constitute the person's object of thought and so have an individual character; their formation and the very uttering of them into speech is necessarily accomplished by means of individual conscious acts, and therefore belong to the individual domain. Any coercive suppression of or indoctrination aimed at the individual's ideas is an infringement upon or invasion of the individual domain. However, the individual's formation of his own ideas always presupposes systems of knowledge and thought that pre-exist the said individual, and always involves the constraint of the actual form of being. At the same time, after the individual shapes his own ideas, he may also influence others in the public sphere in different ways through a variety of forms of expression, transmission, and communication, and therefore ideas have a public character as well.

The relatedness of the individual domain and public spheres not only appears at the level of ideas, but also much more profoundly in the practical domain. Here worthy of mention is the practical activity of the economic domain. In the case of producing materials for private possession, the planning of production and the trade and circulation of the product all belong to private business activity. What a business produces and what price the product is traded for is all determined by the owners of the business, which others may not meddle with. However, the business activity of a company also constitutes a unit of the whole social economic structure; its production activities and the circulation of its products are always constrained by different economic entities and the whole economic structure, and so influence other economic processes in the social sector in different ways. Here, private economic activity and public economic activity share an intrinsic link.

The aforesaid case demonstrates that the individual domain and public sphere cannot be strictly separated and yet cannot be entirely converted into one another. However, when distinguishing the private domain and public sphere, some philosophers fail to note the intrinsic relatedness of the two. Ideas concerning the relation between politics and ethics make this point quite clear. When discussing the relationship between politics and morals, Rawls makes a distinction between the person as moral agent and the citizen as political subject, insisting that the moral individual is linked to moral character, whereas the citizen is a political and legal identity and thus mainly involves political rights and duties.[26] For Rawls, justice is mainly manifested in the public sphere. In correspondence with this distinction between the political and the moral, Rawls proclaims: "the public conception of justice should be, as far as possible, independent of any controversial religious or philosophical doctrine."[27] Here, the political is mainly attributed to the public sphere, and the moral and religious to the private. According to this understanding, human character and virtue, as properties of the individual domain, are linked mainly to private beliefs and choices, and stand in no substantial relation to the political practice of the public sphere.

Actually, the citizen of the political and legal domains does not exist in a separate form from the person of the moral domain: they are both different ways of the same individual "to be" in the world. As a concrete being, human being always participates in different practical lives and develops multiple identities or roles in the multifaceted unfolding of social practice; the citizen of the political domain and the person of the moral domain could also be seen as different "identities" or roles in the broad sense. As different modes of the same being, these different roles or identities are ontologically related, and their relatedness makes the existential realm undergirding such identities inseparable from them. Confucius once proclaimed, "the ruler must be a ruler, the minister a minister, the father a father, and the son a son."[28] Here, ruler, minister, father, and son are roles or identities; the former two exist in a political relationship and the latter two exist in an ethical relationship. When Confucius links the ruler and minister to the father and son, he is in substance affirming the fusion of the political and the ethical domains. As a matter of fact, Confucians were some of the earliest to recognize the unity of the political and ethical domains, Even though blending the ethical and the political may in some cases interfere with a penetrating grasp of political practice, it still certainly reveals the interrelatedness of the two.

Historically speaking, while affirming the interrelatedness of politics and ethics, Confucianism also examined the multiple facets of their connection in political practice. When discussing the process of ordering the state, Mencius particularly points out the interrelation between moral character and the norms at work in this process: "The compass and the carpenter's square are the culmination of squares and circles; the sage is the culmination of the ethical disposition of humanity; if one wishes to be a ruler, one must fulfill the duties proper to a ruler; if one wishes to be a subject, one must fulfill the duties proper to a subject.

In both cases all one has to do is to model oneself on Yao and Shun."[29] The compass and carpenter's square are the standards according to which wood workers measure the circular and the square; by extension, as the general standard of conduct, the sage reflects the perfected ideal of human character; "to model oneself on" means to comply with and imitate. Mencius draws a correlation between the sage and the compass and carpenter's square, which implies the following: in types of political practices such as "being a ruler" and "being a subject," standards of conduct may obtain the form of moral character. In other words, moral character can be endowed with the meaning of being standard or normative: when the sage becomes the object of imitation, he simultaneously plays a guiding and constraining role in relation to the political practice of how to "be a ruler" and how "to be a subject."

Investing human character with the meaning of being a standard means to confirm the role of moral character in the process of political practice. In another respect, other problems pertain to the role of norms themselves such as how they are to constrain and regulate. Mencius uses technology or technical activity as an example, elucidating it in the following way: "Is the maker of arrows really more unfeeling than the maker of armor? The arrow-maker is afraid that his arrows may not harm people; the maker of armor that humans may be harmed. The case is similar with the shamen-doctor and the coffin-maker. Thus, in technical crafts, one cannot be too careful."[30] The one who crafts bows and arrows always hopes the bows and arrows he fashions will put men to death, and the one who crafts helmets and armor always worries that the helmets and armor that he fashions cannot prevent men from suffering injury by bows and arrows; this is not due to the fact that the makers of bows and arrows are more cruel than those making helmets and armor; it is rather their undertaking of a specific "technical craft" that makes them such. Here, Mencius seems already to have noticed that "technical crafts" or technology as procedural structures have their own models of operation. As soon as one falls entirely into "technology" one will always unwillingly fall under its control. In brief, "technology" is originally for people's use, but without the constraint of moral principles, technology may lead to a denial of human being. The statement "in technical crafts, one may not be too careful" is grounded in this fact. Activities that use technology are public in a broader sense. However, their rational orientation is inseparable from the values within the individual. In broad terms, political practices also encompass procedural activities linked to "technology." Such practices not only involve the relationship between the individual domain and public sphere, but the relationship between political activities and moral ideas as well. Mencius also had this precisely in mind when he spoke of self-cultivation: "The post of the ruler is to cultivate his own moral character so that peace and justice may prevail throughout the world."[31] To make peace and justice prevail throughout the world is a political practice in the broad sense, and cultivating moral character is the individual perfecting his own moral virtue. To take the cultivation of moral character as the precondition of making the world just is to further demonstrate that political practice is inseparable from moral constraint.

For Mencius to think that the result of cultivating one's own moral character is a just and peaceful world undoubtedly shows an overestimation of the role of moral cultivation. However, affirming the significance of cultivating moral character in political practice is nonetheless important. Humans are at once both beings in legal-political relationships and also beings with their own moral tendencies. As two interrelated aspects of the being of humans, these attributes are not strictly separable from one another; this way of being, ontologically speaking, determines the political life and moral life of humans to be inseparably intertwined. In regard to the performance and activity of institutions themselves, although it does indeed involve impersonal formalized structures without human character, human participation is nonetheless involved everywhere. The moral character and virtues of humans themselves, as the participating agents, influence the participatory process to different degrees. In this sense, the rational activity of institutional organizations has its formalized and proceduralized preconditions, but requires the checks and balances and guidelines of morality as well; without the constraint of moral factors, the rationalization of the operations of political institutions can only be realized at the technical or technological levels, and thus cannot avoid one-sidedness. At the same time, under the condition that only the form and procedure of institutional activities are considered, there is no way to adequately realize a substantial justice that embodies values.

The link between individual cultivation and the public realm not only appears in the domain of political practice, but also involves social life in a much broader sense. For modern society, carrying out public policy requires gaining support and understanding from ordinary members of society, and so the inner character and spiritual state of human beings have a role in this process, which cannot be disregarded. Will Kymlicka gives us a concrete analysis of this:

> Consider the many ways that public policy relies on responsible personal lifestyle decisions: the state will be unable to provide adequate health care if citizens do not act responsibly with respect to their own health, in terms of maintaining a healthy diet, exercising regularly, and limiting their consumption of liquor and tobacco; the state will be unable to meet the needs of children, the elderly, or the disabled if citizens do not agree to share this responsibility by providing some care for their relatives; the state cannot protect the environment if citizens are unwilling to reduce, reuse, and recycle in their own consumer choices; the ability of the government to regulate the economy can be undermined if citizens borrow immoderate amounts or demand excessive salary increases; attempts to create a fairer society will flounder if citizens

are chronically intolerant of difference and generally lacking in a sense of justice.[32]

From choosing one's way of life to confirming one's ethical responsibilities in one's own family, and from environmental awareness to consumer decisions—all these areas first appear as ideas to be conceived in the individual domain; however, at the same time they constrain and influence practices of the public sphere in different ways and to different degrees. Here, consciousness, moral character, and the ideas of the individual sphere all undoubtedly manifest substantial roles in relation to the social life of the public sphere, and the interaction between the individual's sense of justice and fair society reveals this link at a profound level.

In the theory of citizenship, priority is given to the citizen's character. As the precondition of obtaining political and legal status, citizenship is not simply a static attribute; it is rather intimately bound to practical activities. Bryan Turner notices this when he states, "Citizenship may be defined as that set of practices (juridical political, economic, and cultural) which define a person as a competent member of society."[33] Only in practical activity is the individual able to actually integrate into social life and become a member of such political communities as the nation-state. Distinguished by actualization in practice, the formation and confirmation of citizenship involves many facets of intelligence and character. William Galston thinks that to qualify as a citizen one needs to have the following virtues: general virtues (courage, law-abidingness, loyalty); social virtues (independence and open-mindedness); economic virtues (work ethic, capacity to delay self-gratification, adaptability to economic and technological change); and political virtues (capacity to discern and respect the rights of others, willingness to demand only what can be afforded, ability to evaluate the performance of those in office, willingness to engage in public discourse).[34] Taylor then sees the capacity to generate an effective influence upon policy makers as a quality citizens should have.[35] Virtues as individual properties belong to the private domain, but they also involve different layers of social life: the diversity of virtues in some sense corresponds to the diversity of levels of social life. The effective unfolding and activity of a certain field of social life requires that individuals possess corresponding qualities, and whatever kinds of qualities an individual has always generates corresponding influences upon social life. In brief, the spiritual qualities that the participators in social life possess will necessarily make their own mark upon the unfolding of social life itself.

Some philosophers have failed to adequately account for this relationship between individual character and social life (including political practice). Proceeding from the distinction between the public sphere and private domain, they tend to disregard the effect the inner character and spiritual qualities of the individual have upon the public sphere or merely emphasize the public sphere's molding of the individual. In the work of Rawls, we can see this tendency to some extent. Political-social structure is the main field that Rawls focuses upon. For him, one of the functions of this structure is to mold citizens as individuals: "the institutions of the basic structure have deep and long-term social effects and in fundamental ways shape citizens' character and aims, the kinds of persons they are and aspire to be."[36] On the one hand, as already mentioned, for Rawls, moral character belongs to a form of being outside of the political domain. On the other hand, individual character can be molded by the social-political structure, and so the public sphere presents itself as having a one-sided effect upon the individual domain here. Although this conception differs from the public sphere infringing upon the individual domain, it still fails to concretely grasp the interaction between the public and private domains.

As the actual conditions of accomplishing oneself and accomplishing things, the public sphere and private domain have different dimensions. In regard to their form of being, the relation between the two seems to present both externality and internality. Consisting of the individual's passions, desires, beliefs, orientation, values, character, virtues, and so on, the private sphere exists in the form of ideas; at this level, the private sphere is within the individual's spiritual world, and is thus distinguished by internality. By comparison, the public sphere concerns communication, communal life, public participation, and other such social interactions and social practices, and thereby transcends the individual domain and its internal dimension, and is distinguished by externality. Corresponding to this is the relationship between the person and society: In contrast to the personal dimension of the private domain, the public sphere is a social realm. Of course, the distinction between the two is only relative: the ideas that persons think about belong to the individual domain, but as soon as they are expressed, they enter the public sphere. In this sense, the individual domain and public sphere are distinguished upon lines that do not separate clear-cut spatial zones; at the level of substantial content, they are distinguished through different attributes of being such as individuality and publicity. As for the process of accomplishing oneself and accomplishing things, a confirmation of the individual domain entails a concern for the unique individuality of human beings. In connection with the examination put forward in chapter 6 regarding the relationship between the individual and individuality, a further distinction must be made at the general level between human nature and the unique individuality of human beings. At the general level, human nature expresses the essence of the human species, which distinguishes human being from other beings (things), while the unique individuality of human being, which is connected to the specific process of the individual's being, including her active role, identity, and spiritual world in the social structure, expresses the concreteness of her being. While the individual domain and the unique individuality connected to it determine the process of accomplishing oneself to always be based upon the individual's desires, ideals, autonomous choices, and pursuits, the link between the being of the individual domain and the being of the public sphere makes the process of accomplishing oneself inseparably tied to the guidance and constraint of society from beginning to end.

The unity of individual choice, social guidance, self-determination, and social constraints expresses the link between the individual domain and the social realm mainly with respect to the process of accomplishing oneself. From a much broader perspective, however, the individual domain and the social realm also involve the process of accomplishing things. As a matter of fact, actualizing social justice in practice has the meaning of accomplishing things. As for social justice itself, its realization likewise concerns both the individual and public spheres. According to its substantial meaning, justice not only concerns individual rights, but also the establishment of a rational order in the social sphere, and is thereby intrinsically linked to both the individual and public spheres. Individual refinement unfolds into various sides. On one side, it is based upon the individual's unique individuality, but on the other side, it is also inseparable from actual conditions, which include the reasonable acquisition and possession of developmental resources. So, it is evident that this entails the fusion and interaction of the individual and public spheres, the integration and interaction of accomplishing oneself with the process of accomplishing things, and the integration and interaction of self-realization with social justice. As to its actual form of being, the unity of the individual and public spheres manifests itself as social justice and simultaneously constitutes the conditions of possibility of justice.

Meaning and Freedom

With the unification of the individual and public spheres as a precondition, justice pervades different facets of social life, and in a sense expresses the order of society. However, at the historical level, justice is also just one historical form in the process of social transformation, whose being is not ultimate in nature. As the product of historical development, justice itself is also to be overcome in accompaniment with further historical evolution.

The historicality of justice is first of all tied to the historicality of the ground of being and cause of justice. As explained previously, at the substantial level, justice concerns the acquisition, possession, and distribution of the various resources that the being and development of humans require. Concretely speaking, it presupposes a scarcity of resources and the tension between a finitude of resources and the developmental needs of human beings: When the resources possessed by a society of a particular age can no longer adequately satisfy all the developmental needs of its individual members, the fair acquisition and distribution of limited resources becomes society's pressing problem; this condition also constitutes the necessary historical ground of justice. When the development of a society makes its resources substantially capable of satisfying the need to accomplish oneself and accomplish things, and the tension between the actual resources that society possesses and the development of individuals is thereby substantially alleviated, the principle of justice itself also is no longer presented as the regulating principle that society needs and thereby fades out of history.

Here we can see that the overcoming of justice first presupposes the accumulation and adequate development of social resources. With regard to the acquisition and distribution of resources, the principle of justice is getting what one deserves, and getting what one deserves is also precisely having the right or the entitlement to acquire, the foundation of which lies in rights. Under the condition that the resources society possesses cannot satisfy the developmental needs of individuals, distributing according to the rights that persons have is ordinarily understood as the principle that protects fairness. However, as soon as social resources are adequately developed and accumulated, the distribution of resources itself no longer requires the ground of rights, and can be undertaken according to the needs of the being and development of individuals. Marx demonstrates this point when he links together "all the springs of co-operative wealth flowing more abundantly" and distribution "to each according to his need."[37] As the principle of distribution of resources on the basis of need, distributing according to need undoubtedly goes beyond the horizon of justice whose basis is rights, and manifests an equality at the level of substance.

Justice is mainly tied to the possession, acquisition, and regulation of already existing resources. By contrast, "distribution according to need" and the substantial equality tied to it, as an overcoming of justice, is first of all based on the development and accumulation of resources themselves. Considering historical development, the development and accumulation of resources clearly demonstrates its fundamental meaning. But, can the development of society's resources provide these conditions for overcoming justice? Some philosophers are very doubtful of this point. In this area, Cohen is certainly a representative. According to Cohen's understanding, Marx's conception that the problem of justice can be eliminated under the conditions of a higher degree of material wealth is nothing but a "technological fix." In his eyes, all sources of social wealth may never flow abundantly.[38] One of the grounds of Cohen's argument here is that such phenomena as the current ecological crisis have already prevented us from sharing Marx's optimism regarding material possibility.[39] In brief, for Cohen, the development of material wealth is necessarily limited, and hence there is no way to truly realize the substantial equality based on it.

Here it seems that we first need to make a distinction between the infinite rise of material wealth or social resources and the limitlessness of their development.

An infinite rise of social resources or material wealth implies an unlimited expansion and increase in quantitative terms through the unregulated consumption of matter and energy, whereas the limitlessness of development refers to the fact that the development of material wealth is constantly transcending already-given limits, which means that there is no way to determine a limit or end to them beforehand. The former entails the optimistic belief that material wealth could reach quantitative infinity in a certain period of time, while the latter affirms the processual nature of the development of material wealth, rejecting the artificial prescription of limits and ends. Historically speaking, following the gradual deepening of our knowledge of the world and the daily intensification of our powers to reform the world, humankind always continuously overcomes pre-existing limits and moves toward new stages of development. Problems that arise at a certain stage can always be gradually solved at further stages of development. In a negative respect, the consequences of the modern industrial revolution and their overcoming can serve as a historical example: in the early stages of the unfolding of the industrial revolution all kinds of problems emerged, including the pervasive shroud of smoke, dust, and other pollutants in the urban air, mass deforestation, the saturation of lakes and streams with polluting chemicals, and the list goes on, but following the further deepening of modernization, such phenomena gradually became history in the states where modernization took off the earliest. Similarly, all the new ecological problems that we face today are also given more and more concern day by day and plans for their solution have started to gradually arise, even though the total resolution of these problems will be a long and slow process. In positive terms, although the increase of material wealth is indeed constrained by energy sources and resources, this does not mean that we may suppose the end of such a development on these grounds. With regard to energy sources, if we only keep our eyes on traditional sources of energy such as coal and oil, the world will undoubtedly face such problems as energy shortages, and such problems will become increasingly prominent in the future, since the reserves of traditional energy sources such as oil are certainly limited. However, if diverse energy sources such as solar power, wind power, and tidal power are cultivated, this problem will substantially transform: for humankind, such sources of energy as solar power are nearly inexhaustible. Modern technology already shows that the actual utilization of energy such as solar power will not pose irresolvable obstacles, despite the various technical problems we face today. As a matter of fact, the development of new sources of energy is on the verge of a breakthrough as we speak. Humankind's cognitive and practical sphere once only unfolded in a limited space for a considerable period of time, but since the modern age, humans have gradually moved from one side of the globe to the other and are currently going beyond it, leaping toward the vast universe. Myths such as the flying of Chang'e to the moon and the content of sci-fi novels were once seen as nothing but distant dreams for the longest time, but much of what has been imagined within them has today already transformed into reality. Every time people try to prescribe an end to the development of some domain, further development always leaps over it. History continuously proves that prescribing the limits and supposing the ends of humankind's cognitive and practical domains with already available knowledge concerning the world and already available capacities to reform the world are over-dogmatic.

Ways in which social resources and material wealth can develop could be further distinguished into the expanding realization of the one-sided exploitation of nature and the reaching of an increase by means of relying on cyclical utilization and the recycling of resources. The former appears as the one-sided consumption of resources, the consequence of which is unsustainable development; the latter then aims at the renewability of resources and the sustainability of development. For resources, limits on their increase first arise from their unregulated consumption and exploitative utilization: Under the model of one-sided consumption, resources clearly imply the possibility of being consumed to exhaustion. If the one-sided mode of consumption is overcome, and other modes of development are adopted such as recycling, resource reusability, renewability, and sustainability, then limits on their increase in the aforesaid sense no longer appear in fateful form, and on the contrary, "the abundant flow" of "all sources of collective wealth" can be expected on adequate grounds, and cannot be simply dismissed as some opiate or "technological fix." Of course, the process of development always involves the relationship between Nature and human society; there is always some tension between Nature and human needs and ends. Nature will not spontaneously satisfy human needs, and will also not simply harmonize with human ends with an approving tone. On the other hand, it is impossible for humans to exhaustively know Nature at some stage, and knowing the self and knowing the world (including Nature) has its historicality at different periods of time. In connection with this background condition, as Nature and humans move toward coinciding, they can never entirely avoid dividing. In effect, ever since humankind, as Nature's "Other," moved beyond Nature, historical development has always been a process of Nature and humans continuously dividing and re-coinciding, a process of re-establishing unity after some tension emerges. This continuous re-establishing of unity between Nature and humans in the process of developing will undoubtedly proceed in a new form in future societies. At the same time it shows that the elevated increase and development of social resources and material wealth will itself be realized in a dynamic balancing process.

In the context of accomplishing oneself and accomplishing things, there is a historical connection between increasing resources and the process of transforming things in-themselves into the actual world (things for-us). As the historical achievement of accomplishing oneself (refining oneself) and accomplishing things (reforming the world), the mode of being characterized by the elevated growth of resources or the "abundant flow" of material wealth simultaneously exhibits the actual character of a world of meaning that transcends the ideal dimension. As for the historical evolution of society, a world of meaning in this form is both the product of accomplishing oneself and accomplishing things and also constitutes the starting point of the process of accomplishing oneself and accomplishing things as things for-us. Referring to human being refining the self and humanizing things in-themselves (making things suit human needs), the process of accomplishing the self and accomplishing things intrinsically accompanies the history of humankind itself, and is thereby essentially endless. Moreover, the genesis of a world of meaning has no predictable endpoint.

As the concrete genesis of a world of meaning, the significance of the growth of resources is first exhibited in the satisfaction of the needs of the being and development of individuals. This simultaneously concerns the problem of how to understand developmental needs. Oriented toward accomplishing oneself and accomplishing things, developmental needs are themselves historical and are tied to one's ideals, life-orientation, and pursued goals, and the establishment of ideals and goals always stipulates corresponding needs. At the historical level, primitive humans did not have the need to grasp information technologies or enjoy modern arts. As for the relationship between needs and ideals, for those people committed to the pursuit of self-realization in the actual world, a concern for transcendence in the religious sense will not become the predominant need of their life. In connection with the fact that needs are constrained by ideals, human needs intrinsically involve the question of how to rationally guide them. If every person on earth were to have the goal of possessing the moon or owning Mars, then no matter how abundantly all the sources of wealth are flowing, the conditions needed to reach such goals will never be entirely satisfied. Here, we can see that the rational guidance and establishment of worthy ideals and worthy goals are of pressing importance: whether or not the elevated growth of social resources and material wealth can adequately fulfill the developmental needs of human beings is intimately bound to the rational determination of the status of needs themselves. Furthermore, how to rationally establish worthy ideals is a problem as well. If divorced from the possibilities reality actually provides, ideals are not only impossible to realize, but conflicts between different ideals are similarly unavoidable. Reaching the unity of what is good and what is true in the process of accomplishing oneself and accomplishing things, and thereby shaping worthy ideals whose content is what is good and forming goals on the basis of what is real, while preventing conflicts from emerging between values, reality and different ideals is a process complementary to the adequate development of social resources and material wealth. Through the interaction of the two in the process of history, a mutually agreeable relationship can gradually form between the resources society provides, individual needs, and worthy ideals. In summary, in future societies, the overcoming of justice and the realization of substantial equality at once presupposes the abundant flow of all sources of collective wealth while also involving the rational guidance, regulation, and evaluation of ideals and needs; if the latter facets are ignored, adequately satisfying human needs through the elevated growth of material wealth and thereby realizing substantial equality will devolve into nothing but an abstract and romantic dream.

The abundant growth of social resources or material wealth and the regulation of the value of individual needs provide the preconditions of alleviating the tension between the limited nature of resources and the needs of individual development, and henceforth, make overcoming justice possible. As argued earlier, the principle of justice is always linked to rights, so whether resources are distributed according to the individual's right of free development or resources are regulated according to the right of the individual to acquire from society resources for development, the emergence of justice is always based on individual rights. Now, rights intrinsically imply tension and conflict: they consist in the affirmations and demands of humans themselves, and there is always disparity between the demands of different individuals, and so upholding and protecting one's rights inevitably leads to disparity and conflicts between individuals. Allen Buchanan once pointed this out: as a bearer of rights, one is always the party of a potential conflict.[40] One of the functions of the principle of justice consists in regulating and alleviating the tensions and conflicts that may arise from differing rights. In this sense, the relationship between justice and rights seems twofold: it begins with the affirmation of and respect for the legitimate rights of individuals and also regulates the relationship between different individual bearers of rights.[41]

Corresponding to this relationship between justice and rights, going beyond the principle of justice simultaneously means overcoming the perspective centered on rights. When the tension between the limited nature of resources and the needs of human development is historically alleviated and substantial equality becomes social actuality, needs themselves will start to occupy the center of concern. According to its intension, rights are first of all tied to the identity, qualifications, and demands of human beings, and thus much more directly involve relations pertaining to jurisprudence. By contrast, a need is a determination of values. Differing from demands of subjective meaning, needs are much rather the conditions of the being of humans at the ontological level: with regard to the most basic sense of survival, one's being "needs" air, sunlight, and water; such needs constitute the basic conditions of the being of humans. Rights express the demands of human values, whereas needs constitute the basic ground or ontological origin of values. As the unity of ontological and axiological properties, needs have metaphysical meaning, which at the metaphysical level means affirming the value of the being of humans at the level of needs. From the historical perspective, the principle of justice centered on rights will gradually disappear following the refocusing of social values, that is, away from individual rights and onto human needs.

The process of accomplishing the self and accomplishing things based on needs will not of course just suddenly emerge in a future society. As a matter of fact, in the historical evolution of society, we have already seen this tendency. In this respect, an issue worthy of mention is the relationship between the family and individual development. As one of the basic units of society, the family and the different members of the family face the problem of acquiring and distributing resources. However, even in the conditions of a market economy, the acquisition and distribution of resources within a family is also not undertaken on the basis of rights. Rather, at the substantial level it is undertaken on the basis of the actual needs of the different family members. Implied within this model of resource acquisition and distribution is the principle or conception of responsibility. Rights emphasize the entitlements and demands of the self; by contrast, responsibility refers to a concern for the other, and through the distribution of resources this responsibility or concern is embodied in a focus upon the actual needs of related family members. In comparison with other modes or units of social beings, the family's arrangement of developmental resources for its own members mainly arises out of responsibility, based on need, and in this social structure and through its operating, we can see some overcoming of the principle of justice based on rights. At the level of substance, the family is not predominantly grounded in the principle of justice. This fact also shows that through the evolution of society itself, moving toward a substantial equality focused on need and genuinely realizing the value of the being of humans is not entirely without historical preconditions and intrinsic grounds.

In a much broader sense, this unity between a concern for needs and a consciousness of responsibility also reflects the concept of the way of co-humanity (*rendao* 仁道). Historically speaking, early on in pre-Qin China, the founder of Confucianism, Confucius himself raised the principle of co-humanity, and Mencius furthered it, tying the doctrine that human nature is originally good (all humans have an affective mind that is sensitive to others) to the idea of humane governance, which unfolds the idea of co-humanity that Confucius established in terms of the relationship between the emotional affects of the inner mind and the society external to it. In the Confucian belief of the Han dynasty that "one must lead with philanthropic concern and teach with benevolence,"[42] or in that of the Song dynasty that "the people are my siblings, and things are my co-participants,"[43] the principle of co-humanity is concretely elucidated. The basic spirit of the principle of co-humanity lies in a respect for and a confirmation of the intrinsic value of each and every individual; it both affirms the individual's desire for self-realization and also demands that individuals genuinely accept the value of the being of one another. This not only entails the rational presupposition that human being is an end in itself but also entails a consciousness of responsibility in the mutual concern between individuals. Worthy of notice here is that Confucians who advocate the principle of co-humanity also stress the priority of family ethics. This relation between the two also in a way shows at the substantial level the interrelation between the principle of co-humanity, overcoming the basic unit of rights, and confirming the value of individuals. It is not hard to see that in the historical evolution of society, the principle of co-humanity, and the principle of justice hold different dimensions of value. When social development offers the genuine realization of the value of the being of humans with historical conditions, the principle of justice grounded in rights will lose its ground of being and will be overcome, and in this form of society, the principle of co-humanity, referring to the intrinsic confirmation of the value of being, will be embodied in a much more profound sense and on a more real foundation.

What needs to be pointed out is that on a more real foundation and in a much more profound sense, realizing the axiological tendency entailed by the principle of co-humanity is inseparable from the abundant growth of social resources and material wealth. It will only be possible to switch our focus from rights to needs and realize the development of individuals based on the intrinsic value of the being of humans when the resources society possesses are capable of satisfying the needs of the mutual accomplishment of self and things. Marx also stresses this point when he makes "the abundant flow of all sources of collective wealth" serve as the historical precondition of distributing "to each according to his need." If the adequate realization of the value of the individual's being is discussed in isolation from the growth of material wealth and social resources, values will inevitably devolve into abstract pursuits on the conceptual and spiritual level, and will henceforth be unfit for historical actualization. As an ideal of value in history, the Confucian principle of co-humanity does show this tendency in some sense. With the internal human nature of the affective mind as the starting point, the concept that "those espousing co-humanity love other humans" expresses nothing but an ideal concern, and accomplishing oneself and accomplishing things then simply consists in the elevation of spirit, and the actual conditions of individual development fails to enter the horizon. Realizing the axiological tendency entailed by the principle of co-humanity on a more actual foundation and in a much deeper sense simultaneously implies overcoming this aforesaid abstractness of the principle of co-humanity.

With the elevated growth of social resources or material wealth as a historical precondition, the true realization of the value of the being of humans concretely unfolds as the free development of human beings, which refers to individuals and also unfolds between individuals. When *The Doctrine of Mean* (zhongyong 中庸) summarizes the unity of accomplishing oneself and accomplishing things as "the way of integrating the inside and the outside" (*he neiwai zhi dao* 合内外之道) it already touches upon this relationship at the speculative metaphysical level. Marx, on the other hand, considers human development from a more concrete historical perspective. When discussing society's future form of being, he puts forward the concept of "an association of free men,"[44] and gives the following explanation of its intrinsic characteristic: "we shall have an association, in which the free development of each is the condition for the free development of all."[45] Considering the values it implies, free development implies understanding human being as purposive being, while the realization of all the sides of one's own intrinsic potential and the fulfillment of the needs of each individual's development with the resources society possesses thus constitute the actual supports of this process. In an association of free human beings, the tension between social resources and the needs of individual development is substantially alleviated, and the conflicts and contradictions between individuals that arise from the limited nature of resources lose the ground [from which they arise], and so, the realization and confirmation of the value of one's own being and that of others or the species not only coincide, but become the reciprocal presupposition of one another as well: my free development is no longer a limitation placed on the Other, but rather constitutes the condition of the other's free development. In the same way, the development of other people likewise has the same meaning for my own development. It is precisely through such an interaction that the association of free human beings reveals its value and historical content.

As a historical process, accomplishing oneself and accomplishing things is intrinsically tied to the integration and interaction of the free development of each with the free development of all. Although social justice indeed constitutes the precondition of accomplishing oneself and accomplishing things for a certain period of time, rights occupying the center of concern precludes social justice from overcoming the formal sense of equality and the procedural level of fairness, and also cannot guarantee that the meaning of one's being can be fully realized. Compared to the formation of society under the principle of justice, the association of free human beings makes the realization of the value of being at the substantial level become possible. The aim of the free development of human being is not only to refine human being but to reform the world as well. In this process, the being of humans and the being of the world are invested with deeper meaning and value in the activity of human creation, by virtue of which the genesis of a world of meaning is elevated to the level of truly harmonizing with human nature. With the interaction of the free development of each with the free development of all as its precondition, the self and the Other (society), the individual domain and the public sphere, the ideal world of meaning and the actual world of meaning gradually approach intrinsic unity, and as the process of generating a world of meaning, accomplishing oneself and accomplishing things truly begins to unfold into a state of freedom.

Notes

Foreword

1. Yang Guorong, "Metaphysics: Reconstruction and Reflection," *Contemporary Chinese Thought*, special issue, *Yang Guorong's Concrete Metaphysics* 43, no. 4 (Summer 2012): 7–26.
2. Yang Guorong, "The Maturation of the Self and the Refinement of Things: The Generation of the World of Meaning," *Contemporary Chinese Thought*, special issue, *Yang Guorong's Concrete Metaphysics* 43, no. 4 (Summer 2012): pp. 51–85. [Revised according to this edition.]
3. Yang Guorong, *Lixing yu jiazhi: Zhihui de licheng* [Reason and values: the path of wisdom] (Shanghai: Sanlian, 1998), 445. This essay was published in German translation in *Minima Sinica* (2002) 1: 65–92.

Introduction

Here and throughout the text, the translator has directly rendered the original Chinese as it is currently edited (2015) by Donald Sturgeon on the Chinese Text Project website (www.ctext.org). The first number refers to the book number, and the second to the passage number, respectively.

1. Translation: Here and throughout the book, the author's most frequently used term is *ren* (人), which has no exact English counterpart. Chinese translators use *ren* to translate many English words, including humans, man, human being, human beings, and one—as in someone (*you ren*) and everyone (*meige ren, suoyou ren*). It is a gender-neutral mass noun, like the English term "water," so it is indifferent to the distinction between plural and singular and that between definite and indefinite, and is therefore capable of translating both "human being" and "human beings," "the human being" and "a human being" without any confusion. The only English mass noun that has the equivalent usage is the gender-neutral use of the term "man" without article. And the historical connotations of the word "man" also make it a most suitable counterpart for *ren*. However, in order to avoid the masculine color of the term "man" along with his masculine reflexive pronoun "himself," which *ren* does not have, I have translated it varyingly as "human being," "humans," and "one" depending on the context consistent with the standard translation of those different English words into philosophical Chinese.

2. *Jiji* (既济) and *weiji* (未济) are originally the last two hexagrams of *The Book of Changes* (*zhouyi* 周易). *Ji* (济) here means successfulness and completion and emphasizes the positive significance this has for human beings (see Yu Fan, *Collected Commentaries on Zhouyi*). Taking *weiji* (未济) as the last hexagram, *The Book of Changes* affirms that the world is open to the future and hence understands the world as an infinite process. In this sense Cui Ha states, "It ends with *weiji* due to the infinity of things" (see the chapter *Jiji* in *Collected Commentaries on Zhouyi*). I borrow *jiji* and *weiji* here mainly to emphasize the distinction between what is completed and what remains incomplete. See *Xu Jinting, zhouyi jinzhu jinshi* (Taibei: Taiwan Shangwu Yinshuguan, 1974), p. 378.

3. When discussing the rectification of names, Xunzi asserts: Although all things are innumerable, there are times when we wish to speak of them all in general, so we call them "things" and "things" is the most general term. Xunzi, 22.7, ed. Donald Sturgeon, Chinese Text Project, http://ctext.org/xunzi/zheng-ming (2015).

4. Martin Heidegger, *What Is a Thing?*, translated by W. B. Barton Jr. and Vera Deutsche (South Bend, IN: Regnery/Gate Way Inc., 1967), p. 5.

5. Heidegger, *What Is a Thing?* p. 244.

6. Hanfeizi, 21.15, ed. Donald Sturgeon, Chinese Text Project, http://ctext.org/hanfeizi/yu-lao (2015).

7. Wang Yangming, *Collected Works of Wang Yangming* (Shanghai: Shanghai Guji Chubanshe, 1992), p. 47. Wing-tsit Chan's translation is the following: "the thing is an event." See Wing-tsit Chan, *Instructions for Practical Living* (New York: Columbia University Press, 1963), p. 104.

8. Wang Fuzhi, *Commentary on Zhang Zai's Correction of Youthful Folly*, in *Collected Works of Chuanshan*, Book 12 (Changsha: Yuelu Shushe, 1996), p. 115.

9. Translator: Here, the term translated as "Nature" is the Chinese character *tian* (天), which in the context of Confucianism means something like Heaven due to having moral connotations, but in most other contexts, especially in that of Daoism, it has more cosmic meaning like the term "the heavens," but with the nuance of including the earth and earthly life by nourishing it and uplifting it. For this reason, the best translation into Western conceptual terminology would be Nature. Here, the term rendered as Nature in-itself (*tian zhi tian* 天之天), coming from Wang Fuzhi, could more literally be translated as "natural Nature" in contrast to humanized Nature or Nature for human being (*ren zhi tian* 人之天).

10. Concerning the distinction between "Nature in-itself" and "Nature for human being," see Wang Fuzhi, *shi guangchuan, wangchuanshan quanshu* [*Extensive Commentary on the Book of Poetry, Collected Works of Chuanshan*, Book 3] (Changsha, Yuelu shushe, 1996), p. 463.

11. "Xici I," in *yizhuan* ["The Great Treatise I," in Commentary on Yijing], Chapter 11, ed. Donald Sturgeon, Chinese Text Project, http://ctext.org/book-of-changes/xi-ci-shang (2015). [Translator: The author is adapting this quote for his own purposes. The original form of this sentence is not imperative but declarative and contains a subject. James Legge's translation on the Chinese Text Project goes as follows, "The *Yi* [*The Book of Changes*]" opens up (the knowledge of the issues of) things, [and] accomplishes the undertakings (of men)."

12. *Zhouli*, 6.5 ["Record of Arts and Technology," in *The Rites of Zhou*], ed. Donald Sturgeon, Chinese Text Project, http://ctext.org/rites-of-zhou/dong-guan-kao-gong-ji (2015).

13. See Wing-tsit Chan, *A Source Book in Chinese Philosophy* (Princeton: Princeton University Press, 1963), p. 108 (translation modified).

14. Martin Heidegger, *Contributions to Philosophy*, trans. P. Emad and K. Maly (Bloomington: Indiana University Press, 1999), p. 8.

15. In *Introduction to Metaphysics*, Heidegger poses the question "why is there being instead of nothing" as the basic or primordial question of metaphysics. Comparatively speaking, Heidegger's treatment of the meaning of being in *Contributions to Philosophy* is undoubtedly more important. In fact, it seems the more substantial question of philosophy should be stated as follows: why does actual being involve meaning instead of having nothing to do with meaning at all? Understanding the answer to this question involves the actual background of accomplishing oneself and accomplishing things.

16. See Karl Marx and Friedrich Engels, *Capital: A Critique of Political Economy Vol. III*, trans. Ernest Mandel, Ben Fowkes, and David Fernbach (London: Penguin Books in association with New Left Review), p. 959.

17. Grasping the meaning of being always involves "intuitively comprehending" in the broad sense, and the "intuitive comprehension" linked to the self-investigation of the meaning of being is a much more embodied type of comprehension that permeates the process of elevating individual spirit.

18. Heidegger's approach here seems to differ from Husserl's. In fact, Husserl's suspension of being and Heideggers concern with being not only show differences in methodology and ontology but in tendency of thought as well. However, as this book will discuss later, Heidegger's understanding of being mainly falls under the scope of Dasein, whose authentic mode of being is the inner experience of individual existence.

1. Meaning in the Context of Accomplishing Oneself and Accomplishing Things

1. According to its everyday usage, "What does it mean?" refers to both "What is it" at the level of fact as well as "What significance does it have?" at the level of value. In this book, "What does it mean?" is posed mainly in the sense of "What significance does it have?" rather than "What is it?"

2. [Translator: The Chinese term rendered as "meaning" here and throughout the text is *yiyi* 意义. *Yiyi*, however, has broad connotations, capable of translating both English terms "meaning" and "sense." Aside from the paragraphs in which the author discusses Frege, Deleuze, and Husserl, whose standard translations into English use the word "sense" quite strictly, I have rendered the term invariably as "meaning," when it is used as a philosophical term, for the sake of consistency and at the author's request. The reader should flexibly bear in mind, though, that "sense" is a viable translation in some contexts, especially when discussing language or understandability and incomprehensibility.]

3. Martin Heidegger, *Being and Time*, trans. Joan Stambaugh (Albany: State University of New York Press, 1996), p. 142.

4. See Heidegger, *Being and Time*, p. 298.

5. Ibid., p. 143.

6. Jin Yuelin, *Zhishi Lun* [A theory of knowledge] (Beijing: Shangwu yinshuguan, 1983), p. 414.

7. Ibid., p. 416.

8. Meaning in the ends-values dimension always has its complexity. From one angle it would seem as if a phenomenon or an action were meaningless only to find out from another angle later on that it indeed presents a certain kind of meaning. For instance, in the Chinese myth of the bird Jingwei who filled up the sea with stones, we see the obvious futility of Jingwei's actions and the lack of practical effect that her individual capacity would produce in relation to the aim: the agent repeatedly quarries stones in order to realize the unrealizable goal of filling up the sea. In this sense, Jingwei is but fetching glasses of water to put out an ocean of fire: her action is meaningless at the level of ends and values. However, in terms of the spiritual forces that such a gesture expresses, we can say that it has its positive value, which from another angle could be expressed as displaying the resolute will power needed for humans to reform objects, and through encouraging others to dig deep into their souls for strength, this resolution and will power further demonstrates its worth in influencing practical processes. The intrinsic moral behind the myth of Jingwei filling up the sea lies mainly in the latter respect.

9. See Yang Guorong, *Lunli yu cunzai* [Ethics and being], chapter 1 (Shanghai: Shanghai Renmin chubanshe, 2002).

10. See Albert Camus, *The Myth of Sisyphus and Other Essays* (New York: Knopf, 1955), p.120.

11. Of course, in so far as the falsification of a proposition can also serve as a starting point for further cognition, falsification can also have an affirmative meaning.

12. [Translator: Mao Zedong (Chairman Mao) once wrote an influential report on the peasant movement mentioned here, with which the author's generation is quite familiar.]

13. Karl Marx and Friedrich Engels, *Economic and Philosophic Manuscripts of 1844*, trans. Martin Mulligan (Amherst, NY: Prometheus Books, 1988), p. 108.

14. Robert Nozick once labeled this type of meaning as "personal significance, importance, value, mattering." See Nozick, *Philosophical Explanations* (Oxford, UK: Clarendon Press, 1981), p. 574.

15. See Gottlob Frege, "The Thought: A Logical Inquiry," in *Mind* 65, no. 259 (1956): 295.

16. See Jin Yuelin, *Zhishi lun*, pp. 472–476.

17. Marx and Engels, *Economic and Philosophic Manuscripts of 1844*, p. 108.

18. Here, a distinction must be made between sound in general and music in particular. To those without a musical background, music will appear as a kind of sound, which could be endowed with different kinds of meaning or understood to have different kinds of meaning. However, such kinds of meaning would of course differ from the meaning that it would have as music.

19. [Translator: See *The Analects*, 7:14. Confucius once praised the music of Shao, as the music from Shun, one of Confucius's ideal kings, for being both perfectly beautiful and perfectly good (*The Analects*, 3:26).]

20. [Translator: See *The Analects*, 15:11, where Confucius also criticized the music of Zheng for being wanton.]

21. See Bertrand Russel, *Mysticism and Logic and Other Essays* (New York: Doubleday & Company, Inc., 1957), pp. 8–11.

22. "Xici 1.4," in the *Yijing*, ed. Donald Sturgeon, Chinese Text Project, http://ctext.org/book-of-changes/xi-ci-shang (2015).

23. Ibid.

24. Ibid.

25. "Xici 1.3," in the *Yijing* [Book of changes], ed. Donald Sturgeon, Chinese Text Project, http://ctext.org/book-of-changes/xi-ci-shang (2015).

26. Ibid.

27. John Dewey, *Experience and Nature* (La Salle, IL: Open Court, 1987), p. 186.

28. See J. Macquarrie, *God-Talk: An Examination of the Language and Logic of Theology* (New York: Harper & Row, 1967), p. 63.

29. From a broader perspective, language also involves the function of stimulation, the point of which is to awaken movement in thought or consciousness. This stimulating function may be seen in the cognitive sphere (inciting intuition, imagination, insight, etc., into action) or in the moral and aesthetic sphere of practice (calling up moral consciousness or stirring up an aesthetic experience). What Ogden and Richards explained as the function of words to excite feelings and attitudes also seems to involve this stimulatory function of language. From the perspective of the way in which language is used, language characteristically unfolds on the three planes of description, expression, and prescription, and in actual communication each of these three usages could of course have some kind of stimulatory function.

30. From the theoretical perspective, confirming a word's indirect reference as the indirect meaning of a word also empowers the ongoing response to the argument of skepticism. Skepticism often argues that words and concepts are unable to effectively refer to objects based

on the disparity between the limitations of the meaning of a word or a phrase and the richness of the object's properties. As Zhuangzi argued, "that which can be discussed with words are but the rough outline of things; whereas the intentional power of the mind can reach the fine pulse of vitality in things; but, that which neither intentional awareness can reach nor words denote is not limited to the rough and the fine"(*Zhuangzi*, 17.4). According to this argument, words can merely touch upon the "rough outline" of things (external properties), and that which is not limited to the rough and the fine are for words ungraspable. The intrinsic problem of this viewpoint lies in merely affirming the direct reference of words without giving adequate attention to the function of indirect reference and indirect meaning.

31. C. K. Ogden and I. A. Richards, *The Meaning of Meaning—A Study of the Influence of Language upon Thought and of the Science of Symbolism* (London: Routledge & Paul, 1952), p. 149.

32. See A. J. Ayer, *Language, Truth, and Logic* (New York: Dover Publication, 1952), pp. 107–108.

33. *Lüshi chunqiu* [Master Lu's spring and autumn annals], 1.2.1, ed. Donald Sturgeon, Chinese Text Project, (2015).

34. *The Analects*, 13:3.

35. Ibid., 12:11.

36. "Xici I, 1.12" in the *Yijing*.

37. Wang Fuzhi, *Zhouyi waizhuan* [Outer commentary on the *Yijing*], *Chuanshan quanshu* [Complete works of Chuanshan], Book 1, vol. 5 (Changsha: Yuelu shushe, 1996), p. 1029.

38. See Charles W. Morris, *Foundation of the Theory of Signs* (Chicago: University of Chicago Press, 1938), p. 23.

39. On the naturalization of the relationship between signifier and signified, see R. Barthes, *Elements of Semiology*, trans. Annette Lavers and Colin Smith (New York: Hill and Wang, 1991), p. 51.

40. Ludwig Wittgenstein. *Tractatus Logico-Philosophicus*, 3.3, trans. C. K. Ogden (New York: Dover Publication, Inc., 1999), p. 39.

41. R. Barthes, *Elements of Semiology*, p. 10.

42. Martin Heidegger, *The Principle of Reason*, trans. Reginald Lilly (Bloomington: Indiana University Press, 1996), pp. 3, 120.

43. D. Davidson, *Essays on Actions and Events* (Oxford, UK: Clarendon Press, 1982), p. 3.

44. Edmund Husserl, *Logical Investigations*, trans. Dermot Moran (London: Routledge, 2001), p. 283.

45. Wilhelm Dilthey, *The Formation of the Historical World in the Human Sciences*, trans. Rudolf A. Makkreel and Frithjof Rodi (Princeton, NJ: Princeton University Press, 2002), p. 276.

46. Michael Polanyi and Harry Prosch, *Meaning* (Chicago: University of Chicago Press, 1975), p. 178.

47. Ibid., p. 179.

48. Ibid., p. 182.

49. For instance, when discussing language, Polyani affirms the role of human being's attention to and integration of linguistic symbols in the genesis of linguistic meaning. See Michael Polanyi, *Knowing and Being: Essays by Michael Polanyi*, ed. Marjorie Grene (Chicago: University of Chicago Press, 1969).

50. C. S. Peirce, "How to Make Our Ideas Clear," in *Charles S. Peirce Selected Writings* (New York: Dover Publications, 1958), p. 124.

51. Ibid.

52. See W. James, *Pragmatism and the Meaning of Truth: Works of William James,* http://intersci.ss.uci.edu/wiki/eBooks/BOOKS/James/The%20Meaning%20of%20Truth%20James.pdf (2010), p. 74.

53. H. G. Gadamer, *Truth and Method,* trans. J. Weinsheimer and D. G. Marshall, revised edition (London: Continuum, 2004), p. 299.

54. H. G. Gadamer, *Philosophical Hermeneutics,* trans. and ed. David E. Linge (Berkeley: University of California Press, 1976), p. 56.

55. Gadamer, *Truth and Method,* p. 108.

56. Gadamer, *Philosophical Hermeneutics,* p. 57.

57. Edmund Husserl, *The Essential Husserl: Basic Writings in Transcendental Phenomenology,* trans. Donn Welton (Bloomington: Indiana University Press, 1999), p. 29.

58. Edmund Husserl, *Collected Works: Volume II, First Book,* trans. F. Kersten, (The Hague: M. Nijhoff, 1983), p. 325.

59. Ibid., p. 107.

60. Ibid.

61. Ernst Cassier, *An Essay on Man: An Introduction to a Philosophy of Human Culture* (New Haven, CT: Yale University Press), p. 26.

62. Ernst Cassier, *The Philosophy of Symbolic Forms,* vol. 1, trans. Ralph Manheim (New Haven, CT: Yale University Press, 1965), p. 111.

63. Ibid., p. 88.

64. When Brentano discusses the issue of intention, he finds the characteristic of intention in "reference to content" and "direction toward an object." In broader terms, "Every mental phenomenon includes something as object within itself, although they do not all do so in the same way. In presentation something is presented, in judgment something is affirmed or denied, in love loved, in hate hated, in desire desired and so on" (F. Brentano, *Psychology from an Empirical Standpoint,* trans. D. B. Terrell, L.L. McAlister, and A. Rancurello [London: Routledge, 1995], p. 68.) Here he notices that intention always concerns a corresponding content and object and is not the empty flow of consciousness of nothing.

65. Husserl's late phase, marked by his turn to a theory of the life-world, seems to show signs of a genuine overcoming of this tendency.

66. The contemporary philosopher of science Paul Feyerabend is a perfect exemplar of this trend, which can be seen in his work *Farewell to Reason.*

67. See J. Derrida, "Différance," in *Margins of Philosophy,* trans. Alan Bass, pp. 3–27, (Chicago: Chicago University Press, 1982).

68. See Martin Heidegger, *Nietzsche,* vols. 3 and 4, trans. David Farrell Krell (San Francisco: Harper & Row, 1979), p. 3.

69. Friedrich Nietzsche, *The Will to Power,* trans. Walter Kaufmann, ed. R. J. Hollingdale (New York: Vintage Books, 1968), p. 9.

70. Ibid., p. 23.

71. Friedrich Nietzsche, *The Will to Power,* trans. Walter Kaufmann, ed. R. J. Hollingdale (New York: Vintage Books; 1968), p. 13.

72. Ibid., pp. 10, 11.

73. Ibid., p. 16.

74. Ibid., p. 9.

75. Ibid., p. 316.

76. Ibid., p. 18.

77. Ibid., p. 519.

78. Ibid., p. 35.

79. The concluding note of the whole book goes as follows: "Then one can certainly wager that man would be erased, like a face drawn in sand at the edge of the sea (Michel Foucault, *The Order of Things: An Archaeology of the Human Sciences* [New York: Random House, 1994], p. 387).

80. Karl Marx, *Grundrisse: Foundations of the Critique of Political Economy* (Rough Draft), trans. M. Nicolaus (London: Penguin Books; in association with New Left Review, 1993), p. 158.

2. Human Capacities and a World of Meaning

1. [Translator: What is translated here as "human nature" is the ancient Chinese concept *xing* 性. The reader, however, should bear in mind that this concept of human nature predominantly does not appear in the context of essentialism in Chinese philosophy; aside from Mencius's interlocutor Gaozi, who attempts to generalize *xing* and make it appear as an abstract essence, Mencius and nearly every thinker in China uses it refer to natural human tendencies that are nurtured through social learning and discipline, including natural biological drives sexual and metabolic, and natural dispositions whose strength in each individual remains variable depending on the social environment in which they develop; they are dispositions sensitive to triggers in social circumstances like excitement or calm, rage or panic, selfishness or empathy, and so on. Far from an immutable nature, it is understood strictly in relation to the nurturing mechanisms of society, which can be seen clearly in the debate between Mencius and Xun Zi over whether *xing* 性 is "originally" good or bad in the moral sense of being pro-social or anti-social, and what role society plays in strengthening or weakening or even overriding such tendencies. In this chapter, the author points out the variety of cognitive capacities of human nature from the background of those affective capacities just mentioned while underscoring the role of social learning in their development. It is this nurturing of human nature that the author calls *cheng*, which we have rendered as cultivating, refining, and accomplishing throughout the text.]

2. Some contemporary philosophers have also given some attention to human capacities. For instance, John McDowell, who emphasizes the role of conceptual capacity from the perspective of the process of cognizing, confirms that "objects come into view for us only in actualizations of conceptual capacities that are ours" (John McDowell, *Having the World in View* [Cambridge and London: Harvard University Press, 2009], p. 43). Conceptual capacity could be seen as a concrete form of human capacities; the actualization of conceptual capacity then concerns the actual use of human capacities in the process of cognizing. Although McDowell's point of concern lies in affirming the conceptual content contained in experience, his idea nonetheless notices that human capacities and their actual employment constitute the conditions of possibility of knowing in the broad sense.

3. In a recent work, Li Zehou already proposed the concept of human capacities, however, his understanding seems to be limited to practical reason, and his way of posing the idea also appears to be a summation of Kant's view of practical reason. In fact, Li clearly distinguished "human capacities" from cognitive capacities and aesthetic capacities; he wrote: "What Kant called practical reason, we call human capacities, which are characterized by the condensation of reason, which must be distinguished from the internalization of reason (cognition) and the fusion of reason (aesthetic appreciation)" (Li Zehou, *Li Zehou jinnian dawenlu* [Academic Interviews of Li Zhehou in Recent Years], Tianjin: Tianjin shehui kexueyuan chubanshe, 2006, p. 213). Although Li Zehou's position on this matter changed later on, affirming that human

capacities include the internal structure of reason, the condensation of reason, and the fusion of reason, his emphasis is still placed on the ethical domain, discussing morality from the perspective of human capacities, human feelings, and the ideas of good and evil; on the other hand, he also ties human capacities closely to reason (See Li Zehou, *Additional clarification of "Interview on Ethics," Zhexue dongtai* [Philosophical Trends], no. 11, 2009). His understanding of human capacities seems too narrow. I understand human capacities in the broader sense, similar to the capacities I have discussed in chapter 9 of *Cunzai zhi wei* [*The Dimension of Being*] (Beijing: Renmin chubanshe, 2005) and *What Is Philosophy For? Shehui kexue* [*Social Sciences*], no. 1, 2006.

4. Here, "the already known" concerns empirical knowledge at the cognitive level but also includes value recognition at the evaluative level; what I call "achieved knowledge in the broad sense" includes both the former and the latter.

5. Aristotle, *The Basic Works of Aristotle, Metaphysics,* trans. Richard Mckeon (New York: Random House, 1941), p. 778. 1025b25.

6. Ibid., p. 1112. 1181b10.

7. Although in some respects, there were modern philosophers who also noticed the connection between human capacities and human activity, like Vico, who connects human capacities to the process of transforming virtue into action. (See G. Vico, *On the Most Ancient Wisdom of the Italians: Drawn out from the Origins of the Latin Language,* trans. J. Taylor [New Haven, CT: Yale University Press, 2010], p. 103.) Yet, "action" here mainly concerns such acts as perceiving and imagining. Vico makes a further clarification of his viewpoint, pointing out that the "the soul is a power [*virtus*], vision is an act [*actus*], and the sense of sight is a faculty [facultas]" (Ibid., p. 103; [Trans. in brackets; for the original Latin, see G. Vico, *De antiquissima italorum sapientia,* ed. M. Sanna (Roma: Edizioni di storia e letteratura, 2005), p. 112.]). This sort of activity seems to go no further than cognizing in the broad sense.

8. Immanuel Kant, *Critique of Pure Reason,* trans. Norman K. Smith (New York: St. Martin's Press, 1969), p. 146.

9. Ibid. p. 143.

10. Ibid. pp. 182–183.

11. Of course, as I will show later on, while emphasizing dichotomies overall, Kant also touches on a few aspects of human capacities, and not without insight. At the same time, Kant's later posthumous works also touch upon the connection between knowledge and human being's powers (see Immanuel Kant, *Opus Postumum* [Cambridge, UK: Cambridge University Press, 1993], p. 230). However, it seems Kant never had the chance to adequately unfold his thought regarding this topic.

12. Karl Marx and Friedrich Engels, *Capital: A Critique of Political Economy,* trans. and ed. Ernest Mandel, Ben Fowkes, and David Fernbach (London: Penguin Books, in association with New Left Review, 1990), p. 959.

13. [Translator: This explanation is based on the linguistic phenomenon that in Chinese "perceiving" (*gan-zhi*) consists of the characters "sensing" (*gan* 感) and "knowing" (*zhi* 知).]

14. See chapter 1, the section "Signs, Value, and Meaning."

15. Kant distinguished between sensibility, understanding, and reason. For him, reason, in contrast to sensibility and understanding, involves the transcendent. What I mean by reason in this discussion differs from his in this respect. In essence, what Kant called "understanding" is similar to what I call "reason" here in many ways. (See Immanuel Kant, *Critique of Pure Reason,* trans. Norman K. Smith [New York: St. Martin's Press, 1969], pp. 93, 147.)

16. Following Kant, Hegel makes a break with another distinction between reason and understanding. In his view, understanding dissociates form from content and the universal from the particular, whereas reason is concrete since it overcomes the disjunctive and abstract na-

ture of understanding and reveals the unity of form and content and the universal and the particular. (See G. W. F. Hegel and W. Wallace *Hegel's Philosophy of Mind* [Oxford: Clarendon Press], pp. 89, 90.) Aiming at concreteness, reason according to this perspective is linked to the capacity of dialectical thinking in an extended sense.

17. Nozick brought up two rules of reason. First, "Do not believe *h* if some alternative statement incompatible with *h* has a higher credibility value than *h* goes." The second, "Believe *h* only if the expected utility of believing *h* is not less than the expected utility of having no belief about *h*. (See Richard Nozick, *The Nature of Rationality* [Princeton: Princeton University Press, 1993], pp. 85–86.) While the first rule is mainly related to epistemology and logic, the second rule concerns the axiological meaning of rationality. Whether or not these rules adequately grasp the meaning of rationality is of course still open to debate, but insofar as they affirm that rationality is not limited to cognitive and logical relations in the narrow sense due to involving the domain of values, they are not without insight here.

18. When discussing the relation between practical wisdom and virtue, Aristotle states that virtue makes us aim at the right mark, and practical wisdom makes us take the right means, and virtue determines the end and practical wisdom makes us do the things that lead to the end (see Aristotle, *Nicomachean Ethics,* trans. Richard McKeon [New York: Random House, 1941], pp. 1144a, 1145a). In substance, reason in the broad sense seems to involve both of virtue and practical reason.

19. David Hume, *A Treatise of Human Nature* (Oxford: Clarendon Press, 1896), p. 239.

20. Ibid., p. 217.

21. Immanuel Kant, *Critique of Pure Reason,* trans. N. K. Smith (New York: St. Martin's Press, 1965), p. 112.

22. Ludwig Wittgenstein, *Zettel,* 621, trans. G. E. M. Anscombe (Oakland: University of California Press, 1970), p. 109e.

23. See Kant, *Critique of Pure Reason,* pp. 146–147. Of course, for Kant, this function of the imagination is inseparable from the inclusion of a priori structure or form.

24. Kant, *Critique of Pure Reason,* p. 487.

25. Wittgenstein, *Zettel,* p. 119e.

26. George Berkeley, *Principles of Human Knowledge and Three Dialogues,* ed. Howard Robinson (Oxford: Oxford University Press, 2009), p. 26.

27. Ludwig Wittgenstein, *Zettel,* p. 111e.

28. [Translator: *The Analects,* 6:30.]

29. Paul Ricoeur, *Imagination in Discourse and in Action,* in *Rethinking Imagination,* ed. G. Robinson and J. Rundell (London: Routledge, 1994), p. 128.

30. [Translator: The term *xin* 心 here is usually translated as "heart-mind" in English, following Roger Ames, to show that the classical Chinese conception of the mind was not dualistically defined in opposition to the body and was always conceived as the embodied seat of the affects and never just as the agent of withdrawn reasoning. Indeed, this character derived from a graph depicting a heart. The translator chooses to render this term as "the affective mind" in the sense in which John Protevi speaks of the mind as "embodied, embedded, extended, enacted, and affective" (see John Protevi, *Life, War, Earth* [Minneapolis: University of Minnesota Press, 2013]). Here, the affective mind emphasizes that the mind in the classical Chinese conception is the subject of affective states, which aside from rage, excitement, arousal, joy, and sorrow, the affective condition favoring rational reflection would be "the calm state" (*jing* 靜), and as opposed to a purely rational motivation for moral action, as in Kant's conception, the concept of *xin* as affective mind would include empathy as an affect motivating moral action. The Author frequently turns to this classical Chinese conception to show these embodied and affective dimensions of the mind.]

31. Wei Qipeng, *Mawangdui hanmu boshu huangdishu jianzheng* [Commentary on *The Four Books of Yellow Emperor* (Beijing: Zhonghua shuju), p. 83.
32. See N. Chomsky, *Language and Mind*, (Cambridge, UK: Cambridge University Press, 2006), pp. 106–113.
33. See ibid., pp. 78–85.
34. Mencius, *Mencius,* trans. D.C. Lau (London: Penguin Classics, 2004), 2A, 2 (translation modified).
35. Davidson, "Rational Animals," in *Actions and Events: Perspectives on The Philosophy of Donald Davidson*, ed. B. McLaughlin (Oxford: B. Blackwell, 1984), p. 477.
36. W. V. Quine, "The Flowering of Thought in Language," in *Thought and Language*, ed. J. Pleston (Cambridge, UK: Cambridge University Press, 1997), p. 171.
37. C. K. Ogden and I. A. Richards, *The Meaning of Meaning: A Study of the Influence of Language Upon Thought and of the Science of Symbolism* (London: Routledge & Paul, 1952), pp. 9–10.
38. [Translator: The Chinese word rendered as "lived experience" here and elsewhere as "bodily experience" is *tiyan* 体验. The reader should bear in mind that this term refers to the lived experience of the embodied mind through situations requiring both cognitive and practical effort rather than to the purely rational experience of reflective thought about objects.]
39. [Translator: *Huainanzi,* 13.10.]
40. *Mencius,* 7A, 1.
41. Zhu Xi, *Zhuzi yulei* [Classified Conversation of Zhu Xi], Book 8 (Beijing: Zhonghua Shuju, 1988), p. 142.
42. Ibid., Book 11, p. 182.
43. Ibid., Book 8, p. 140.
44. Hans-George Gadamer, *Truth and Method,* trans. Joel Weinsheimer and Donald G Marshall (London: Continuum Books, 2004), p. 60.
45. Hannah Arendt affirms that judgment is the basic form of man's spiritual activity, but she also adds that judgment has nothing in common with logical operations, which seems to ignore the connection between judgment and logical thinking. See Arendt, *The Life of Mind* (New York: Harcourt Brace Jovanovich, 1978), p. 215.
46. Kant distinguished between the two forms of employment of the power of judgment. He states, "If the universal (the rule, principle, law) is given, then judgment, which subsumes the particular under it, is *determinative*. . . . But if only the particular is given and judgment has to find the universal for it, then this power is merely reflective" (Immanuel Kant, *Critique of the Power of Judgment,* trans. Werner S. Pluhar [Indianapolis: Hacket Publishing Company, Inc., 1987], pp. 18–19). From the perspective of the way they grasp being, the former uses the universal to govern the particular, whereas the former seeks to subsume the particular under a universal that it must discover.
47. Immanuel Kant, *Critique of Pure Reason,* trans. N. K. Smith (New York: St. Martin's Press, 1969), p. 177.
48. Kant links the use of judgment in the domain of reality to harmonizing with universal law, and takes this to be the intrinsic property of the "rationalism" of judgment. See Immanuel Kant, *Critique of Practical Reason* (Cambridge, UK: Cambridge University Press, 1997), p. 61.
49. Kant, *Critique of the Power of Judgment,* p. 33.
50. Ibid., pp. 36–37.
51. Ibid., pp. 20–21.
52. Ibid.
53. Kant, *Critique of Pure Reason,* p. 177.

54. From the anthropological perspective, Kant determines taste, as the aesthetic power of judgment, to be a human faculty. In contrast to Kant's emphasis on form and conditions in the epistemological domain, his anthropological perspective emphasizes the attributes and faculties, which "humankind" has; the formal nature of concepts and categories certainly generates a contrast in relation to the facultative nature of the power of judgment. This undoubtedly shows an aspect of the intrinsic perspective through which Kant understands the power of judgment. See Immanuel Kant, *Anthropology from a Pragmatic Point of View*, trans. Victor Lyle Dowdell (Carbondale: Southern Illinois University Press, 1978), p. 14.

55. [Translator: The term translated here as "spirit or mind" is the compound Chinese word *jingshen*, which has no exact counterpart in English. The first character in the compound, *jing*, means vitality, while the connotations of the second character, *shen*, overlap in a complicated way with those of the Latin derivative "spirit." Together, the word *jingshen* is perhaps closest in meaning and usage to the German word *Geist*, but the reader should bear in mind that due to the extra ingredient of *jing* in the blend, *jingshen* also carries with it a more mundane sense, similar to that of the non-religious usage of the English word "spirit" in the common phrase "that's the spirit!" Here, spirit refers to an uplifting direction of the mind, i.e., a mentality positively directed toward a mission to be accomplished. It is precisely in this everyday sense of "spirit" as a determinate direction of mind along with the philosophical sense of *Geist* that the author intends to use this term.]

56. [Translator: The classical Chinese concept *benti* (本体) is a complicated one, which no English translation is capable of fully rendering. The phrase *benti* is composed of two characters: by distinguishing with a horizontal line the root region of the pictographic characterization of a tree (木—>本), *ben* means the "root," "origin," "foundation," and "beginning" of a natural process of growth, whose complement is the term *mo* (末), which, by distinguishing with a horizontal line the opposite end of the tree's branching (木—>末), signals the consequent effect, result or end of a natural cycle of growth; the character *ti* (體) in *benti* is usually translated well by the English term "substance" and it is usually defined in contradistinction from its philosophical counterpart *yong* (用), which usually translates well as function. However, in the context of classical Chinese philosophy, *benti* means the fundamental substance of human spirit. Moreover, *bentilun* (the study of *benti*) is now the standard translation of *ontology*, and so now refers to everything from the underlying substance to the fundamental structure of being. We have chosen the translation "fundamental substance of being" when it stands alone to express the nuances of the classical Chinese conception of being, which the author explains in a footnote to the paragraph that follows, but we translate it simply as "fundamental substance" when it is used specifically in combination with "spirit" to express the fundamental substance "of spirit."]

57. Wang Yangming, "Instructions for Practical Living," *Complete Works of Wang Yangming*, supplement (Shanghai: Shanghai guji chubanshe, 1992), p. 1167 (translation modified).

58. It should be shown here out of convenience that the concept of *benti* in this context is not the same as the concept of substance in Western philosophy. The latter is often determined to be the ultimate substratum of being (see Aristotle, *The Basic Works of Aristotle: Metaphysics*, 1003a25, p. 731, and 1017b23-25, p.761); whereas the former corresponds to effort (*gongfu* 功夫) and means the original form of spirit and the stable tendencies of the mind. As stated previously, the fundamental substance of being (*benti*) is mainly understood as the foundation and ground of cognitive and practical activity or effort (*gongfu*) (see Yang Guorong, "Introduction," in *The Dimension of Being* [Beijing: Renmin chubanshe, 2005]).

59. Ludwig Wittgenstein, *Notebook: 1914–1916* (Oxford: Basil Blackwell, 1979), p. 82.

60. Wang Yangming, "Da Wei Shishuo" [Reply to Wei Shishuo], *The Complete Works of Wang Yangming* (Shanghai: Shanghai guji chubanshe, 1992), p. 217.

61. Zhu Xi, *Zhuzi yulei*, Book 126, p. 3021.

62. Ibid., Book 62, p. 1497.

63. While denying that consciousness and its acts give vitality to language, Wittgenstein also emphasizes that the nature or essence of language is its "use" (see Wittgenstein, *The Blue and Brown Books* [New York: Harper & Row Publishers, 1965], pp. 3–4). Although this opinion touches on the relation between language, consciousness, and thinking, insofar as it invokes the extrinsic use of language to dispel the intrinsic form of consciousness and spirit, it also expresses some tendency to "take functioning as nature."

64. In *The Concept of Mind*, Ryle distinguished between "knowing that" and "knowing how," and mainly linked human capacities to knowing how. This viewpoint came to be widely accepted. In fact, knowing that and knowing how cannot be strictly separated, and thus human capacities do not only involve knowing how. "What/that" is mainly considered to be an epistemological question, and "how" is mainly seen to be a question concerning methodology; however, in reality, knowledge about an object always involves meaning that pertains to methodology: When knowledge is applied in the process of knowing and practicing, it gains methodological meaning. On the other hand, understanding "how" to do something also presupposes having some knowledge about that something. Here, knowing that and knowing how are intrinsically related. Furthermore, knowing, being, and doing are likewise inseparable: knowledge about being (facts) always entails knowledge of how something should be done. For example, knowing that some plant is poisonous is first of all knowledge about "being" (a fact), but it implies within itself knowledge about how one ought to do something (for instance, avoid eating the said plant). This case shows another aspect of the relationship between "knowing that" and "knowing how." Aside from this, "knowing how" also contains both theoretical and practical levels. At the theoretical level, it includes a grasp of the various rules and procedures involved in the process of "doing" something; on the practical level it involves the proper application of this knowledge in the process of "doing" something; the former is closer to "knowing that," while the latter is closer to the narrow sense of "knowing how." Here, we notice the intrinsic connection between the two once again. Lastly, as far as the relationship between cognition and capacities is concerned, this connection between knowing how and knowing that always involves human capacities both in the case of having knowledge of how and in the case of having knowledge of that. In fact, human knowledge (including knowledge of how and that) not only pervades the process of practice and transforms into concrete capacities; it becomes the real construction of human capacities by fusing into the spiritual substance of man. See G. Ryle, *The Concept of Mind* (London and New York: Routledge, 2009).

65. *Zhuangzi*, 1.1, ed. Donald Sturgeon, Chinese Text Project, http://ctext.org/zhuangzi (2015).

66. Gadamer noticed the role of a perspective. However, his understanding of a perspective seems to contain a twofold nature. On the one hand, he affirms that a perspective is generative and formative rather than forever set and unchanging, but the other hand, he mainly emphasizes the communication between a past perspective and a present perspective and the meshing of an already existing text and the process of understanding it. Gadamer's notion of a "fusion of horizons" seems to emphasize both of these aspects. See Gadamer, *Truth and Method*, translation revised by J. Weinsheimer and D. G. Marshall (London: Continuum, 2004), pp. 306–307, 374, 394–395.

67. *Zhuangzi*, 17.5, ed. Donald Sturgeon, Chinese Text Project, http://ctext.org/zhuangzi/floods-of-autumn, (2015).

3. Systems of Norms and the Genesis of Meaning

1. [Translator: The ancient Chinese concept of *li* 理 has a long and complicated history, which would never show in any translation. Its meaning could be expressed as the "patterns" processes exhibit as well as "the structuring principles" that generate and hence explain such patterns. Chinese translators use it to translate everything from axiom (*gongli* 公理) and reason (*lixing* 理性) to rational (*heli* 合理). For the author's purposes, the English word *principle* is the best match.]

2. From this perspective, we claim that some scholars have failed to truly grasp the issue when explaining why human beings have normative problems through the notion that we are self-conscious rational animals (see C. M. Korsgaard, *The Sources of Normativity* [Cambridge, UK: Cambridge University Press, 1996], pp. 46–47).

3. The concrete forms of norms could be analyzed from different perspectives. G. H. von Wright divides norms into three general types, that is, rules (mainly game rules, grammatical rules, and rules of logic), prescriptions (such as commands and permissions), and directions (such as technical norms) and he also makes a distinction between three types of minor norms, that is, customs, moral principles, and ideal rules (see G. H. von Wright, *Norm and Action: A Logical Enquiry* [London: Routledge and Kegan Paul, 1963], pp. 15–16). On the basis of the different objects upon which, the domains in which, and the ways in which norms act, further distinctions between norms could also be made such as those characterizing the cognitive, moral, aesthetic, legal, religious, ritual, customary, and technical domains: norms of the cognitive domain are mainly related to truth and falsity; norms of the moral domain concern good and evil in the broad sense; aesthetic rules are associated with artistic production and aesthetic appraisal; legal norms deal more with the confirmation of lawfulness and legitimacy; religious laws are based on transcendent aims; ritual norms are associated with the distinction between the civilized and the uncivilized; customary prescriptions aim at cultural identity; technical rules aim at the assurance of effective technical operations; and so on. Here examining the general character of norms at the rational level leaves out a detailed discussion of the concrete forms of norms.

4. *Mencius*, 4A, 9.

5. Wang Fuzhi, *Zhangzi zheng meng zhu* [Commentary on Zhang Zai's *Correction of Youthful Folly*], vol. 1, *Chuanshan quanshu*, book 12 (Changsha: Yuelu shushe, 1996), pp. 32–33.

6. *Mencius*, 1A, 6.

7. See C. M. Korsgaard, *The Sources of Normativity* (Cambridge, UK: Cambridge University Press, 1996), pp. 92–113.

8. Zhu Xi, *Zhuzi yulei*, Vol. 114, p. 2760.

9. Zhu Xi, *Zhuzi quanshu* [Collected Books of Zhuzi], vol. 1, *Lunyu huowen* [Dialogues on the Analects], book 4 (Shanghai: Shanghai guji chubanshe, 2002), p. 613.

10. Zhu Xi, *Zhuzi quanshu*, vol. 19, book 2, *Daxue huowen I* [Great Learning], p. 527.

11. Zhu Xi, *Zhuzi quanshu*, vol. 1, *Lunyu huowen*, book 4, p. 613. Considering its connotations, "cannot but do so" approximates what is necessarily so, and belongs to the category of norms in the strong sense (commands, orders); and what "the self cannot outstrip" approximates what is necessary (a tendency the individual cannot choose to either manifest or not). Putting the first on par with the second is the theoretical orientation of mistaking what ought to be for what necessarily is, which such statements as "cannot but" and "cannot outstrip" clearly demonstrate.

12. Kant also in a sense shows this tendency to view what ought to be as what necessarily is. When discussing rules, Kant claims that rules, so far as they are objective, can also be called

laws (see Immanuel Kant, *Critique of Pure Reason*, trans. N. K. Smith (New York: St. Martin's Press, 1965), p. 147). But as compared with a rule's implication of what ought to be, laws manifest what must necessarily be, so to take rules for laws means to include what ought to be in what must necessarily be. In fact, Kant's moral philosophy to a considerable extent presents an understanding of what ought to be as what necessarily is, and as this text mentions later on, Kant's understanding of the moral law makes this point obvious. Out of convenience, it should be pointed out that Korsgaard differs from Kant substantially on this issue of understanding the nature of norms, even though he recognizes his philosophical standpoint as Kantian.

13. Ludwig Wittgenstein, *Philosophical Investigations*, trans. G. E. M. Anscombe (Malden: Blackwell, 1958), §199, p. 80e.

14. Ibid., §202, p. 81e.

15. Ibid., §219, p. 85e.

16. *Mencius*, 6A, 4.

17. Confucius, *The Analects*, 2, 7.

18. "Smaller Rules of Demeanor," in *Book of Rites*, ed. Donald Sturgeon, Chinese Text Project, http://ctext.org/liji/shao-yi (2015).

19. Li Gou, *Li Gou ji* [Collected Works of Li Gou] (Beijing: Zhonghua shuju, 1981), p. 66.

20. Zhang Zai, *Zhang Zai ji* [Collected Works of Zhang Zai] (Beijing: Zhonghua shuju, 1978), pp. 264, 37.

21. Confucius, *The Analects*, 7, 14.

22. *The Analects*, 3:25.

23. The music of Shao refers to music from the Shun dynasty according to legend. The music of Wu refers to the music of the first king of Wu of the Zhou Dynasty.

24. *The Analects*, 15:11.

25. *The Analects*, 17:18.

26. [Translator: The character *jing* (经) though figuratively means rules, stems from an ancient graph characterizing the fixed warp set for a weft to weave around, and the character *quan* (权) in this context means to bend; here, the bending of the weft (that is, the fluid unfolding of circumstances) in and out, around the fixed warp, but also means to weigh, that is, to balance rules and circumstances.

27. *Mencius*, 7A, 26.

28. Wang Fuzhi, *Zhangzi zheng meng zhu*, vol.1, *Chuanshan quanshu*, book 12, p. 72.

29. *Xunzi*, 9.19.

30. [Translator: Though the prevailing translation of *yi* (義) into English is righteousness, this substantivization of the English adjective "righteous" does not show the complexity of the original concept, especially in Xunzi here. The character *yi* (義) originally derived from a graph showing a warrior, most likely in a military march, adorned with flare, which as *shuowen jiezi* (说文解字) explains, is the display of authoritative might. By extension, *yi* points to one's righteously obtained position of power [in the hierarchy], from which the connection between being-righteous and the rightful division of labor can be gleamed.

31. *Xunzi*, 19.1.

32. Considered historically, some norms first spontaneously take shape in the process of social practice, and then thereafter they are gradually accepted, approved, and self-consciously enunciated, acquiring the form of norms. This includes the two aspects of practical need and historical choice: whereas the spontaneous formation of a norm in the evolution of society expresses a practical need, for society to further its formalization, acceptance, and approval, is presented as a historical choice. So, the system of rite and right (*liyi* 礼义) could also in a sense be seen as the product of the interaction of these two aspects.

33. J. Raz, *Practical Reason and Norms* (London: Hutchinson of London, 1975), p. 52.

34. Kant, *Grounding for the Metaphysics of Morals*, trans. James W. Ellington (Cambridge, MA: Hackett Publishing Company, 1993), p. 30.
35. Ibid., p. 38.
36. Immanuel Kant, *Critique of Pure Reason*, trans. N. K. Smith (New York: St. Martin's Press, 1965), p. 135.
37. See Yang Guorong, *Lunli yu cunzai* [Ethics and Being] (Beijing: Beijing daxue chubanshe, 2010), esp. chaps 3 and 8.
38. *The Analects*, 8:8.

4. Meaning in the World of Spirit

1. Edmond Husserl, *The Essential Husserl: Basic Writings in Transcendental Phenomenology*, ed. Don Walton (Bloomington: Indiana University Press, 1999), p. 338.
2. Zhang Zai, *Zhang Zai ji* [Collected Works of Zhang Zai] (Beijing: Zhonghua Shuju, 1978), p. 7.
3. [Translator: Here, modifying the term Nature (*tian* 天) are the two terms *zhi* (秩) and *xu* (序). In modern Chinese, the word for "order" of whatever kind is the compound *zhixu*, but here, Zhang Zai seems to be using these terms separately to refer to the spatial order of Nature *tianzhi* and the temporal order of Nature *tianxu*, respectively.
4. Ibid., p. 19.
5. Gao Zhennong, *Dacheng qixin lun jiaoshi* [The Awakening of Faith in the Mahayana: Collation and Commentary] (Beijing: Zhonghua shuju, 1992), p. 116.
6. Fa Zang, "Xiu Huayan anzhi wangjin huanyuan guan" [The Perspective of Returning to the Origin through Discarding All Delusions with Huayan's Miraculous Practice], in *Zhongguo fojiao sixiang ziliao xuanbian*, Vol. 2, Book 2, Ed. Jian Shijun and Lou Yulie, (Beijing: Zhonghua shuju, 1983), pp. 107–130.
7. Wang Fuzhi, *Zhangzi zhengmeng zhu* [Commentary on Zhang Zai's Correction of Youthful Folly], in *Chuanshan quanshu* [Complete Works of Chuanshan], book 12 (Changsha: Yuelu shushe, 1996), p. 143.
8. Strictly speaking, as Wittgenstein points out, there is no such thing as a private language that exists only in a particular individual and can be understood only by this individual.
9. Wang Fuzhi, *Du sishu daquan shuo* [Discussions in Reading the Great Collection of Commentaries on the Four Books], in *Chuanshan quanshu* [Complete Works of Chuanshan], book 6 (Changsha: Yuelu shushe, 1996), p. 1077.
10. Ibid., p. 1091.
11. See Yang Guorong, *Dao lun* [A Treatise on *Dao*] (Beijing: Beijing daxue chubanshe, 2011), chapter 2.
12. See K. Marx and F. Engels, *Karl Marx and Frederick Engels: Selected Works in One Volume* (New York: International Publishers, 1968), p. 435.
13. See Wang Yangming, *Instructions for Practical Living and Other Neo-confucian Writings*, trans. Wing-Tsit Chan (New York: Columbia University Press, 1963), p. 14. [Translator: Wang renders *yi* as "will," which is also an excellent translation; the semantic range of *yi*, however, fits that of "intention" in innumerable aspects as well, hence the slight modification.]
14. Wang Fuzhi, *Du sishu daquan shuo*, *Chuanshan quanshu*, book 6, p. 607.
15. See Wang Yangming, *Instructions for Practical Living and Other Neo-Confucian Writings*, p. 189.

16. See K. Marx and F. Engels, *Economic and Philosophic Manuscripts of 1844*, trans. Martin Mulligan (Amherst, NY: Prometheus Books, 1988), p. 108.

17. Dai Mingyang, *Ji Kang ji jiaozhu* [Collected Works of Ji Kang: Collation and Commentary] (Beijing: Renmin Wenxue Chubanshe, 1962), p. 217.

18. Ibid., p. 199.

19. Ibid., p. 214.

20. See *The Analects*, 14:12.

21. *The Analects*, 8:8.

22. *The Analects*, 7:14.

23. *Xunzi*, 20.6.

24. Kant, *Opus Postumum* (Cambridge, UK: Cambridge University Press, 1993), p. 248.

25. Wing-tsit Chan, trans. and ed., *The Platform Scripture* (New York: St. John's University Press, 1963), p. 73 (translation modified).

26. Ibid., p. 79.

27. Ibid., p. 91.

28. Ibid., p. 83.

29. The unity of presentation and intentionality is related to the unity of the given and the taken in the epistemological sense. (See Yang Guorong, *Dao lun*, chapter 3.)

30. Husserl's phenomenology in some respects already accounted for the interrelatedness of the presentation of meaning and the giving of meaning in intentional activity, but as chapter 1 of this book has argued, Husserl's phenomenology gives priority to the giving of meaning in connection with his suspension of being and his emphasis on the constitution of consciousness, thereby failing to evaluate the status of the thing's presentation. In this respect, it is obviously hard to say that his phenomenology truly grasped the unity and interaction of the two in the process of generating meaning or sense.

31. *Mencius*, 6A, 7. See *A Source Book in Chinese Philosophy*, trans. Wing-tsit Chan (Princeton, NJ: Princeton University Press, 1963), p. 56 (translation modified).

32. Of course, as far as etymology goes, the term *jingjie* already emerged prior to the transmission of Buddhism into China. However, the original meaning of this term principally had to do with territory and boundaries, and some of the Han dynasty scholars used this term in precisely this sense. For instance, in the *Zhouli Zhushu* (*Commentary on the Rites of the Zhou: Scroll 24*) Zheng Xuan adds an explanatory comment to the sentence *bu da feng* from the Zhouli, stating: "bu da feng [Perform a divination concerning the expansion of the boundary—trans.] means the state boundary (*jingjie*) has been invaded, consult the oracle to divine [the future of] a military expedition to correct it." *Jingjie* also means state here, specifically, the territorial boundaries of the state. Following the transmission of Buddhism, this word became used to translate and interpret Buddhist concepts, and its meaning did transform thereby. However, the original meaning of *jingjie* still survived side by side with the Buddhist usage, which can be seen in several statements well after Buddhism took root. For example, in *Wang Yangming Quanji* (the *Collected Works of Wang Yangming*), Wang Yangming mentions "The territory (*jingjie*) of Guangdong." (For reference, see *Wang Yangming Quanji: Anxing zhangnan daoshou xunguan daizui dubin chaozei* [Shanghai Guji Chubanshe, 1992], p. 535.) Such phenomena illustrate the complexity of linguistic evolution.

33. See *Dacheng miyan jing* (Mahayana Sutra of Mystic Glorification), Taisho-Pitaka (No. 440), Chinese Buddhist Electronic Text Association, www.cbeta.org/index.htm (2015).

34. *Ru lengqie jing* (The Sutra on Entering the Land of Lanka), vol. 5, Taisho-Pitaka (No. 67), Chinese Buddhist Electronic Text Association, www.cbeta.org/info.htm (2015).

35. Shi Puji. *Wudeng huiyuan* (Five Collected Records of Chan's Words and Deeds), vol. 3, (Beijing: *Zhonghua shuju*, 1983).

36. "Huayan yicheng jiaoyi fenqi zhang" (Huayan's Teaching of the Single Vehicle and Distinctions), in *Zhongguo fojiao sixiang ziliao xuanbian*, Vol. 4, ed. Jian Shijun and Lou Yulie, (Beijing: *Zhonghua shuju*, 1983), pp. 179-199.

37. Considered on a broader level, Buddhism brings the external state into a domain of understandable meaning by determining the external state with the notion of conditioned arising, that is, explains the phenomenal world as arising from conditions; on the other hand, Buddhism also determines the internal state with the notion of Nirvana, thereby investing the state with value. In this way, the distinction between internal state and external state also touches on different senses of the world of meaning.

38. See *The Platform Scripture*, p. 83.

39. Zhu Xi, "Reply to Zhang Qinfu," in *Zhu wengong wenji* (Collected Works of Zhu Xi), book 21, p. 1314.

40. Wang Fuzhi, *Chuanshan Quanshu*, vol. 10, *Du sishu daquan shuo*, book 6, p. 624.

41. *The Analects*, 4:2.

42. Wang Fuzhi, *Chuanshan Quanshu*, vol. 10, *Du sishu daquan shuo*, book 6, p. 627.

43. Ibid.

44. *Mencius*, 7A, 1.

45. *Mencius*, 4A, 12.

46. Wang Fuzhi, *Chuanshan Quanshu*, vol. 10, *Du sishu daquan shuo*, book 6, p. 1119.

47. Zhang Zai, *Zhang Zai ji*, p. 24.

48. Feng Youlan, *Sansongtang quanji* (Collected Works in Three Pines Hall), vol. 4 (Zhengzhou: Henan Renmin Chubanshe, 1986), p. 549.

49. Zhang Zai, *Zhang Zai ji*, p. 376.

50. Kant, *Opus Postumum*, p. 239.

51. Ibid., p. 232.

52. Ibid., p. 238.

53. *Mencius*, 4B, 19.

54. *Mencius*, 4B, 28.

55. See chapter 2.

56. Heidegger, "The Question Concerning Technology," in *The Question Concerning Technology and Other Essays*, translated and with an Introduction by William Lovitt (New York: Garland Publishing, Inc., 1977), p. 20.

57. Heidegger, "Science and Reflection," p. 169.

58. *Zhuangzi*, 8.3.

59. Huang Zongxi, "Epigraph for Historigrapher Bian Yuwu," in *Huang Zongxi quanji* [Collected Works of Huang Zongxi], book 10 (Hangzhou: Zhejiang guji chubanshe, 1992), p. 421.

60. Nie Bao, "Reply to Chen Mingshui," *Shuangjiang nie xiansheng wenji* [Collected Works of Neibao], vol. 11.

5. Meaning and Reality

1. Husserl once defined the word "actual" from the perspective of logic in the following way: "The predicate 'actual' does not determine the object but means: I do not imagine, I do not carry out an act of quasi-experience or of quasi-explication and predication; I do not speak about fictive objects but about objects given in conformity with experience." [Edmund Husserl, *Experience and Judgment: Investigations in a Genealogy of logic*, trans. and ed. L. Landgrebe, J.S. Churchill, and K. Ameriks (Evanston, IL: Northwestern University Press,

1997), p. 301.] In regard to his linking what is actual with one's experience in order to distinguish it from a general objective determination, his understanding does notice in a way the intrinsic sense of "actuality." But Husserl does not adequately account for the link between actuality and the broad sense of humanized reality.

2. Heidegger once insisted that Being or the manifestation of Being needs man (see M. Heidegger, G. Neske, and E. Kettering, *Martin Heidegger and National Socialism: Questions and Answers* [New York: Paragon House, 1990], p. 82). Perhaps a more precise way of saying it would be: Being can only obtain its actual mode in and through man.

3. K. Marx and F. Engels, *Economic and Philosophic Manuscripts of 1844*, trans. Martin Mulligan (Amherst, NY: Prometheus Books, 1998), p. 108.

4. *Mencius*, 6B, 25.

5. See *Zhuangzi*, 23.2.

6. See Karl Marx, *Capital: A Critique of Political Economy*, trans. B. Fowkes, vol. 1 (Harmondsworth, UK: Penguin, 1976), p. 290.

7. When discussing the issue of meaning, Michael Polanyi thinks that every achievement of any sort of meaning should be seen as the epitome of reality itself (see Michael Polanyi and Harry Prosch, *Meaning* [Chicago: The University of Chicago Press, 1976], p. 182). As this book discussed in the first chapter, this idea views every meaning to some extent as reality's determination of itself, which unavoidably neglects the link between meaning and human being's creative activity.

8. Hegel, *Hegel's Philosophy of Nature: Being Part Two of the Encyclopaedia of the Philosophical Sciences (1830)*, trans. A. V. Miller (Oxford: Oxford University Press, 2004), p. 3.

9. See Wang Yangming, *Instructions for Practical Living and Other Neo-confucian Writings*, trans. Wing-Tsit Chan (New York: Columbia University Press, 1963), p. 14 (translation modified).

10. Ibid.

11. Williams James, *Pragmatism* (New York: Dover Publications, 1995), p. 96.

12. Habermas once asked the following question: "How is it possible to go beyond pragmatism and turn to defend a realist position?" (J. Habermas, *Duihua lunli yu zhenli wenti* [Ethics of Discourse and the Problem of Truth] [Beijing: Zhongguo renmin daxue chubanshe, 2005], p. 47). As opposed to traditional realism, which stresses the in-itself nature of being, pragmatism stresses the being for-us dimension of being, which could be seen as a "turn," and going beyond this turn to defend realism would mean affirming both the being for-us and being in-itself of being. Although the main concern of Habermas did not lie in how to understand being, his idea mentioned here implicitly involves the issue of how to unify the being for-us dimension of being and the being in-itself dimension of being.

13. See Heidegger. *Being and Time*, trans. Joan Stambaugh (Albany: State University of New York Press, 1996), p. 11.

14. Ibid., p. 10.

15. Karl Jaspers, *Philosophy*, trans. E. B. Ashton, vol. 1 (Chicago: The University of Chicago Press, 1969), p. 49.

16. Nelson Goodman, *Of Mind and Other Matters* (Cambridge, MA: Harvard University Press, 1984), p. 29.

17. Ibid., p. 34.

18. Ibid., p. 42.

19. Wang Chong, 14.5.

20. Ibid., 41.14.

21. Ibid., 12.1.

22. Hegel, *Hegel's Philosophy of Nature*, p. 4.

23. Ibid., p. 5.

24. Ibid., p. 7. Hegel furthermore distinguishes the theoretical spirit from the practical spirit [translated as theoretical and practical mind in the William Wallace version], thinking that the former does not treat the object subjectively, while the latter begins with its own aims and interests. (See G. W. F. Hegel, *Hegel's Philosophy of Mind: Being Part Three of the Encyclopaedia of the Philosophical Sciences,*' trans. William Wallace [Oxford, UK: Clarendon, 1971], pp. 64–102). This seems consistent with the distinction between the theoretical attitude and the practical attitude.

25. When discussing intentional acts from the perspective of "direction of fit," Searle distinguishes the different forms of relations between mind and things, among which two are worth a closer look: "mind-to-world" and "world-to-mind." In the consciousness or intention of the content of a proposition, the issue concerns the fittingness of the mind to the world. Take for instance the consciousness or idea of the content of such propositions as "it's raining"; i.e., the type we form when observing external objects—whether it is true or false depends on whether it fits the actual state of the external world—but, the intention or consciousness of modal content such as desires more directly concern the issue of whether or not the external world fits the mind. For instance, the content of the proposition "I want to drink water" is an intention, which concerns the issue of whether or not the world can provide the subject with water to satisfy his desire. (See John Searle, *Mind—A Brief Introduction* [Oxford, UK: Oxford University Press, 2004], pp. 117–122). Whereas the theoretical attitude corresponds to the mind-to-world direction of fit, in an extended sense, the world-to-mind direction of fit involves the practical attitude.

26. *Li ji*, 9.20.

27. Heller Agnes, *Everyday Life* (London: Routledge & Kegan Paul, 1984), p. 3.

28. K. Marx, *Grundrisse: Foundations of the Critique of Political Economy (Rough Draft)*, trans. M. Nicolaus (London: Penguin Books in association with New Left Review, 1993), p. 92.

29. *Li ji*, 9.5.

30. Ibid., 1.47.

31. Ibid., 1.49.

32. Ibid., 1.40.

33. Ibid., 16.3.

34. Ibid., 3.72.

35. *Li ji*, 9.6.

36. Zheng Xuan. *San li zhu* [Commentary on the Record of Rites], (Beijing: Beijing daxue chubanshe, 1999), p. 65.

37. *Li ji*, 4.200.

38. Ibid., 26.7.

39. Ibid., 44.1.

40. K. Marx and F. Engels, *Economic and Philosophic Manuscripts of 1844*, trans. Martin Mulligan (Amherst, NY: Prometheus Books, 1988), pp. 101–102.

41. *Xunzi*, 19.3.

42. Ibid., 19.1.

43. See Johann Christoph Friedrich von Schille, *On the Aesthetic Education of Man*, trans. Reginald Snell (Mineola, NY: Dover Publications, 2004), p. 80.

44. Alfred Schutz, *Collected Papers I: The Problem of Social Reality*, ed. Maurice Natanson (The Hague: Martinus Nijhoff, 1962). Although he mentions many forms of reality, Schutz considers everyday life as the predominant form.

45. See John R. Searle, *The Construction of Social Reality* (New York: The Free Press, 1995), pp. 31–58.

46. K. Marx, *Capital: A Critique of Political Economy*, ed. F. Engels, trans. S. Moore and E. B. Aveling (Mineola, NY: Dover, 2011), p. 197.

47. K. Marx, *The Eighteenth Brumaire of Louis Bonaparte* (New York: International Publishers, 1963), p. 15.

48. *The Analects*, 2:12.

49. *The Analects*, 1:12.

50. *The Analects*, 17:11.

51. *Li ji*, 1.9.

52. Ibid., 42.1.

53. *Zhuangzi*, 16.3.

54. Ibid., 17.7.

55. Ibid., 24.10.

56. Ibid., 8.3.

57. Daoism emphasizes natural principles in the debate concerning Nature and humans, but this does not mean that Daoism denies every form of being related to society. At the level of content, Daoism stresses rather that such social forms of being should harmonize with natural principles.

58. See Hegel, *Hegel's Philosophy of Nature*, p. 17.

59. *Li ji*, 9.18.

60. Ibid., 26.7.

61. Of course, such critiques are also historically limited themselves.

6. Meaning and the Individual

1. See Suárez, *On Individuation, Metaphysical Disputation V: Individual Unity and Its Principle*, trans. J. J. E. Gracia (Milwaukee, WI: Marquette University Press, 1982), p. 31. Francoise Suárez (1548–1617) was a Spanish philosopher who had an important influence in the history of philosophy, profoundly impacting Christian Wolf, for instance, who regarded his meditations on metaphysical questions to be of considerable depth, and also Heidegger, who regarded the wisdom, profundity, and uniqueness with which he posed problems to top Aquinas (see Heidegger, *The Fundamental Concept of Metaphysics* [Bloomington: Indiana University Press, 1995], p. 51). In *Being and Time*, Heidegger furthermore expressed his view that the metaphysics of Suarez was the middle term between ancient Greek ontology on the one hand and modern metaphysics and transcendental philosophy on the other (see Martin Heidegger, *Being and Time* (Albany: State University of New York Press, 1996], p. 19).

2. Strawson sees the person as one of the individual's basic modes of being, when discussing the person in the sense of an individual, Strawson regards the concept of a person to be the primitive concept of an entity, and may be applied to an individual entity. Explaining this primitiveness, Strawson remarks: "All I have said about the meaning of saying that this concept is primitive is that it is not to be analysed in a certain way or ways" (P. E. Strawson, *Individuals: An Essay in Descriptive Metaphysics* [London and New York: Routledge, 2003], p. 104). What is not analyzable consists mainly in logical properties, and implied behind this understanding of a person is a determination of the individual. Considering the actual mode of being, the distinctive feature of the individual (including the person) lies in that it is a primitive unity, and this characteristic of individual beings has more original meaning than the non-analyzable characteristic of properties in the logical sense. Strawson's use of analysis as an approach to metaphysics thus seems to have precluded his understanding of the individual to go beyond the merely logical context of being.

3. See J. E. Gracia, *Individuality: An Essay on the Foundation of Metaphysics* (Albany: State University of New York Press, 1988), p. 234.

4. When discussing the notion of individuals, Strawson never makes a distinction between individuals and particulars. Though in the book *Individuals* he directly discusses particulars, he understands material bodies to be basic particulars (see P. E. Strawson, *Individuals*, p. 39). This idea immediately raises theoretical problems at least in terms of logic.

5. Jin Yuelin, *Lun Dao* [A Treatise of Dao] (Beijing: Shangwu yinshuguan, 1987), p. 128.

6. See Leibniz, *Discourse on Metaphysics and Other Essays* (Indianapolis, IN: Hackett, 1991), p. 9.

7. See B. Bosanquet, *The Principle of Individuality and Value* (London: Macmillan, 1912), p. 40.

8. Ibid.

9. See J. E. Gracia, *Individuality*, p. 139.

10. Arthur Pap, *Elements of Analytic Philosophy* (New York: Macmillan, 1949), p. 208.

11. In his discussion on the alteration of the individual, Jin Yuelin notices a distinction between principle and potentiality (see Jin Yuelin, *Lun Dao*, pp. 201–203; and "A General Rule Governing the Occurrence of Potentiality," in *Jin Yuelin xueshu lunwen xuan* [Selected Academic Papers of Jin Yuelin] (Beijing: Zhongguo shehui kexue chubanshe, 1990), pp. 335–350].

12. Heidegger, *What is a Thing?* trans. W. B. Barton, Jr. and Vera Deutsch (South Bend, IN: Gateway Editions, Ltd., 1967), p. 244.

13. Gilles Deleuze, *The Logic of Sense,* trans. M. Lester with C. Stivale (New York: Columbia University Press, 1990), p. 182.

14. K. Marx and F. Engels, *Economic and Philosophic Manuscripts of 1844* (Amherst, NY: Prometheus Books), p. 109.

15. Ibid.

16. See J. Searle, *Mind: A Brief Introduction*, pp. 196–198.

17. See John Locke, *An Essay Concerning Human Understanding*, vol. 1 (Mineola, NY: Dover Publications, Inc., 1959), pp. 448–451.

18. Charles Taylor, "What Is Human Agency?" in *The Self: Psychological and Philosophical Issues*, ed. Theodore Mischel (Oxford, UK: Basil Blackwell, 1977), pp. 103–135.

19. Dan Zahavi, *Subjectivity and Selfhood: Investigating the First-Person Perspective* (Cambridge, MA: The MIT Press, 2005), p. 76.

20. See B. Bosanquet, *The Principle of Individuality and Value*, p. 70.

21. See Heidegger, *What Is a Thing?* p. 15.

22. Huang Zongxi, "Master Liu's Explanation of *Mencius*," vol. 4, book 1, in *Huang Zongxi quanji* [Collected Works of Huang Zongxi] (Hangzhou: Zhejiang guji chubanshe, 1985), p. 101.

23. K. Marx, *Grundrisse: Foundations of the Critique of Political Economy (Rough Draft),* trans. M. Nicolaus (London: Penguin Books in association with New Left Review, 1993), p. 156.

24. K. Marx, *Grundrisse*, p. 161.

25. K. Marx and F. Engels, *Economic and Philosophic Manuscripts of 1844*, p. 105.

26. K. Marx, *Grundrisse*, p. 158.

27. *Zhuangzi*, 11.5.

28. Ibid., 24.10.

29. Ibid., 26.8.

30. Zhang Zai, *Zhang Zai ji* [Collected Works of Zhang Zai] (Beijing: Beijing Shuju, 1978), p. 27.

31. According to *Zhuangzi*, the natural human being does not separate herself from the origin (See *Zhuangzi*, 33.1). The authentic person treats human being from the perspective of

Nature and does not approach Nature from the perspective of human [society] (see *Zhuangzi*, 24.13). "The natural human being" is one who lives in harmony with Nature or identifies with Nature.

32. *Zhuangzi*, 12.2.
33. *Xunzi*, 9.20.
34. Ibid., 10.1.
35. K. Marx, *Grundrisse*, p. 157.
36. K. Marx, *Grundrisse: Foundations of the Critique of Political Economy (Rough Draft)*. Ibid., p. 242.
37. K. Marx, *A Contribution to the Critique of Political Economy*, trans. N. I. Stone (Chicago: Forgotten Books, 2012), pp. 22–23.
38. K. Marx and F. Engels, *Makesi En'gesi quanji* [Collected Works of Marx and Engels] (Beijing: Renmin chubanshe, 1998), p. 360.
39. K. Marx, *Grundrisse*, p. 162.
40. K. Marx, *The German Ideology*, ed. C. J. Arthur (New York: International Publishers, 1972), p. 53.
41. K. Marx, *Grundrisse*, p. 162.
42. Ibid.
43. Ibid., p. 172.
44. Ibid., p. 711.
45. Ibid., p. 706.
46. There is a point in common shared by the positive and negative modes of freedom here and Isaiah Berlin's distinction between negative freedom and positive freedom, but they are not completely identical. Berlin's distinction, though not entirely limited to the political realm, focuses mainly upon it. The two modes of freedom discussed here are positioned in the context of the free development of individuality. On the whole, Berlin mainly holds a critical position in relation to positive freedom and strongly defends the significance of negative freedom. By contrast, the author tends to overcome both of them, which will be shown in detail in the following.
47. See Isaiah Berlin, *Four Essays on Liberty* (Oxford, UK: Oxford University Press, 1969), pp. 131–32.
48. See Ibid., pp. 127, 131.
49. Ibid., pp. 171–172.
50. *The Analects*, 6:30.
51. *The Analects*, 12:2.

7. Accomplishing Oneself and Accomplishing Things

1. J. Habermas, *The Structural Transformation of the Public Sphere*, trans. Thomas Burger (Cambridge, MA: MIT Press, 1993), p. 12.
2. Hannah Arendt, *The Human Condition*, trans. M. Canovan (Chicago: Chicago University Press, 1998), p. 72.
3. Will Kymlicka, *Contemporary Political Philosophy: An Introduction* (Oxford, UK: Oxford University Press, 2002), p. 394.
4. Ibid., p. 52.
5. J. Habermas, "The Public Sphere," in *New German Critique*, No. 3 (Autumn, 1974), p. 50.

6. With this said, this book will not continue to make strict distinctions separating the private domain from the individual domain on the one hand and the public sphere from the social sphere on the other.

7. Ban Gu, *Han shu* [History of the Han Dynasty], Vol. 52. Edited by Donald Sturgeon. Chinese Text Project. http://ctext.org/han-shu/wang-shang-shi-dan-fu-xi-zhuan (2015).

8. Dong Zhongshu, *Chunqiu fanlu* [Luxuriant Gems of the Spring and Autumn Annals], 29.1.

9. See Anthony Giddens, *The Constitution of Society: Outline of the Theory of Structuration* (Cambridge, UK: Polity Press, 1986), p. xxxi.

10. Contemporary philosophers present us with a spectrum of perspectives with which to explore justice. In contemporary critical theory, Holt stresses the priority of "recognition" in justice, whereas Fraser insists on the irreducibility of recognition and redistribution, while adding as a third dimension the issue of representation and entitlement to representation (see Axel Honneth and Nancy Fraser, *Redistribution or Recognition? A Political-Philosophical Exchange* (London: Verso, 2003), pp. 5–149; and Nancy Fraser, *Scales of Justice: Reimagining Political Space in a Globalizing World* (New York: Columbia University Press, 2009), pp. 12–34.] However, in this understanding, the basic issue is still inseparable from the acknowledgment, reasonable possession, and fair distribution of social resources: "recognition" primarily concerns cultural identity and "the struggle for recognition" (including recognition of equal cultural identity), the essential meaning of which is not simply a competition for abstract status, but for the right to take a fair share of resources: "redistribution" in the narrow sense directly involves the readjustment of economic resources, while entitlement to representation concerns the reasonable sharing of political resources. Here we can see the meaning of the reasonable possession of resources for the problem of justice.

11. Plato once presented justice as rendering to each man what most befits him, which in substance means to get what one deserves (see *The Collected Dialogues of Plato: Republic* 332c [Princeton, NJ: Princeton University Press, 1961], p. 581). Aristotle saw the essence of justice in the principle of treating equal persons equally (*The Basic Works of Aristotle: Politics* 1282b30 [New York: Random House, 1941], p. 1193), and the concrete meaning of equal treatment is manifested in the distribution of shares on the basis of what is deserved (see Aristotle, *The Basic Works of Aristotle: Nicomachean Ethics* 1131a25, p. 1006). Both views focus on different senses of the right of the individual.

12. John Rawls, *A Theory of Justice*, rev. ed. (Cambridge, MA: Harvard University Press, 1999), p. 503.

13. Ibid., p. 220.

14. Ibid., p. 53.

15. Robert Nozick, *Anarchy, State, and Utopia* (New York: Basic Books, Inc., 1974), p. 151.

16. Ibid., p. 155.

17. Robert Nozick, *Anarchy, State, and Utopia* (New York: Basic Books, Inc. 1974), p. 172.

18. *Xiao jing*, 1.1.

19. Kant once put forward the following critique of the idea of one's self-ownership, insisting that "he [man] is not his own property," because "if he were his own property, he would be a thing over which he could have ownership . . . for it is impossible to be a person and a thing, the proprietor and the property" (see Kant. *Lectures on Ethics,* trans. Louis Infield [Cambridge, MA: Hackett Publishing Company, 1963], p. 165). This simultaneously concerns the logical and axiological perspectives: From the axiological perspective, human being is not a thing, and taking oneself to be a possession implies equating human being with a thing; from the logical perspective, simultaneously being both proprietor and possession entails a logical contradic-

tion. Kant's view here offers a perspective with which to analyze Nozick's argument and see the logical and axiological problems his concept of self-ownership runs into.

20. Marx and Engels, *Karl Marx and Frederick Engels: Selected Works in One Volume* (New York: International Publishers, 1968), p. 324.

21. *Mencius*, 6A, 7.

22. *Mencius*, 4B, 32.

23. John Rawls, *A Theory of Justice*, p. 87.

24. Passerin D'Entreves already pointed out the link between natural law and the idea of rights, and insisted that the modern theory of natural law is not a theory of law at all, but a theory of rights (see Passerin Alessandro D'Entreves, *Natural Law: An Introduction to Legal Theory Philosophy* [New Brunswick: Transaction Publishers, 1994], p. 61).

25. John Rawls, *A Theory of Justice*, p. 396.

26. John Rawls, *Political Liberalism* (New York: Columbia University Press, 2005), p. 175.

27. Ibid., p. 9.

28. *The Analects*, 12:11.

29. *Mencius*, 4A, 2.

30. *Mencius*, 2A, 7.

31. *Mencius*, 7B, 32.

32. Will Kymlicka, *Contemporary Political Philosophy* (New York: Oxford University Press, 1990), pp. 285–286.

33. Bryan Turner, *Citizenship and Social Theory* (London: Sage Publications, 1993), p. 2.

34. Will Kymlicka, *Contemporary Political Philosophy* (New York: Oxford University Press, 1990), pp. 288–289.

35. See Charles Taylor, "The Liberal-communitarian Debate," in *Liberalism and the Moral Life*, ed. N. Rosenblum, (Cambridge: Harvard University Press, 1989), p. 178.

36. John Rawls, *Political Liberalism*, p. 68.

37. Karl Marx and Frederick Engels, *Selected Works in One Volume*, p. 325.

38. G. A. Cohen, *Self-ownership, Freedom, and Equality* (Cambridge, UK: Cambridge University Press, 1995), pp. 116–156.

39. Ibid., pp. 10–12.

40. See Allen E. Buchanan, *Marx and Justice: the Radical Critique of Liberalism* (London: Methuen, 1982), pp. 75–76.

41. While noting that rights cause conflicts, Buchanan also conceives of justice as making subjects become uncompromising rights-holders and hence as making conflicts unavoidable. This conception seems to disregard the regulative function of justice, (Ibid. p. 178).

42. Dong Zhongshu, *Chuqiu fanlu*, chapter 41.

43. Zhang Zai, *Zhang Zai ji*, p. 62.

44. Karl Marx and Frederick Engels, *Karl Marx and Frederick Engels: Selected Works in One Volume*, p. 15.

45. Karl Marx, *Capital: A Critique of Political Economy*, trans. B. Fowkes, vol. 1 (Harmondsworth: Penguin, 1976), p. 171.

Bibliography

Agnes, Heller. *Everyday Life*. London: Routledge & Kegan Paul, 1984.
Arendt, Hannah. *The Human Condition*. Translated by M. Canovan. Chicago: Chicago University Press, 1998.
Aristotle. *The Basic Works of Aristotle, Metaphysics*. Translated by Richard Mckeon. New York: Random House, 1941.
———. *The Basic Works of Aristotle, Nicomachean Ethics*. Translated by Richard Mckeon. New York: Random House, 1941.
Ayer, A. J. *Language, Truth, and Logic*. New York: Dover Publications, 1952.
Ban Gu. *Han shu* [History of the Han Dynasty], Vol. 52. Edited by Donald Sturgeon. Chinese Text Project. http://ctext.org/han-shu/wang-shang-shi-dan-fu-xi-zhuan (2015).
Barthes, Roland. *Elements of Semiology*. Translated by Annette Lavers and Colin Smith. New York: Hill and Wang, 1991.
Berkeley, George. *Principles of Human Knowledge and Three Dialogues*. Edited by Howard Robinson. Oxford, UK: Oxford University Press, 2009.
Berlin, Isaiah. *Four Essays on Liberty*. Oxford, UK: Oxford University Press, 1969.
Bosanquet, B. *The Principle of Individuality and Value*. London: Macmillan and Co., 1912.
Brentano, F. *Psychology from an Empirical Standpoint*. Translated by D. B. Terrell, L. L. McAlister, and A. Rancurello. London: Routledge, 1995.
Buchanan, Allen E. *Marx and Justice: the Radical Critique of Liberalism*. London: Methuen, 1982.
Camus, Albert. *The Myth of Sisyphus*. New York: Knopf, 1955.
Cassier, Ernst. *An Essay on Man: An Introduction to a Philosophy of Human Culture*. London: Yale University Press, 1944.
———. *The Philosophy of Symbolic Forms: Vol. 1*. Translated by Ralph Manheim. London: Yale University Press, 1965.
Chan, Wing-tsit. *Instructions for Practical Living*. New York: Columbia University Press, 1963.
———, trans. *The Platform Scripture*. New York: St. John's University Press, 1963.
———. *A Source Book in Chinese Philosophy*. Princeton, NJ: Princeton University Press, 1963.
Chomsky, Noam. *Language and Mind*. Cambridge, UK: Cambridge University Press, 2006.
Cohen, G. A. *Self-ownership, Freedom, and Equality*. Cambridge, UK: Cambridge University Press, 1995.
Confucius. *The Analects of Confucius*. Translated by Roger Ames and Henry Rosemont Jr. New York: Random House, 1998.
Dacheng miyan jing [Mahayana Sutra of Mystic Glorification]. Taisho-Pitaka, No. 440. Chinese Buddhist Electronic Text Association. www.cbeta.org/index.htm (2015).

Dai Mingyang. *Ji Kang ji jiaozhu* [Collected Works of Ji Kang: Collation and Commentary]. Beijing: Renmin Wenxue Chubanshe, 1962.
Davidson, Donald. *Essays on Actions and Events*. Oxford, UK: Clarendon Press, 1982.
———. "Rational Animals." In *Actions and Events: Perspectives on the Philosophy of Donald Davidson*. Edited by B. McLaughlin, pp. 473–480. Oxford, UK: B. Blackwell, 1984.
Deleuze, Gilles. *The Logic of Sense*. Translated by M. Lester with C. Stivale. New York: Columbia University Press, 1990.
Derrida, Jacque. "Différance." In *Margins of Philosophy*. Translated by Alan Bass, 3–27. Chicago: Chicago University Press, 1982.
Dewey, James. *Experience and Nature*. La Salle, IL: Open Court, 1987.
Dilthey, Wilhelm. *The Formation of the Historical World in the Human Sciences*. Translated by Rudolf A. Makkreel and Rodi. Princeton, NJ: Princeton University Press, 2002.
Dong Zhongshu. *Chunqiu fanlu*, Chapter 41. Edited by Donald Sturgeon. Chinese Text Project. http://ctext.org/chun-qiu-fan-lu/wei-ren-zhe-tian/zh (2015).
Fa Zang. "Xiu Huayan anzhi wangjin huanyuan guan" [The Perspective of Returning to the Origin through Discarding All Delusions with Huayan's Miraculous Practice]. In *Zhongguo fojiao sixiang ziliao xuanbian*, Vol. 2, Book 2. Edited by Jian Shijun and Lou Yulie. Beijing: Zhonghua shuju, 1983.
Feng Youlan, *Sansongtang quanji* [Collected Works in Three Pines Hall]. Vol. 4. Zhengzhou: Henan Renmin Chubanshe, 1986.
Feyerabend, Paul. *Farewell to Reason*. London: Verso, 2002.
Foucault, Michel. *The Order of Things: An Archaeology of the Human Sciences*. New York: Random House, 1994.
Fraser, Nancy. *Scales of Justice: Reimagining Political Space in a Globalizing World*. New York: Columbia University Press, 2009.
Frege, Gottlob. "The Thought: A Logical Inquiry." *Mind* 65, no. 259 (1956): pp. 289–311.
Gadamer, Hans-George. *Philosophical Hermeneutics*. Translated by David E. Linge. Berkeley: University of California Press, 1976.
———. *Truth and Method*. Translation revised by J. Weinsheimer and D. G. Marshall. London: Continuum, 2004.
Gao Zhennong. *Dacheng qixin lun jiaoshi* 大乘起信论校释 [The Awakening of Faith in the Mahayana: Collation and Commentary]. Beijing: Zhonghua shuju, 1992.
Giddens, Anthony. *The Constitution of Society: Outline of the Theory of Structuration*. Cambridge, UK: Polity Press, 1986.
Goodman, Nelson. *Of Mind and Other Matters*. Cambridge, MA: Harvard University Press, 1984.
Gracia, J. E. *Individuality: An Essay on the Foundation of Metaphysics*. Albany: State University of New York Press, 1988.
Habermas, J. *Duihua lunli yu zhenli wenti* [Ethics of Discourse and the Problem of Truth]. Beijing: Zhongguo renmin daxue chubanshe, 2005.
———. "The Public Sphere." *New German Critique*, no. 3 (Autumn, 1974): pp. 49–55.
———. *The Structural Transformation of the Public Sphere*. Translated by Thomas Burger. Cambridge, MA: MIT Press, 1993.

Heidegger, Martin. *Being and Time*. Translated by Joan Stambaugh. Albany: State University of New York Press, 1996.
———. *The Fundamental Concept of Metaphysics*. Bloomington: Indiana University Press, 1995.
———. *Nietzsche: Vols 3 and 4*. Translated by David Farrell Krell. San Francisco: Harper & Row, 1979.
———. *The Principle of Reason*. Translated by Reginald Lilly. Bloomington: Indiana University Press, 1996.
———.*The Question Concerning Technology and Other Essays*. Translated and with an Introduction by William Lovitt. New York: Garland Publishing, Inc., 1977.
———. *What is a Thing?*. Translated by W.B Barton Jr. and Vera Deutsch. South Bend: Regnery/Gate Way, Inc., 1967.
Heidegger, Martin, G. Neske, and E. Kettering. *Martin Heidegger and National Socialism: Questions and Answers*. New York: Paragon House, 1990.
Hegel, G. W. F. *Hegel's Philosophy of Mind: Being Part Three of the Encyclopaedia of the Philosophical Sciences*. Translated by William Wallace. Oxford, UK: Clarendon, 1971.
———. *Hegel's Philosophy of Nature: Being Part Two of the Encyclopaedia of the Philosophical Sciences (1830)*. Translated by A. V. Miller. Oxford, UK: Oxford University Press, 2004.
Hegel, G. W. F., and W. Wallace. *Hegel's Philosophy of Mind*. Oxford, UK: Clarendon Press, 1894.
Honneth, Axel, and Nancy Fraser. *Redistribution or Recognition? A Political-Philosophical Exchange*. London: Verso, 2003.
Huang Zongxi. "Epigraph for Historigrapher Bian Yuwu." In Huang Zongxi quanji [Collected Works of Huang Zongxi]. Book 10. Hangzhou: Zhejiang guji chubanshe, 1992.
"Huayan yicheng jiaoyi fenqi zhang" [Huayan's Teaching of the Single Vehicle and Distinctions]. In *Zhongguo fojiao sixiang ziliao xuanbian*. Vol. 4. Edited by Jian Shijun and Lou Yulie. Beijing: *Zhonghua shuju*, 1983.
Hume, David. *A Treatise of Human Nature*. Oxford, UK: Clarendon Press, 1896.
Husserl, Edmund. *Collected Works: Volume II, First Book*. Translated by F. Kersten. The Hague: M. Nijhoff, 1983.
———. *Experience and Judgment: Investigations in a Genealogy of logic*. Translated and edited by L. Landgrebe, J. S. Churchill, and K. Ameriks. Evanston, IL: Northwestern University Press, 1997.
———. *The Essential Husserl: Basic Writings in Transcendental Phenomenology*. Translated by Donn Welton. Bloomington: Indiana University Press: 1999.
———. *Logical Investigations*. Translated by Dermot Moran. London: Routledge, 2001.
James, William. *Pragmatism*. Mineola, NY: Dover Publications, 1995.
———. *Pragmatism and the Meaning of Truth: Works of William James*. http://intersci.ss.uci.edu/wiki/eBooks/BOOKS/James/The%20Meaning%20of%20Truth%20James.pdf
Jaspers, Karl. *Philosophy*. Translated by E. B. Ashton. Vol. I. Chicago: The University of Chicago Press, 1969.

Jin Yuelin. *Jin Yuelin xueshu lunwen xuan* [Selected Academic Papers of Jin Yuelin]. Beijing: Zhongguo shehui kexue chubanshe, 1990.

———. *Lun Dao* [A Theoretical Discussion on Dao]. Beijing: Shangwu yinshuguan, 1987.

———. *Zhishi lun* [Theory of Knowledge]. Beijing: Shangwuyin Shuguan, 1983.

Kant, Immanuel. *Anthropology from a Pragmatic Point of View*. Translated by Victor Lyle Dowdell. Carbondale: Southern Illinois University Press, 1978.

———. *Critique of the Power of Judgment*. Translated by Werner S. Pluhar. Indianapolis, IN: Hackett Publishing Company, 1987.

———. *Critique of Practical Reason*. Translated by Mary Gregor. Cambridge, UK: Cambridge University Press, 1997.

———. *Critique of Pure Reason*. Translated by N. K. Smith. New York: St. Martin's Press, 1965.

———. *Grounding for the Metaphysics of Morals*. Translated by James W. Ellington. Indianapolis, IN: Hackett Publishing Company, 1993.

———. *Lectures on Ethics*. Translated by Louis Infield. Indianapolis, IN: Hackett Publishing Company, 1963.

———. *Opus Postumum*. Cambridge, UK: Cambridge University Press, 1993.

Korsgaard, C. M. *The Sources of Normativity*. Cambridge, UK: Cambridge University Press, 1996.

Kymlicka, Will. *Contemporary Political Philosophy: An Introduction*. Oxford, UK: Oxford University Press, 2002.

Laozi. Edited by Donald Sturgeon. Chinese Text Project. http://ctext.org/dao-de-jing (2015).

Leibniz, G. *Discourse on Metaphysics and Other Essays*. Indianapolis, IN: Hackett Publishing Company, 1991.

Li Gou 李觏. *Li gou ji* 李觏集 [Collected Works of Li Gou]. Beijing: Zhonghua shuju, 1981.

Li ji [Book of Rites]. Edited by Donald Sturgeon. Chinese Text Project. http://ctext.org/liji (2015).

Locke, John. *An Essay Concerning Human Understanding*. Vol. 1. Mineola, NY: Dover Publications, Inc., 1959.

Lüshi chunqiu [Master Lu's Spring and Autumn Annals]. Edited by Donald Sturgeon. Chinese Text Project. http://ctext.org/lv-shi-chun-qiu (2015).

Marx, Karl. *Capital: A Critique of Political Economy*. Vol. 1. Translated by B. Fowkes. Harmondsworth, UK: Penguin, 1976.

———. *Capital: A Critique of Political Economy Vol I*. Translated and edited by Ernest Mandel, Ben Fowkes, and David Fernbach. London: Penguin Books in association with New Left Review, 1990.

———. *Capital: A Critique of Political Economy Vol III*. Translated and edited by Ernest Mandel, Ben Fowkes, and David Fernbach. London: Penguin Books in association with New Left Review, 1990.

———. *Capital: A Critique of Political Economy*. Translated by S. Moore and E. B. Aveling. Edited by F. Engels. Mineola, NY: Dover Publications, 2011.

———. *A Contribution to the Critique of Political Economy*. Translated by N. I. Stone. Forgotten Books, 2012. http://www.forgottenbooks.com/readbook/A_Contribution_to_the_Critique_of_Political_Economy_1000372438#3 (2015).

———. *The Eighteenth Brumaire of Louis Bonaparte*. New York: International Publishers, 1963.

———. *The German Ideology*. Edited by C. J. Arthur. New York: International Publishers, 1972.
———. *Grundrisse: Foundations of the Critique of Political Economy (Rough Draft)*. Translated by M. Nicolaus. London: Penguin Books in association with New Left Review, 1993.
Marx, K. and F. Engels. *Economic and Philosophic Manuscripts of 1844*. Translated by Martin Mulligan. Amherst, NY: Prometheus Books, 1998.
———. *Karl Marx and Frederick Engels: Selected Works in One Volume*. New York: International Publishers, 1968.
———. *Makesi En'gesi quanji* [Collected Works of Marx and Engles]. Beijing: Renmin chubanshe, 1998.
McDowell, John. *Having the World in View*. Cambridge, MA: Harvard University Press, 2009.
Mencius. *Mencius*. Translated by D. C. Lau. London: Penguin Classics, 2004.
Nie Bao. *Shuangjiang nie xiansheng wenji* [Collected Works of Neibao]. Vol. 11. *Zhongguo guji Quanlu*. http://guji.artx.cn/Article/13142.html (2015).
Nietzsche, Friedrich. *The Will to Power*. Translated by Walter Kaufmann and edited by R. J. Hollingdale. New York: Vintage Books, 1968.
Nozick, Robert. *Anarchy, State, and Utopia*. New York: Basic Books, Inc., Publishers, 1974.
———. *The Nature of Rationality*. Princeton, NJ: Princeton University Press, 1993.
———. Ogden, C. K., and I. A. Richards. *The Meaning of Meaning: A Study of the Influence of Language upon Thought and of the Science of Symbolism*. London: Routledge & Kegan Paul, 1952.
Pap, Arthur. *Elements of Analytic Philosophy*. New York: Macmillan, 1949.
Plato. *The Collected Dialogues of Plato: Republic*. Princeton, NJ: Princeton University Press, 1961.
Polanyi, M. and H. Prosch. *Meaning*. Chicago: The University of Chicago Press, 1976.
Quine, W. V. *Thought and Language*. Edited by J. Pleston. Cambridge, UK: Cambridge University Press, 1997.
Rawls, John. *A Theory of Justice*. Rev. ed. Cambridge, MA: Harvard University Press, 1999.
———. *Political Liberalism*. New York: Columbia University Press, 2005.
Raz, J. *Practical Reason and Norms*. London: Hutchinson, 1975.
Ricoeur, Paul. *Rethinking Imagination*. Translated by G. Robinson and J. Rundell. London: Routledge, 1994.
Ru lengqie jing [The Sutra on Entering the Land of Lanka]. Taisho-Pitaka, No. 67. Chinese Buddhist Electronic Text Association. www.cbeta.org/index.htm (2015).
Ryle, G. *The Concept of Mind*. London, UK: Routledge, 2009.
Schiller, J. C. F. *On the Aesthetic Education of Man*. Translated by Reginald Snell. Mineola, NY: Dover Publications, 2004.
Schutz, Alfred. *Collected Papers I: The Problem of Social Reality*. Edited by Maurice Natanson. The Hague: Martinus Nijhoff, 1962.
Searle, John. *The Construction of Social Reality*. New York: The Free Press, 1995.
———. *Mind: A Brief Introduction*. Oxford, UK: Oxford University Press, 2004.
Shi Puji. *Wudeng huiyuan* [Five Collected Records of Chan's Words and Deeds]. Vol. 3. Beijing: Zhonghua shuju, 1980.

Strawson, P.E. *Individuals: An Essay in Descriptive Metaphysics.* London and New York: Routledge, 2003.
Suárez, Francis. *On Individuation, Metaphysical Disputation V: Individual Unity and Its Principle.* Translated by J. J. E. Gracia. Milwaukee, WI: Marquette University Press, 1982.
Taylor, Charles. *Liberalism and the Moral Life.* Edited by N. Rosenblum. Cambridge, MA: Harvard University Press, 1989.
———.*The Self: Psychological and Philosophical Issues.* Edited by Theodore Mischel. Oxford, UK: Basil Blackwell, 1977.
Turner, Bryan. *Citizenship and Social Theory.* London: Sage Publications, 1993.
Vico, G. *On the Most Ancient Wisdom of the Italians: Drawn out from the Origins of the Latin Language.* Translated by J. Taylor. New Haven, CT: Yale University Press, 2010.
———. *De antiquissima italorum sapientia.* Edited by M. Sanna. Rome: Edizioni di storia e letteratura, 2005.
Wang Fuzhi. *Zhangzi zheng meng zhu* 张子正蒙注 [Commentary on Zhang Zi's Correction of Youthful Folly], *Chuanshan quanshu* 船山全书, Book 12, Vol. 1. Changsha: Yuelu shushe, 1996.
———. *Shi guangchuan* [Extensive Commentary on the Book of Poetry], *Chuanshan quanshu* [Complete Works of Chuanshan], Book 3. Changsha: Yuelu shushe, 1996.
———. *Du sishu daquan shuo* [Discussions in Reading the Great Collection of Commentaries on the Four Books]. *Chuanshan quanshu* [Complete Works of Chuanshan], Book 6. Changsha: Yuelu shushe, 1996.
Wang Yangming. *Instructions for Practical Living and Other Neo-confucian Writings.* Translated by Wing Tsit-Chan. New York: Columbia University Press, 1963.
———. *Wang yangming quanji* [The Complete Works of Wang Yangming]. Shanghai: Shanghai guji chubanshe, 1992.
Wei Qipeng. *Mawangdui hanmu boshu huangdishu jianzheng* [Commentary on The Four Books of the Yellow Emperor, Written in Silk Unearthed from a Han Dynasty Tomb in Mawangdui]. Beijing: Zhonghua shuju.
Wittgenstein, Ludwig. *The Blue and Brown Books.* New York: Harper & Row Publishers, 1965.
———. *Philosophical Investigations.* Translated by G. E. M. Anscombe. Malden: Blackwell, 1958.
———. *Zettel,* 621. Translated by G. E. M Anscombe. Oakland: University of California Press, 1970.
Wright, G. H. *Norm and Action: A Logical Enquiry.* London, UK: Routledge and Kegan Paul, 1963.
Xiao jing [Book of Filial Piety]. Edited by Donald Sturgeon. Chinese Text Project. http://ctext.org/xiao-jing (2015).
Xu Jinting. *Zhouyi jinzhu jinshi.* Taibei: Taiwan Shangwu Yinshuguan, 1974.
Xunzi. *Xunzi.* Edited by Donald Sturgeon. Chinese Text Project. http://ctext.org/xunzi (2015).
Yang Guorong 杨国荣. *Chengji yu chengwu: yiyi shijie de shengcheng* 成己与成物：意义世界的生成.Shanghai: Huadong shifan daxue chubanshe 华东师范大学出版社, 2009.
———. *Cunzai zhi wei* [The Dimension of Being]. Beijing: Renmin chubanshe, 2005.

———. *Daolun* 道论 [*A Treatise on Dao*]. Shanghai: Huadong shifan daxue chubanshe 华东师范大学出版社, 2009.
———. *Lixing yu jiazhi: Zhihui de licheng* [Reason and values: the path of wisdom]. Shanghai: Sanlian, 1998.
———. *lunli yu cunzai* 伦理与存在 [Ethics and Being]. Shanghai: Huadong shifan daxue chubanshe 华东师范大学出版社, 2009.
———. "The Maturation of the Self and the Refinement of Things: The Generation of the World of Meaning." *Contemporary Chinese Thought* 43, no. 4 (2012): pp. 51–52.
———. "Metaphysics: Reconstruction and Reflection." *Contemporary Chinese Thought* 43, no. 4 (2012): p. 16.
———. "What Is Philosophy for?" *Shehui kexue* [Social Sciences], no. 1 (2006).
Zahavi, Dan. *Subjectivity and Selfhood: Investigating the First-Person Perspective*. Cambridge, MA: The MIT Press, 2005.
Zhang Zai. *Zhangzai ji* 张载集 [Collected Works of Zhangzai]. Beijing: Beijing Shuju, 1978.
Zheng Xuan. *Zhouli Zhushu* [*Commentary on the Rites of the Zhou*]. Beijing: Beijing daxue chubanshe, 1999.
Zheng Xuan. *San li zhu* [Commentary on the Record of Rites]. Beijing: Beijing daxue chubanshe, 1999.
Zhongyong. Edited by Donald Sturgeon. Chinese Text Project. http://ctext.org/liji/zhong-yong?searchu=%E4%B8%AD%E5%BA%B8&searchmode=showall#result (2015).
The Zhou Book of Change, Vols. I and II. Translated by Fu Huisheng. Hunan: Hunan People's Publishing House, 2008.
Zhuangzi. *Zhuangzi*. Translated by Wang Rongpei. Hunan: Hunan People's Publishing House, 1999.
Zhu Xi. *Zhu wengong wenji* [Collected Literary Works of Zhu Xi], Book 21. Shanghai: Shanghai guji chubanshe, 2010.
Zhu Xi. *Zhuzi quanshu* [Collected Books of Zhuzi], vol. 1, *Lunyu huowen* [Dialogues on the Analects], book 4. Shanghai: Shanghai guji chubanshe, 2002.

Index

A priori, 13–14, 71–73, 78, 79, 97–99, 101, 277
Abstract [abstraction], viii, ix, 6, 14, 17, 93, 141, 147, 154, 179, 189, 212, 229, 267
Action, 16, 39–40; and moral language, 44–45, 51; and communication, 83; norms in the process of, 113–114; [doing], 117; [human activity], 134, 136; practical, 187; of bodies, 214
Actual [actuality], 1, 5, 7–12, 20–22, 24, 30, 32, 40, 45–48, 52–54, 76–79, 178–180, 186; form of being and the world, 7, 11, 20–22, 41, 178, 187, 198, 268; [actualize, actualization], 14, 29, 73, 90, 92, 109, 111, 142, 155, 210, 236, 241
Aesthetic(s), 38, 52, 59; taste, 91, 122, 223; judgment, 95–97; consciousness, 128, 158, 179
Affairs (*shi*), 3–5
Aristotle, 70, 186
Attitude, 44–48; toward the world, 105–107; practical and theoretical, 185–186, 189; toward oneself and others, 241
Authoritarianism, 12–13, 66–68
Ayer, A. J., 44

Barthes, Roland, 50
Benti "the fundamental substance": of being, 100–105, 100n56, 165; of the mind or spirit, 105, 110, 153, 156
Berkeley, George, 81
Body, 23–24, 73–75, 78, 87; bodily [embodied] experience, 91–92, 112–113
Bosanquet, B., 211
Buchanan, Allen, 265
Buddhism, 148–149; Hua Yan, 149; Chan, 161, 162; Zhu Xi's critique of, 103

Camus, Albert, 34
Cassier, Ernst, 59
Cause: and effect, 59; of beings, 50; of action, 234; efficient, material, formal, final, 196–199
Chengxin "prejudiced mind," "made-up mind," 109
Chomsky, Noam, 88
Cohen, G., 261
Common sense, 17–18, 110, 145–151, 194–196

Communication, 83, 88–90, 100, 110, 132, 152, 163, 196, 203, 243
Conflict, social, 195, 210, 213, 264–265
Confucius, 38, 45–46, 82, 125, 128, 156, 160, 165, 226, 236, 265, 272
Consolidation: of wisdom and knowledge into perspective, 107, 110–111; of the historical experience of the species, 134; of historical achievements, 194–195, 214
Continuity, 23–24, 86; of individual life, 190; spatio-temporal, 216; of personality, 217
Contradiction, 10, 31–32, 43, 75, 79, 141, 211

Dao, 3, 8–9, 84, 90–93; from the perspective of, 109; of necessity and of what ought to be, 116–117; everydayness of, 168; of humans, 147, 191; of co-humanity, 266
Dasein, "being-there," 8, 21, 30, 175, 183–184
Davidson, Donald, 51, 89
Deleuze, Gilles, 214
Dependence: personal, 65, 173, 225, 227, 230–231, 234, 237; objective [sachlicher], 65, 174, 229, 233
Derrida, Jacque, 61
Development: multi-sided (multifaceted, whole-sided, all-sided), 20, 175, 205, 227, 231–238; individual, 24–25, 223, 225–240; social, 119, 140–143, 201, 207, 223–231, 233, 240, 245; of social resources, 262–268
Dewey, John, 41, 76
Dilthey, Wilhelm, 54
Diversity, 31–33, 95; of cognitive and practical processes, 118; of norms, 148
Division, 159, 164, 177; of labor, 195, 233
Dong Zhongshu, 225

Effectiveness, 15, 77–78, 115, 139
Emotion, 36, 42, 44–45, 215, 220, 240; emotional state, 157
Empiricism, 77; empiricist, 136, 223
Equipment, 118, 244; equipmentification, 229–230
Estrangement, 22, 145, 172, 174, 185
Existentialism, 22, 188

Experience, lived, 91–94, 91n26, 98
Externalization, externalizing: of knowledge and wisdom, 17, 112, 138; of meaning, 19, 52, 177; of human capacities, 90

Fa Zang, 149, 152, 164
Feng Youlan, 167–168
Filial Piety, "*xiao*," 53–54, 121–122, 157
Foucault, Michel, 65
Freedom, 12–13, 21, 25, 28, 237; realm of, 72–73, 140; of the imagination, 92; feeling of, 97; free development, 25, 234, 237–238, 250–253, 265–268; positive and negative, 230, 234–237, 234n46
Frege, Gottlob, 36, 46, 48
Function, assignment, 199–201

Gadamer, Hans-George, 56–58, 93
Giddens, Anthony, 245–246
Good, the, 15, 52, 77; morally, 22, 33; and evil, 40, 76
Goodman, Nelson, 84

Habermas, J., 238
Harmony, harmonize, harmonic mixture, 5–6; of capacities, 15, 76; between *yin* and *yang*, 91; with norms, 100; combine harmonically, 131–132; with human need, 140, 169; with human nature, 205–206, 263, 268; with nature, 226
Hegel, G. W. F., 21, 182, 189, 205
Heidegger, M., 2, 8–10, 30, 51, 61, 107, 162, 165–166, 183–184, 213
Huang Zongxi, 175, 221
Humanization, 2, 41, 140, 180, 186, 190, 195, 202, 205, 207; humanized actuality, 3–6, 11, 22, 26, 52, 144, 154, 177–179; humanized form of being, 180–183, 190, 194, 204–205, 207
Hume, David, 77–78
Husserl, Edmond, 51, 58, 146, 271

Idea, ideas, 28; actualization of, 29, 53; internalization and internality of, 109, 110
Ideal, ideals, 6, 10–12, 181; pursuit of, 160–161, 168–172; human character, 175
Identity: enduring, 23–24; law of, 10, 31; of thought, 75; cultural, 115; collective, 130; self-identity, 211–213; social, 214, 246; personal, 218–219, 224
Imagination, 71–72, 79–87, 159–160
Insight, 15, 85, 87

Integration, 53; of empirical content and conceptual form, 80–81, 103; of ethical norms with concrete situations, 94–96; of the psychological with the logical, 103; of individuals, 115; of concepts with conscious activity, 150; of man and woman, 193; of human being with the world of objects, 195; and differentiation, 113; of rational and irrational, 231; of accomplishing oneself and accomplishing things, 260; of linguistic symbols, 268
Internalization, 17; of concepts and ideas, 99–102; of norms, 126

James, William, 183
Jaspers, Karl, 184
Ji Kang, 159
Jin Yuelin, 36–37, 141, 209
Jingjie, "state of mind," "spiritual state," "state," "states," 18, 52, 123, 142, 149, 164–166, 164n32; the human, 170–176
Jue (awareness), 152–153
Justice, 25–26, 204–205, 247–268

Kant, Immanuel, 2, 13–14, 71, 75, 79–81, 97–98, 134–136, 161, 169–170, 182
Korsgaard, C. M., 118–119, 123
Kymlicka, Will, 257–258

Labor, 12, 180; abstract, 228–229; alienation of, 19, 65, 172, 174; division of, 195, 233
Language, 41–50; deep structure of, 88; thought and, 102; private, 134, 151; descriptive, 42–45, 142; prescriptive, 45–46; expressive, 43–45
Lao Zi, 9
Law, laws: of logic, 10, 31, 51, 75; of being, 117; natural, 120, 122, 252; moral, 134–136
Learning, 91–93, 103; line/path of, 168–169, 171
Legitimacy, 76–78
Leibniz, G., 211
Li, "principle," 45, 103–104, 112; of Nature, 120–126; of consistency, 129–121; and what is righteous, 163
Li, "ritual propriety," 53–54, 112, 121, 127, 131, 133, 137, 139, 156, 160, 191; "rites," "rituals," 91, 94–95, 202–206
Li Gou, 127
Li ji [Book of Rites], 127, 191–193
Life: biological, 5, 296; everyday, 145–146, 168, 189, 192–198, 242; social, 133, 191, 218–219, 239;

individual, 93, 190, 198, 249; private, 243–245; public, 243
Limits, 86–87, 89, 108; of a perspective, 110, 186; limited resources, 263, 265, 268
Locke, John, 217, 252
Loss: of meaning, 121, 61–62, 65; gain and/or, 45, 139; of balance, 189
Lüshi Chunqiu, 45

Marx, Karl, 14–15, 24, 35, 38, 55, 72–73, 158, 173, 178, 190, 193–194, 200, 214–215, 222–235, 250, 260, 267–268
Mencius, 88–89, 92, 116, 118, 124–126, 162–163, 166–170, 250–251, 255–257
Metaphysics, 18; the metaphysical view of the world, 147–151
Music, 38, 45–46, 159, 161; rites and, 204–205

Nature, in-itself and for human being, 3–11, 29, 53–57, 144, 177–181, 186–190, 193, 198, 200, 207, 230; the Way of, 9, 69, 110
Needs: human, 4, 6, 45, 56, 115, 139–141, 153–155, 169, 177–179, 185, 190, 195–196, 203, 207, 246–247, 250–251, 263; practical, 16; spiritual, 38; psychological, 62; metaphysical, 235; purpose and, 116, 120; developmental, 260, 264; individual, 265–266, 268
Nie Bao, 175
Nietzsche, Friedrich, 61–66
Nihilism, 12–13, 61–68
Norms, 16–17, 26, 45–46, 112–144, 245–247
Nozick, Robert, 76, 248–252

One-sided, 8; understanding of meaning, 12, 55–60; understanding of the individual, 212, 231, 233; development of the individual, 234
Openness [open nature of], 60–68, 151, 166, 239; opening up, 2, 4–5, 8, 15, 18, 20, 51
Order: practical order of affairs, 3–4; socio-political, 45–46, 115, 120, 132–133, 191–195, 254; of logic, 61, 85; spatial and temporal, 145–146, 148–149
Other, the, others, 17–18, 82, 223; in isolation from, 132; being-with, 176; dependence upon, 223, 229–230; being-for, 226; helping, 236; respecting, 241, 258; understanding and being understood by, 244; being partially owned by, 249; influencing, 254

Pap, Arthur, 212
Particularization, 209–210

Passion, 64, 72, 77, 78, 231, 259
Perception, 37, 71–75, 78–83, 126, 131
Perspective, 18, 105–111, 158
Plato, 187
Polyani, Michael, 55
Possibility: possible realm, 15; and imagination, 79–83, 87, 79–90; world of, 83, 87
Powers: essential, 1, 14–15, 19–20, 52–54, 70–72; intrinsic, 96–99; creative, 207, 215
Psychological, the, 4, 23, 42, 99–104, 150–151, 156, 172, 181, 217, 243
Purposive, purposiveness, 23–24; dimension of accomplishing oneself and things, 33–34, 51; of capacities, 72–73; rationality, 77–78; and norms, 112, 114; and need, 115–116; of human beings, 169–170; Chinese philosophy and, 226–227; Marx and, 230, 237, 268

Qi "energy," 116, 131, 147–148
Quine, W. V., 89
Qun "group," "grouping," 132, 133

Rawls, John, 247–255, 259
Raz, J., 134
Reason: rational, rationality, 61, 66; perception and, 73–78; theoretical and practical, 97
Reference, direct and indirect, 42, 43n30, 74
Relativism, 67
Ren "being-humane," "humane," "humanity," 53–54, 92, 114, 124–125, 170, 221
Resources, social, 25–26, 235, 245–254, 260–268
Ricoeur, Paul, 82
Rights, 66–67, 132, 169–170, 199, 221–222, 247–255, 258–268
Rules, 81, 85, 95–100, 117–143; bending of, 129, 129n26
Ryle, G., 106n64

Schiller, J., 97
Schutz, Alfred, 199n45
Science, 17, 146–147, 172–176, 188–189; Heidegger's critique of, 220
Scientism, 8, 22, 77, 288–289
Searle, J., 199–202, 216–218
Self-awareness, 93, 109, 124
Significance, 36–37
Signs, 41; mathematical, 35, 37; image-, 39–40; linguistic, 43, 53–54; natural, 49–50
Species, 36–37, 47, 72, 88, 209–213, 221, 244, 259
Strawson, P.E., 209n2

Structure: of spirit, 99–105, 110; of consciousness, 119, 126; internal conceptual, 129; hierarchical, 131, 203; social, 133
Suárez, Francoise, 208–209
Subject: of meaning, 6, 37; moral, 19, 72, 157; aesthetic, 97, 158–159; of lived experience, 91; subjective, 36, 55, 86, 140
Survival, 8, 28, 155, 169, 171, 191, 196, 207, 246, 252, 265

Taylor, Charles, 219
Technology, 172–176, 188, 256, 262
Tool, tools, 19, 72, 74, 78, 173–174, 190
Transcendence: of being, 107; seeking, 148; of the Other, 221; the transcendent, 9, 21; world, 63–65; ground of moral principle, 82, 105, 121–123, 132; plane, 163–262; speculation, 184; being, 242
Transmission: transmit, 90–92, 99, 154; historical, 193–195, 200
Truth, 52, 56, 59, 73, 76–77, 163, 179
Turner, Bryan, 258

Understanding, 10–12, 15–18, 21–22, 31–33, 35, 37, 40–41; of signs, 48–51; and values, 54; of texts, 57–58, 61; rational, 64; human, 71, 75, 150, 152, 157, 167; categories of, 81; the other, 82–83, 100; imagination and, 87; and sensibility, 115; of norms, 119, 122, 130
Universal: concrete, 23, 211, 213; principles, 141–142, 151–152; norms, 123, 132, 134–135, 140–143, 202, 245
Utilitarianism, 246, 249

Vico, G., 71n7
Virtue, 70–71, 102, 127, 138, 153, 166–168, 170, 218–224; public, 239–240

Wang Chong, 184–185, 187
Wang Fuzhi (Wang Chuanshan), 3, 46, 116, 129, 150–151, 153, 157, 165–168
Wang Yangming, 3, 101–103, 156–157, 182–183
Wisdom, 15, 69, 110, 138
Wittgenstein, Ludwig, 21, 47, 79, 82, 102, 123–124, 133–134
World-picture, picture of the world, 17–18, 52, 76, 142, 147–158

Xin "the affective mind": "heart," 17, 19, 22–23; Zhuangzi"s treatment of, 83–84; Mencius's treatment of, 92, 163, 170; Wang Yangming's doctrine of, 101–102, 156; and principle, 112, 123, 126, 137; Zhang Zai's treatment of, 151–152, 168–169; Wang Fuzhi's understanding of, 153, 157; Zhu Xi's understanding of, 165
Xing "human nature": "natural disposition of human beings," 19–22, 69, 110, 115, 225; Mencius on, 92; Neo-Confucian understanding of, 103–105; alienation of, 173–174; according with, 203–205; equality of, 250–252
Xunzi, 131–133, 194–195, 270

Yi "being-righteous," "what is righteous," "righteousness," 92, 113, 124–127, 131–132, 163, 245, 253
Yijing "Book of Changes," 1n2, 39, 46, 147

Zhang Zai, 127, 150, 166–171, 226
Zheng Xuan, 3
Zhu Xi, 3, 103–104, 120–121, 165–167

YANG GUORONG is Zijiang University Professor at East China Normal University in Shanghai and a leading figure in Chinese philosophy. He has published ten books on classical Confucianism, Neo-Confucianism, Daoism, modern Chinese thought, and Chinese and Western philosophy.

CHAD AUSTIN MEYERS is a Ph.D. candidate in Chinese philosophy at East China Normal University. He has published "An Outline of a Concrete Metaphysics" and "Yang Guorong's Concrete Metaphysics" in *Contemporary Chinese Thought*.

www.ingramcontent.com/pod-product-compliance
Lightning Source LLC
Chambersburg PA
CBHW021345300426
44114CB00012B/1087